SELF-HELP
MESSIAH

SELF-HELP
MESSIAH

Dale Carnegie and Success
in Modern America

STEVEN WATTS

OTHER PRESS

NEW YORK

All of the photos are courtesy of Dale Carnegie & Associates, Inc., except for those of Carnegie and Frieda Offenbach, and Carnegie and Linda Offenbach, which are courtesy of Linda Polsby.

Production Editor: Yvonne E. Cárdenas
Text Designer: Chris Welch
This book was set in 10.5 pt Sabon by Alpha Design & Composition of Pittsfield, NH.

10 9 8 7 6 5 4 3 2 1

Library of Congress Cataloging-in-Publication Data

Watts, Steven, 1952-
Self-help Messiah : Dale Carnegie and success in modern America / by Steven Watts.
pages cm
Includes bibliographical references and index.
ISBN 978-1-59051-502-0 — ISBN 978-1-59051-503-7 (e-book)
1. Carnegie, Dale, 1888-1955. 2. Success. 3. Conduct of life. 4. Teachers—
United States—Biography. 5. Orators—United States—Biography.
6. Authors, American—20th century—Biography. I. Title.
CT275.C3114W37 2013
973.91092—dc23
[B]
2013003227

For all of my teachers, friends, and colleagues
at the University of Missouri

Contents

PART TWO: WINNING FRIENDS AND INFLUENCING PEOPLE

Helping Yourself in Modern America

On a cold January evening in 1936, a great horde descended on the Hotel Pennsylvania in New York City. Three thousand people crammed into the grand ballroom and onto the balcony encircling it, while hundreds more stood shivering on the sidewalk outside, unable to find even standing room as the hotel staff frantically wedged the doors shut and hoped the fire marshal would not appear. The throng was responding to a series of full-page ads in the *New York Sun* that promised "Increase Your Income," "Learn to Speak Effectively," "Prepare for Leadership."

Yet the crowd did not spring from the ranks of the working class or the desperately unemployed who were struggling to survive in the dark days of the Great Depression. It came from a more prosperous stratum, but one equally anxious about sliding into failure—entrepreneurs, businessmen, shopkeepers, salesmen, middle managers, white-collar executives, professional men. As the audience listened attentively for the next hour, fifteen figures paraded before the single microphone on the stage and gave three-minute testimonials. Understanding the principles of human relations, the speakers proclaimed, had pointed them toward success. A druggist,

1

a chain-store manager, an insurance man, a truck salesman, a dentist, an architect, a lawyer, a banker, and several others explained that learning how to deal with people had dramatically enhanced their careers and changed their lives.

After these endorsements, a short, trim man with steel-rimmed glasses, ramrod posture, and a sincere, soothing voice with a slight Midwestern twang took the stage. Dale Carnegie, creator of the self-improvement course being praised, admitted that he was gratified by the large audience. But, he added quickly, "I have no doubt as to why you are here. You are not here because you are interested in me. You are here because you are interested in yourself and the solution to your problems." He assured the crowd that each listener could learn the techniques that had improved so many lives. Each could understand how to be a good listener, make people like them instantly, develop an enthusiastic attitude, handle difficult personal situations, and win others to their way of thinking. Each could be successful. Every student taking his course, he declared in conclusion, "begins to get self-confidence. After all, why shouldn't they— and why shouldn't you?" The throng leapt to its feet in thunderous applause and most of them rushed to tables at the back of the room to sign up for the class. In subsequent years, more than eight million students would graduate from the Dale Carnegie Course in Effective Speaking and Human Relations.[1]

One year later, an even bigger event sent Carnegie rocketing to national fame. In January 1937, his book *How to Win Friends and Influence People*, which codified the lessons of the Carnegie Course, shot to the top of the best-seller list. It would go through seventeen editions its first year, and Leon Shimkin, Carnegie's editor, sent him a somewhat dazed letter in March 1937, after the book had already sold a quarter of a million copies in only three months. "If one year ago a friend of mine were to have told me that today I was going to send to an author the 250,000th copy of his book I would have either referred him to the nearest psychiatrist or to Robert Ripley for a believe-it-or-not-cartoon," he wrote. *How to Win Friends* would go through dozens of reprintings in subsequent years, ultimately selling more than thirty million copies worldwide over the next few decades. It became one of the best selling nonfiction books in American history—it sells in the six figures yearly even now—with some ranking it only behind the Bible and Dr. Benjamin Spock's *Practical Guide to Baby and Child Care*.[2]

At the heart of *How to Win Friends* lay a message that massive numbers of readers found irresistible: One could find success in the modern world by developing attractive personal traits, bolstering self-confidence, improving skills in human relations, getting people to like you, and adopting a psychological perspective in assessing and meeting human needs. Carnegie insisted that getting ahead in life—securing a better job, making more money, enjoying the esteem of your peers—was simply a matter of retooling your personality. With contagious enthusiasm, he promised that his advice book would help any individual to "get out of a mental rut, think new thoughts, acquire new visions, new ambitions . . . Win people to your way of thinking. Increase your influence, your prestige, your ability to get things done. Win new clients, new customers . . . Handle complaints, avoid arguments, keep your human contacts smooth and pleasant . . . Make the principles of psychology easy for you to apply in your daily contacts."[3]

In such a fashion, Carnegie became one of the most popular and influential figures in modern American history. His message promoting sparkling personality, self-esteem, human relations, and psychological well-being resonated widely and deeply in society, attracting millions of acolytes and elevating him to a pinnacle of influence in shaping modern values. And his legacy was a lasting one.

Life magazine named him one of the "Most Important Americans of the Twentieth Century." A Library of Congress survey placed *How to Win Friends and Influence People* as the seventh most influential book in American history. In 1985, *American Heritage*, the popular history magazine, chose ten books that had most shaped the American character—"not its political life but its cultural, social, and domestic life." Predictably, the list included stalwart volumes such as Mark Twain's *Huckleberry Finn*, Henry David Thoreau's *Walden*, Thorstein Veblen's *Theory of the Leisure Class*, W. E. B. DuBois's *The Souls of Black Folk*, and Ernest Hemingway's *The Sun Also Rises*. It also included Carnegie's *How to Win Friends and Influence People*.[4]

So what explains Carnegie's meteoric rise? Why did millions of ordinary citizens flock to his message of personality development, human relations, and success? Why was he able to become a major cultural figure in modern America? Answers to these questions lay partly embedded in a massive reorientation of American life in the early decades of the twentieth century, the remarkable era during which Carnegie labored and wrote. The United States found itself in the throes of rapid change as it transformed from a rural village republic to an urban society of jarring ethnic diversity, imposing bureaucratic structures, and bewildering social problems. From the 1880s to the 1920s, precisely the years of Carnegie's youth and young manhood, the United States experienced not only massive industrialization, mass immigration, and the closing of the frontier but the rapid growth of a modern consumer economy. In contrast to a nineteenth-century landscape of vigorous market exchange regulated by an economic calculus of scarcity, the early twentieth century presented an expansive new world of material abundance where the purchase and accumulation of consumer goods became the new yardstick for measuring achievement.

More immediately for Carnegie, however, the transformation of the United States from 1880 to 1920 brought a crisis in cultural values. In the Victorian nineteenth century, a mainstream creed of stern morality and studied self-control had defined private morality and regulated public conduct. But by the early 1900s this tradition was unraveling. In a society increasingly devoted to consumer abundance, leisure, and entertainment, a new ethos of self-fulfillment (rather than self-denial) gained growing legions of adherents. The hidebound strictures of "character" receded while sparkling images of "personality" became central to a new code of individualism. The shaping of a healthy, magnetic, charismatic personal image (as opposed to an older tradition stressing internalized moral principles) became crucial to success in an age where self-fulfillment had replaced self-control as the emotional nexus of American behavior. The powers of personality gained additional traction from new bureaucratic institutions and large corporations, with their hundreds of employees engaging in complex interactions, which were employing growing numbers of white-collar workers.

Not surprisingly, in this dynamic new atmosphere, the old American tradition of success seeking became irrelevant. In an earlier era, influential figures such as Benjamin Franklin, in his *Autobiography* and essays such as "The Way to Wealth," and Horatio Alger, in novels such as *Mark, the Match Boy* and *Struggling Upward*, had instructed ambitious Americans that the road to prosperity and respectability lay in forming a solid character based on thrift, industry, self-denial, and moral respectability. But such prudential qualities no longer seemed sufficient in a world where material affluence and personal self-fulfillment, bureaucratic imperatives and leisure opportunities, vast cities and far-flung markets held sway.

Carnegie stepped into this cultural breach. By the 1930s, he had begun to develop a vibrant new formulation of rules for gaining success in this daunting new world. His *How to Win Friends and Influence People* expressed these principles in a breathless, anecdotal style and became *the* guidebook for getting ahead in modern America. In Carnegie's telling words, one could "no longer put much faith in the old adage that hard work alone is the magic key that will unlock the door to our desires." The ability to handle people, he insisted repeatedly, was now the key to achievement, status, and prosperity in this complex urban and bureaucratic society. Modern success depended upon getting along with others, working smoothly in a bureaucratic milieu, and subtly maneuvering to assume leadership among groups of people. Carnegie tailored his advice to fit these demands: "make the other person feel important," "don't criticize others," "establish a positive atmosphere and avoid arguments," "be hearty in approbation and lavish in praise," "let the other fellow feel that the idea is his," and "make people like you." A bit later, when the United States was awash in material prosperity in the aftermath of World War II, Carnegie's second blockbuster book, *How to Stop Worrying and Start Living*, presented strategies for coping with the unexpected emotional pressures and angst accompanying consumer comfort. Such advice, with its reliance on human relations and personality appeal rather than hardy individualism and unflinching morality, found a receptive modern audience.

Yet Carnegie also did more than he knew. The tremendous appeal of his success message gained much of its power from a subtle appropriation of psychological perspectives and techniques. This impulse, once again, embodied an important cultural shift. As a number of critics and historians have observed—most famously, Philip Rieff in *The Triumph of the Therapeutic*—the slow erosion of community ties and religious faith under the pressures of modernity produced "psychological man." This dominant character type grew preoccupied with self-awareness, personal growth, self-esteem, and an unceasing quest for a state of emotional well-being. Psychological man jettisoned morality for therapy. This new therapeutic sensibility spread throughout America during the early 1900s and became a powerful influence on education, child-rearing, political activity, family life, religion, and many other areas of modern life.

Carnegie, who often presented himself as an expert in "practical psychology," emerged as the first great popularizer of this newfound stress on mental health and self-esteem. The popular Carnegie Course tried to eradicate "the inferiority complex" and advertised its reliance on "the significant discoveries of modern psychology." *How to Win Friends and Influence People* instructed readers that when dealing with people "we are not dealing with creatures of logic. We are dealing with creatures of emotion." Invoking the psychological ideas of William James, Alfred Adler, and Sigmund Freud, as well as many lesser figures, the text promised that "positive thinking" and the art of "appreciation—the easiest of all psychological techniques," would create among adherents "a new way of life."

From this collection of cultural ingredients—success ideology, charismatic personality and self-fulfillment, positive thought, human relations, therapeutic well-being—Carnegie ultimately created his greatest legacy: the establishment of a robust self-help movement that has shaped modern American values in fundamental ways. In the wake of his stunning success, a host of dazzling, popular self-help gurus—Norman Vincent Peale, Dr. Joyce Brothers, Dr. Wayne Dryer, Tony Robbins, Robert Schuller, Marianne Williamson, M. Scott Peck, Deepak Chopra, Stephen Covey, Oprah Winfrey, and many others—fanned out over the American landscape in subsequent decades, spreading the message that therapeutic adjustment and personal improvement would produce career success, material prosperity, and emotional self-fulfillment. Carnegie's basic notion, embodied in *How to Win Friends*—that the individual who learns "the fine art of getting along with people in everyday business and social contacts" will enjoy "more profit, more leisure, and, what is infinitely more important, more happiness in his business and his home"—became the urtext of this modern American success creed.

But however powerful the links between Carnegie's success message of therapeutic self-help and the changing circumstances of twentieth-century history, that does not explain all. The compelling ideas in *How to Win Friends* and *How to Stop Worrying* did not appear suddenly, as if by magic, from some process of cultural alchemy. Nor was Carnegie an intellectual who systematically thought his way to new conclusions. Instead, his revolutionary notions about success in the modern world took shape, in part, from his unique genius for soaking up new, controversial ideas that were floating around in the broader cultural atmosphere and synthesizing them into a popular form. But they also appeared from a more direct source: the cauldron of his own experience, the events of his own remarkable personal life. For Carnegie had a rags-to-riches story rivaling anything in a Horatio Alger novel.

Born deep in the American rural hinterland, he grew up in grinding poverty surrounded by religious revivals, temperance crusades, and political Populism—the dissenting spasms of a beleaguered rural population being pushed to the margins of a modernizing nation. After fleeing this tradition in search of opportunity, he cycled through a series of jobs in search of a vocation suited to the volatile, transformative society of the early 1900s. He tried to be an automobile salesman in a new age of mobility; a dramatic actor and tabloid journalist in a culture increasingly devoted to images and impressions; an adult-education teacher for those seeking practical guidance in navigating an unfamiliar world; an entertainment manager in a new culture celebrating leisure and celebrity; an alienated, expatriate novelist looking for inspiration abroad; a business guru catering to economic expansion and prosperity in the 1920s. Carnegie's varied endeavors—from delivering boyhood speeches against "demon rum" at fiery tent meetings to popularizing Lawrence of Arabia in the aftermath of World War I, from teaching public speaking to restless white-collar clerks to joining the Lost Generation of American writers abroad, from publishing magazine sketches of successful entrepreneurs to advising giant American corporations—illuminated the swirling changes, the opportunities and dislocations, of America's changing milieu in this era and provided the basic stuff of his formulations.

Carnegie's labors to shape his persona also contributed to the new social ethos proclaimed in *How to Win Friends*. While maintaining the old Protestant tradition of self-regulation—dating back to the Puritans, it enjoined individuals to examine themselves obsessively for evidence of virtuous values and behavior—Carnegie gave it a modern twist. Maintaining a file entitled "Damned Fool Things I Have Done" throughout much of his adult life, he recorded dozens of mistakes in his conduct that he vowed to correct. But whereas traditional Protestants had identified moral or spiritual failings, Carnegie focused on social faux pas that gave offense to others—forgetting people's names, blurting out negative comments, failing to make friends feel comfortable, arguing instead of tactfully suggesting, overlooking others' viewpoints, making sweeping statements that irritated someone. With Carnegie, the stress shifted from shaping one's inner moral character to shaping the impressions that one made upon other people—what he described in his diary as "the biggest problem I shall ever face: the management of Dale Carnegie." Therein lay the central project of his private life, and also of America's modern culture of self-fulfillment: presenting a positive personal image and pleasing personality.

Thus the story of Dale Carnegie is, in essence, the story of America itself in a dynamic era of change. Throughout the early twentieth century he helped redefine the American Dream and plotted a new pathway by which to get there. A self-made man, he became the successor to Franklin and Alger as the modern formulator of success in a society devoted to its pursuit. Dismantling older attachments to economic self-sufficiency, stern moral character, and self-denial, he glorified new attractions of material abundance, human relations, and self-fulfillment. The first great popularizer of the modern cult of personality, he helped weave psychological viewpoints and therapeutic uplift into the fabric of modern life. As the father of the self-help movement, he launched a massive crusade promoting personal reinvention that swept through modern life during the twentieth century and reshaped our basic values. Carnegie did not leave American culture where he found it.

But the tale of this central figure in modern American life began in a rather unlikely place. In the late 1800s, the rural country of northwestern Missouri was deeply provincial—in fact, barely removed from the frontier—and remained far from the bustling urban centers that were beginning to alter the nineteenth-century republic. There, a second son was born to a pious but impoverished farm family struggling to survive in a rather forbidding environment. From his parents, and from his surroundings, the boy imbibed a traditional set of values that would shape his entire life. Some of them would remain a source of profound inspiration. But others would trigger a passionate reaction and slowly push him in new directions.

PART I

FROM CHARACTER TO PERSONALITY

1

Poverty and Piety

n *How to Win Friends and Influence People,* Dale Carnegie lionized a prominent business figure in early twentieth-century America. Charles Schwab, he wrote, the top manager at Andrew Carnegie's huge steel company before becoming head of U.S. Steel, was perhaps the first person in the country "paid a salary of a million dollars a year, or more than three thousand dollars a day." Why this beneficent sum? Because he knew more about steel manufacturing than other executives? Nonsense, said Dale Carnegie. Schwab had told him that there were many men working at Carnegie Steel with more knowledge about making this product. Instead, wrote Carnegie, Schwab believed that "he was paid this salary largely because of his ability to deal with people." The wealthy executive elaborated, claiming that "his smile had been worth a million dollars." In Carnegie's words, Schwab's "personality, his charm, his ability to make people like him were almost wholly responsible for his extraordinary success." But it was that million dollars a year that stuck in Carnegie's head, the result that provided ultimate confirmation of this individual's worth and achievement.[1]

In his second influential advice book, *How to Stop Worrying and Start Living*, Carnegie promoted another principle he held dear: the need for spiritual values to provide emotional peace of mind. He carefully explained that he was not embracing traditional Christianity but had "gone forward to a new concept of religion. I no longer have the faintest interest in the differences in creeds that divide the churches. But I am enormously interested in what religion does for me" in creating "a new zest for life, more life, a larger, richer, more satisfying life." Carnegie noted that during his workaday life he would frequently drop into a church—the denomination did not matter—and engage in quiet meditation and prayer. As he explained, "doing this helps calm my nerves, rests my body, clarifies my perspective, and helps me revalue my values."[2]

Carnegie's enthusiastic endorsement of economic abundance and emotional well-being—in fact, they were two halves of his modern creed of success-seeking—sprang directly out of his childhood experiences. As a boy, he suffered the consequences of persistent poverty as his father, a hardscrabble dirt farmer with a dogged work ethic, struggled mightily but unsuccessfully to earn a living. From his mother, a devout and dynamic lay preacher of the Gospel, he learned the virtues of evangelical Protestantism and self-examination. This tense juxtaposition of stern religiosity and economic failure, hard work and hard times, self-control and personal defeat produced a profound ambiguity in Carnegie's experience of childhood. On the one hand, in later life he waxed lyrical about joyful romps in rural pastures, woods, and creeks where he would "smell the apple blossoms in the orchard and listen to the song of the brown thrasher." He cherished memories of a pious mother who read from the Bible and offered prayers of thanks for their modest food and shelter, and a generous father who, even while his own family had little, went to the local town and gave "the children of poor families shoes and warm clothing" at Christmas. On the other hand, he bitterly recalled a grim childhood characterized by a struggle to survive on a small farm. "My parents slaved sixteen hours a day, yet we constantly were oppressed by debts and harassed by hard luck," he wrote.

> One of my earliest memories is watching the floodwaters of the 102 River rolling over our corn and hayfields, destroying everything. The floods destroyed our crops six years out of seven. Year after year, our hogs died of cholera and we burned them. I can close my eyes now and recall the pungent odor of burning hog flesh . . . After ten years of hard, grueling work, we were not only penniless; we were heavily in debt. Our farm was mortgaged . . . No matter what we did, we lost money.[3]

Not surprisingly, the ongoing tension between poverty and piety during Carnegie's childhood nourished doubts and anxieties. As he admitted later, "I was full of worry in those days." Affection for his parents and respect for their traditional virtues—industriousness, family solidarity, spiritual striving, persistence in the face of daunting odds—provided a sense of basic morality and emotional grounding that stabilized him throughout life. At the same time, this sensitive child could not understand why their efforts, and their upstanding values, seemed to produce only failure. This painful disjuncture in his youthful psyche became one of the most important factors in his life. It provided the impetus, and the raw emotional material, for what would gradually emerge as his life's project: reformulating the meaning of success in modern America, and blazing a new trail by which to get there.

James Carnagey and Amanda Harbison first became acquainted in a fashion common among rural folk in the late 1800s. They both boarded at the Lynch farm near the town of Maryville, in extreme northwest Missouri not far from the Iowa border, where he worked as a hired hand and she as a schoolteacher who also did sewing and other domestic labor in return for a room and food. Mrs. Lynch told Miss Harbison, when she first arrived, about a nice-looking, hardworking young man who helped her husband with chores and recommended that she "set [her] cap for him." Her words proved prophetic. Within a short time, the young people became enamored of each other and struck up a romance.[4]

James William Carnagey was the eldest child in a large family of six sisters and three brothers. He had been born in February 1852 and raised in rural Indiana. Like most farm boys in the nineteenth century, he received only a rudimentary education. Attending school for portions of five or six years, he learned the basics of reading, writing, and arithmetic, but "never heard of Dickens or Shakespeare," as his son later discovered. Instead, James devoted himself to the backbreaking work that marked the typical small-farm regimen—milking cows, feeding hogs, planting corn, harvesting wheat and oats, threshing grain, chopping firewood, repairing fences, and a hundred other daily tasks. But rural life suited him. In the mid-1870s, James left Indiana to work at a sawmill owned by the Montana Beaverhead Company in Trapper Gulch, Montana, where he "snaked" logs down mountainsides and tended charcoal pits. After several years there, at his father's suggestion, he returned to the Midwest to check out the farm land in northwest Missouri, which was considerably cheaper than land in Indiana. The young man decided to stay in the area.[5]

Amanda Elizabeth Harbison was a native Missourian. Born in February 1858 in the northern part of the state, she was the eldest girl among eight siblings. In 1861, with the outbreak of the Civil War, her father, Abraham, moved the family to Henderson County, Illinois, just across the Mississippi River—he was drafted during the conflict but hired a substitute—before returning to northwest Missouri around 1870. As a youth, Amanda imbibed stern religious principles and a love for education, both of which would stay with her throughout her life. Around 1880, she accepted a position as a teacher at a small country schoolhouse near Maryville and met the young man who would become her husband.[6]

James and Amanda began courting soon after her arrival at the Lynch farm, but the relationship (again in the fashion of traditional rural folk) evinced more pragmatism than passion. The couple began planning marriage, but Amanda developed deep second thoughts before receiving reassurances from her father. "Jim Carnagey is a very good man," he told his eldest daughter. "He is honest. He works hard. He doesn't drink or gamble or chew or smoke. I know he'll make you a good husband. He is one of the finest men I know." Dale put it more descriptively several decades later. His parents' courtship was "far from being a Romeo and Juliet of the cornfields," he related. "It was, instead, a solid, kindly, cooperative, and Christ-like union." The couple married on January 1, 1882, and it proved to be a suitable pairing. "If they ever had one quarrel or spoke one unkind word to each other, I do not remember hearing it," Dale noted.[7]

In November 1886, a first child, Clifton, arrived to the young couple. They were living on a small farm near a crossroads hamlet named Harmony Church, which stood about ten miles northeast of

Maryville and only seven miles from the Iowa state line. Two years later, Dale Harbison Carnagey was born on November 24, 1888. One of the worst blizzards in recent memory was raging, and when Amanda went into labor a neighbor galloped away on horseback through the snow to summon the nearest doctor from the village of Parnell, Missouri. "I have always been in a hurry, so I arrived before the doctor did," Dale liked to say.[8]

In many ways, Dale led an idyllic youth deep in the rural hinterland. When he was old enough to walk, he loved to be outdoors, enjoying the beauties of nature on a daily basis. This experience was amplified when his father tried to advance the family fortunes in the early 1890s. "When I was five years old, father bought a beautiful farm that I shall remember all my life," Carnagey recalled. It featured a house and a barn perched on a high hill that sloped down to beautiful, level farmland that was accented with a sluggish stream meandering through it. Dale particularly remembered "gorgeous sunsets that splashed the sky with the colors of a painting by Turner." He spent endless hours fishing and swimming in the 102 River, so named by the Mormons because it was the 102nd river or stream they crossed on their journey from Nauvoo, Illinois, to Great Salt Lake, Utah. He trekked to grammar school with nearby farm kids and enjoyed picnics with them in Coulter's Woods. Dale had a special fondness for local patches full of large, juicy watermelons that were cooled in a water tank before being devoured on warm summer evenings. Even when the weather turned cold, the natural world could seem enchanted to the impressionable boy. He would awaken to a snow-covered "fairyland" where the tracks of rabbits and wild birds could be seen everywhere. "When father put on his felt boots and rubbers and started for the barn to feed the stock," Dale recalled, "the scene was a living Currier and Ives print."[9]

Dale Carnagey as a toddler (holding the hatchet), posing with older brother, Clifton.

A warm, secure family atmosphere enhanced his childhood experience. Dale appreciated his father's work ethic, noting a few years later that "if father built a fence it would last forever, for I used to think that he was the most particular man in the world about getting the posts straight and building the fence as though it

Dale as a little boy (front), Clifton, and his parents, James and Amanda.

was to hold mad bulls." But it was with his mother that he enjoyed a special bond. "I was greatly influenced by her in every way," he once declared. "No one ever had a more loving mother than I did . . . I can't imagine what my life would be like if I had not had Amanda Elizabeth Harbison Carnagey for my mother." She especially influenced his education. In Dale's view, she was "one of the most exciting teachers I have ever known," regularly reading favorite books aloud to him: *Uncle Tom's Cabin*, *Robinson Crusoe*, *The Swiss Family Robinson*, *The Prince of the House of David*, *David—the Way of the Cross*, *Black Beauty*, and the temperance novel *Ten Nights in a Barroom*. She also trained him to memorize and recite religious "pieces" for church gatherings. "The first time I ever made an appearance on the platform, facing the audience, Mother said as I walked up the aisle, 'Here comes my boy, my precious boy,'" her son recalled later. But then when he began to speak "my memory failed me and I said to my mother, 'My, ain't it hot up here.'" A bit later, the youngster made his first public address and, reflecting his mother's religious fervor, it was entitled "The Saloon, the Offspring of Hell."[10]

The son also inherited the mother's enthusiasm for life, a key trait that would define him as an adult. He described her as "the sparkplug of our family" and observed that he "either inherited or acquired her boundless energy and excitement about life . . . She did everything with earnestness. She often sang as she worked." Through example and instruction alike, Amanda conveyed to her bright offspring a sense that life was something to be embraced as an opportunity and molded by action. She personified steadfastness in facing the world—he would later describe Amanda as having "the courage of 17 Bengal tigers"—and her perseverance served as a "shining example" to her son.[11]

But another factor sullied Dale Carnagey's childhood. Life was hard in rural Missouri in the late 1800s, and reminders of its fragility, hardships, and dangers came often. His maternal grandmother, who was in her nineties, lived with the family for several years and would entrance the boy with scary stories of life on the frontier, such as when her brother was kidnapped by Indians and forced to live with them for fourteen years. Disease provided a constant threat as various maladies regularly swept through the local population and carried off vulnerable children. The Mizingo family, who lived across the road from the Carnageys, lost a daughter to smallpox and the horrifying details burned themselves into the boy's memory. "Her dead body was so foul and stinking that two men held their noses as they rushed into her bedroom, picked up the four corners of the sheet, and dropped her body into a crude wooden box," he remembered. "She was buried at night under the apple trees in a nearby orchard. Since I lived directly across the road, I could hear the clods rattle down on her coffin." For days Dale's mother lived in terror because her son had visited the Mizingo house only a day before the disease appeared. In a region only barely removed from its frontier atmosphere, violence also exploded with disturbing frequency. For decades, Carnagey carried with him the memory of murders, rapes, and violent family feuds that exploded nearby with disturbing regularity.[12]

Farm life also presented the boy a brutal work regimen with few amenities. From a young age, he hauled manure from the barn, cowshed, and chicken houses and helped milk the cows and chop and stack firewood. He found farm labor to be dirty and exhausting, and distastefully remembered being covered in dust from plowing the fields behind a horse. Running water did not exist, of course, and like all farmers the Carnageys had no inside toilet. Later, Dale vividly remembered the first time he used an inside flush toilet at a dry goods store in Maryville. "There was a roar. Everyone in the store could hear it. To me it sounded as if the town's water tower had fallen down. I walked out of the store, my face burning with embarrassment," he recalled. A single wood stove provided the only source of heat in the Carnagey farmhouse, and the boy spent many winter nights huddled under the covers in a freezing bedroom.[13]

The same forces of nature that inspired euphoric visions of beauty in his youth also induced spasms of fear. During the spring and summer seasons, violent storms with high winds and thunder would sweep in from the west and fill the horizon with violent flashes of lightning. The Carnageys would rush from the house into the storm cellar, which would be lined with preserved food, to ride things out. After one such event, Dale couldn't find his little dog, Tippy. He finally saw his lifeless body laying near the porch—the animal had been struck by lightning. He pleaded with his pious mother to pray to God for the return of his little dog, but she replied gently that the Almighty did not raise dogs from the dead. "But Tippy is a lot better than many people," the heartbroken youngster replied. "This was the greatest tragedy of my early life," he recalled later.[14]

The winter season could send temperatures plummeting to painful depths. After emerging from a frigid house in the early-morning hours, the boy had to walk more than a mile to school in bone-chilling temperatures and often through deep snow. "Until I was fourteen, I never had any rubbers or overshoes. During the long, cold winters, my feet were always wet and cold," he reported. "As a child, I never dreamed that anyone had warm, dry feet in the winter." And the frigid temperatures, of course, made farm work even more difficult during this season. His father raised Duroc hogs, for instance, and the sows often had their litters in February, when temperatures commonly hovered near zero. To keep the piglets from freezing to death, James would bring them into the house and put them in a basket behind the kitchen stove, covered with a burlap sack. It was Dale's job to take care of them. Just before bed, he would take the basket of piglets out to their mother in the barn to nurse. "Then I went to bed, set the alarm for three o'clock; when it went off I got out of bed in the bitter cold, took the pigs out for another hot meal, brought them back, set the alarm for six o'clock, and got up to study . . . At the time I thought that was a great hardship."[15]

Boyhood accidents illustrated the dangers of rural life. Once, young Carnagey mounted a horse on a cold winter day and as he swung into the saddle the animal bolted. Falling backward, he had one foot stuck in a stirrup and was dragged quite a distance at high speed through the frozen mud before he was able to extricate his foot. The encounter left him bruised and a bit dazed. Another time he was less fortunate. On the day after Christmas 1899, he was playing with his cousin in the attic of an abandoned log cabin down the road from his house. He was wearing on the forefinger of his left hand a ring—a family heirloom—that his father had given him. Urged on by his cousin, he stood on the windowsill of the attic and jumped to the ground, but when he did so the ring caught on a nail embedded in the log he had been grasping. His finger was torn off. The terrified youth ran to his house bleeding profusely and shouting for help. His mother wrapped the stump tight as his father hitched up a team to the wagon, and they drove hurriedly to Maryville. "I prayed and yelled and screamed every step the horses took in that hour-long trip to town. I was taken to Dr. Nash's office in Maryville," he remembered fifty years later. "As he took off the handkerchief that had been wrapped around my bleeding finger, some of it clung to the bone. The agony was terrible." The doctor sedated the boy with chloroform before cleaning the wound and making a neater amputation. For the rest of his life, Carnagey would gesture with his right hand while subtly hiding his left one.[16]

But another factor created the deepest, most enduring emotional pain for this Missouri farm boy: his family's poverty. Unable to make a profit and increasingly mired in debt, like many small farmers in the late 1800s, James Carnagey's hard work took him nowhere. Floods washed out his crops periodically, diseases killed his hogs, and the vagaries of the agricultural market brought little or no profit at harvest time. Once, he tried raising cattle but was unable to sell them for what it cost to fatten them up. Another time, he bought a group of young, untrained mules and labored

As a schoolboy in the mid-1890s, Dale already displayed a wide-eyed curiosity about the world.

prodigiously to break them for farm use, only to find that, once again, he was unable to sell them for enough to cover the cost of their feed. James complained bitterly that "he would be better off financially if he had taken a shotgun and killed the mules the day he bought them."[17]

Desperate, the family did its best to survive through self-sufficiency and barter. The Carnageys raised their own fruit and vegetables, and smoked their own ham and bacon. They traded butter and eggs for coffee, sugar, and salt at Kirk's Grocery and for shoes from the local cobbler. But such efforts brought little beyond bare survival. Homer Croy, a lifelong friend of Dale's who grew up nearby, recalled an embarrassing sign of the Carnageys' economic hardship. "My first memory of his family was seeing them drive into town Sunday morning with a horse on one side of the pole and a mule on the other," he wrote. This mismatch displayed to all "how impoverished the family was."[18]

Dale, intelligent and sensitive, found it hard to face the deprivation and small humiliations that accompanied his family's poverty. The Carnagey boys had very little. Amanda made all of their clothes out of cloth bartered from local stores and they had to endure holes in the bottom of shoes and patches on the seat of pants. Toys and treats, of course, came only rarely. Dale would cry when his father came home from town without bringing him a cheap piece of candy, which deeply hurt James. One Christmas, his parents gave him a tiny trunk less than a foot high, which included a little tray, and the boy treasured it as one of his most prized possessions. An enormous thrill came from riding in the wagon into Maryville on occasion, and his father giving him a dime to spend in whatever way he wished. But such extravagances were rare, and the abiding sense of physical want and emotional trauma was palpable. "I was ashamed of our poverty," he admitted later.[19]

Eventually dwindling economic resources caught up to the Carnagey family. In early 1900, after several years of heartbreaking failures, James was so deeply in debt that he was forced to sell the farm he had purchased with such high hopes in the early 1890s. After paying off his creditors, the family was left with a few pieces of furniture, a wagon, and a couple of horses. Even Dale's stalwart mother broke down, hugging her sons as she sobbed, "You boys are the only things we have left in the world now." The family rented another farm in the Maryville area and tried to start over. But "Father's spirit was broken at the failure he was making of his life," the son described, and this image of failure burned itself into his youthful psyche.[20]

The crisis affected his parents differently. James turned to politics by associating with the Populist movement. Many small farmers scrambling to survive in the 1880s and 1890s had determined that the financial and political power structure of Gilded Age America—particularly the banks, the railroads, and a Republican Party devoted to the protective tariff favoring manufacturers and the gold standard—were responsible for their economic problems. They revolted. Organizing politically, they pushed forward by organizing the People's Party in the early 1890s and then backing William Jennings Bryan as a Populist standard-bearer in the Democratic Party a bit later. The Populists sought redress for their grievances in free silver, government regulation of railroads and financial institutions, and collective tactics in the marketplace. James became an ardent supporter of Bryan in his 1896 presidential bid against Republican William McKinley. He took a wooden box top, wrote "Bryan and Prosperity" on it, and nailed it to a tree by the road. But the election turned out badly; James and his boys heard the news of Bryan's defeat while gathered around the telephone in the local general store on election night. Disgusted, James turned his sign over, wrote "McKinley and Starvation, Farm for Sale," and nailed it back on the tree.[21]

Eventually James gave way to despair. Mired in debt with no escape route in sight, he grew depressed. Threats and intimations of self-harm became frequent as he suggested he might hang himself from the branches of a large oak tree on their farm. Amanda worried that whenever her husband went to the barn to feed livestock and took longer than expected in returning, "she would find his body dangling from the end of a rope." James himself admitted to his son that after returning from a bank in Maryville, which had threatened to foreclose on his farm, he stopped his wagon on a bridge over the 102 River, got out, "and stood for a long time looking down at the water, debating with himself whether he should jump in and end it all."[22]

Amanda responded to the family's economic adversity in a strikingly different fashion. Already a religious woman, she raised her piety to an even higher pitch. Forbidding both dancing and card-playing, she turned her home into a fortress of faith and a bastion of strict morality. She led her family in frequent prayers for God's love and protection and read a Bible chapter aloud to her sons every night before they went to bed. A great supporter of reading and education, she subscribed to the Moody Colportage Library, a series of inexpensive religious books endorsed by the noted evangelist Dwight L. Moody, and acquainted her husband and sons with its didactic volumes. One of her favorites was an anti-dancing tract, *From the Ballroom to Hell*, which Dale read with misplaced energy—he reported later that he had been entranced in a decidedly non-pious way by the "pictures of girls in short skirts going to hell." Amanda also served as a disciplinarian. Endorsing the Bible injunction to "spare the rod and spoil the child," she switched both of her sons when they misbehaved, although it pained her to do so. But Amanda's moral firmness produced a sunny, optimistic outlook toward life rather than a sour, pinched one. As Dale recounted, "Neither floods nor debts nor disaster could suppress her happy, radiant, and victorious spirit."[23]

Amanda's religious enthusiasm also prompted her to widespread involvement in church affairs in the community around Maryville. She played the organ in a variety of country churches and taught Sunday school throughout her adult life. More important, she became a skilled lay preacher who, in the words of a family friend, "could get up on the platform and speak as well as any man. And she did. Sometimes she came to Brother Lytle's pulpit at our Methodist Church and preached sermons as good as his . . . She put fire and drive and earnestness into them." As her fame spread, Amanda traveled into nearby Iowa and Nebraska for speaking engagements and once even to Illinois when friends raised enough money to send her there to participate in revival meetings. She particularly embraced the temperance movement and its crusade to root out demon rum—Carrie Nation, the hatchet-wielding opponent of liquor establishments, became a special hero—and Amanda fought local saloons "tooth and nail," in the words of one observer.[24]

Young Dale absorbed one positive lesson from his parents' struggles: a profound regard for their selflessness. Even in the depths of their poverty, he reported, his father and mother somehow would scrape together some money every year to send to the Christian Home, a nearby orphanage in Council Bluffs, Iowa. Later in life, when the prosperous son sent his parents a Christmas check for a few small luxuries, he would shake his head to learn of how his parents would use part of the money to buy groceries or coal for local families who were struggling. Such virtue made an indelible impact. After Dale became famous, he gave a talk in New York in which he described his parents' selfless natures. He choked up and tears ran down his face. "My parents gave me no money nor financial inheritance," he said after regaining his composure, "but they gave me something of much greater value—the blessing of faith and sturdy character."[25]

Thus Carnagey grew up immersed in the traditional culture of nineteenth-century America as he internalized a strong religious ethic. Eventually he would reject many of the specifics of Protestant theology—he would joke that he "had been brought up to believe that only Methodists were sure to get into heaven"—but a yearning for spiritual solace and connection would endure. "My mother wanted me to devote my life to religious work. I thought seriously of becoming a foreign missionary," he noted. While he had no interest in a religious career, he nurtured this didactic impulse in a different form. In his hands, the cultivation of human relations and the achievement of success became a kind of secular salvation. As he wrote exuberantly in *How to Win Friends and Influence People*, the adoption of his techniques would create a kind of transformative religious experience: "I have seen the application of these principles literally revolutionize the lives of many people."[26]

As a youth, Dale also developed an affinity for verbal expression and contention. His schoolteacher mother had a way with words that rubbed off. "I was a born arguer. For years I loved a verbal joust. I argued at home, in school, and on the playground," he admitted. "I had the typical 'I'm from Missouri, you have to show me' attitude." In the same vein, he absorbed from his mother a taste for performing in public as "she always had me speaking pieces in Sunday School and church entertainments." These expressive qualities, which he came to see as "a blessing in disguise," would shape a future interest in debating and his career in public speaking.[27]

Young Carnagey exhibited a large element of charm in his personality, another trait that he inherited from Amanda. As a young boy, after caught misbehaving, he sweet-talked his mother as she was about to apply the switch. "I asked her if I couldn't have a cookie and lie down on the couch and rest a while before she switched me," he reported. "That got the better of her. She had to laugh, and I got out of the switching." Lighthearted and an occasional prankster, he once caused great hilarity at his small country school when he killed a rabbit, skinned it and cut up the carcass, and stealthily put the meat in a bucket sealed with a lid atop the heat stove. By the time the teacher and his fellow students became aware of the odd smell, it was too late. A surge of steam blew off the lid as hot water and pieces of boiled rabbit shot up to the ceiling. The teacher was not amused but the other students certainly were. "Education ought to be fun," he remarked. "It was—that afternoon."[28]

But Dale also developed a powerful sensitivity to humiliation. As a youngster first going to school, he was embarrassed to use the communal outhouse because the older boys would stand around and jeer at the younger ones. Instead, in an act of desperation he lay down on the far side of the schoolhouse when nature called. "Presently, a little stream of water began to trickle out from under me in the dust," he described. "Some of the older boys spotted this. They all began to whoop and holler, and point at me and call me names. Never before or since have I been so humiliated. It brought tears of shame." The schoolyard also brought relentless teasing about his large, protruding ears—years later he remembered the name of his primary tormentor, an older student named Sam White—which reduced him to cringing. His family's poverty, of course, provided an abiding source of distress and he felt a growing sense of inferiority about his rustic background and rough manners. Around age thirteen, for instance, while working in the fields, he spied a pretty girl coming down the road in a buggy and decided to attempt gallantry by tipping his hat. When she got to him, however, panic set in and he missed the brim and knocked his hat completely off. The girl laughed mockingly and drove off, leaving him acutely embarrassed.[29]

Revealingly, for an individual who later would develop a blueprint for success in the corporate, urban, white-collar world of the twentieth century, Dale also developed a pronounced aversion to the physical labor necessary to rural success in the nineteenth century. "As a young lad, I hated anything that even remotely resembled work," he freely admitted. "The work I loathed was churning the cream into butter, cleaning out the hen house, cutting weeds, and milking cows. Above all else, I hated to chop wood. I despised it so bitterly that we would never have any firewood stored up in advance." James continually lectured his youngest son about the necessity of hard work and made him perform a regular regimen of chores. But the boy's heart was not in it.[30]

Gradually, and portentously for his future, Carnagey grew aware of the profound limitations of his rural existence. The occasional trips to Maryville delighted and depressed him in equal measure. He perceived the town to be a bustling metropolis and was enormously impressed with figures such as Daniel Eversole, the proprietor of the local dry goods store, who was a man of great presence and personality. The Linville Hotel seemed an icon of sophistication as Dale peered through the windows and observed well-dressed town dignitaries and visitors sitting in the lobby's plush chairs and smoking fat cigars. This dawning awareness of a bigger world outside of rural Missouri was underlined when he saw a motion picture for the first time in 1899 at his small school. A short Western film, its dazzling climax featured a train hurtling along with two cowboys galloping beside it. The boy was thrilled.[31]

One influence loomed particularly large in expanding Dale's worldview. In the winter of 1901, Nicholas M. Sowder began teaching at the rural school and also became a boarder with the Carnagey family. He first made an impression by directing a dramatic, four-act student play entitled *Imogene, or the Witch's Secret.* Dale played the part of Snooks, the newsboy, and was enthralled, particularly when the play's success prompted Sowder to "go high-hat" and rent a hall in nearby Parnell, Missouri, for several performances and charge admission. This exposure to acting gave young Carnagey "a taste of the thrill that comes from appearing before a crowd," an emotion that would loom large in his future career. Sowder also had important personal interactions with Dale at the Carnagey home. The teacher owned a typewriter and an adding machine, neither of which the youngster had ever seen, and Sowder engaged in long discussions with his bright pupil using complex words such as "intuitive" and "psychology." The wide-eyed student viewed the teacher as a door opening onto a wider world, and years later described Sowder as his "first inspiration."[32]

Ultimately, Dale's boyhood experiences led him to confront a topic that would become central to his later career: What it meant to be successful in America, and how to go about achieving it. Traumatized by his family's failure to prosper, he grew determined to escape the trap of rural poverty and "live in a big city and wear a white collar seven days a week." At the same time, he struggled to accommodate his yearning for affluence with a genuine respect for moral virtues. He was inclined to judge the man with the biggest farm and the most money as the biggest success. But then he noticed that one of the Carnageys' neighbors, a prosperous farmer, was greedy and drove his farmhands relentlessly to work harder. "The poor devil was devoured by a blind, fanatical desire for more money, more money, more money! If he had accumulated a million dollars, he would still have been driven for more," he wrote. When compared to the unselfishness of his parents and many other ordinary farm folk, such values seemed less attractive.[33]

A keen observer of human nature even as a youth, Carnagey perceived that people derived meaning and fulfillment from things other than wealth. His father's Duroc hogs and white-faced cattle won a number of blue ribbons over the years at county fairs and livestock shows. James mounted the ribbons on a sheet of white muslin, and whenever a visitor came by the house he would proudly exhibit the prizes. Dale drew an important conclusion: Each individual seeks a feeling of distinction, of being recognized for some kind of achievement, worthiness, or attractiveness, no matter how small. The lesson would stick with him.[34]

Struggling to accommodate piety and poverty, virtue and failure, hard work and humiliation, Dale Carnagey reached a turning point in his youth. In the spring of 1904, when he was sixteen, his family left their rented farm near Maryville, loaded their belongings into a railroad boxcar, and headed toward Warrensburg, Missouri, about a hundred and seventy miles to the southeast. The farmland there was no better than in northwest Missouri, but his parents had a larger aim. They wanted to give their sons a college education, and a state teachers college was nearby. For the first time, the poor farm boy from the rural margins of society came into direct contact with the larger world he had only envisioned up to this point. It would be the first step on his own road to success.[35]

2

Rebellion and Recovery

A mong the many principles of self-improvement strewn throughout *How to Win Friends and Influence People*, the importance of taking up fresh ideas and considering a new approach to life stood high on Dale Carnegie's list. He talked frequently about the need to abandon an archaic, ineffective worldview and adopt a new mind-set more conducive to success. The "indispensible requirement" for getting the most out of his book, Carnegie stressed, was having "a deep, driving desire to learn, a vigorous determination to increase your ability to deal with people." He urged readers to keep in mind "the rich possibilities for improvement that still lie in the offing" and reminded them, "You are attempting to form new habits, you are attempting a new way of life." But Carnegie recognized that adopting new viewpoints was extremely difficult because of innate human intransigence. "Most of us are prejudiced and biased. Most of us are blighted with preconceived notions," Carnegie wrote. "And most citizens don't want to change their minds about their religion or their haircut or Communism or Clark Gable."[1]

Adopting new ideas depended on generating sufficient self-confidence and self-esteem, both in yourself and in others. Carnegie saw it as a fundamental impulse in human nature that everyone wanted a feeling of distinction. "You want the approval of those with whom you come in contact. You want recognition of your true worth," he contended. "You want a feeling that you are important in your little world." Thus the sensitive, or perhaps shrewd, success seeker must approach the world confidently but with a determination to "make the other person feel important, and do it sincerely." At all times you must tell yourself to be "hearty in your approbation and lavish in your praise." After all, Carnegie observed, "We nourish the bodies of our children and friends and employees; but how seldom do we nourish their self-esteem."[2]

This twin emphasis on rethinking one's approach to the world and bolstering self-esteem stemmed from the author's difficult adolescence. At age sixteen, he enrolled at a small Missouri college and almost immediately suffered an intense personal crisis. Fueled by his academic studies, he began to question the religious principles he had been taught during childhood. Humiliated by family poverty that was all too clearly reflected in his threadbare personal appearance, he suffered an "inferiority complex" with regard to his fellow students, an emotional malady that sent him reeling. These challenges propelled him into outright rebellion against the traditions with which he had grown up and created a tense conflict with his family, particularly with his pious mother. Yet young Carnegie soon found relief, and a strong measure of self-esteem, by embracing public speaking. He discovered a talent for addressing and convincing others, and success in this popular collegiate activity eventually made him one of the most respected students on campus. Moreover, his embrace of a progressive version of public speech—it stressed communication, a conversational style, and the expression of personality over old-fashioned, theatrical oratory—laid the foundation for his later career. Ridding himself of much of the baggage of nineteenth-century cultural tradition, and possessed of a new sense of self-worth, young Carnegie took another important step on his journey to success. Reshaping his own worldview became the basis for convincing others to do so too.

In 1904, when the Carnagey family pulled into Warrensburg, they found a modest town of around five thousand inhabitants nestled among gently rolling hills on the western edge of the Ozark Mountains as they began to flatten out approaching the Kansas plains. The governmental seat of Johnson County, it sat in west central Missouri about sixty-five miles southeast of Kansas City. It had been founded in the 1830s, and then gained an economic boost in 1864 when the Missouri Pacific Railroad established a depot there, and by the turn of the century it had become a typical, prosperous small Midwestern town. It contained several churches representing every Protestant denomination, a grain elevator and flour mill, a foundry, a small woolens factory, three hotels, a number of banks, a library, two newspapers, and small merchants of every variety.[3]

But its central feature, and the reason the Carnageys had moved there, was a college. The State Normal School in Warrensburg had been founded in 1871—one of two in the state devoted to training teachers for an emerging public system of grammar schools and secondary schools—and by late in the decade it was thriving. Tuition was free, and in return students were expected to take a teaching position in Missouri after graduation. In the fall of 1904, a student body of around eight hundred and a faculty of forty met for classes on a compact campus consisting of several large, sandstone buildings constructed in the Lombard-Venetian style of late-Victorian architecture. A large pond and an open athletic field added attractive physical features to the layout.[4]

The State Normal School described its mission as contributing to "an educated citizenship" in Missouri by training qualified teachers for the public schools. It drew students from around the state, particularly rural areas in the central agricultural region and Kansas City. In the early 1900s, as was typical of most normal schools in this era, freshman and sophomore students took classes at the level of what today we would call the eleventh and twelfth grades, while juniors and seniors studied at the modern-day equivalent of the first two years of college. Students pursuing the elementary course, such as Carnagey, graduated with Regents Certificates while more advanced students received a Bachelor of Pedagogy. Typically, students proceeded lockstep through a variety of courses in rhetoric, mathematics, psychology, history, literature, and science during the first two years, followed by more advanced elective courses and ever larger doses of teacher training in the final two years. By providing well-rounded educations to future teachers and then dispersing them throughout the state, the school aimed its efforts "with the general welfare always in view."[5]

In the spring of 1904, James and Amanda Carnagey settled about three miles south of Warrensburg. They had secured a small farm that had a traditional two-story clapboard house along with a barn and a scattering of outbuildings. James continued his lifelong struggle to eke out a living on the land, as he had in earlier years, by cultivating mixed crops and raising livestock, while Amanda managed the household and became involved in local church activity. But the reason the couple had moved from Maryville was to provide educational opportunity for their sons, and that fall both boys enrolled in college. Clifton was an indifferent student, but Dale was delighted to be on a college campus. It greatly broadened his view of the world and satisfied a yearning for new experiences that the isolated youth had first glimpsed through some of his mother's books and in his conversations with Mr. Sowder. His college studies in science, history, and literature took him into intellectual realms far removed from the one-room schoolhouses and the Sunday school classes in small country churches of his youth. They changed the trajectory of his life and, in his words, "altered my sights and widened my horizons."[6]

At the same time, however, college life presented a stern trial for the farm boy. It offered a daily ritual of humiliation that was rooted in the old bugaboo of his family: poverty. Only a handful of students lacked the modest funds necessary for room and board in Warrensburg, and Carnagey was one of them. He had to ride a horse to campus every morning to attend classes. An obvious problem emerged—what to do with the animal during the day and how to feed him? So the youth found a man with a barn and a vacant stall near the college, and every week James would bring in a load of grain and hay for his son to use for his horse. Then in the afternoon, after classes, Dale would ride home. Back on the farm, he would slip on his overalls, milk the cows, cut the wood, slop the hogs, and then study late into the night by the light of a coal-oil lamp. His equine transportation and rustic schedule were impossible to hide from his classmates, and the smirks of more sophisticated students soon caused him great embarrassment. He began to see himself as a social outcast and, as he recalled years later, developed "an inferiority complex."[7]

One issue particularly embodied the boy's social anxiety. "Above all else I was ashamed of my clothes," he confessed. "I was growing rapidly. When I first got my clothes they were too large—then they fit perfectly for several months and finally they were too little." Not only were his clothes ill fitting, they were shabby—home sewn, with threadbare cloth and washed-out colors from long use, and even patched on occasion. For a rural youth trying to fit in on a college campus that he viewed as the epitome of sophistication and knowledge, the situation opened a raw psychological wound. He was so self-conscious about his attire that going to the front of the class for blackboard exercises became mortifying. "I can't think of the problem [at hand]," he burst out to his mother at one point. "I am only conscious of the fact that my clothes don't fit and that the students are laughing at me behind my back." Amanda broke down in tears upon hearing this. "Oh Dale, I wish we could get better clothes for you but we just can't!" she cried. In turn, this lament filled the son with remorse about "how cruel I was without intending to be."[8]

A dawning attraction to young women further sharpened Carnagey's acute sensitivity to his outsider status. After settling into life at the State Normal School, he began to notice the array of pretty, intelligent coeds in his classes and asked a number of them to go out on dates. A long series of rebuffs ensued. "I remember a girl by the name of Patsy Thurber," he reported ruefully. "I asked her to go buggy riding with me and she turned me down. And some of the other girls in town turned me down." Such rejection not only underlined his feelings of inferiority but made him even more tongue-tied when he tried to chat up his female classmates. Soon his anxiety became obsessive. "I worried for fear no girl would ever be willing to marry me," he explained later. "I worried about what I would say to my wife immediately after we were married. I imagined that we would be married in some country church and then get in a surrey with fringe on the top and ride back to the farm. But how would I be able to keep the conversation going on that ride back to the farm? How? How? I pondered over that earth-shaking problem for many an hour as I walked behind the plow." For a boy in the throes of adolescent angst, romantic rejection made life appear bleak.[9]

While social strains undermined his self-confidence, Carnagey underwent an intellectual trial of equal magnitude, one that threatened the very foundation of his upbringing. As he advanced through the State Normal School curriculum, he suffered a crisis of religious faith. His studies called into question the traditional Protestant doctrine with which he had been raised and shed new, unflattering light on the intense religious beliefs of his mother. In later years, he described how the familiar worldview of his boyhood began to collapse around him:

> I studied biology, science, philosophy, and comparative religions. I read books on how the Bible was written. I began to question many of its assertions. I began to doubt many of the narrow doctrines taught by the country preachers of that day. I was bewildered . . . I didn't know what to believe. I saw no purpose in life. I stopped praying. I became an agnostic. I believed that all life was planless and aimless. I believed that human beings had no more divine purpose than had the dinosaurs that roamed the earth some two hundred million years ago. I felt that someday the human race would perish—just as the dinosaurs had . . . I sneered at the idea of a beneficent God who had created man in his own likeness.[10]

By the time he left college, Carnagey's turn against traditional religion became so strong that he began to openly proclaim it to his horrified mother. When Amanda objected to the theater, for instance, he replied mockingly, "I'll bet that the plays of Shakespeare and the play *Ben Hur*, by Lew Wallace, have preached more sermons and touched the lives of more people than the preaching of the evangelists you mention." When Amanda denounced dancing as a pathway to damnation, now her son could barely conceal his contempt. "If there is any place that they are going to keep me out of after death because I danced and went to the theatre, I am frank to say that I want to be kept out, for I never could be happy and congenial with such people holding such views," he declared. "They don't do those things in my heaven." The church as an institution was a hundred years behind the times, young Carnagey now insisted, and its narrow policies not only were alienating young people but were "too absurd to be countenanced by any intelligent person." He proclaimed indignantly, "Most of these God-given laws that we hear so much about were made by some ignorant fogey and then attributed to God."[11]

Staggered by social rejection and floundering in intellectual doubt, Carnagey sought a way out. He desperately wanted to overcome the stigma of poverty and funnel his intellectual stirrings into positive action. Roiling in uncertainty, he searched for a course of action to overcome his inferiority complex and achieve success. In his words, "I looked around unconsciously for a compensation for my life, whether it was because my clothes didn't fit, or that girls turned me down for dates, or the fact that I had to live on a farm. I was determined to put myself on the map." More deeply, he also sought a measure of respect from his fellow students: to prove "I was just as good as they were."[12]

Unexpectedly, he received a jolt of inspirational energy. Two visiting speakers to the school touched a nerve in this young man trying to find his way in the world and find himself in the process. One evening he went to hear a Chautauqua speaker at the college— Carnagey described him admiringly as "riding around in trains and living in hotels and wearing a white collar and all"—who told

a story about a boy who worked as a janitor to pay for his college education, was ashamed of his clothes, and could not muster
enough money to take a girl on a respectable date. After detailing
this grim scenario for fifteen minutes, he proclaimed, "That boy is
standing before you tonight!" A short time later, Carnagey heard
another lecture delivered by a vice president of the Chicago and
Alton Railroad, which described his rise to prominence after beginning as a lowly brakeman. The student was mesmerized by these
tales of opportunity awaiting in the outside world. Previously, he
believed that "you had to be a rich man's son to get to the top and
that a poor boy didn't have much of an opportunity." But now he
felt a surge of courage and hope from this pair of speakers. "The
first, because I felt that if he could push himself out of poverty and
make his living as a speaker, I could do the same," he explained.
"The second, because he assured me that poverty at the beginning
did not stop a determined man from reaching the top."[13]

Fired by these visions of a brighter future, Carnagey had an
epiphany. Many of the popular students on campus, of course,
were the football, baseball, and basketball players, and the farm
boy admitted that he had neither skills in, nor a flair for, sports. But
then he noticed something else:

> I looked around and saw that the men who had won the de
> bating and public speaking contests were regarded as the in
> tellectual leaders in college. They were in the limelight; they
> stood up and addressed an audience of a thousand people.
> Everybody knew them! Everybody knew their names! They
> were pointed to as they walked across campus. I said, "maybe
> I can do that" because my mother had taken me around to
> Sunday School affairs and I had spoken pieces, and I had

engaged in amateur [theatrical] performances. I had discovered that I could at least stand up and speak with a little more vitality and enthusiasm than the average speaker.

So he plunged ahead by drawing upon a happier legacy from boyhood—his way with the spoken word—and moved it to the center of his endeavors. Public speaking became his means to respectability and success.[14]

But he struggled mightily in his quest to find redemption through oratory. There were a number of annual, hotly fought campus-wide speaking competitions—a debating contest, a declamatory contest, and a general public-speaking contest—but entering them was no simple matter. In this era, when social fraternities were only just appearing, "literary societies" dominated the social map at the State Normal School. There were six of them that were officially recognized: the Athenian, the Baconian, and the Irving for young men; and the Campbell, the Osborne, and the Periclean for young women. Controlled by the faculty and supervised by the head of the Department of Expression, each society had a hall of its own and convened a regular series of programs that included readings, orations, debates, and choral singing. Every year, the literary societies also organized the various campus contests in oratory, debate, and declamation. To win the campus prizes, a student first had to emerge as a winner from this sextet of organizations, a difficult task for a relatively untutored and inexperienced student like Carnagey.[15]

He had joined the Irving Literary Society, named after the popular early nineteenth-century Knickerbocker writer Washington Irving. The Irvings stressed the strong fellowship and enviable achievements within their group, as they proudly described it in *The Rhetor*, the State Normal School yearbook: "Irving! What a suggestion of strength, courage, perseverance, patience, endurance!"

During his first two years on campus, Carnagey entered the public-speaking competition within the Irvings, hoping to emerge as its representative in the campus contests. He failed miserably. On top of his social frustrations, these setbacks were terribly discouraging and he grew increasingly morose. His defeat in 1906 was particularly devastating. "I was so crushed, so beaten, so despondent, that I literally thought of suicide," he recalled many years later. "Sounds silly? Not when you are seventeen or eighteen and suffering from an inferiority complex!"[16]

Added pressure came from the fact that the State Normal School nurtured a tradition of oratorical excellence. The spoken word was highly valued among these prospective teachers, and students vied for distinction and attended the competitions in large numbers. One observer claimed that in Warrensburg "oratory was more highly esteemed than in any town in the state" and that each year the winners "were carried on the shoulders of the crowd and bonfires sent aloft in their honor." In fact, one of the most famous addresses in nineteenth-century America had been delivered in the town. In 1869, lawyer George Vest—he would go on to win election to the United States Senate from Missouri ten years later—represented a client who had sued a neighboring sheep farmer for shooting his beloved hunting dog, Old Drum. In his summation, Vest presented an eloquent "Tribute to the Dog" that reduced the jury to tears and won the case. Its famous phrase, "man's best friend," quickly entered the popular lexicon. The speech itself soon rolled off the printing press and became a staple of American rhetoric as thousands of schoolboys around the country set to memorizing and reciting it in countless oratory contests. The speech certainly embedded itself in Carnagey's mind—thirty years later he featured it in his syndicated newspaper column, reprinting the text and urging readers to "cut it out and paste it in your scrapbook."[17]

Eventually, however, through sheer hard work, Carnagey began to scramble upward in the public-speaking hierarchy at the State Normal School. He pushed ahead, in his own words, with "the inspirational example of my mother always before me." He memorized a number of surefire pieces—not only "Tribute to the Dog" but Richard Harding Davis's "The Boy Orator of Zapata City" and Lincoln's "Gettysburg Address"—and practiced them fervently in every spare moment. He declaimed to the woods and pastures as he rode his horse to and from the college campus. He practiced his delivery while milking the cows on the family farm. When finished with evening chores, he mounted a bale of hay and delivered eloquent speeches to the curious livestock bedding down in the barn. The fledgling orator also critiqued visiting lecturers. A speaker on Alaska, he noticed, frequently lost his audience when "he neglected to talk in terms of what his audience knew." The visitor described this massive territory as having an area of half a million square miles and a population of sixty-five thousand, statistics that meant little to the average listener. Carnagey concluded that a better approach would have been to note that Alaska was the size of Vermont, New Hampshire, Maine, Massachusetts, Rhode Island, Connecticut, New York, New Jersey, Pennsylvania, Maryland, North Carolina, South Carolina, Georgia, Florida, Mississippi, and Tennessee put together, with a population only the size of St. Joseph, Missouri. Listeners, he speculated, would have instantly grasped this comparison and been awed.[18]

Carnagey's persistence soon paid off. Listeners began to notice that this rough-edged, ill-clad farm boy, while presenting a set piece identical to his competitors, "could recite it with more fire and pathos than any of the others." To his delight, he finally won the competition within the Irving Literary Society and then ascended to the campus contests. In 1907 he claimed victory in the declamatory contest, which involved memorizing a piece of literature and then interpreting it in front of an audience. Then he won the debating contest the following year. Equally gratifying to his self-esteem, in the wake of these successes other students began to come to him for tips and training. During his final year in college, Carnagey won the debating contest while one of his trainees won the public-speaking contest and another the declamatory contest. With his profile elevated by these triumphs, he branched out by writing pieces of his own and delivering them at country churches and social gatherings in the area. With a new sense of self-confidence, he confessed, "I got a thrill out of appearing before audiences and I was determined from then on that I would make my livelihood doing that."[19]

Success as a public speaker also changed Carnagey's social life. The self-conscious, poorly dressed rube, who had been an object of condescension or mockery only a short time before, now became a big man on campus. In 1907, classmates elected him vice president of the sophomore class and he was memorialized in the yearbook with this bit of doggerel: "Our Vice President, Carnagey, is sure to win fame / makes all of us students think he can declaim." Another sign of a growing reputation came when classmates began to tease him about his enthusiasm, a now-characteristic trait that occasionally could go to excess.[20]

The following year brought further acclaim as the Irving Literary Society held him up as an example of their organizational excellence. "Mr. Carnagey has been striving for honors ever since he entered this institution—not for himself alone, but for the Society—and he has now, though yet a junior in the course, succeeded in carrying off first honors in two contests, last year in declamation and this year in debate," they wrote proudly in a campus publication. In the 1908 *Rhetor*, he was proclaimed one of the "Junior

Stars" of the class: "Dale Carnagey—As Winning Debater." He also became the object of more playful swipes from fellow students. Under the title "We Wonder," *The Rhetor* pondered "What Dale Carnagey's next scheme to work the faculty for a holiday will be." It named him a member of the facetious "Ever-Active Investigation Committee" and poked fun at his self-confidence in a section entitled "Constant Companions . . . Dale Carnagey and 'Egoism.'" The most prophetic comment, however, came in the listing of the junior class members along with a characteristic saying: "Dale Carnagey . . . 'I will sit down now, but the time will come when you will hear me.'" Perhaps most gratifying to this adolescent, as he admitted in an interview many years later, "the girls began buzzing with compliments for that nice Carnagey boy with all the talent."[21]

But there was more to his success. While Carnagey's emergence as a public-speaking star at the State Normal School was primarily a product of his personal emotional needs and determination to succeed, it also resonated more broadly. His private victory, in fact, reflected an important public trend in American education. In concert with other developments, it hastened the collapse of traditional Victorian culture.

At the turn of the century, as historian Daniel Boorstin has noted, American public speech was still dominated by a standard of formal oratory in place since the early 1800s. The popular *McGuffey Readers*, for instance, which first appeared in the 1830s and went on to shape education for several generations, had instructed boys and girls in the proper method of "reading as a rhetorical exercise" and delineated the rules for oral presentation regarding "Articulation, Inflection, Accent, Emphasis, Modulation, and Poetic Pauses." Mastery of these rules of formal declamation helped determine advancement through the primary and secondary grades, while universities stressed rhetoric, elocution, and oratory as essential subjects and drew upon the classical models of Cicero and Horace. This tradition of "great orations in the bombastic style," as Boorstin termed it, held sway in this important area of public discourse.[22]

Young Dale Carnagey entered college, however, precisely at a fluid moment when the oratorical tradition was losing its grip. In the early years of the new century, educational interest in revamping the traditional teaching and practice of rhetoric was growing significantly. Critics of Victorian formalism were beginning to replace old-fashioned "oratory" with a new model of "public speaking," thus beginning a revolution that over the next few decades would establish a conversational tone, a relaxed atmosphere with an audience, and open, honest speech as keys to effective communication. Eventually Carnagey would become a prime mover in this process, but during his college years in the early 1900s he stepped into the arena just as the first stages in the transition were playing out. Many of the old rules of gesture, breathing, and inflection were still being drilled into students, but teachers of "expression" and rhetoric were also importing new elements that aimed to relax some of the old strictures and imperatives. At the forefront of this revisionist crusade stood the disciples of a European voice and acting teacher.[23]

The Delsarte System, named after François Delsarte, a French theorist of vocal music and operatic acting, emerged as a progressive method of speech training in the United States during the late nineteenth century. Originally, Delsarte had presented a complex, cosmic pseudo-philosophy stressing the intertwining of vocal sounds and movement in expressing the deepest human impulses of mind and soul. But under the aegis of American interpreters such as Steele MacKaye, this approach evolved into a system of

physical training where gesture, pantomime, and emotion became
conduits for human "expression." By the 1880s and 1890s Delsartians had become an important influence in shaping acting, dance,
and, most important for young Carnagey, oratory. The practice of
MacKaye's "harmonic gymnastics," or physical exercises designed
both to relax the body and to focus one's mental powers on elocution, gesture, and effective expression, became a key pedagogical
tactic. In some hands, the Delsartian method became a parody of
late-Victorian gentility, with a highly artificial inventory of statue
posing, tableaux, and mechanical poses. But for most Delsartians,
this approach represented a shift away from Victorian restraint and
formalism. The system offered several new principles with liberating potential: freeing the voice and body from restrictive habit and
making them responsive to a deeper "mental cause"; training the
voice and body to be responsive to the spontaneous expression of
ideas; encouraging the free play of individualism; and utilizing the
voice and body for a delivery that was "natural," which meant a
"conversational" tone achieved through studied technique.[24]

Thus the Delsarte System served as a bridge between the high formalism of nineteenth-century Victorianism and the socially grounded
realism of twentieth-century modernity. As such, it reflected a broader
transformation in American culture. Many fields of endeavor in this
era of great change—education, the law, philosophy, historical study,
political ideology—witnessed a similar shift away from formal cat-
egories, abstract principles, moral imperatives, and static, immutable
systems of thought. A new sensibility stressed the need to confront
social reality, test ideas for their efficacy in the real world, and accept
the notion that truth *happened* to an idea rather than residing inher-
ent in it. From "legal realism" to "progressive education" to philosophical "pragmatism" to "progressive history," nearly every area of
cultural endeavor took on this new instrumentalist coloration. The

teaching of oratory fit the larger pattern. The Delsartians reflected an emerging antiformalist, post-Victorian sensibility that deemphasized technical displays and embraced a psychological approach tying together body and mind.[25]

At the State Normal School in 1904, as at many other educational institutions, the influence of Delsarte was palpable. Frederick Abbott, the school's professor of Dramatic Expression and the Speech Arts, was leading the charge. A diminutive man with thick, wiry hair and a dynamic, inspiring presence, he had trained under F. Townsend Southwick, one of America's leading Delsartians, at Southwick's New York School of Expression in New York City. Abbott spent much of the 1890s touring the United States and Canada as a lyceum speaker, and then moved into pedagogy, filling a number of teaching positions in the following years. He arrived at the State Normal School in 1905, and quickly became a major influence on Carnagey's development as a public speaker.[26]

Abbott assigned Southwick's textbook, *Elocution and Action*, in his classes. In fact, Abbott had written an advertising blurb for his mentor's text several years earlier, describing it as "in accordance with the 'new elocution'" and reporting, "I have used it with splendid results with my pupils." From Southwick's text, Carnagey learned a dislike for overblown displays of passion, a Victorian staple, and an appreciation for "a solid foundation of conversational delivery. Emotion that is genuine will find its own outlet, if the channels of expression are free." He learned that an overemphasis on technique would result in "loss of spontaneity, which is more valuable than grace or mechanical perfection." He learned the importance of speaking slowly because if "we are careful to do this, we need not shout nor strain the voice, but we can use our every-day conversational tone and be perfectly at ease." Finally, he learned to connect spoken words with inner emotions so as to "really feel what you would express and express only what you feel. This is the secret of natural delivery."[27]

Carnagey became a convert to Abbott and Southwick's "new elocution." He retained the studied physical posture of traditional formalism but aimed for a more natural, conversational delivery while spicing up his presentations with elements of emotion, particularly enthusiasm. He saw himself as part of a revolution in public speaking that rejected the "verbal fireworks" of the nineteenth century and sought "to let go, to be spontaneous, to break through my shell of reserve, to talk and act like a human being." Carnagey also drew upon his mother's influence. During his childhood, she had nudged him toward a more natural style in delivering his "pieces" at religious gatherings. While other boys had adopted florid physical movements while speaking, Amanda "scorned these silly tricks. Poetry had to be spoken with the proper singing quality, and a speech made with the meaning clear and eloquent. And without the extravagant gestures."[28]

By the time he had completed his college studies and entered the wider world, Carnagey's rejection of formalism in rhetoric and elocution was complete. By 1912, he had become a fledgling speech instructor and even the faintest vestiges of traditional, stilted oratory drew his ire. He urged his mother, for example, to abandon her plans to send a young female ward for speech lessons. "Those elocution teachers that you have out in those small towns are worse than nothing," he warned. "Don't let anyone spoil her by teaching her a lot of rot." In another missive, he stressed that misguided elocution lessons were worse than none and contended that "a bad teacher, like a bad doctor, may do you harm."[29]

Eventually Carnagey's embrace of modern public speaking, with its practical bent and emphasis on individuality and communication, caused him to rethink his entire view of college education. Looking back at his college experience, he wrote many years later, he could recall only one sentence that stuck in his mind. His history professor had told him, "Carnagey, you are going to forget practically everything you learn here; and you ought to forget it, anyway, because very little of it is important. The really significant thing is what kind of man you are making of yourself while learning these things." This became the lynchpin for Carnagey's utilitarian view that academic learning—he described it as a "medieval" system that filled students' heads with useless facts—should give way to an emphasis on personal development in college studies. Public speaking had filled this role for him, providing confidence and skills in dealing with people that were "of more practical value to me in business—and in life— than everything else I had studied in college put all together."[30]

In such fashion Carnagey's college experience framed a critical transition in his life. Socially, it brought into focus a desperate yearning to escape his family's heritage of rural poverty and presented the possibility of future success. Intellectually, it convinced him that the narrowly religious worldview of his parents was ill suited to the dynamic modern world of the early twentieth century. Culturally, it nudged him away from the moral strictures and genteel formalism of nineteenth-century Victorian culture. Overall, college provided a quantum leap in self-respect to this impoverished farm boy and prompted a dawning sense that a new world was opening up and that he could be a part of it. Bolstered by his achievements in public speaking and eager to strike out on his own, Carnagey sensed that success was his for the taking. Confident in his abilities and impatient with his past, he was ready for even bigger changes.

An opportunity presented itself in 1908 when a fellow student told Carnagey about a moneymaking opportunity that seemed tailor-made for his verbal skills. He leaped at the chance and fled from the family cocoon. Determined to get ahead, he moved hundreds of miles away physically and even further emotionally.

3

Selling Products, Selling Yourself

n *How to Win Friends and Influence People*, Dale Carnegie often delved into the world of sales. "Thousands of salesmen are pounding the pavements today, tired, discouraged, and under-paid," he claimed. "Why? Because they are always thinking only of what they want" and don't understand the people to whom they are trying to sell. But the guidelines in his book could remedy this situation. "Countless numbers of salesmen have sharply increased their sales by the use of these principles. Many have opened up new accounts—accounts they had formerly solicited in vain," he exclaimed. "Men are frequently astonished at the new results they achieve. It all seems like magic." The first step was to understand that in modern America, discovering people's desires was crucial. Every-one had their own problems and "if a salesman can show us how his services or his merchandise will help us solve our problems, he won't need to sell us. We'll buy." But the skilled salesman also knew that people's desires could be encouraged and inflated. As Carnegie pro-claimed, in one of his favorite maxims, "arouse in the other person an eager want. He who can do this has the whole world with him."[1]

The second step was equally important. Successful salesmen needed to sell themselves as well as their products, Carnegie shrewdly observed. A major section of *How to Win Friends* was devoted to "Six Ways to Make People Like You," and it included advice on "how to make people like you instantly." The author offered tips for advancing in the sales game, such as soliciting a "yes response" immediately from a potential buyer because this would "set the psychological processes . . . moving in the affirmative direction" and make it more likely that he would buy your product. Carnegie even included a surefire letter for use in sales promotions. It began, "I wonder if you would mind helping me out of a little difficulty?" It went on to ask clients how successful the product had been and if there were additional services that could be supplied, and then closed with: "If you'll do this, I'll surely appreciate it and thank you for your kindness in giving me this information." Carnegie added, in parentheses, "Note how, in the last paragraph, [the letter] whispers 'I' and shouts 'you.'" These techniques aimed to make the other person feel important but also set the salesman to conveying a positive, compelling image of himself to a client.[2]

In a broad sense, Carnegie, with his usual acumen, had grasped a crucial historical truth: Early twentieth-century America was embracing a new kind of economy where consumer abundance was the order of the day and salesmen played a key role in lubricating the flow of goods. But he also understood that selling consumer goods had become linked to emotional self-fulfillment and the ideal of a compelling personality. As with many other themes in his famous book, Carnegie's formulation was less the result of a systematic analysis of modern life and more a result of his own past experience. As his college career came to a close, the young man, weary of poverty and eager to partake of the prosperity beckoning all around, took the plunge into the world of salesmanship. This endeavor proved frustrating, but it provided ideas and techniques that became an integral part of his famous success message. As he would make clear in later years, selling yourself in a modern America of abundance held the key to achievement and advancement.

In the spring of 1908, Dale Carnagey was ready for a change. Having confronted an acute crisis of confidence in college over his religious background and feelings of social inferiority, he had embraced public speaking as a means to distinction and molded himself into a champion debater and orator. He expected to finish his course work, graduate, and become a schoolteacher with a long-term goal—set sometime in the hazy future—of becoming a Chautauqua speaker. But Carnagey still was haunted by the specter of poverty that had hung over his family since his boyhood. He had no money, few possessions, and his parents were struggling to hold on to their farm.

Thus when a classmate, in casual conversation, mentioned an opportunity for moneymaking, Carnagey was receptive. Frank Sells, a fellow member of the Irving Literary Society, related that he had spent part of the previous year selling courses for the International Correspondence School in Denver, Colorado. The company paid the princely sum of $2.00 a day for room and board, while the salesman pocketed the commissions from any sales he made. After noting that a beginning schoolteacher made only $60.00 a month, an amount matched by the Correspondence School's expense account alone, Carnagey quickly calculated the advantage and moved decisively.[3]

Full of enthusiasm but naïve, he applied for the job in a rather unorthodox fashion. Not realizing that it was bad form to seek a position by mail, he dashed off a letter—along with a crude résumé—to the International Correspondence School in Denver and asked for a sales position. The company decided to hire this neophyte sight unseen. Only later did Carnagey learn that its managers had ignored his effrontery because they felt that someone who had won several public-speaking awards had the stuff to be a good salesman. Elated, he finished his spring semester courses, received his Regents Certificate, which made him a graduate of the "elementary course" and entitled him to teach, and prepared to leave home for the first time at age nineteen. On May 23, 1908, his family accompanied him to the Warrensburg depot, and as he boarded the train, his mother wept to see her youngest child depart on this new adventure. She seems to have sensed the finality of what her son later described as "leaving the family nest forever, to try out my wings in the world."[4]

Carnagey's journey to Denver almost parodied the old story of the backward country boy arriving in the big city. He brought with him every penny he had—around twenty dollars—in a small cloth bag that Amanda had made for him. It hung on a string around his neck under his shirt, in his words, "so none of the city slickers would rob me." After riding the rails for a day and a half, he secured a cheap room at a boardinghouse in Denver and lay awake his first night "awestruck by the largest city I had ever seen and . . . too frightened to turn out my light." About midnight, when a loud pounding on the door convinced him that he was about to be robbed and killed, he cried out, "What do you want??" The night watchmen yelled back, "Turn out that light!" The chagrined young man admitted, "I was probably the greenest country kid that had ever wandered into Denver in many a moon."[5]

Carnagey faced the world with a determination to succeed. Photographs from this era show a young man of modest stature, neatly dressed in a dark suit, a shirt with a high, starched collar, and a bow tie. His medium-length hair was parted on the side and swept back, sometimes with a slight pompadour, a style that emphasized his sharp features, aquiline nose, and protruding ears. With his head cocked to the right and tilting slightly upward, he gazed out at the world earnestly, intensely, somewhat quizzically. Young Carnagey attempted to project an air of gravitas befitting a man of the world. At the same time, however, he betrayed a certain false bravado with this air of worldly confidence. A hint of insecurity peeked out from behind the serious façade of the boy orator with the gift of gab.

In many ways, Carnagey's alliance with the International Correspondence School was a perfect match. His driving ambition to escape a family background of poverty and move up in the world reflected perfectly the company's mission. The ICS had been founded in 1891 in Scranton, Pennsylvania. Aimed at working-class individuals who sought to move upward into more prestigious jobs, it offered a variety of courses in practical subjects such as accounting, mechanical drawing, barbering, embalming, pharmacy, real estate sales, bookkeeping, stenography, surveying, plumbing, building contracting, electrical lighting management, gas engineering, and dozens of others. To make the offerings even more attractive to a clientele of modest economic means, one could enroll in a course on the installment plan and pay the fee over a period of months. As a 1905 ICS advertisement asked dramatically, "On Which Side of the Desk Are You? The man before the desk works with his hands and is paid for his *labor*. The man behind the desk works with his head and is paid for his *knowledge* . . ."[6]

Students would receive in the mail a series of Instruction and Question Papers from ICS, which offered exactly the information they needed. Each unit was accompanied by a test that the student would complete and return to the company, where scores

In 1910 Carnagey left college to work a large territory in the Great Plains as a traveling salesman.

of graders sitting five abreast at desks checked the work. Higher-ranking instructors and principals then evaluated it again. A student progressed upward at his or her own pace through ever-more sophisticated layers of information until completing the course. By the early 1900s, every year about a hundred thousand new students were enrolling in more than three hundred ICS courses emanating from thirty-one branch schools established around the country in cities such as Denver. Eager for practical education and upward economic mobility, throngs of largely white, native-born industrial workers and laborers—as well as a few clerks and low-level office workers—flocked to the ICS, seeing it as an opportunity for self-improvement.[7]

Displaying his trademark enthusiasm, Carnagey rushed into his sales territory in western Nebraska eager to sell this program for success, and to launch his own upward mobility in the process. Establishing a base in the small town of Alliance, he scoured the surrounding area looking for clients. But as the young man quickly discovered, it was not a locale rich with possibilities for selling home-education courses. In his words, "It was a dry, parched, burned-out country where wild horses roamed. Much of it was so bad that even the homesteaders who lived there had to struggle daily to eke out just a bare living on the dry, sandy land." But he was not easily discouraged. He scurried in and out of retail stores trying to sell clerks and checkers a course in retail sales management. He spied men in the countryside painting a barn and tried to sell them a course in commercial sign painting. He dropped by machine shops and tried to sell the mechanics a course in engineering. "I worked desperately hard," he described. "I was pathetically eager to succeed." Despite such dogged efforts, however, he sold hardly any courses. Discouragement set in. "I was a flop," Carnagey confessed. "The farmers I called on thought more about the drought than education, and would no more buy my course than they would jump off a ten-story building—if they could find a ten-story building."[8]

After several months, Carnagey gradually surrendered to despair. Dragging back to his hotel room every evening with an empty sales book, he grew disheartened, then depressed as his sales career seemed to be collapsing before it even got off the ground. "Try as

I would," he reported, "it was mostly failure and discouragement and this was my first job! I longed to give it up and go back to the farm and to the emotional security of my mother and father, but I was ashamed to do that." The situation became so bleak that after one particularly unrewarding day, he returned to his lodging and threw himself onto the bed and sobbed over his fading fortunes. His prospects for the future, which had seemed so bright only a short time before, now seemed to mock his pretensions.[9]

And as if this travail was not enough, Carnagey became involved in another imbroglio. Near the conclusion of his college career at the State Normal School, a professor of biology, Benjamin L. Seawell, somehow had convinced the youth to become involved in a gold-mining venture with promises of great profit from a meager investment. So Carnagey, along with his parents—all of whom had great trust in the judgment and integrity of this professional academic—somehow scraped together $100 to contribute to this venture. But the mine did not pan out and the young man's letters home were filled with frantic inquiries about their vanished funds: "What have you heard regarding the gold mine? It seems to me we ought to be getting some results . . . Push the news from the gold mine on as fast as you get it." James Carnagey finally succeeded in chasing down Seawell, who had moved from Warrensburg and taken a position at another small college in Missouri. In a return letter, the professor insisted that this business failure was not his fault. The gold-mining enterprise was legitimate, he insisted, and the only reason he could deduce for its failure to produce was "that some stealthy and criminal native, with no other motive than to get a job on the dredge, must have salted our prospective samples." Indignantly he announced "my own clear conscience in the case." Dale Carnagey was not mollified, scribbling angrily across the front of Seawell's letter, "I want no more worthless stock. I want some hard cash out of him." The episode offered a warning about how dangerous the pursuit of profit could be. Carnagey admonished himself, "I am constantly astonished at how people who have a little hard-earned money will listen to the slick talk of some smooth crook and then take and spend the savings of a lifetime without getting the advice of their bankers." It was a hard-won lesson about human trust and the vagaries of the marketplace.[10]

Then Carnagey found a sudden solution to his problems. While traveling his territory, he met a veteran salesman in the hotel in Scottsbluff, Nebraska, and struck up a conversation. Soon the despondent youth began pouring out the story of his failure to sell correspondence courses and lamenting his future prospects. After hearing his tale, the older man "gave me some advice that proved to be another turning point in my life," in Carnagey's words. The salesman, who worked for the National Biscuit Company, did not mince words. "You haven't got a real job, boy," he said. "It is awfully difficult to sell educational courses to these farmers, grocery clerks, potato growers, and cattle ranchers in the sandhills of Nebraska. You ought to be selling some necessity like meat or canned foods. Why don't you get yourself a regular job? I think a lad with your energy and enthusiasm could succeed if he sold something everybody wanted." This frank assessment prodded Carnagey to action, while the words of encouragement soothed his lacerated confidence. He decided to sell something more tangible and began to plan a foray to Omaha to find a more dependable, lucrative job in its booming meatpacking industry.[11]

While Carnagey's tenure with the International Correspondence School appeared to be a short-lived disaster, it provided some important, enduring lessons. He imbibed, for instance, the ICS's definition of its mission as one to provide "practical men with a technical education, and technical men with a practical education."

This utilitarian philosophy aimed not at instilling abstract ideas or developing the student's mind in some broad sense but, in the company's slogan, to help students "put the knowledge obtained into practical use." In addition, Carnagey internalized the ICS's sunny promotion of individual social advancement, which was reflected in an Algeresque pamphlet that it sent to everyone who answered one of its ads or signed up for one of its courses. Entitled *1,001 Success Stories*, it was filled with personal testimonials from students who had taken the correspondence courses and subsequently risen within the white-collar world of American enterprise. Carnagey may even have seen a journal that began to appear from the ICS's Encouragement Department just as he was leaving the company. It was entitled *Ambition: A Journal of Inspiration to Self-Help*. Burrowing deep into his worldview, the ICS sensibility of utilitarian success and inspiration helped create the foundation for his public-speaking courses, and then his success program presented in the mammoth best seller, *How to Win Friends and Influence People*.[12]

Keen to procure a more reliable, profitable sales position, Carnagey sought employment with one of the trio of big meatpacking companies located in Omaha: Armour, Swift, or Cudahy. He went to a local stockyard in western Nebraska and found a livestock dealer who was shipping two carloads of wild horses to Omaha and needed someone to feed and water them on the trip. The payment was free train transportation. Carnagey took the job, performed the task, and found himself in Omaha a few days later. Realizing that he did not really know how to apply for a job, he dropped into a local hardware company for an interview to gain some experience. After this dry run, he approached Swift and then Cudahy, both of whom rejected his application to be a salesman. At the

offices of Armour and Company, however, he encountered Rufus
E. Harris, the sales manager, who proved more sympathetic. When
Harris heard about the applicant's success as a public speaker in
college, he offered him a position because, in Carnagey's words,
"he thought a kid who could speak better than anyone in college
might become a good salesman."[13]

Founded in 1867 in Chicago by Philip D. Armour and several
of his brothers, Armour and Company had expanded throughout
the late 1800s to become a giant in the meatpacking industry. It
specialized in a variety of fresh and canned meats, and was in the
forefront in the development of refrigerator cars to transport car-
casses and in using meat by-products to produce other items such
as glue, lard, buttons, soap, and fertilizer. In the 1880s, Armour and
Company created a number of branch houses around the country
as distribution centers to assist with sales, storage, and delivery. In
1897, it built a large meatpacking plant in Omaha to take advantage of the stockyards already established there to collect livestock
from the Great Plains. By the time Carnagey joined the company in
the fall of 1908, Armour's Omaha facility was booming as one of
the largest meatpacking operations in the country.[14]

Given a salary of $17.30 per week plus expenses, and assigned
to a sales territory in the badlands of the Dakotas, a rejuvenated
Carnagey set out once more to sell. Armour products were precisely the kind that his salesman mentor had advised—beef, pork,
lard, and soap, staples that generated a steady demand among store
owners and merchants. If the youthful salesman was enthusiastic
about his new position, his parents were incredulous. When James,
who was lucky to clear thirty dollars a month from his farm,
learned the amount of his son's weekly salary, he was so astonished
that he told Amanda the company could not possibly keep up that
rate of pay. But they were gratified when their son proved able to

live off of his expense account and send most of his salary home to help them pay their mortgage. For Carnagey, however, the prod to success was more personal than benevolent. He was fiercely determined to recover from his disastrous first foray into sales with ICS. "I was so desperately eager to make good on this job that I would let nothing stop me," he recounted.[15]

In fact, as Carnagey ventured out as a representative of Armour and Company, he was swept up in a booming expansion of American business. The period from 1890 to 1920 saw a significant shift in the economy away from a production-centered system of small entrepreneurs and toward a consumer-oriented system of large, bureaucratic corporations. As the early twentieth century unfolded, economic endeavors increasingly revolved around large companies that created and disseminated a swelling cornucopia of consumer goods: ready-made clothing, canned food, refrigerators, vacuum cleaners, washing machines, electric sewing machines, cameras, record players, toys and games, and a host of others. As this vast array of items poured out of the nation's factories, there were department stores, chain stores, and mail-order houses that sprang up as commercial conduits to funnel them to consumers. This new economy of mass consumption was best reflected, perhaps, by the automobile, particularly Henry Ford's Model T, introduced in 1908, but many other companies followed the same path: Singer Manufacturing, Eastman Kodak, National Cash Register, Coca-Cola, Wrigley, American Tobacco, H. J. Heinz, Kellogg, and Armour. Such corporations extended their economic reach into the nation's hinterlands, spreading a vast banquet of products before eager middle-class consumers.[16]

In this explosive growth of a consumer economy, two endeavors proved particularly dynamic. First, advertising began to take shape in its modern form. Whereas advertising in the 1800s had focused on the practical virtues of a given product—its strength, quality, durability, usefulness—by 1900 the promotion of goods had dropped utilitarianism for emotional symbolism. Modern advertising increasingly trumpeted the idea that commercial products could bring personal enhancement, private satisfaction, and emotional happiness. It took shape as a species of commercial therapy promising an array of self-fulfillment: fantasies of play and fun, romantic encounters, displays of increased social status, emblems of progress and sophistication. Advertisements for dresses and sport jackets, deodorant and shampoo, cigarettes and golf clubs, vacuum cleaners and refrigerators, automobiles and pool tables shifted their calculus of appeal from meeting practical needs to fulfilling personal desires. They promised a better life.[17]

Second, salesmanship emerged as a key activity for conveying consumer goods from manufacturers through retailers to the hordes of ordinary middle-class and working-class citizens eager to enjoy the fruits of abundance. In the 1800s, individual salesmen had traveled the countryside as peddlers, "hawkers," and "drummers" bringing a limited cache of goods to small groups of buyers at village stores or rural farmsteads. But beginning around 1900, large manufacturing companies began to organize dozens or even hundreds of salesmen and create elaborate systems where routes were planned, retail customers were targeted, and a paper trail of sales slips and reports tracked their every move. "The birth of modern salesmanship occurred in the decades around the turn of the century," Walter A. Friedman, the leading historian of the subject, has observed. "The country, as envisioned by the pioneers of modern selling, now comprised sales 'territories.' Citizens were not steelworkers, bankers, or housewives but 'prospects.'" Psychologists, economists, and newly emerging marketing experts studied and refined the bureaucratic rationalization of selling. This activity gave rise to trade journals—*Salesmanship* in 1903, *Salesman* in 1909, and *Salesmanship: Devoted to Success in Selling* in 1915—that discussed new issues and trends in the field. The professionalization of salesmanship was intrinsic to the broader expansion of a corporate, consumer economy. As Friedman concluded, "The 'visible hand' of management . . . could not have succeeded in many industries without the 'visible handshake' of a team of salesmen out on the road."[18]

Dale Carnagey headed out on his determined quest to sell Armour products as part of this great sales revolution in the early 1900s. He found life on the road to be full of challenges. Working his territory in South Dakota, he quickly discovered that weather in the northern Great Plains could impede and exhaust even the hardiest traveling salesman. The winter months saw an onslaught of bitter, unrelenting cold. His letters home from December to February were filled with regular notices of hardship: "I am snowbound here today and probably will be tomorrow, too"; "I went wolf hunting last Saturday and had to wade in snow over a knee deep." In January 1909, he was stranded in a hotel in Pierre, South Dakota, for several days by a howling blizzard. Having read all the available books and magazines and growing stir crazy, he finally decided to walk to the train station in the ferocious gale and plot his escape. The clerk warned him not to go, pointing out the temperature was seventeen degrees below zero, "that I couldn't see my hands in front of me and that I might get off the sidewalk and lose my way, start going in circles, and end up freezing to death." Carnagey ventured outside anyway and suffered the consequences: He froze the tiny blood vessels in his ears. "To this day, I will walk down the street with my hands cupping my ears on days when other people don't even feel slightly uncomfortable," he related more than forty years later.[19]

At the opposite extreme, large portions of the summer could be blazing hot and dry. "We have been having some fearful hot weather here—105 degrees in the shade," he wrote to his mother in August 1909. "[Let anyone] come to Dakota for a year and then just plain old Missouri will look good." But Carnagey did not allow weather to slow him down. "I was ambitious," he noted. "Some of the other salesmen in that territory didn't bother to go out on sizzling summer days when the temperature soared to over a hundred, or in the bitter winter cold when it dropped below zero. Extremes of weather never kept me indoors if there was a possibility of making a sale or catching a train to the next town."[20]

Carnagey also learned that transportation could be problematic as he struggled to reach the far-flung towns in this vast region. There was only one regular passenger train, and it traveled at night. But "butchers and grocers were not open at night, so that night train was no good to me," he explained. "So I had to ride in the caboose of a [daytime] freight train, and while the train was taking on freight or unloading freight or switching cars, I had to run uptown to the butcher shops to sell them fresh beef and pork, and to the grocery stores to sell canned meats, cheese, and lard." He had only a rough idea of how much freight needed to be loaded or unloaded, and thus how long the train would be stopped. So upon dashing back to the station he often found himself swinging onto the platform of the caboose as it was pulling out of the station and rapidly picking up speed. "The wonder is that I wasn't thrown under the cars and ground into mincemeat," he observed later.[21]

Carnagey soon realized that the life of a traveling salesman in the West was often solitary and irregular, beset by loneliness, long workdays, crude lodgings, and erratic meals. In one frontier town, he was forced to share a room with another man as the proprietor stretched a bedsheet over a wire that he strung across the center of it. "There was no privacy. Every time I moved, the man on the other side of the sheet could see the big shadows I made against the sheet," he described. He also suffered from catarrh, a chronic inflammation of the mucous membranes in the head, which was finally alleviated by the removal of his tonsils. But Carnagey was determined to persevere over all such obstacles. "I was so eager to make good that long hours, uncomfortable beds, and missing meals meant nothing to me," he wrote. "I didn't mind . . . It was infinitely easier than the backbreaking work of cutting weeds and brush on the farm." Only occasionally did he succumb to loneliness, as he did in July 1910. "As I sit here waiting for my train I will write to what I have at last come to realize is the best friend that I have ever had or ever will have—my mother," he confessed.[22]

As Carnagey gradually built a regular sales route among the retail stores throughout the badlands, he was able to establish a base of operation in Pierre, South Dakota. He traveled to towns such as Redfield, Philip, Huron, Wall, and Wolsey, but then returned to Pierre for most weekends, where he was able to enjoy a number of social activities with a circle of new friends. Most of them centered on the First Baptist Church. Skeptical of traditional Protestant doctrine after his college studies, he attended church less for spiritual edification and more as a way to fend off his mother's inquiries about the state of his soul. "I will try to take the plan of asking 'what would Jesus have me do' in my work," he reassured her wearily in a letter home. "It makes one want to try to do better to read your letters." "Don't read my Bible as much as I ought to," he confessed at another point, before adding, "I attend Sunday School all the time and wouldn't think of missing it." In letters home, he described enthusiastically the numerous gatherings and outings hosted by "the young ladies' and young gentlemen's Sunday School class." At one such gathering at a young woman's home, he reported how he "put on my white shirt and white vest and dressed up better than I had for six months." Clearly, Carnagey's church attendance was a matter of social companionship rather than doctrinal devotion.[23]

Within a few weeks of beginning his stint with Armour and Company, Carnagey had established connections with merchants, applied his determined work ethic, and settled into a comfortable network of friends. His sales career began to thrive. Letters home were filled with descriptions of hard work and feeling "mighty tired" at the conclusion of his workdays. But they were also filled with proud accounts of sales success. In the summer of 1909, he told Amanda, "I stood 6th out of the 112 route salesmen in pure lard last month." In early February 1910 he reported that he stood tenth overall among the Armour sales force in terms of volume and profit, and then third overall a few weeks after that. By the summer of 1910, he informed his family, "I have had extra fine luck this week selling goods and I believe that the records will give me first place."[24]

While some of his success could be attributed to hard work and a good product, it also stemmed from learning tricks of the sales-man's trade. As he traveled about meeting with store owners and shopkeepers, Carnagey grasped the need to establish personal re-lationships and then maintain them in order to sell goods. Success demanded a pleasant personality, ease in meeting and conversing with people, using stories and anecdotes to hold attention, and con-veying an infectious zeal for one's product. Aided by his experience with public speaking and his natural enthusiasm, Carnagey became a deft practitioner of these skills. He sensed that the art of selling lay in meeting human desire, a topic that many psychologists (and advertisers) were beginning to explore in the early 1900s. As one observer would note years later, Carnagey's *How to Win Friends and Influence People* "draws in part on lessons the author learned working as a salesman for Armour." Smiling, becoming interested in other people, avoiding arguments, remembering people's names, encouraging others to talk about themselves, being a good listener, using encouragement and praise, dramatizing your ideas, and making the other person feel important—all of these techniques were honed in the dusty towns and bustling general stores of the South Dakota of the early 1900s.[25]

Carnagey's success as a salesman brought a new sense of financial security and sophistication. On this front, he had much ground to make up. As his Armour sales flourished, he began to bring home handsome paychecks, but never having had any money before he remained woefully ignorant of the rudiments of personal finance. In August 1909, he confronted an embarrassing problem in a letter to his parents:

> Here is a question I am ashamed to ask anyone else, so I will ask you. I have put my last three salary checks in the National Bank of Commerce at Pierre and I have also put $10 of my expense account in there . . . Here is my question. When I put my money in there how do I know I can ever get it out? They gave me a receipt for it and if they should say they owed me nothing I could do nothing. I don't just have to rely on their word, do I? Be sure to answer this.

The inexperienced young man, at age twenty-one, did not know how banks worked.[26]

Within a few months, however, Carnagey was facing the world armed with a growing arsenal of financial and business knowledge. He opened bank accounts in South Dakota and Missouri and deposited hundreds of dollars into them, while also learning to navigate the system of sales slips and letters of credit involved with Armour and Company. By early 1910 he was sending his parents checks for $370.00 to pay on their farm and reminding them about another $200.00 he had asked to be deposited in his Citizens Bank account. Even more revealingly, he asked his father to "sign a note for this $570.00 promising to pay on demand without interest and also a note promising to pay that $420.00 on the settlement of the estate or something to that effect." He explained his rationale: "It can't hurt anything to do business on business-like principles. I've learned that since I went to working for a wholesale house." Here appeared a new Dale Carnagey—a man of the world with a grasp of business and an air of sophistication, a man who was confidently throwing off the old family albatross of poverty.[27]

For all his success as salesman and the welcome flow of money into his pockets, Carnagey grew increasingly restless with selling meat. His heart was not entirely in it. In many ways, he remained a frustrated performer who yearned to do something more expressive, a skilled public speaker who longed for the approval of the crowd. In letters home, he talked frequently of "going back to school as soon as possible" after working to "earn a few dollars." He regularly attended Chautauqua meetings, where he "heard some very fine things," or lectures such as the one by a Baptist minister in Pierre who had traveled around the world and who "spoke last night on the Hawaiian Islands. It was simply fine." Whenever possible, he made public presentations himself. In February 1910 he sent his parents a copy of the program from a meeting at the Pierre Baptist Church where he recited a poem of his own composition entitled "The Sunday School Boy." At the conclusion, he reported proudly, "the Superintendent of the Sunday School and the President of the

Class both came to me at once and they wanted to get a copy of the poem and have it printed . . . Others said it was the best thing on the program." He added playfully, "Didn't know I was a poet, did you?" Later in the year, he appeared at a church benefit show, where he again presented one of his own poems along with a scene from Shakespeare's *As You Like It*.[28]

In fact, as Carnagey admitted later, during his entire stint as a salesman "I was still interested in public speaking and dramatics." When a freight train on which he was traveling had a longer layover than expected, he used to practice aloud, in his words, "some of the Shakespearean declamations I had spouted in college." One time, this penchant for public speaking sparked a comical incident that almost landed him in deep trouble. He was in Redfield, South Dakota, when his freight train was delayed unexpectedly. So he killed the time by wandering into the train yard and "rehearsing a scene from *Macbeth*: 'Is this a dagger that I see before me? The handle toward my hand? Come, let me clutch thee. I have thee not, yet I see thee still. Art thou not, fatal vision, sensible to feeling as to sight? Or art thou but a dagger of the mind, a false creation, proceeding from a heat-oppressed brain?' " As the young man went through the scene, he spoke loudly and forcefully, paced about, and punctuated his words with broad, dramatic gestures. All at once a police car pulled up and four officers jumped out, demanding to know what he was doing and why he was frightening women. Carnagey replied that he didn't know what they were talking about. It turned out that Redfield contained an insane asylum, and a pair of women living in a house adjoining the train depot had reported that an escaped patient was yelling and throwing himself around. When the young man explained his actions, the police did not believe him. They demanded identification and, in Carnagey's words, "they were positive I was off my rocker." Only when he showed

them his Armour order book and letter of credit did they relent. As
he concluded, "I was released after being warned to watch my step.
As I walked back across the tracks to my train, I was conscious of
the puzzled and still suspicious eyes of the police on my back."[29]

By the fall of 1910, his sales skills had produced striking success. In his assessment, his two years with Armour and Company
brought "tremendous self-confidence because I took a territory that
had been standing in 25th place among the 29 rural routes leading
out of South Omaha, and brought that territory into first place."
Rufus Harris, the company's sales manager, was so impressed that
he recommended Carnagey be given a management position at the
sales office in Omaha. But the young man declined. His restlessness
with the meat-selling business had grown acute, and by the late fall
of 1910 he had concocted an ambitious plan. He had saved enough
money to return to his first love—public speaking—so he decided
to resign his position and go to Boston, where, in his words, he
would "attend one of the schools of expression and learn to interpret poetry so that I might go out on the Chautauqua circuit
and make my living interpreting poems and stories I had written
myself."[30]

At this point Carnagey had a fortuitous encounter. While traveling from Blunt to Pierre in the caboose of a freight train, he
found himself sitting alongside Reverend Russell, a lecturer from
the Episcopal Church who was traveling to give a presentation. As
they talked, Carnagey shared his plan for heading to Boston in a
few weeks to enroll in a school of expression. But Russell suggested
another course of action. According to Carnagey, the older man argued that "I would get much better training if I attended the American Academy of Theatrical Arts in New York City, the most famous
dramatic training school in the United States. He said I would get
everything there that I could get in Boston plus training for the

stage. I decided to go to New York." It was a momentous decision that, in Carnagey's words, "changed the course of my life."[31]

The young man's parents were stunned when he informed them of his plans, especially his mother. Not only was he abandoning a lucrative position but he was entering into the morally dubious field of stage acting. Amanda bluntly told her youngest son that "a stage career was sinful" and prayed that God would guide him to the correct decision. But Carnagey maneuvered subtly to gain her approval. "I will say that I do pray over the proposition and want you to. I do not want to go unless it is for my good. I am sure I am willing to do whatever God shows me in his will. It is far nobler work than selling meat," he wrote to Amanda. He suggested that stage training could lead to more acceptable endeavors and "I may benefit from it in Lyceum business work." After several weeks of debate, however, the young man played the trump card: his own happiness. "I hate to go into a profession against your will but when choosing a wife or profession one does well to please themselves," he wrote Amanda. "So I am going to the American Academy of Dramatic Arts in January." His mother finally resigned herself to her son's decision after praying to God that "His will, not hers, be done."[32]

So after resigning his sales position with Armour and Company in November 1910, Carnagey returned home to spend the Christmas holiday with his mother and father. He stayed through the New Year to join his parents in celebrating their twenty-ninth wedding anniversary, and then he boarded a train for New York City during the first week of January. Amanda, although accepting her son's decision, had a sense of the finality of this move and was distraught. "Mother kissed me goodbye with tears rolling down her cheeks," he related. "She sobbed and sobbed, 'Oh Dale, I may never see you again.'" But the young man was committed. He had saved

a considerable amount of money—enough to pay the tuition of
four hundred dollars at the American Academy of Dramatic Arts,
with enough left over to live cheaply for a year—and was confident
that a bright future awaited him. So for the next few days, he traveled by rail from Kansas City to New York, sitting in a day coach
because he was unable to "afford the luxury of a Pullman berth."[33]

Carnagey arrived at Penn Station in New York City about midnight on January 10, 1911. It was a classic scene pulled directly
from the long tradition of success-seeking in American culture.
In 1723, Benjamin Franklin had stepped onto the Market Street
wharf and walked into Philadelphia, dirty and bedraggled, having spent his last pittance of money on "three great puffy rolls,"
two of which he carried under either arm while he devoured the
third. After conquering this leading colonial city in America, he
would become the early republic's leading avatar of personal social mobility and achievement. In the mid-1800s, Horatio Alger
novels were filled with dramatic examples of the young man come
to the big city to make good. *Ragged Dick, or Street Life in New
York* (1867) showed its hero, Richard Hunter, counseling a rube
just arrived in New York City who was wearing an ill-fitting suit
and a bewildered look from already having been swindled out of
fifty dollars by a slick confidence man. Alger's *Struggling Upward*
(1890) followed the adventures of Luke Larkin, a virtuous young
man who overcame a crisis in his village home before ascending to
a respected financial position on Wall Street.[34]

Now the youth from rural Missouri replicated this legendary scenario in the early twentieth century. Arriving by train in the middle
of the night, wearing a cheap, wrinkled, dirty suit topped off with a
derby hat, he carried two cheap suitcases filled with all his earthly
belongings and "was astonished when a porter wanted to carry my
bags." Walking out of the station and into the bright-lit streets of

Gotham left him thunderstruck. "I had never before seen a city that could compare to New York. The hurrying people and the noise in Pennsylvania Station astounded me," he wrote. "I walked through the station and along the streets that night, completely agog by the lights and the sounds and the people. I was the perfect picture of a hayseed from the country, awed at the sights of Manhattan."[35]

Thus Dale Carnagey abandoned the world of sales for the world of the theater. This weighty shift in his life was both exhilarating and frightening, but it was less final than it seemed. In fact, as the future would demonstrate, he would carve out an influential, unique career that combined his skills as a salesman with his talent for personal expression. The result would be a highly influential cultural role, and a book that redefined the model of selfhood in modern America. But as Carnegie emerged into the swarming metropolis of New York City in 1911, it was only the beginning of a long and twisting journey.

4

Go East, Young Man

Dale Carnegie understood better than most that the presentation of self had become an important aid to success in the modern world. In an atmosphere where personal images meant everything, the ability to project an attractive persona often spelled the difference between achievement and advancement, or stagnation and failure. Polishing one's appearance and striving to appear confident, solicitous, charismatic, optimistic, enthusiastic, and engaging required both commitment and skills. And who better demonstrated these traits than an actor? The essence of this craft relied on taking the malleable nature of selfhood and molding it into whatever a role required. Thus it was no accident that *How to Win Friends and Influence People* frequently highlighted actors and entertainers.

Carnegie suggested that acting skills should be employed to make a particular impression on others. Influencing people required a pleasant, smiling demeanor that created a happy, affirmative atmosphere, of course, but what if you did not feel like smiling and being pleasant? Carnegie urged playing a part: "Act as if you were already happy, and that will tend to make you happy." The striver for success needed to arouse in others an eager want for his products or ideas, but what if the goods were intrinsically unexciting and his formulations were bland? Carnegie proclaimed, "This is the day of dramatization. Merely stating a truth isn't enough. The truth has to be made vivid, interesting, dramatic. You have to use showmanship. The movies do it. Radio does it. And you will have to do it if you want attention."[1]

Carnegie also contended that the interaction between performer and audience provided a model for broader social relations in modern America. The success seeker, as entertainer, sought to amuse, impress, or edify his clients or co-workers in the same fashion as a play or a show. Carnegie noted that Howard Thurston, the most famous magician of the age, attributed his success to his ability to put his personality and his great love for people across. He never entered the stage without repeating, "I love my audience. I love my audience." Carnegie believed that modern business had become a stage for such performances. He even recommended *Showmanship in Business* (1936), a book that illustrated the many ways that corporations were using the drawing power of entertainers to sell their goods. In fact, the dynamics of performer and audience had penetrated so deeply into modern consciousness that, in the famous words of William Shakespeare, "All the world's a stage, and all the men and women merely players . . . And one man in his time plays many parts." Carnegie recognized that a performative dynamic in human relations had become crucial to modern advancement, and he urged readers to "be a good listener" and "make the other person feel important." In his cogent assessment, "Many persons call a doctor when all they want is an audience."[2]

In part, Carnegie's deep interest in acting and audiences captured an important historical development: the emergence of a broader culture of entertainment and leisure around the dawn of the twentieth century. With the steady erosion of Victorian culture from 1890 to the 1910s, an older tradition of genteel, uplifting diversions had given way to a new sensibility of exuberant energy, uninhibited sensuality, irreverent fun, and invigorating experience. This sea change inspired a mass culture of commercialized leisure—popular theater, radio, amusement parks, sporting events, nightclubs, and the movies. By the 1930s, the entertainment culture had become ubiquitous and Carnegie, ever sensitive to the shape of popular culture, folded its influence into the pages of *How to Win Friends.*[3]

But Carnegie's emphasis on the stage and the dynamics of acting also came most directly from his earlier life. As a young man of twenty-two, he fled from his religious, Victorian family background in the rural Midwest. He fled from the mere making of money in a new consumer economy, even though he had proved to be a master salesman in the vast spaces of the Great Plains. He fled from the rural hinterland of the Midwest and the Great Plains to the east, to the center of the historical transformation that was recasting American society in the mold of urban, commercial, and leisure values. Determined to express himself and entertain others, he enrolled in acting school.

Dale Carnagey's initial, exhilarating arrival in New York City in January 1911 soon turned into a painful episode of acculturation. Walking out of Penn Station into the bright lights of America's largest metropolis for the first time was tremendously exciting, but that feeling quickly faded when he tried to find lodging. The man in the information booth at the train station told him where to find inexpensive hotels, but the youth was totally unprepared for the scale of expense. The first hotel he visited cost $1.50 per night, a figure that left him dazed. In South Dakota, he had stayed at the finest hotels for only fifty cents, but when he mentioned that figure hotel clerks only laughed. Finally, a sympathetic one steered him toward the Mills Hotel, where the bedraggled youth finally procured lodging for fifty cents—among two-decker bunk beds that were stacked several to a room.[4]

The discouraging ordeal continued the next morning when Carnagey struggled to locate an inexpensive meal. After much searching, he finally found a small, cheap restaurant and had a breakfast of cornmeal mush, one egg, and a cup of bad coffee for fifteen cents. This startling introduction to urban life sobered the aspiring young man. "I could see that my money was going to vanish quickly in New York, so I held onto it even more tightly," he noted. "If I went broke, I had no one to turn to. Father couldn't send me money. He didn't have any."[5]

But Carnagey, persistent and ambitious, was determined to succeed in the world of the creative arts. So after finishing his disheartening breakfast on the morning of January 11, 1911, he appeared at the American Academy of Dramatic Arts, located in the Carnegie Building (named after industrialist Andrew Carnegie) on Seventh Avenue, stretching between West Fifty-Sixth and West Fifty-Seventh Streets. He was taken to see Franklin H. Sargent, the president of the institution, for an interview. According to Carnagey's account, they chatted for a few minutes and then the instructor gave the prospective student a rather unusual assignment to test his mettle: "Imitate a chair." Carnagey apparently did so with convincing aplomb because he was accepted into the school on the spot. (Twenty-five years later, as a world-famous author, he re-created his chair imitation for a reporter from *The Saturday Evening Post* and she described it as "a fascinating thing to see.") But then the young man made a mistake due to inexperience.

Neither he nor his parents, of course, had ever paid for anything in installments, so he handed over the entire course fee of four hundred dollars at the onset, only later learning that most of the students paid as they learned. So Carnagey launched his career as an actor on a shoestring, having only a few hundred dollars in savings to live on for the next year.[6]

But he chose a first-rate institution. The first professional acting school in the United States, the American Academy of Dramatic Arts had been founded in 1884 by Steele MacKaye, the same American disciple of Delsarte who had created the modern public-speech model Carnagey encountered in college. Within a few years, Sargent, one of MacKaye's followers, took over the institution and served as its director for the next several decades. The academy offered a rigorous standard of professional training and would produce many of the leading lights of the American stage

A self-consciously serious Dale Carnagey in New York looking for success as an actor, salesman, teacher, and journalist.

and movie screen throughout the twentieth century: William Powell, Anne Bancroft, Spencer Tracy, Rosalind Russell, Jason Robards (senior and junior), Grace Kelly, Hume Cronyn, Lauren Bacall, Kirk Douglas, Colleen Dewhurst, and Robert Redford among dozens of others.[7]

So while Carnagey treated his acceptance by the academy in a whimsical fashion, it was more of an achievement than he let on or may even have realized. In fact, this institution did not admit students on the basis of a five-minute conversation but rigorously screened applicants before they were allowed to enroll. Each applicant was given an entrance examination containing questions about personal background (geographical home, education, previous occupation, age, health) and personal goals (aims, ambitions, personal traits, experience in the theater). The academy faculty looked closely at these exams in an attempt to assess a student's capability. They also tested applicants by asking them to recite or read extracts from plays with which they were familiar, and then to do some "acting at sight" by interpreting from a script they were given to read cold. Writing in 1911, Sargent explained that aspiring students were "thoroughly examined as to dramatic capabilities, selected as naturally qualified for a theatric career, severely discouraged if not qualified, and carefully prepared for that career if sufficiently promising."[8]

When Carnagey entered the academy, he encountered a curriculum that had been revamped in the 1890s to reflect Sargent's determination to professionalize the training of actors. The school's yearly schedule was separated into two six-month terms. The first term, which Carnagey completed in the summer of 1911, featured basic studies in the actor's craft, such as developing the physical body and the voice for theatrical expression, and learning various skills in practical stagecraft. (The second term, for which he did not enroll, emphasized advanced classroom study and the actual production of plays.) He received extensive instruction in voice articulation, pantomime, improvisation, dramatic reading, makeup, and dancing and fencing, which were believed to enhance a graceful physical carriage. He also took the famous Life Studies course, which sent students prowling the streets of New York to observe the gestures, movements, linguistic styles, accents, and emotional displays of a wide variety of people in order to re-create natural, realistic representations onstage.[9]

In other words, the academy aimed its pedagogy at professional training. Rather than following old-fashioned methods of theatrical stock companies—Sargent denounced them as a haphazard, "medieval" process of initiation into a "guild"—this modern institution sought to sharpen systematically an array of expressive talents in the prospective actor. The academy taught acting as "an expression of the 'total' man—the union of imagination, mind, feeling, and technique," as one observer put it. In a public pronouncement, Sargent explained his school's rigorous agenda as "condensed experience, plus disciplined faculties and an established art creed. Such training should accomplish in one year what would require several years of ordinary theatrical experience."[10]

As with the teaching of public speech, however, larger cultural changes lay behind the curriculum. MacKaye, the leading American proponent of Delsarte, had infused the principles of his French mentor throughout the school's varied activities. Similarly to Delsartian revisions to oratory, this acting program stepped away from older Victorian traditions of genteel restraint and artificial decorum. MacKaye sought a "science of movement" in acting that did not rely upon the stock Victorian menu of melodramatic poses and grandiloquent gestures. Instead, the Delsartian actor tried to channel thought, sentiment, and emotion through the physical body

and sought to "produce greater sincerity and naturalism in acting." MacKaye's maxims would "render an actor more lifelike and
would eliminate the posturing and artificiality too often observed
on the stage" during the Victorian nineteenth century.[11]

Sargent further sharpened this modern paradigm. Dismissing
the mechanical conveyance of emotion, he stressed that "life-like
creation of expression can only develop from within," and thus
form a foundation for creating compelling, believable characters
onstage. The actor must tap internal emotional resources, or what
the academy's *Annual Catalogue* described as "the powers of personality itself—the inner and deeper natures." Sargent, writing
in the *New York Dramatic Mirror* just as Carnagey entered the
academy, asserted that only through the "development of personal
character ... and the temperamental powers of the individual"
could an actor rise to new heights of power and persuasion. A journalist who visited the academy at this time discerned this central
impulse at work in all its varied endeavors. He noted that students
were seldom told how to do things but encouraged to think for
themselves. At this school, "individuality is regarded as a sacred
thing ... obstructions have been cleared away and it is at liberty
for the first time to express itself."[12]

So when Carnagey began his course of study, he entered a vibrant, innovative institution that was helping to transform the
American theatrical world, an experience that proved equal parts
thrilling and daunting. He took a room in a dingy, cramped room-
ing house in the West Forties and walked every morning to the
Carnegie Building, along with dozens of talented, ambitious, aspiring actors. Edward G. Robinson, who would emerge as a major
star of the stage and screen over the next two decades, had entered
the school the previous year, while Carnagey's classmates included
Guthrie McClintic, later a distinguished producer, and Howard

Lindsay, who would become a famous playwright in his collaborations with Russel Crouse as the co-author of *Life with Father*, the Pulitzer Prize–winning *State of the Union*, and the libretto for *The Sound of Music*, among many other films and plays. Sometimes the intensive training regimen overwhelmed Carnagey. "I find I know less about acting every day," he wrote to his parents in early April, and admitted to suffering bouts of discouragement. He also stewed about making a living in the theater, confessing, "This business is just a gamble at best."[13]

But Carnagey responded enthusiastically to the academy's pedagogical agenda. The Life Study course, for instance, opened up an entirely new realm of experience for a young man who had grown up within the homogeneity of the rural Midwest. "Have just returned from a life study tour down on the East Side amongst Jews and Italians, then down through the Bowery and Chinatown," he wrote home in April. "[A]ll the yelling and jabbering and trading you ever heard tell of. It is sure a fine place for character study." These jaunts caused him to explore the connection between people's physical traits and their inner qualities. "Notice the walk of different people and see how shiftlessness, selfishness, ambition, etc. show themselves through the walk," he observed. "Begin to notice the lines on people's faces . . . Try to imitate people's voices. Every man you see is a book 'where men may read strange matters.'"[14]

Most interestingly for his later work, Carnagey embraced the academy's emphasis on self-expression as the key to skilled acting. Upon first arriving at the school, the neophyte had adopted a foolish plan to study the famous actors of the day, copy their most effective techniques, and then make himself into "a shining, triumphant combination of all of them." He gradually discovered, however, that simply borrowing from others violated the essential requirement for the academy-trained actor: summoning your own emotions and finding your own voice. But he wasted several weeks imitating other people before "it penetrated through my thick, Missouri skull that I had to be myself, and that I couldn't possibly be anyone else."[15]

In fact, his stint at the American Academy of the Dramatic Arts indelibly stamped his developing worldview in two significant ways. First, the academy's teaching methodology of gently guiding students as they discovered their own inner resources—Sargent declared that skilled instructors "can only draw out and encourage or discourage tendencies in the pupil . . . Best teaching throws all on the pupil"—became a fundamental principle of Carnagey's later courses in public speaking and human relations. So, too, did the academy's stress on practical instruction, an approach that insisted on translating theory into practice. Second, the school's stress on expressing personal qualities and projecting inner emotions became a powerful influence on Carnagey's notions of image and personality, pivotal themes in *How to Win Friends and Influence People.* The idea of self-consciously shaping an image for presentation to others clearly hastened the young man's abandonment of the old-fashioned, Victorian standard of "character" with stern moral values and genteel decorum, and his endorsement of a modern, malleable ethos of "personality" where sparkling, attractive social masks could be taken off and on at will.[16]

But for all its long-term impact, Carnagey's experiment with acting lasted only a short time. After six months of training at the American Academy of Dramatic Arts, he won a part in a traveling show entitled *Polly of the Circus* and went on the road. Beginning in August 1911, he became part of an acting troupe of twenty-seven cast and crew and would remain with it for the next forty-two weeks. For a young man afire with creative energies and ambitions, it was a dream come true.

In a sense, Carnagey's involvement with this project was ironic. His dramatic training had involved the firm rejection of Victorian tradition, but the vehicle for his first sally onto the stage was quite the opposite. *Polly of the Circus* was an old-fashioned melodrama, replete with the moral flourishes, stereotyped characters, and sentimental messages characteristic of the nineteenth-century theater. He described it as "a clean, moral play" to reassure his worried mother. Written by Margaret Mayo, the play had been a hit on Broadway in 1907, starring Mabel Taliaferro and Malcolm Williams in the lead roles. The plot told the story of Polly, a beautiful circus rider who was knocked unconscious in a fall and taken to the home of Reverend John Douglass to recuperate. A romantic attachment developed, but Polly fled, fearing that their relationship would stain the character and social standing of her suitor in the town where he lived. He followed her, however, only to witness a second, life-threatening accident in the circus ring that brought the pair together, and then reunited them in wedded bliss. *Polly of the Circus* enticed audiences with both its scintillating depiction of a forbidden love affair and its spectacular circus scenes full of trapeze artists, animal trainers, acrobats, clowns, and a full contingent of performers.[17]

Carnagey departed New York with the troupe in the summer of 1911 and made his first appearance onstage on August 17 in Elmira, New York. He had a minor role in the production, the part of Dr. Hartley, the town physician clad in a Prince Albert coat, who was summoned to examine Polly after she took her first nasty spill from the horse. Since actors in secondary roles were expected to fill in as extras, Carnagey also played a circus performer—outfitted in red tights with silver spangles—who helped carry an unconscious Polly out of the arena when she was reinjured in the final, climactic scene that led to her reunion with Reverend Douglass. He also chipped in as an assistant stage manager. For these various labors he received a salary of $25 a week, and out of which he had to pay for his own room and meals.[18]

Life on the road was an adventure for the young man. He enjoyed the camaraderie and new experiences but had to watch every penny, eating inexpensive meals and sharing rooms at second-rate boardinghouses as the company traveled around the country. He usually roomed with Howard Lindsay, who was cultivating his skills as an aspiring playwright by writing for long stretches every day in their dingy little room. Lindsay remembered Carnagey as a loquacious, engaging young man whose enthusiasm often overwhelmed his manners. "Dale was quite a talker. I would not say that he had any gift of conversation; he didn't. He made speeches. At the dining table a knife or fork never impeded his gestures. I remember chiding him about this until he did put the silver down before bringing his hands into play to emphasize a point in his oratory," Lindsay related.[19]

While Carnagey was on the road, a stream of letters to his parents kept them apprised of his whereabouts. He appeared in a string of performances stretching from New York and New Jersey in the east, to West Virginia in the south, to Kansas City, Wichita, and Oklahoma City in the Midwest. Hijinks helped relieve the monotony of lengthy rail travel that took the troupe from theater to theater. At two in the morning on New Year's Day 1912, for instance, he was awakened by some of his male comrades, who then carried him uproariously through the train dressed only in his pajamas and nightcap. "Then they took me and threw me in the berth with that old maid in our company and then took me out and took all my clothes off and put me in bed with one of the men," he wrote. "Boys will be boys."[20]

But while Carnagey had given his heart to the theater he did not commit his wallet. During his entire tour as an actor, he also worked a sideline job as a salesman. He sold neckties, carrying with him a large bag of samples and spending spare time persuading local haberdashers to place orders. According to Lindsay, "he didn't make enough to justify the amount of work he put in." Carnagey also peddled a line of trunks and suitcases for a time, and then sold awnings for two different companies. The work was difficult.[21]

Then his brief acting career fizzled as no parts opened up after *Polly of the Circus* completed its run. Even before that, however, the young thespian had become disenchanted with the professional stage. On the road, he became acquainted with several aging actors whose devotion to their calling brought only financial instability and precarious social standing. "I remember a gray-haired man in our cast who must have been in his seventies," Carnagey wrote. "His family lived in New London, Connecticut, but he spent his life traveling all over the United States on one night, or one week, stands and he saw them for a total of only five or six weeks of the year." So when the tour ended, Carnagey spent a couple of weeks back in New York halfheartedly combing through the trade papers and visiting producer's anterooms looking for another acting job. But he already had reached a conclusion about his future: "The theater seemed entirely too uncertain for me and I left."[22]

Carnagey turned his attention elsewhere, instinctively reaching out to the meatpacking industry, the profitable venue he had left behind a year earlier. He went to Paterson, New Jersey, to inquire about a sales position at the Armour and Company offices there while also contacting the local Cudahy outlet. He had dinner with an acquaintance who was a manager at the Beech-Nut Packing Company. Based on his earlier record of achievement in sales, Carnagey received promising feedback about potential jobs, a development that bolstered his confidence and eased his disappointment about his failed theatrical dreams. "I am in no hurry about going to work . . . and I guess I will have no trouble in getting it," he told his parents in March 1912. "When I left Armours I never thought that I would ever want to refer to my record with them again. You see that I am using it mighty soon."[23]

So with an awkward combination of resignation and chagrin, self-justification and optimism, Carnagey changed course and headed back into the world of salesmanship. But instead of the meatpacking industry, he opted to break into an exciting new field that was transforming daily life in the United States in the early twentieth century. As would be true throughout most of Carnagey's adulthood, his instinct for identifying cutting-edge developments in American society was sharp.

When Carnagey looked to revive his career as a salesman, he saw great opportunities, as did the great hordes of young men who had begun flocking from the countryside by the turn of the century. Attracted to the bustling excitement in America's rapidly swelling urban centers, they were eager to immerse themselves in a dynamic new environment of social and economic change. Several important developments faced them. Exploding economic growth had resulted from booming industrial production and a rapid expansion of the consumer marketplace, while massive waves of immigration from southern and eastern Europe fed a steep rise in population. In addition, the emergence of great bureaucracies—business corporations, public school systems, the Progressive Era regulatory state—was reshaping the structure of public life in the United States.[24]

But perhaps the most striking development was the gasoline-powered transportation that had begun to remake American life in the early 1900s. Henry Ford had introduced the inexpensive, mass-produced Model T in 1908 as an affordable vehicle for citizens of modest economic means, and it swept all competitors before it during the following decade. Following in Ford's footsteps, other automobile manufacturers began springing up throughout the United States as their machines steadily replaced horses and steam engines. The impact of the automobile radiated widely, transforming not only transportation but suburban residential patterns, the steel and petroleum industries, the growth of new service industries in lodging and gas stations, the advance of credit systems, and the construction of roads and streets. "Automobility," as one observer has defined the impact of the car, not only broadened the parameters of experience for millions of middle-class and working-class citizens but formed the backbone of social and economic life in twentieth-century America.[25]

So Carnagey decided to venture into the automobile industry. Over the next few years, he became involved in three separate projects involved with car sales. First, shortly after returning to New York from the *Polly of the Circus* tour, he entered into a business partnership. In May 1912, an acquaintance named Parmalee suggested they go into business together, with him providing the capital and Carnagey doing the legwork with selling and advertising. Parmalee had procured several secondhand cars and trucks, and believed they could turn a tidy profit reselling them. Carnagey agreed, so the pair procured a small office, a desk, and a file cabinet, and hired a secretary to handle correspondence. They called it the Meriden Motor Company.[26]

Carnagey was pleased at his business prospects. He liked being his own boss and leaped into promoting Meriden vehicles. "Have worked hard for 3 & ½ days this week on this advertising business. I have several good prospects and I may be able to close some of them later," he reported. "I can't expect to start into a new business like this and make it pay right at first."[27]

But selling motor vehicles was a difficult undertaking, as the young man discovered. Part of the problem lay in his aversion to machinery, an attitude that caused him to confess, "I didn't know what made an automobile truck run, and I didn't want to know." Moreover, he found it difficult to muster enthusiasm for selling only to make a profit, just as at the end of his stint with Armour and Company, when his real interests lay elsewhere. "There was nothing wrong with selling trucks, especially if you wanted to make money," he explained. "I wanted to give lectures and write books. I was not as much interested in making money as making an interesting and significant life for myself." Mishaps made matters worse. In early 1913, for example, he sold a used car and promised to deliver it to the buyer the next day. But then he discovered that the vehicle had been left out in bitterly cold temperatures and water had frozen in the engine and ruined it. He agreed to fix the car, but "this fellow got scared and before I could get a hold of him he went and bought another car and I lost out. Such are the troubles of the used car game."[28]

In February 1913, Carnagey left the Meriden partnership for his second venture in the motor vehicle field: a position with the International Motor Company, an automobile concern located only a few blocks away. He was hired to manage sales of secondhand cars, and he brimmed over with confidence about affiliating with an already thriving business. "Every used car that is sold through their New York office I will get a rake off of," he wrote his parents. "I put in all the newspaper advertising that I think is necessary and they pay for it. They also pay me for any carfare that I spend in taking parties around to look at cars and they said that they would

arrange after a while to have a car and driver at my disposal when
I wanted to show a man a car."[29]

Reveling in these perks, Carnagey saw a bright future ahead. "I
am in an infant industry with one of the best concerns in the world
and I am my own boss and I can do just as I please and can go out
in the park for a stroll whenever I want to or anything else," he reported. "I am my own boss and they are not paying me a salary, and
all I have to do is to produce results, and this I am confident I can
do." He became convinced that, working on commission, he could
make $1,800 during his first year, and possibly $3,000 or $4,000 a
year within a short time. During the first couple of weeks, he sold
two cars, which seemed to confirm his confident outlook. Then
things fell apart. After a month, and no further sales, Carnagey
was let go. The manager called him in and said a decision had been
made to eliminate all secondhand sales. The young man, his pride
injured by this rather unceremonious dismissal, became extremely
touchy about the entire episode. "Kindly allow me to disabuse the
minds of all of you in regard to my leaving the position that I had
with the International Motor Company," he declared indignantly
to his family. "I was not fired. No one took my place. They simply
did away with the second hand department."[30]

Carnagey quickly rebounded, finding a sales position with the
Packard Motor Company two weeks later. The arrangement was
difficult from the outset. The sales manager offered him a salary
of $1,500 a year, but Carnagey asked for a higher sum. When the
manager refused, the applicant grudgingly agreed. But it did not sit
well, and he told his family, "I will make good with them first, and
then with the record I have I can easily get another position if they
do not want to come across with a good salary."[31]

While he struggled to find his footing in the automobile game, he
found greater satisfaction in a vibrant social life. Since first arriving

in the metropolis, the sociable young man had thrown himself into various activities. He also became something of a ladies' man. While taking the Life Study course at the American Academy of the Dramatic Arts, he toured Manhattan's East Side "several times with the ladies." His correspondence revealed a host of female entanglements, past and present. Writing to the young people's group at the Baptist Church back in Pierre, he noted a former sweetheart: "I love Effie as truly as I love anyone . . . I never *can* love anyone more than I did her." A letter to his mother discussed "that married woman that you were worrying about in South Dakota. She never comes into my mind once a month . . . Now as to the Jewess, didn't I tell you that I had given her up?" He made constant references to his dates with "a little Irish girl," "the French girl," and a young woman he took to a play before going to her home where he "met some delightful ladies." On occasion he left New York for out-of-town dates, as when he "went up in the country about 40 miles to see a girl today. Good old-fashioned family. Girl is a school teacher."[32]

One weekend in 1913 overflowed with romantic liaisons. "On Saturday, Miss Stewart, my Jersey City friend, came by the house and rapped on the window as I live on the ground floor. She came in and gossiped for a while. I kissed her and sent her home," Carnagey related in a letter to his family. "Then another friend of mine, a beautiful little Canadian girl, came in to practice my 'talking song' with me on the piano . . . After the song I left a kiss on her cheek and sent her home, and in the evening I was out with another girl . . . and I kissed her good night, too. So you see, I am rather well supplied with lady friends at present."[33]

On occasion, Carnagey's relationship with young women became more involved. During his first two years in New York, he spent a good deal of time with a Miss Botsford going to plays, dances, and lectures. He also briefly entered an entertainment partnership involving dramatic and comedic readings with a Miss Banghart. "Now mother, as to the girls, I will say that I always have been a fool about them and always want to be, and expect to disgrace all of you when I get married," he confessed at one point. "You can't say it has not been because I have not looked around, though."[34]

Carnagey also engaged in many church-related activities. He heard a sermon by the famous evangelist Billy Sunday, regularly attended Sunday school at a Baptist church near his room and went to the YMCA to hear visiting ministers. But clearly, much of this activity had more to do with socializing than piety. He loved Sunday school dances at the Baptist church, chiding his mother, "A lot of this old tommy rot that a lot of these backwoods preachers preach about the dance and theater is a fake, and the sooner they stop it the sooner will a lot of reasoning people come with them." He took Miss Botsford to church socials, where she appeared as "a Bible visitor" giving talks on Old Testament characters, and to mission nights where missionaries told tales about their endeavors.[35]

Despite this whirl of activity, Carnagey took pains to stay in contact with his parents and remain involved in family issues. He regularly gave his parents' Belton farm—south of Kansas City, where they had moved from Warrensburg—as his home address to a number of business contacts, but sternly warned, "I WANT NONE OF MY MAIL OPENED that comes to me at Belton. None whatsoever. My mail is private." He continued to send his parents small amounts of money when possible to help with expenses, with the assurance that they need not worry about paying back either the principle or interest during their lifetime. He also urged Amanda and James, rather pompously, to be content with their position in life. While the wealth of others might make them feel like failures, he noted, a modest life had many virtues. "All the world is seeking happiness, and a very wise man once said, 'he is happiest who wants least,'" the son enjoined. "Moral—want less."[36]

But unknown to the outside world, Carnagey's own happiness was crumbling. He presented a brave front, particularly to his parents, talking confidently about the world of car sales and claiming that success waited right around the corner. "At my age, it is not a question so much of how much are you making this year as it is a question of how much are you placing yourself in position to earn 10 years from now," he rationalized. "In other words, are you on the right path. I believe that I am." Even amid the debacle at the International Motor Company, he maintained that things "shall work out splendidly."[37]

Behind the brave words, however, lay grim circumstances that were closing in on him. By 1913, Carnagey's private reality had become equal parts career disappointment, emotional despair, and material poverty. He moved to a tiny room in a sordid roach-infested tenement house on West Fifty-Sixth Street to save money. A large number of neckties, left over from his earlier sales project, hung on pegs in the wall, and when he picked one every morning as he dressed for work, dozens of bugs would scatter in every direction. As his funds dwindled, he ate at cheap, dirty restaurants, brooded about the daily grind of working in a job he despised, and trudged home nearly every night with a severe tension headache. He fell into a depression that was, in his words, "fed by disappointment, worry, bitterness, and rebellion. I was rebelling because the dreams I had nourished back in my college days had turned into nightmares. Was this life? Was this the vital adventure to which I had looked forward so eagerly?"[38]

Carnagey's mounting troubles came to a head when his efforts at Packard collapsed. "It is an economic revolution for a man to throw out his horses and put in these expensive things," he observed. "It is the hardest kind of salesmanship to get a man to do it." The young man proved unable to accomplish the job, and as sales dried up he fell into despair. "What was I to do? Where was my future?" he lamented.[39]

In October 1913, Carnagey, facing bleak prospects, finally quit his job at Packard. He claimed, with some justification, that his heart lay elsewhere, writing, "If I had become a millionaire at salesmanship, I never would have been happy." Sick of trying to sell products he did not care about, he wanted to pursue the life of reading, writing, and lecturing he had dreamed about in college. In fact, even before the disaster at Packard, he had begun to explore a number of options in this area.[40]

Early in 1913, Carnagey persuaded the New York City Board of Education to pay him for a number of evening lectures in the spring. He then delivered two talks on "The Passing of the Cowboy and His Country" at ten dollars per appearance. He picked up another cowboy lecture during the summer, which was attended by an assistant superintendent. He was impressed and told the young speaker to contact him in several months about presenting several talks on "American Men of Eloquence."[41]

Encouraged, Carnagey sent out fliers to various organizations advertising a variety of talks and dramatic readings he was prepared to present. The Royal Arcanum, a fraternal organization, became a regular client. He spoke to them on "Development of the Art of Self-Expression" and was so well-received that he returned at a later date to speak on "Patrick Henry—The Orator." A local chapter of the Masons engaged him to read the lengthy poem *King Robert of Sicily*, by Henry Wadsworth Longfellow, at one of their banquets. "I did it and I think I read it very well," he reported. "I got a very swell dinner thrown in, of course, and I was paid $5 for the reading." The New York Telephone Company invited him to present a lecture on the history of oratory. These small successes inspired him to form a dramatic partnership with a female friend, Miss Stewart, and they sent out circulars to ministers and mayors in surrounding towns to stir up interest in readings and other types of entertainment.[42]

As Carnagey sought to make a living by his creative wits, he made overtures to several universities in New York. He applied to both Columbia University and New York University to teach extension courses for adults in the evening. The aspiring teacher drew up outlines for courses in salesmanship and advertising— somewhat ironically, of course, in light of his recent failures—and presented them to school officials. But, as he observed dryly much later, "these universities decided they could struggle along some- how without my help."[43]

So he switched direction to try his luck as a student, hoping "to keep myself touched up and get in a college atmosphere again." Concerned about tidying up his college record, he contacted the Missouri State Normal School and received assurances that with the completion of requisite course work in New York the Warrens- burg institution would grant him a regular college degree instead of the lesser Regents Certificate he had received in 1908. So Carnagey enrolled at Columbia University and signed up for English Compo- sition, Short Story Writing, and Dramatic Composition. Simultane- ously, he enrolled at New York University for an evening class in magazine writing.[44]

Carnagey also probed the possibilities for becoming a writer. He first envisioned becoming a drama critic for one of the New York newspapers, but this dream was squashed when he contacted the editors of the *Dramatic Mirror* and the *Dramatic News*. "I soon found out that one had to become famous in some out of town paper, or would have to have a big pull when some dramatic critic died to get his place," he reported ruefully. One editor told him bluntly, "you stand about as much chance as a snowball in Hell." So he turned to another scheme, which he confided to his childhood friend Homer Croy, who had achieved success as a novelist and journalist in New York. Over dinner, Carnagey expressed a desire "to do some writing for the magazines and if I can make that win I will give up all my time to it." But such a plan, of course, would require much time and effort to come to fruition.[45]

Thus Carnagey's dramatic move to New York from the rural Midwest seemed to fall flat, producing little either in the creative world or in salesmanship. Spinning his wheels, the ambitious young man was existing hand to mouth on modest stipends picked up from occasional public talks. He was living in squalid conditions with no escape in sight. In the midst of this precarious situation, he wrote a revealing letter to his brother, Clifton, who was suffering his own career crisis as he careened from job to job as, successively, a land speculator, an apprentice lawyer, and a drummer in a jazz band. "You will never make any more in life than you are making now until you stick to one thing a little longer," wrote the younger sibling to the older. "These things all look rosy enough at first just as that gold mine did, but you see how most of these things turn out . . . Now I am putting this matter up to you strongly for it is time that you became a man and ceased to dream such wild dreams." Carnagey's missive could just as well been addressed to himself.[46]

Nonetheless, he remained determined to succeed. "I am looking for something big and there are a lot of big things in a city like this," he declared. That insistence on finding "something big," and the ambition and enthusiasm that fueled it, sustained him and would prove to be a lifelong source of personal strength. "I think that the only thing that God endowed me with was a little ability to shoot off my mouth," he joked to his parents. "I am pretty well decided that a little teaching and salesmanship will be my life's work, and if I essay on anything else it will be this lecture work here and a little writing."[47]

In fact, Dale Carnagey's eventual blueprint for distinction would be constructed of precisely these elements—teaching, salesmanship, lecturing, and writing. Almost by accident, this brighter future first began to glimmer in an endeavor he had begun as a sideline to pick up a few extra dollars in the fall of 1912. It would prove to be his path to secular salvation and success.

5

Teaching and Writing

At the outset of his landmark 1936 book, Dale Carnegie explained two key elements informing its message. First, he credited his experience as a teacher for discovering the principles regarding "the fine art of getting along with people." The Dale Carnegie Course in Effective Speaking and Human Relations, with its thousands of students enrolled over the previous two decades, comprised a "laboratory of human relationships for adults" and he had studied its results carefully. Initially the course had been designed to help people express themselves clearly and develop poise when appearing before a group, but gradually it had evolved into a broader exercise in helping people to get along with and influence others. As a result, Carnegie had learned that knowledge alone was insufficient for advancement in the modern world—it also required human relations skills. After instructing several engineers' groups, for example, it became clear that the most successful engineers were frequently not those with the greatest technical knowledge. They were individuals who had "the ability to express his ideas, to assume leadership, and to arouse enthusiasm among men." This lesson stuck with him.[1]

Second, Carnegie stressed that the process of writing itself had shaped the nature of his advice. In the preface, entitled "How This Book Was Written—and Why," he told readers, "I myself had been searching for years to discover a practical, working handbook on human relations. Since no such book existed, I have tried to write one for use in my own courses. And here it is." As a writer, he worked hard to convey useful ideas in a lively style that avoided the flaw shared by thousands of books published every year: "most of them were deadly dull." He tried to explain clearly, and describe colorfully, the tried-and-true principles that seemed to "work like magic." The acid test for his writing, he told readers, was practicality. "If by the time you have finished reading the first three chapters of this book—if you aren't then a little better equipped to meet life's situations, then I shall consider this book to be a total failure," he declared. "For 'the great aim of education,' said Herbert Spencer, 'is not knowledge but action.' And this is an action book."[2]

Carnegie's emphasis on the importance of teaching and writing in *How to Win Friends* was well-placed, and it had a long history in his personal life. When he gave up acting, and then car sales in the early 1910s, he turned to these two endeavors. He first procured a part-time position as an instructor for adult-education classes, a position that soon turned into something much more. Then, a short time later, he began writing for magazines in an attempt to reach a popular audience, which led to the publication of his first book. In both areas he began to develop several shadowy themes—personal development, confidence building, positive thought, human relations—that soon took more solid form. They moved the young man significantly closer to his eventual role as America's modern guide to success.

In later years, after Dale Carnagey became a world-famous author and speaker, he liked to tell a story about how he gave up salesmanship and began teaching speech to adults. He described an epiphany that he had in 1912 when he was struggling in New York. Agonizing about what he would do with his life, he came "to the Rubicon—to that moment of decision which faces most young people when they start out in life. So I made my decision . . . I would make my living teaching adult classes in night schools. Then I would have my days free to read books, prepare lectures, write novels and short stories." This dramatic decision, he contended, had roots in his college experience, when he had dreamed of accomplishing grand things. "You were going to have time to read books. You were going to have time to write books," he had told himself. Now the time had arrived to make it happen. "This is the turning point in my life! I don't want to make money, but I do want to live."[3]

His tale performed the traditional function of myth—telling the story of a daunting crisis that first threatens destruction to a heroic protagonist, then pushes him to craft a resolution that inspires ordinary mortals. But as with most myths, the tale was only partly true. Its substance was accurate, but the drama was exaggerated. In fact, Carnagey's emergence as a teacher of public speaking in 1912 was a much quieter, slower, and indefinite process. It lasted because, unlike his other career efforts, it combined his various enthusiasms and talents. Teaching provided a means by which he could reach people in the practical fashion he had come to value, and by which he could reach personal success as well.

In the autumn of 1912, Carnagey made his first stab at teaching. Having been turned down as an instructor for evening extension courses at Columbia University and New York University, he aimed at a more modest target. New York had several YMCAs that offered a variety of courses and lecture series in the evening, and he approached them with offers to present a class on public speaking. They all rejected him. Finally, he went to the smallest YMCA in the city, on 125th Street, and made his offer. The director, Maynard Clemens, was unimpressed, noting that earlier attempts at public-speaking classes had failed because of weak appeal. But Carnagey pleaded for a chance. Clemens agreed to think it over and invited the young applicant to a social evening later in the week, asking him to prepare a talk or a stunt to amuse the group. So Carnagey appeared and presented James Whitcomb Riley's popular poem "Knee-Deep in June" and "Giddyap, Napoleon, It Looks Like Rain," a humorous song from a 1907 show, both to piano accompaniment. The audience was so delighted that Clemens asked him to give an evening lecture to the young men who roomed at the YMCA, who were hard put to find entertainment. This talk, too, received an enthusiastic reception.[4]

After witnessing Carnagey's enthusiasm and panache, Clemens relented and agreed to give him a trial run as a teacher. The young man requested two dollars a night for the class, but the director balked at paying a guaranteed fee, instead saying that the best the YMCA could do was 80 percent of the total proceeds. Carnagey later joked that a skeptical Clemens was thinking "80 percent of nothing." The skepticism seemed warranted when only half a dozen people signed up for the class, but the optimistic instructor believed that success would draw in more students. Moreover, he clearly viewed this as a moneymaking project to supplement his other endeavors, rather than as a final career commitment. "I thought I might make $25.00 a week out of it—it was all I wanted to make," he observed. "In this way, my days would be free for reading and writing."[5]

This venture into teaching adult courses made more sense, perhaps, than his other initiatives because of its connection to his life, training, and talents. He had first made a mark with his flair for

public address at the State Normal School, and now he asked himself, "Why shouldn't I avail myself of the thing I knew best and
teach public speaking?" One issue particularly struck him. "As I
looked back and evaluated my own college training, I saw that the
training and experience I had had in public speaking had been of
more practical value to me in business—and in life—than everything else I had studied in college all put together," he wrote. "Why?
Because it had wiped out my timidity and lack of self-confidence
and given me the courage and assurance to deal with people."[6]

But the Dale Carnagey who embarked upon this teaching experiment was also a markedly different person from the greenhorn
who had alighted in New York City a short time before. In certain respects, he retained many of his earlier personal characteristics: a contagious enthusiasm that made optimism about life his
default position, a verbose temperament that attacked difficulties
and issues with a torrent of words, a desire to be liked that pushed
him in the direction of performing for people, a native intelligence
that created an aura of competence, and a sincere sensibility that
radiated concern about others. At the same time, in less evident
ways, the young Midwesterner had hardened. Reaching a series
of career dead ends had shaped darker attributes that occasionally emerged—a deep-seated insecurity, a tendency toward emotional despair, a cynicism about the motivations of others, a sense
of being chastened by worldly experience, and an awareness that
youthful dreams often faded in the face of reality.

Carnagey's complex persona was reflected in a more mature
physical appearance. By 1912, photographs showed him to be a
man rather than a youth, the result both of aging into his mid-
twenties and enduring some hard knocks in life. Gone were the
signs of boyish bravado, the cocky and playful poses, the brash
air of inevitable success. He now appeared serious and seasoned,

dressed neatly in light trousers and a dark coat accented by a tie and pocket handkerchief. With his hair cut shorter and neatly parted on the side, thin-set lips, and large ears, he looked out at the world through wire-rimmed spectacles with a cool, thoughtful, calculating expression. He seemed both determined and slightly wary.

In many ways, the YMCA provided the perfect venue for Carnagey's entry into teaching. Founded in 1844 in London, the Young Men's Christian Association had begun as a group offering religious fellowship and instruction to young single males who had flocked to the city seeking jobs during the expanding Industrial Revolution. This included both factory laborers and those in the entrepreneurial class, all of whom required protection from "urban

A nattily attired Carnagey with several YMCA officials outside his first teaching venue.

vice and debauchery." The institution spread internationally, arriving in the United States in 1851 and establishing itself in many northern cities. The YMCA allied itself with evangelical Protestant churches, and by the turn of the century it had expanded to include recreational, athletic, social, and educational endeavors in the service of spiritual salvation, moral uplift, and character formation. Businessmen applauded these "manhood factories" for their "promotion of Protestant virtues such as thrift, honesty, temperance, industriousness, and benevolence" and contributed financially to the construction of YMCA buildings, where activities were hosted and rooms were rented to young men. With its Christian sensibility, moral agenda, and practical outreach, the YMCA offered a natural arena for this transplanted Midwesterner with his pious background and longing for self-improvement.[7]

The nature of Carnagey's evening class at the YMCA had an immediate impact on his approach to teaching. The great majority of students were adults in low- or mid-ranking positions in the rapidly expanding business world of the early twentieth century. They did not want to become orators but sought career advancement. As Carnagey recognized quickly, technical instruction in breath control, stance, gesturing, and voice projection "wasn't what my pupils—average young fellows trying to get ahead, clerks and salesmen and mechanics—really wanted and needed. It wouldn't help the man trying to sell insurance to puff out his cheeks and recite 'Horatio at the Bridge,' however eloquently." This workaday audience did not want to make speeches but to speak with colleagues and customers in a compelling fashion. In Carnagey's amused words, his earliest class consisted "mainly of businessmen and employees who wanted to be able to stand up on their feet and say a few words at a business meeting without fainting from fright . . . or call on tough customers without having to walk around the block three times to get up courage." Their instructor, who only a few years before had quailed in college because of his inferiority complex, instinctively responded to this need.[8]

Carnagey's initial experience with his pupils opened his eyes. At his first class session on the evening of October 22, 1912, in an upstairs room at the 125th Street YMCA, he began in traditional fashion. Drawing on his college experience, he began to deliver a lecture he had prepared on the history and fundamental principles of public speaking. After expounding on these themes for a while, however, he noticed that the students were fidgeting in their seats, looking restless and bored. He grew fearful, knowing, in his words, that "they were paying their tuition on an installment basis—and they stopped paying if they didn't get results—and since I was being paid not a salary but a percentage of profits, I had to be practical if I wanted to eat." So on an impulse, fueled by some desperation, he quit lecturing and asked a student to stand up and give a brief, impromptu talk. When the flustered pupil asked what he should talk about, Carnagey told him to speak about himself, his background, his life. After the pupil did so for a few minutes, the instructor went around the room and had each of the students do the same. To his surprise, they spoke reasonably well and grew more comfortable as the exercise progressed. "Without knowing what I was doing," Carnagey wrote, "I stumbled on the best method of conquering fear." Student participation—getting them to talk about themselves or things they cared about—steadily moved to the forefront of his teaching method.[9]

Subsequent experiences in the classroom produced other principles of pedagogy. Carnagey had the idea of asking pupils to talk about something that made them mad, a technique that soon created a scene where the "YMCA boys jumped to their feet, one after another, and unleashed their hidden indignations in a growing roar of eloquence that soon had them shouting one another down." Another time, he cleverly drew out a retired naval officer, who had droned on and fumbled for words in previous class sessions, by having another student, a "Greenwich Village soapbox radical," give a talk criticizing the American government. He did so with relish. The angry navy man leaped to his feet and patriotically defended his country, speaking with "more fire, more excitement, more sincerity than most professional speakers use. He wasn't good—he was superb!" Another classroom incident where a student convinced his classmates that scattering fireplace ashes on one's lawn would create "bluegrass"—they believed this fantastic claim unanimously because "he was so sure and so enthusiastic about it"—convinced the instructor of the tremendous impact that came from a speaker's "sincere belief." All of these episodes pushed Carnagey to promote "emotion" and "enthusiasm" as keys to successful public speaking.[10]

Thrown into this cauldron of experience, an astute Carnagey quickly began to cobble together a new template for teaching his course. He concluded that fear of standing alone before others and making a talk was the biggest problem confronting his students, so he began requiring each student to talk briefly at every session to overcome it. Because of this, he also became convinced that large classes were counterproductive. "One of the YMCA's in New York put on a course that did far more harm than good," he reported. "They had 500 students in a class and the professor would call ten or fifteen of them at a time up on the platform. He would make them read out of a book, make identical gestures. This was sheer, crass, commercial, and unforgivably bad teaching." Moreover, Carnagey began to identify sincerity, emotion, and enthusiasm as the key personal ingredients for successful public speaking. This approach, he found, worked wonders. "I soon found that they were teaching themselves ten times as much as I could ever teach them," he observed. In later years, he confessed that his method came "through trial and error and the response of the students. I was learning and discovering a successful method even while I was teaching it."[11]

Carnagey's innovative methods began to bear fruit, and his classes prospered along with his financial status. Student enrollment grew slowly but steadily. A new course beginning in February 1913 had tripled in size with eighteen enrollments, he reported, while the 125th Street YMCA also agreed to sponsor a debate class, which enrolled twenty pupils. Moreover, the Brooklyn YMCA came on board and agreed to host another public-speaking course in the spring of 1913 with an expected enrollment of twenty-five. Carnagey's pay rose steadily on the shoulders of this expansion. He received $59 for twelve lessons at the 125th Street Y and $99 for twelve lessons in Brooklyn, and he was hopeful that "my debate class will net me from $7 to $9 per night." By mid-May 1913 he was hopeful of bringing home $12 per night during the following fall.[12]

That next fall saw Carnagey's teaching endeavors branch out even more. After being contacted, he opened up courses in Newark and Baltimore and traveled by train to conduct them. By the end of 1914, he was teaching at YMCAs in Philadelphia and Wilmington, Delaware, as well, earning upward of $500 a month, and renting office space in Carnegie Hall. Other opportunities began to pop up. With his reputation spreading by word of mouth, and the assistance of some advertising circulars, individuals began contacting him for private speaking lessons. So did organizations. For example, Carnagey was solicited to provide instruction on public speaking to functionaries at Tammany Hall, the notorious Democratic political machine that still dominated New York City politics. The connection made him uneasy. "If I can make a little money training

Tammany Hall speakers, I see no reason why I should not," he wrote defensively to his parents. "Besides, it is a fine way to get prestige. [William Jennings] Bryan had to cooperate with Tammany the first time that he ran, for he had to have their support until he got big enough to fight them."[13]

By 1914, Carnagey had moved into a new social milieu that proved receptive to his basic message of public speaking as a confidence-building form of personal expression. The students in his YMCA classes—white-collar workers, modestly positioned but eager to move ahead in the corporate world—sensed that effective communication and skilled human relations would boost their ascent to success. Sensing it as well, their teacher began to tailor his approach to meet that need. An emphasis on sincerity, enthusiasm, personal expression, and confident interactions with others became the foundation of Carnagey's public-speaking pedagogy. His workaday audience, faced with the new demands of selling in a consumer economy and maneuvering in a corporate bureaucracy of early twentieth-century America, responded enthusiastically. Twenty-five years before his famous book, *How to Win Friends and Influence People*, he had begun to fashion the principles that defined it.

But the new perspective that came from his teaching endeavors at the YMCA was further enhanced by another endeavor. In this same period, eager to revive his creativity, Carnagey began writing for magazines. In a spate of articles published over the next few years, he began exploring how successful individuals in modern America had made it. Intentionally reaching out to a popular audience, he unintentionally internalized many of the lessons he uncovered.

In a letter to his mother in the autumn of 1913, Carnagey wrote offhandedly, "I am sending you a copy of *Leslie's Weekly* for Oct.

18th. You will note my piece on 'War' in it." This blasé air of indifference barely masked the aspiring writer's thrill at seeing his first publication. The brief antiwar editorial essay reflected his Populist, evangelical upbringing with its Bryanesque suspicion of armed conflict. "In Nazareth a carpenter laid down his saw to preach the brotherhood of man," he noted, and followed with horrified descriptions of warfare's victims—destroyed property, "a widowed mother crying," "fatherless children," "sick, disabled, and dead men." Its stilted prose style smacked of Victorian tradition with an abundance of ornate, sentimental language and emotional effusions. In a melodramatic conclusion, for example, Carnagey declared, "When mankind rises above creeds, colors, and countries; when we are citizens not of a nation but of the world, the armies and navies of the earth will constitute an international police force to preserve the peace and the dove will take the eagle's place."[14]

But the merits of Carnagey's "War" piece were less important than its appearance. With this effort, he launched a career in journalism. *Leslie's Illustrated Weekly*, a popular periodical, had been founded in 1855, and by the turn of the century reached an audience of some sixty-five thousand readers with its topical stories and lavish illustrations. Carnagey was delighted to appear in print before such a large number of readers. With typical enthusiasm, the young Midwesterner envisioned a future of literary distinction, but experience had taught him the necessity of restraint. "I do not expect to sell every article that I write by any means," he told his family. "I shall have to drill myself in that, the same as I would to be a lawyer."[15]

In the wake of this initial effort, he published eleven more magazine pieces from 1914 to 1918. This work appeared in a dynamic new journalistic venue. Around 1900, a number of developments in American life—rapid urbanization, growing

numbers of white-collar workers, the swelling appeal of commercial entertainment—had triggered a massive change in the
magazine market. Older, genteel periodicals such as *The Atlantic*,
Scribner's, *Harper's*, and the *Century*, with their agenda of improving the taste of respectable Victorian readers with pieces of literary
merit, moral uplift, and philosophical reflection, began to shrink
in popularity. Simultaneously, beginning in the 1890s, a new type
of magazine burst into American life. Publications such as *Mc-
Clure's*, *Cosmopolitan*, *Ladies' Home Journal*, *Illustrated World*,
World Outlook, *American Magazine*, *The World's Work*, and *The
Saturday Evening Post* presented a very different sensibility. Cheap
and with large circulations, they were produced at cost and made
money from advertising, which appeared in large volume with appeals aimed at connecting readers to the new consumer economy.
With a general-interest approach, these magazines' varied stories
and articles revolved around presenting the inside story, describing
bold personalities, conveying timely tales of "real life" in America,
adopting a personal and authentic voice, and supplementing colorful writing with vivid photographs or sketches. They also delighted
in detailing examples of self-improvement in the dynamic milieu of
early twentieth-century America. These popular magazines generated a large audience not among the old-fashioned "gentle reader"
of an earlier era but among new white-collar professionals, managers, and executives who were erecting the new social order. In them,
Carnagey found an ideal outlet for his work.[16]

Several themes and concerns characterized Carnagey's journalistic efforts. Nearly all of them explored bigger-than-life personalities and explained how they overcame obstacles to achieve success,
distinction, or celebrity. In "Fighting for Life in Antarctic Ice," published in *Illustrated World* in September 1915, he related the thrilling story of Dr. Douglas Mawson, who fought his way to survival

and "vanquished starvation and death" after being accidentally stranded during the expedition of Sir Ernest Shackleton. Writing for *American Magazine* in October 1914, Carnagey examined the unique and colorful life of "The World's Best-Known Hobo," Leon Ray Livingston, who had become famous traveling the world as a tramp, then writing books about his wanderlust adventures, and becoming friends with figures such as Theodore Roosevelt, Jack London, and Thomas Edison. Similar stories treated Sarah J. Atwood, a tragically widowed mother who went on to found one of the biggest employment agencies in the United States, and C. S. Ward, the most successful fund-raiser of the era who employed heartfelt appeals and elaborate organization to gather unprecedented sums of money for benevolent projects.[17]

Carnagey penned a fascinating article for *Illustrated World* in December 1915. Entitled "Sharpshooting the Future," it scrutinized a technological invention that promised to remedy a major social problem—the difficulty young people had in finding a suitable vocation. Modern America, the author argued, was full of people who could not find a job appropriate to their talents or who had chosen unwisely. He began with a telling example that reflected his own recent experience: an automobile salesman who hated his work and suffered through his daily tasks "like a raw-shouldered horse whose collar sets wrong." But now a new machine—it consisted of two jars filled with a mercury-and-salt solution, into which an individual would place a finger from each hand; then a mild electrical current was run through the whole, and changes in resistance would be measured—promised to assist. It was based on the principle that the electrical resistance of the human body varied under the slightest emotional changes, so when images were shown on a screen the response could be measured on a scale ranging from exaltation to depression. Carnagey believed that this contraption promised to provide "scientific vocational guidance" to confused young people by plumbing their psychological and biological impulses.[18]

In other magazine pieces, Carnagey explored some of the fresh opportunities for success appearing in modern commercial entertainment and business. The new industry of moviemaking, he suggested in 1916, had opened doors for screenwriters, who were scrambling to take advantage of "filmland's easy money." The growing popularity of theater likewise opened opportunities for playwrights who could summon both "inspiration and perspiration," original conceptions and hard work. Similarly, business had opened doors to people with imaginative ideas. In an admiring article on a successful banker, Carnagey surveyed his subject's "campaign of *ideas*, which I have been waging incessantly" and the great accomplishments that attended it. Pushing innovations such as interest on time deposits, friendly service, and opening the bank one night a week, he had worked himself to the top of his field like many such figures in the large, complex bureaucratic organizations coming to dominate finance, production, and trade.[19]

Carnagey made it clear that moneymaking set the standard for distinction in this white-collar world. High salaries or generous payments for creative work was the trophy awarded to successful people, as the titles of several of his articles revealed: "Rich Prizes for Playwrights," "How I Laid the Foundation for a Big Salary," "Money Made in Writing for the Movies." He noted that successful playwrights often had "a larger income than the occupants of a certain white house on Pennsylvania Avenue" and that busy screenwriters "are fairly rolling in money." As a businessman told him, "From my first job as a handy-boy about a bank in my home town at a wage of fifteen dollars a month, up to my present position as president of a corporation at sixty thousand dollars a year, there is a trail so clear."[20]

In his scrutiny of contemporary social and economic advancement, Carnagey tried to identify the personal characteristics of successful individuals. He concluded that enthusiasm, self-confidence, and friendliness were most critical. Master fund-raiser C. S. Ward, for instance, looked for ardent, eager, confident men to head his local canvassing committees, "men who think in big sums and have forgotten the meaning of f-a-i-l-u-r-e." But Carnagey also observed that smooth, solicitous interactions with others particularly characterized successful individuals. Sarah Atwood, for example, not only hired hundreds of men for stupendous projects but often went out to live with them on the job, opened a small store to provide daily necessities, learned many of their first names, and "was always ready with a cheerful greeting." They idolized her. A prominent banker related that while his work ethic had impressed superiors, his career took off only when he pushed a new ethic of positive interaction with customers. "Sociability and courtesy, I believed, were valuable commercial assets," he told Carnagey. "With a smile, I inquired into the customer's interests and tried to make his visit to our bank pleasant."[21]

At the same time, Carnagey raised a difficult issue that would disquiet his thought and work during the rest of his life: To what extent should the aspiring success seeker balance concern for others with self-interest? His subjects often displayed an admirable, old-fashioned disinterestedness. Ward declared, "I would leave this work immediately if I thought I was merely raising money. It is raising men that appeals to me." On the other hand, Carnagey admitted that self-regard often seemed the key impulse motivating people to action, as merchants recognized when they advertised.

"The greatest drawing card imaginable, if practical, would be to have a photograph of every desired customer in the window," he wrote. "When it comes right down to brass tacks, we are more interested in ourselves than anything else." In fact, the young journalist suggested that advertising and publicity had emerged as powerful forces in modern life precisely because they approached people not as moral entities but as creatures driven by powerful emotional needs and unconscious desires. Department store managers, for instance, used vivid colors, moving objects, and human figures to attract notice subconsciously. Venues for advertising were "unworked mines rich in treasure," Carnagey concluded.[22]

In writing for a popular audience, Carnagey developed an early version of the breathless, anecdotal, human-interest style for which he would later become famous. A playwright's comment about amateur writers—they "have good ideas, but they don't know how to express them; they write long speeches and wander and flub-dub around, start nowhere and get there, just talk"—seems to have made an impact. Carnagey, aiming deliberately at a mass audience of average readers, adopted a brisk prose enlivened by colorful personality sketches, human-interest angles, and self-assured conclusions. Confident rather than reflective, evocative rather than analytical, Carnagey's prose reached out to grab readers' interest and hold it. He described Atwood as hiring enough laborers "to junk the Sierra Nevadas, or to build another Panama Canal," and Reverend Russell Conwell, recently written off during a health crisis, as "about as dead as a Pittsburgh steel factory during a rush season." When a businessman launched a successful publicity campaign, Carnagey wrote, "The effect of that advertisement was beyond all expectations! Newspapers wrote editorials on it; a local evangelist used the figures to show how near one might be to hell; people who had never saved a dollar before opened up accounts, hundreds of them." This colloquial, perky prose, as it continued to develop in subsequent years, became a secret to his popular appeal.[23]

Carnagey's journalistic efforts reached their apex in the last magazine article he wrote during the 1910s. In November 1918, he published "My Triumph Over Fears That Cost Me $10,000 a Year" in *American Magazine*. The story of an anonymous businessman who overcame his fears and climbed to the top of his profession, the piece detailed how learning to speak in public provided an important means to acquiring distinction. Its theme—a method for the individual to climb to success—reflected the larger concern that was coming to dominate its author's worldview.[24]

The tale opened, in soon-to-be vintage Carnagey style, with the protagonist confessing that feelings of embarrassment, loneliness, and mental anxiety had dampened his enthusiasm for life and imprisoned him in a dead-end job. Then one day his new bride spoke out as they sat moldering in a dingy boardinghouse. "Did you ever notice that most of the boarders here are failures?" she declared. "These people stay on here because they are failures and they are failures because they do stay. Let's get out of here and think success!" Shaken by her outburst and realizing that he "was not a good advertiser" of himself, he decided to transform his life. The couple put up portraits of Napoleon, Abraham Lincoln, Henry Clay, Daniel Webster, and William Gladstone to provide examples of self-confidence. He began a program of nightly study while his wife spent evenings reading aloud from "inspirational books" such as James Allen's *As a Man Thinketh*. When his wife gently pointed out that he did not speak well and impress people, he enrolled in a public-speaking course at the local YMCA. Soon his career took off as he spoke compellingly about policy issues in his company and attracted attention with his "enthusiasm" and "human interest stories." He was soon appointed manager of the company's St. Louis operation and a year later was sent to New York to take charge of the biggest office in the company. Finally, a prominent industrialist hired him as the vice president of one of his companies at a large salary. Now the happy couple sat in their opulent apartment on Central Park West and he credited his wife as the one who "banished my fears and inspired me with confidence."[25]

Obviously, this "true story" of success was a thinly disguised parable about the usefulness of Carnagey's own course on public speaking. Having taken to heart the lesson of self-promotion, he wasted little time in distributing hundreds of reprints of this article. He added to the original manuscript by pointing out that Dale Carnagey was the teacher of the public-speaking course and appended a postscript: "The Y.M.C.A. in your city conducts the nationally known Carnagey Course in Public Speaking—the course studied by the man whose story you have just read. You are invited to attend, without any obligation on your part, one of the sessions of this course at your Y.M.C.A."[26]

Thus Carnagey, in both his teaching and writing in the mid-1910s, examined modern American culture and its emergent calculus of success. He sensed that moving upward now involved not so much determined labor, prudent self-control, and thrift as another constellation of qualities—human relations, advertising, self-promotion, and enthusiasm. As he wrote his parents in the spring of 1913 after his father sold ten acres of land at a considerable profit after holding on to it for several years: "Now you see how money is made," Carnagey noted. "It is not by hard work."[27]

Carnagey's pedagogical and journalistic endeavors, however, soon inspired a more extensive writing project that would take up a good deal of time. Having launched his YMCA courses in 1912, and his magazine articles the following year, he sought to combine his passion for writing with his interest in teaching public speech in innovative ways. The result was his first book.

In 1915, Carnagey co-authored with Joseph Berg Esenwein, a popular "how-to" writer, a book entitled *The Art of Public Speaking*. It aimed for a broad audience of readers who had a yearning for self-improvement, much like his YMCA courses and magazine articles. Published by the Home Correspondence School of Springfield, Massachusetts, the volume was designed to fit into its adult-education program and encompassed many of Carnagey's developing notions about the road to success in modern America.[28]

It is unclear how Carnagey became linked with the Home Correspondence School—probably either through his earlier association with the International Correspondence School or through his growing reputation from teaching evening classes at the YMCA—but there is little doubt that an association with this leading institution in the field of adult schooling gave a stamp of approval to his expertise. The Home Correspondence School had been established in 1897 and by 1910 it had grown to become one of the largest distance education schools in the United States. Enrolling more than fifty thousand students during its first dozen years, the HCS offered more than one hundred courses organized in five departments—Academic and Preparatory, Agricultural, Commercial, Normal, and Civil Service—while enlisting the services of professors from prestigious schools such as Amherst, Harvard, Brown, Hartford Theological Seminary, Cornell, Wesleyan, Dartmouth, and New York University. Typically, an HCS course, at a cost of $20, comprised forty weekly lessons involving reports or tests on each lesson that were graded, commented upon, and returned by instructors. The school clearly aimed to reach aspiring adults who had not attended college but now wanted to enhance their education so they could move upward.[29]

Carnagey's co-author played a prominent role in the HCS program. A native Philadelphian, Esenwein had earned a college degree, worked for the YMCA, and served as a professor of English at Pennsylvania Military College. He then moved into journalism, becoming the manager of *The Booklovers Magazine*; the editor of *Lippincott's Magazine*, an esteemed literary journal, from 1904 to 1914; and the editor of *The Writer's Monthly* in 1915. But he became increasingly devoted to adult education, publishing instructional books on how to address popular audiences, write short stories, and create screenplays for movies. As the director of the Home Correspondence School's literary offerings, he taught a course on short-story writing that promised a chance for potential students to "pull out of the mire of mediocrity; to be a force in the world; to take a new social position." People with imagination and ambition could learn to write "stories that carry his or her personality out into the world." Here was a natural partner for Carnagey.[30]

Carnagey and Esenwein's *The Art of Public Speaking* was intended to serve both as a textbook for an HCS course and as an independent guidebook for aspiring speakers. Throughout its thirty-one chapters, Esenwein focused on technique by discussing "Efficiency Through Change of Pitch," "Fluency Through Preparation," "The Voice," "Influencing by Persuasion," among others. Carnagey eschewed technical advice in his sections to focus on themes that stressed mental preparation and emotional projection—"Feeling and Enthusiasm," "Force," "The Truth About Gesture," "Thought and Reserve Power," "Right Thinking and Personality."

Carnagey argued that the aspiring public speaker should cultivate attitudes and attributes that created a persona of positive, willful, focused energy. These qualities, he insisted, would enhance a reader's performance when he was called upon to address others, whether in work conferences, on social occasions, or at formal professional gatherings. He stressed several specific principles in *The Art of Public Speaking.*

First, Carnagey underlined the importance of projecting a confident air. As he knew from his YMCA courses, fear of simply standing before others and speaking coherently was the major roadblock hindering his students. So in this book he urged speakers to "banish the fear-attitude; acquire the confident attitude." Confidence came from focusing "mental energy" and appearing confident and authoritative: "remember that the only way to acquire it is—*to acquire it.*" Willpower and resolve were essential. "Never tolerate for an instant the suggestion that your will is not absolutely efficient," wrote Carnagey. "The way to will is to will—and the very first time you are tempted to break a worthy resolution, and you will be, you can be certain of that—make your fight then and there. You cannot afford to lose that fight."[31]

He contended that controlling your thoughts offered the best way to create a confident persona. Citing the Book of Proverbs—"As a man thinketh in his heart, so is he"—Carnagey repeatedly insisted that a speaker literally could use his mental powers to shape reality. "All that a man is, all his happiness, his sorrow, his achievements, his failures, his magnetism, his weakness, all are in an amazingly large measure the direct results of his thinking . . . [W]e choose our characters by choosing our thoughts," he wrote at one point. "Our trains of thoughts are hurrying us on to our destiny." He related the story of a student in one of his classes who declared, "I will not be discouraged!" after a string of poor speeches, and worked even harder to improve his performance. "There is no power under the stars that can defeat a man with that attitude," he concluded.[32]

Second, Carnagey maintained that the public speaker should use enthusiasm to create a vital connection to his audience. Insisting that "sincerity is the very soul of eloquence," he urged readers to be absorbed in their subject and to choose language that conveyed their conviction. In one passionate passage, Carnagey drew upon his acting background. "There is only one way to get feeling into your speaking: *you must actually ENTER INTO* the character you impersonate, the cause you advocate, the case you argue—enter into it so deeply that it clothes you, enthralls you, possesses you wholly," he declared. "Genuine feeling in a speech is bone and blood of the speech itself and not something that may be added to it or subtracted at will." Not only audiences but modern society demanded enthusiasm. "Effective speech must reflect the era," he contended. "This is not a rose water age . . . This is the century of trip hammers, of overland expresses that dash under cities and through mountain tunnels, and you must instill this spirit into your speech if you would move a popular audience."[33]

Third, Carnagey insisted that effective speech demanded a projection of inner strength by the speaker. He must realize that "the true source of power lies within himself" and, accordingly, gather, strengthen, and focus his mental resources to truly communicate with an audience. "If the thought beneath your words is warm, fresh, spontaneous, a part of your *self*, your utterance will have breath and life," he maintained. For Carnagey, "The man within is the final factor. He must supply the fuel. The audience, or even the man himself, may add the match—it matters little which, only so that there be fire . . . If your speech lacks fire, it is dead."[34]

Fourth, Carnagey contended that compelling speakers must recognize the limitations of self-assertion and avoid the appearance of conceit and egoism that could alienate an audience. He quoted Voltaire—"we must conceal self-love"—and offered this aphorism:

"Self-preservation is the first law of life, but self-abnegation is the first law of greatness—and of art." A shrewd speaker persuaded people by appealing to their interests and points of view. "The successful pleader must convert his arguments into terms of his hearers' advantage," Carnagey contended. "Mankind are still self-ish. They are interested in what will serve them. Expunge from your address your own personal concern and present your appeal in terms of the general good." This notion of deploying oneself in light of other people's interests and concerns fascinated Carnagey. "A good conversationalist who monopolizes all the conversation will be voted a bore because he denies others the enjoyment of self-expression, while a mediocre talker who listens interestedly may be considered a good conversationalist because he permits his companions to please themselves through self-expression," he wrote. "Dynamite the 'I' out of your conversation."[35]

Finally, Carnagey urged readers to understand that people's psychological makeup offered a key to reaching them. Convinced that people are essentially emotional beings, he maintained that "the public speaker's ability to arouse men to action depends almost wholly on his ability to touch their emotions . . . The speeches that will live have been charged with emotional force." Contrary to old-fashioned thinking, modern research had shown that people seldom relied on reason and logic but were propelled by impulses of which they were only vaguely aware: a "natural respect" for authority, a tendency "to follow the line of least resistance" in mental efforts, emotional reactions that had been shaped by "our environments." So speakers should think like modern advertisers, Carnagey argued, who created publicity slogans that conveyed confidence and relied on the power of suggestion, as with a large department store that spent "fortunes on one advertising slogan: 'Everybody is going to the big store.' That makes everybody want to go."[36]

Carnagey's battery of recommendations culminated in a chapter entitled "Right Thinking and Personality." He announced the main point in the first sentence: "The speaker's most valuable possession is personality—that indefinable, imponderable which sums up what we are, and makes us different from others; that distinctive force of self which operates appreciably on those whose lives we touch," he wrote. "It is personality alone that makes us long for higher things." Here, again, was a marked departure from the Victorian standard of "character"—the set of internalized moral principles that kept the individual on the path of virtue—in favor of a more modern creed. "Let it not be suspected for one moment that all this is merely a preachment on the question of morals," he wrote. Achievement in the modern world "touches the whole man—his imaginative nature, his ability to control his feelings, the mastery of his thinking faculties, and—perhaps most largely—his power to will and to carry his volitions into effective action."[37]

For Carnagey, in other words, "personality" embodied self-expression rather than self-denial. It projected inner emotions and imagination, expressed mental energy and desires, and presented a set of magnetic, authoritative images that would seduce the audience into accepting what the speaker was saying. And he urged aspiring readers to focus their thoughts and willpower with this goal in mind. "You must fight just as though life depended on the victory," he declared, "and indeed your personality may actually lie in the balance."[38]

Thus in the mid-1910s—through new methods of teaching, magazine writing, and his first book—Dale Carnagey created the foundation for the work that would take him to worldwide fame and make him an exemplar of modern American success. At the YMCA, he first engaged a new white-collar corporate world whose inhabitants were hungry for techniques to guide them through an unfamiliar bureaucratic maze of meetings, group work, and human relations. In popular magazines, he engaged a new urban culture of commercialized leisure where audiences were eagerly embracing celebrity, inspiration, and entertainment. In his book, he connected public speech to personality and the dynamics of modern achievement. Such concerns would engage him for the rest of his life.

6

Mind Power and
Positive Thinking

n *How to Win Friends and Influence People*, there appeared on
the first printed page, even before the title page, a promise that
the book would "make the principles of psychology easy for
you to apply in your daily contacts." Then in his introduction, a
few pages later, famed broadcaster Lowell Thomas described the
book's author as a master of "applied psychology." Dale Carnegie
explained in his preface that he had prepared for writing the book
by "plowing through erudite tomes on psychology." He quoted an
observation from William James, the famous psychologist, that
most of us make use of only a small part of our "mental resources,"
and declared, "the sole purpose of this book is to help you discover,
develop, and profit by those dormant and unused assets."[1]

This strong psychological emphasis continued throughout the
book. Carnegie quoted frequently from James, other theorists such
as Sigmund Freud and Alfred Adler, and psychological writers such
as Harry A. Overstreet and Henry C. Link. He discussed the impact
of mental influences on the workings of human relations, admonishing people for their lack of awareness about the great power of
psychological impulses in human affairs. He contended that even

the most educated individuals often "learn to read Virgil and master the mysteries of calculus without ever discovering how their own minds function." Carnegie reserved his greatest enthusiasm, however, for a popular strain of psychological thought that had swept through American culture in the early 1900s: New Thought, or positive thinking. This school maintained that the mind, by focusing on affirmative thoughts, could shape beneficial events in the material world. Carnegie quoted an influential acolyte of New Thought—"Picture in your mind the able, earnest, useful person you desire to be, and the thought you hold is hourly transforming you into that particular person."[2]

Where did Carnegie's preoccupation with psychology—it was a crucial element in everything he advocated in his best-selling book—come from? It originated in the mid-1910s, when the aspiring teacher and writer began a program of intellectual self-improvement that first brought him into contact with this revolution in modern thinking initially launched by Freud, James, and others. As he prepared to write a textbook for his expanding YMCA courses, he immersed himself in popular psychology, particularly New Thought. The result was a cast of mind that stressed mental impulses, emotional needs, and unconscious desires in human behavior. This way of thinking would persist for the rest of his life and influence everything Carnegie wrote about the pursuit of success in modern America.

Dale Carnagey once recalled that as a teenager he had heard his mother speak excitedly about the "new century that was going to usher in great and lasting changes." In his opinion, however, she had underestimated the sweeping transformation that altered the conditions of American life in the early 1900s. "It was more astonishing than even she could have dreamed it would be," he wrote. "The automobile that changed our transportation habits; the vast changes in the way we spend our leisure time—radio, motion pictures, television; the electric light and telegraph, the airplane—inventions and events destined to have a profound effect upon our civilization and all the generations that follow us."[3]

But perhaps the most striking element of modernity for young Carnagey was an intellectual movement overhauling the understanding of human nature and behavior in the early twentieth century. That was psychology, of course, and in the mid-1910s he was fascinated by it. This preoccupation flowed from a broader project. By his own account, eager to move ahead in society, Carnagey had begun a program of study and self-improvement after arriving in New York. He cultivated a habit of making notes, carrying a small notebook in his hip pocket at all times. Whenever he saw something interesting, had a significant idea regarding an important topic, or came across a good story or a striking illustration, he entered it in his notebook. He also began a filing system for keeping track of articles he read, using large yellow manila envelopes as files and filling them with newspaper clippings, magazine extracts, and personal notes.[4]

Along the same lines, Carnagey embarked upon a program of reading. An elderly, eminent public speaker, with whom he had struck up a friendship, urged him to build a "reserve power" of knowledge by reading seriously in history, literature, science, and philosophy. This would provide him the means to enhance his personal "magnetism." The young man did not reveal the identity of this figure, describing him only as "the most notable lecturer in our state," "venerable," "white-haired," and an analyst of the dynamic mental powers of figures such as Rudyard Kipling, the actor Richard Mansfield, and Ida Tarbell. It is likely that Carnagey's anonymous mentor was Orison Swett Marden, the famous lecturer and writer on self-improvement, who matched that description and played a central role in Carnagey's writings on public speaking, where he was frequently quoted and fulsomely praised.[5]

But regardless of his mentor's identity, Carnagey began to read widely in the 1910s as he labored to build up his "mental reserve power." In his words, he entered into "the delightful dominion of books." Establishing a routine of reading on Monday, Tuesday, and Friday evenings, he stocked his storehouse of knowledge and came to appreciate "the difference that one usually feels between the educated and the unread man: the one has a vast store of reserve power; the other's knowledge and experiences have been limited to his own narrow sphere." This self-education project brought Carnagey into contact with a wide sphere of intellectual endeavors as he encountered works in history, philosophy, the natural sciences, technology and inventions, and what would become a special interest, biographies. But significantly, he usually did so secondhand. He demonstrated a preference for compendia and condensations and sketches—his good friend Homer Croy once observed that Carnagey "wants everything condensed: books, speeches, newspapers, magazines. He is condensation's greatest zealot"—and thus devoured volumes such as *Great Books as Life Teachers* by Newell Dwight Hillis and *Ridpath's History of the World* by John Clarke Ridpath. He especially became a fan of the Chautauqua Course of Reading, a program of home study that he highly recommended in his YMCA lessons.[6]

The young man's expanded reading also brought him into contact with contemporary currents of thought, debate, and discussion. Some of this involved current social and political affairs, as evidenced by references to figures such as Theodore Roosevelt and Woodrow Wilson, John D. Rockefeller and Andrew Carnegie. More significantly,

Carnagey was attracted to an important cultural crusade in early twentieth-century America: the New Thought movement, or "positive thinking." Emerging in the late 1800s and gathering influence and adherents in the early 1900s, this loose movement aimed at the acquisition of "health and wealth and peace of mind" through mental power, which held the key to emotional and material abundance. Important advocates included Phineas P. Quimby, the self-educated founder of mental healing; mystical metaphysicians such as Ralph Waldo Trine with his best-selling book, *In Tune with the Infinite*; mind-cure advocates such as Annie Payson Call; and Mary Baker Eddy, the founder of Christian Science. New Thought advocates believed that hidden mental resources could be retrieved and mobilized to increase emotional vigor, social success, and material accumulation. Overall, these positive thinkers stressed the galvanizing, restorative, generative power of the human mind. An eclectic group, some drew upon a religious mind-cure impulse while others mined a vein of old-fashioned Emersonian transcendentalism with its notions of an "oversoul" and intuition as a window into reality. Many drew upon psychology, the new science engaged in the exploration of mental impulses and capacities.[7]

Synthesizing this variety of religious, scientific, and philosophical influences, New Thought spread out over the American cultural landscape in the early 1900s, promoting several broad ideas. Its disciples contended that the human mind was the primary causative force in the universe; that the remedy for human defects and disorders lay in the mental and spiritual realm; and that evil was not a permanent reality in the world but merely the temporary absence of good. Finally, and most important for Carnagey, they insisted that health and material abundance were available to those who mobilized their available mental resources to pursue it. To this end, New Thought disciples underscored the importance of

personal magnetism, positive thinking, and personality development for the aspiring individual. As the movement's influence grew
in the early 1900s, it attracted adherents ranging from the eminent
philosopher and psychologist William James to popular magazines
such as *Good Housekeeping*, which by 1908 ran a regular column
for women entitled "How to Become Beautiful by Thought."[8]

Though never formally affiliated with any New Thought group,
Carnagey displayed a clear affinity for their beliefs. His involvement was somewhat haphazard, of course—he made no pretense
of being an intellectual devoted to sustained, disciplined critical
thought—and he had only a dim awareness of the broader implications of New Thought. But numerous references and citations
in his writing revealed his attraction to, and inspiration by, key
figures, texts, and ideas in this movement. He punctuated practical
directives for aspiring public speakers—develop self-confidence,
conquer fear, generate enthusiasm, radiate sincerity—with a steady
drumbeat of advice on how to do the most important thing of all:
gathering and galvanizing one's mental powers.

In 1915, Carnagey wrote that an individual's neglect of mental development created stagnation but "there is promise of better
things as soon as the mind detects its own lack of thought power."
He recommended several books on "the management of thought,"
and quoted a psychologist who stressed the importance of mustering mental powers: "Mental energy and activity, whether of
perception or thought, thus concentrated, act like the sun's rays
concentrated by the burning glass. The object is illumined, heated,
set on fire." At one point, Carnagey declared bluntly, "Your success or failure as a speaker will be determined very largely by your
thoughts and your mental attitude."[9]

Carnagey's enthusiasm for psychology and New Thought, while
partly a result of intellectual engagement, also developed out of his

growing success with teaching adults. By 1916, he had left behind the intermittent paychecks and cockroach-infested boardinghouses of his early days in New York. Now students were streaming in to sign up for his YMCA courses, and his income rose and solidified. He was able to find a comfortable apartment in Manhattan and rent an office for himself at Studio 824 in Carnegie Hall. Young Carnagey "was doing well," wrote one journalist, and he was able "to hire halls around town where ambitious young men were nightly exhorted to Speak Out, to Go In There and Fight, to Wham It Across, and to Keep Their Hands Out of Their Pockets."[10]

One of Carnagey's students at this time described the confident, inspiring teacher he encountered in the class. Frank Bettger had been a professional baseball player—he was third baseman for the St. Louis Cardinals—when a badly broken arm ended his career prematurely in 1911. Returning to his hometown of Philadelphia, he tried to earn a living as a debt collector and then as a life insurance salesman, but a shy personality hamstrung his efforts and he spiraled downward into hard times. Bettger came to realize, in his own words, that he had to "overcome this timidity and fear of talking to strangers." Hearing about Dale Carnagey's course at the YMCA on Arch Street, and its success in helping people to overcome such problems, he enrolled in 1917. He met the instructor, who immediately put him in front of the class for a brief talk on why he was there. The terrified Bettger survived the ordeal and set to work bolstering his self-confidence. Progress was slow. Then one evening, Carnagey stopped him in the middle of a listless speech and insisted that he "put some life and animation into what you say." In Bettger's words, the teacher then "gave our class a stirring talk on the power of enthusiasm. He got so excited during his talk, he threw a chair up against the wall and broke one of its legs." The aspiring salesman went home and concluded that he needed to put the same enthusiasm into selling that he put into baseball, and went on to become fabulously successful in his field. The decision he made that night under Carnagey's tutelage, Bettger wrote later, "was the turning point in my life."[11]

So successful were Carnagey's teaching efforts that he expanded his public-speaking course into a nationwide endeavor. In 1917, he put together an advertising pamphlet for the Carnagey Course in Public Speaking, which listed endorsements from an array of businessmen in New York, Philadelphia, Baltimore, Newark, and Scranton. He began training instructors and codifying his methods in a series of guidelines, lessons, and pamphlets. Carnagey gathered these materials and published them in 1920 as *Public Speaking: The Standard Course of the United Y.M.C.A. Schools.* This volume—a collection of four "books" and sixteen multi-section "lessons"—offered a complete map of his pedagogical techniques and a sketch of his developing philosophy of individual success and human relations.[12]

The book expropriated large chunks of material from *The Art of Public Speaking,* but it also promoted the classroom techniques he had developed in the trenches—prodding students to conquer their fear, establishing regular bouts of speaking, arousing enthusiasm, encouraging natural delivery and gestures, striving to build confidence and self-expression. These qualities became hallmarks of his post-Victorian approach to instruction.

But perhaps most striking, positive thinking pervaded many portions of *Public Speaking: The Standard Course.* "Every man has in him dormant powers of which he never dreams," Carnagey claimed, and he argued that speaking was "the shaft which, sunken into the mine of our minds, reveals to others the riches planted there." Noting again William James's claim that "the average man develops only ten percent of his mental powers," Carnagey asserted that his greatest reward as a teacher was "an inner realization of my own progress and the uncovering and fruition of my hidden powers." He stressed that liberating muffled mental capacities would create a powerful willpower in the individual. "Will to win and keep on willing; and you will possess a power that is as real as a cannonball," he wrote. "You can't see it. You can't lay your hands on it. You can hardly describe it. But it will make you irresistible."[13]

Carnagey larded the book—even more than his earlier effort with Esenwein—with frequent references to iconic figures in the New Thought crusade. In particular, he embraced a quartet of men who had helped popularize the message that mental exertion and positive thinking would lead to happiness and material success. The first, Reverend Russell H. Conwell, was one of the great success avatars in American history. Born into a farm family of modest means in the Massachusetts countryside in 1843, he had fought in the Civil War and then toured the world and drifted through a variety of vocations as a young man—lawyer, journalist, and finally, Baptist minister. In the 1880s he became head of the Grace Baptist Church in Philadelphia, which he soon built up to a staggering size of more than four thousand members. Conwell, a man of prodigious energy, also founded Temple University and three hospitals in the Philadelphia area. He became most famous, however, for his "Acres of Diamonds" speech, which he first penned in the 1870s before crisscrossing the country to deliver it more than six thousand times in the succeeding decades. (He gave away much of the wealth he earned from this lecture to send poor young men to college.) This legendary address put forward two central ideas, which Conwell presented with great panache and an actor's gift for mimicry and impersonation. First, he declared that opportunity lay everywhere in American society, most likely in one's immediate environment, and that keen attention to producing what people wanted or needed would deliver "acres of diamonds." Second, he denounced the old religious idea that virtue was related to poverty and declared, "I say that you ought to get rich, it is your duty to get rich. Money is power, and you ought to be reasonably ambitious to have it. You ought because you can do more good with it than you could without it."[14]

By the 1910s, however, Conwell began to stress something that New Thought adherents like Carnagey found especially congenial: the crucial role of individual thought and will in achieving wealth. In a 1916 *American Magazine* article, Conwell stressed that "will-power is your greatest asset" and quoted from Proverbs: "As a man thinks, so he is." In a booklet issued the following year, Conwell moved further in this direction. The "first essential" in achieving success was "to gain a full appreciation of the latent or unused force which each individual possesses," he declared. An admiring Carnagey praised Conwell's demonstration that "If the thought beneath your words is warm, fresh, spontaneous, a part of your *self*, your utterance will have breath and life." He also reprinted the entire "Acres of Diamonds" address as a "Special Lecture" in *Public Speaking: The Standard Course*.[15]

A second New Thought hero was Elbert Hubbard, who likewise became an inspiration for Carnagey. Born in 1856 near Bloomington, Illinois, this son of a religious farm family began his career as the successful manager of a soap company. A restless intellect, however, prompted him to abandon business in the 1890s. He became a disciple of William Morris and the Arts and Crafts movement and founded *The Philistine*, an iconoclastic magazine that promoted literary innovations, political reform, and traditions of craftsmanship. Describing himself as "a businessman with a literary attachment," Hubbard became a writer, editor, and publisher and churned out a steady stream of books and articles on success and happiness. He achieved national fame with "A Message to Garcia," an ode to an individual initiative set during the Spanish-American War, which castigated the average American's "inability or unwillingness to concentrate on a thing and do it." This had created an atmosphere, Hubbard argued, where "slipshod assistance, foolish inattention, dowdy indifference, and half-hearted work seem the rule." The successful man, he insisted, was the individual who decided "to be loyal to a trust, to act promptly, concentrate their energies: do the thing [the task] at hand." For Hubbard, "Civilization is one long, anxious search for just such individuals."[16]

Like Conwell, Hubbard developed a New Thought sensibility in the early 1900s. In books such as *Love, Life and Work* (1906) and *The Book of Business* (1913), he stressed that aspiring individuals needed to enhance their mental powers in order to succeed. "Success is the result of mental attitude, and the right mental attitude will bring success in everything you undertake," he instructed. "The Master Man is a person who has evolved Intelligent Industry, Concentration, Self-Confidence, until these things become the habit of his life." Carnagey became a devoted fan of Hubbard. He described "A Message to Garcia" as a "tremendous little tract," and was especially taken with Hubbard's axioms about developing the "right mental attitude." He often utilized this one: "Try to fix firmly in your own mind what you would like to do, and then without violence of direction you will move straight to the goal . . . Keep your mind on the great and splendid thing you would like to do, and then, as the days go gliding by, you will find yourself unconsciously seizing the opportunities that are required for the fulfillment of your desire."[17]

James Allen, the eccentric English writer and metaphysician, became a third New Thought influence on Carnagey. Born in 1864 and orphaned when his father migrated to America and was murdered, Allen left school, became a clerk to support his family, and worked for several British manufacturers until 1902. Interested in spiritual and philosophical issues, he began to write for *The Herald of a New Age*, and he finally quit business to launch his own magazine, *The Epoch*. At the same time, Allen began to write a series of short, reflective, inspirational volumes on individual success and happiness, which poured out over the next nine years until his death in 1912. A slight, frail man with long, dark hair who habitually dressed in a black velvet suit, this sage attracted many disciples in New Thought circles with his various writings extolling the possibilities of mind power.[18]

His best-known work, *As a Man Thinketh*, presented Allen's belief that mental exertions could alter both internal states and external circumstances. The human mind was like a garden, he claimed, and "a man may tend the garden of his mind, weeding out all the wrong, useless, and impure thoughts, and cultivating toward perfection the flowers and fruits of right, useful, and pure thoughts." This would produce much more than abstract goodness. "The outer world of circumstances shapes itself to the inner world of thought," he contended. "Let a man radically alter his thoughts, and he will be astonished at the rapid transformation it will effect in the material conditions of his life." The success seeker needed to begin by shaping his own mind. "All that a man achieves and all that he fails to achieve is the direct result of his own thoughts," Allen maintained. "A man can only rise, conquer, and achieve by lifting up his thoughts. He can only remain weak, abject, and miserable by refusing to lift up his thoughts."[19]

Intrigued by the Englishman, Carnagey tried to unearth information about his mysterious life, even sending inquiries to the editor of *The Business Philosopher: A Magazine Advocating the Principles of Success Through Service*, who had published some of

Allen's writings. Carnagey described Allen's booklet as "exercising a commanding influence in many lives today," and reprinted it as a "special lecture" in *Public Speaking: The Standard Course.*[20]

Orison Swett Marden became the most powerful New Thought influence on Carnagey in the 1910s. Marden's own life was a nearly pitch-perfect rendition of the American anthem of climbing to success. Born in 1850 in rural New Hampshire, he was orphaned at age seven and then circulated through a series of foster homes where he was harshly treated and overworked as a "hired boy." Inspired by the Scottish author Samuel Smiles, whose popular book *Self-Help* he chanced across in an attic, he worked his way through primary and secondary school, Andover Theological Seminary, and Boston University before earning an MD from Harvard Medical School and an LLB from Boston University Law School. In the 1880s and 1890s he pursued an entrepreneurial bent and became the owner of several hotels and resorts before suffering severe setbacks in the Depression of 1894.

Marden quickly restarted his career in Boston as a successful writer with the 1894 publication of *Pushing to the Front, or Success Under Difficulties.* This best seller went through twelve editions in the first year. The tireless author followed up by founding *Success* magazine in 1897 (he would edit it for the rest of his life); contributing regularly to Elizabeth Towne's New Thought magazine, *Nautilus*; and authoring some sixty-five books on success, willpower, and positive thinking before his death in 1924. Originally Marden was a proponent of Victorian hard work and self-denial as a recipe for success, which he illustrated in books such as *Character: The Grandest Thing in the World* (1899). By the early twentieth century, however, he had moved toward an advocacy of personality and its attributes—personal magnetism, popularity, charisma, dynamism—that he elucidated in books such as *The*

Masterful Personality (1921). This shift also became apparent in differences between the 1894 and 1911 editions of *Pushing to the Front*: the former featured chapters such as "Character Is Power," while the latter added chapters such as "Personality as a Success Asset."[21]

Marden became a devotee of New Thought in the early 1900s. In books such as *Little Visits with Great Americans, or Success Ideals and How to Attain Them* (1903), *Peace, Power, and Plenty* (1909), and *The Miracle of Right Thought* (1910), he proclaimed the message of mind power. He urged ambitious readers to focus on "personal characteristics, the varying assortment of which in the individual constitutes what we call his personality, wherein one man differs from another." He offered these principles: "that the body is but the mind externalized, the habitual mental state out-pictured; that the bodily condition follows the thought, and that we are sick or well, happy or miserable, lovable or unlovable according to the degree in which we control our mental processes . . . Before a man can lift himself, he must lift his thought." He concluded that "there is no habit which will bring so much of value to life as that of always carrying an optimistic, hopeful attitude of really *expecting* that things are going to turn out well with us and not ill, that we are going to succeed and not fail, that we are going to be happy and not miserable."[22]

Carnagey frequently acknowledged Marden's impact on his own thinking. He had a much-annotated copy of the 1911 edition of *Pushing to the Front* in his library and adopted much of that book's style: biographical vignettes, human-interest stories, lively writing. He also adopted many of its central themes: enthusiasm, magnetic personality, being agreeable, overcoming fear. Describing the older man as "that great apostle of better things," Carnagey recommended Marden's books to students and quoted him frequently and at length in his writings on public speaking. He recycled numerous Marden aphorisms on the successful individual's need for skills in addressing others. "How many people owe their advancement, their position, largely to their ability to talk well," said one. "Nothing else will call out what is in a man so quickly and so effectively as the constant effort to do his best in speaking before an audience," said another. "The practice of public speaking, the effort to marshal all one's forces in a logical and forceful manner, to bring to a focus all the power one possesses, is a great awakener of all the faculties." Carnagey even reprinted in his *Public Speaking: The Standard Course* a Marden essay entitled "Public Speaking."[23]

Carnagey's involvement with New Thought ultimately brought him into contact with a broader area of fresh intellectual inquiry in early twentieth-century America. The doctrine of mind power, as many observers have noted, had a special connection to the rapidly developing discipline of psychology. According to one historian, "The ideology of success through mind power is intimately bound up with the growth of psychotherapy in the present century." By the early 1900s, a variety of psychologists had begun to probe ever more deeply into the complexity of the human mind, producing the notion that beneath rational thought and calculation lay submerged mental powers that shaped our perception of and action upon the world around us. Those resources could be strengthened if weak, marshaled if disparate, focused if scattered, and cured if ailing. American psychotherapies of many stripes were advanced by figures such as the neurologist James Jackson Putnam; the abnormal psychologist Morton Prince; the psychopathologist G. Stanley Hall; the physician of "the whole personality," Richard Clarke Cabot; the eclectic explorer of the subconscious William James; and the Freudian psychoanalyst A. A. Brill. All of them promoted the broad idea that therapeutic strategies could minister to the mind, enhance its powers, resolve its problems, and hence improve one's quality of life.[24]

Intrigued, Carnagey began rummaging about in psychology, which increasingly permeated his perceptions, analyses, and formulas in the 1910s. In *The Art of Public Speaking*, he regularly cited psychologists and provided brief exegeses of their ideas. Carnagey noted Walter Dill Scott, the eminent psychologist of business and advertising and the future president of the American Psychological Association, on the need to banish fear: "Success or failure in business is caused more by mental attitude even than by mental capacity." He quoted from Daniel Putnam, author of *Elementary Psychology: Or, First Principles of Mental and Moral Science*, on the efficacy of the individual focusing attention to produce "the prime condition of the most productive mental labor." Carnagey drew upon Gerald Stanley Lee's best-selling book, *Crowds: A Moving-Picture of Democracy*, to probe "the psychology of crowds" and quoted its contention that businessmen had surpassed preachers in influencing the modern age because "they are more close and desperate students of human nature, and have boned down harder to the art of touching the imagination of crowds." Carnagey closed his final chapter "Right Thinking and Personality" with a quotation from Stanton Davis Kirkham, the author of *The Philosophy of Self-Help: An Application of Practical Psychology to Daily Life*. It poetically expressed the internal satisfactions flowing from achievement: "now you have become the master . . . You shall lay down the saw and the plane to take upon yourself the regeneration of the world."[25]

In *Public Speaking: The Standard Course*, Carnagey relied even more heavily on psychological themes and interpretations. He discussed "the psychology of gesture," "the psychology of combat," "business psychology," and "Hints on Crowd Psychology." He presented an entire section entitled "Power of Suggestion," in which he explored the growing field of applied psychology and its focus on taking advantage of people's proclivity for irrational decision-making. "Acts of pure reasoning are as rare as romantic thoughts before breakfast," Carnagey asserted. "Most of our actions are the result of suggestion." This process, he explained, involved subtly floating assertions or hinting at ideas that then "embed themselves in our subconscious minds and dictate our actions." Skilled salesmen and effective advertising relied heavily on suggestion, Carnagey explained, and it also constituted "the greatest power of the public speaker. It is a tremendous force that you can employ in your daily dealings with men."[26]

Carnagey frequently spiced up the book with references to an array of psychological experts. Felix Arnold, the author of *Attention and Interest: A Study in Psychology and Education*, attracted notice with his claim that people forgot half of what they had heard within thirty minutes, two-thirds in nine hours, and three-quarters in a week. Carnagey cited G. Stanley Hall, the respected psychologist who brought Freud to the United States for several lectures in 1909, as an authority on "the psychology of dress," whose studies indicated that attractive clothing and good grooming increased both self-respect and the respect accorded by others. The power of suggestion, Carnagey observed, was confirmed by growing numbers of psychologists such as Walter Dill Scott, who contended that the individual "is reasonable, but he is to a greater extent suggestible." Forbes Lindsay, the author of *The Psychology of a Sale: Practical Application of Psychological Principles to the Processes of Selling Life Insurance*, similarly contended that "Suggestion is the most powerful factor in our mental processes and consequently exerts a great influence over our physical actions."[27]

Carnagey's references to two figures particularly illustrated the linkages between psychology and New Thought in the early twentieth century. First, he drew upon William James, the eminent intellectual who probed deeply into human consciousness as a psychologist and philosopher in the late 1800s and early 1900s. James, unlike many serious thinkers, respected New Thought as a legitimate approach for understanding human endeavor. In his famous *The Varieties of Religious Experience*, he described the movement as a quasi-religion that endorsed "the all-saving power of healthy-minded attitudes," demonstrated "an unprecedentedly great use of the subconscious life," and met "the mental needs of a large fraction of mankind." It must be taken seriously, James concluded, since "mind-cure gives to some of us serenity, moral poise, and happiness, and prevents certain forms of disease as well as science does." In "The Powers of Men," another famous essay, James argued that New Thought had begun to uncover and harness "stored-up reserves of energy that are not ordinarily called upon" by humans usually content to "continue living unnecessarily near our surface."[28]

Carnagey revered James, describing him as a "great psychologist." In *Public Speaking: The Standard Course* (as well as in several other books throughout his career), he approvingly cited James's belief that the average individual developed only a small portion of his "possible mental powers." He also appropriated, and misunderstood, one of James's most famous phrases: the "will to believe." Whereas James had used it to define the struggle to adopt religious faith in the modern world, and provided a foundation in philosophical pragmatism for doing so, Carnagey misinterpreted the phrase to mean "the average man likes to hear what he already believes." This became the basis for his contention that speakers needed to gauge the psychology of their audience and appeal to "their tastes, their experiences, and their beliefs." Thus Carnagey's William James was a promoter of mental power and psychological growth.[29]

Second, Carnagey respected H. Addington Bruce, a journalist who had done more than anyone, perhaps, to explain the convergence of New Thought and psychology. A publicist for the Emmanuel Movement, an early twentieth-century crusade that melded religion and psychology, Bruce became the psychological adviser to the Associated Newspapers, a national publishing group. He authored a number of books—*The Riddle of Personality* (1908), *Scientific Mental Healing* (1911), *Nerve Control and How to Gain It* (1919), and several others—that sought to popularize psychology as a species of mind power. He also wrote regularly for popular magazines such as *Appleton's, Good Housekeeping,* and *American Magazine.* Bruce contended broadly that the new explorers of "psychopathology" were establishing a truly scientific foundation for the efforts of mind curists and faith healers. As he contended in his article "Masters of the Mind," psychologists such as Pierre Janet, Boris Sidis, Morton Prince, and Sigmund Freud were showing the world that "the human mind possesses powers which, when scientifically directed, are almost incredibly efficacious in conquering many widespread and baffling diseases."[30]

In Carnagey's reading, Bruce served as an authority on the psychological power of enthusiasm. He quoted the journalist's contention that "Enthusiasm doubles the power to think and do . . . The man or woman of enthusiastic trend always exercises a magnetic influence over those with whom he or she comes into contact." Bruce asserted that enthusiasm would help its possessor to dominate any situation and produce "dollars in your pockets as well as a ruddier glow to your cheeks." This principle fed Carnagey's growing belief that a posture of positive thinking could propel the aspiring individual toward success and linked his public-speaking program more tightly to the larger New Thought.[31]

Carnagey's embrace of the main tenants of New Thought in the 1910s—mind power, positive thinking, psychological amelioration—served to broaden his goal as a writer and teacher. Increasingly, he went beyond public speaking to address a much larger topic: how to become successful in American society. He had long believed that skills in addressing an audience would improve self-confidence and enhance one's public reputation, but now he began to harness those skills to a larger goal of upward social mobility and material gain. "Every time you speak, you are preparing yourself for ultimate success," he now wrote. Carnagey envisioned the first faint outlines of a success ideology rooted in positive thinking and popular psychology, salesmanship and human relations, magnetic personal images and mental power. This modern approach urged adherents to embrace the dynamism of early twentieth-century America. "Grip us with a virile topic. Something with red blood and big biceps. We are Americans," he declared in 1920. "Ragtime is our national music. Baseball and football are our national games. We are not much interested in croquet. It takes something with Yankee dash to hold us." Carnagey may even have glimpsed his own future. "He who can tell us how to earn more money, lengthen our lives, better our health, increase our happiness, is sure of an attentive audience," he wrote. "If you know what people want and can show them that they will get it by following your proposals, success is yours."[32]

As Carnagey advanced in the late 1910s, his achievements as a teacher and writer gained him a significant measure of social respect. It also brought a measure of financial security as the young man escaped the hardship and poverty of his early years in New York and began to live more comfortably. A favorite poem captured his buoyant mood—"Invictus," by William Ernest Henley—and he reprinted it in *Public Speaking: The Standard Course.* This paean to the "unconquerable soul" of the individual became such "a decisive influence in my life" that he also memorized and recited it on numerous occasions. The final stanza offered a stirring conclusion:

> It matters not how strait the gate,
> How charged with punishments the scroll.
> I am the master of my fate;
> I am the captain of my soul.[33]

Carnagey's developing role as a teacher of public speaking, a New Thought disciple, and a writer on success, however, reached an unexpected impasse in the late 1910s. First, the outbreak of war on the world stage acted to disrupt his career progress, and then a more personal difficulty threatened his integrity and professional standing. Ultimately, the two events converged to drive him away from writing and teaching and, indeed, away from the United States entirely for a time. In the long term, this hiatus helped sharpen Carnagey's views of the world and mold the shape of his career. In the short run, however, it threw his burgeoning business into utter disarray.

On April 2, 1917, President Woodrow Wilson went before Congress to ask for a declaration of war against the German Empire and its allies. Armed conflict had been raging in Europe since 1914 as an alliance of Germany, the Austrian Empire, and Turkey battled another comprised of England, France, and Russia. After several years of escalating tension with the Germans over freedom of the seas, the Wilson administration finally decided to enter the fray. Congress approved a war declaration on April 6 by an overwhelming vote, and the president moved quickly to mobilize the economic and military resources of the nation. A key initiative was the Selective Service Act, pushed through Congress in May 1917 and put into action over the next few months. Nearly three million young Americans eventually would be drafted into the armed forces during World War I. Dale Carnagey was one of them.

According to official records, he registered for the draft on June 5, 1917, listing his address as an apartment building in Brooklyn and noting the loss of his finger and "partial support" of his parents as mitigating circumstances. But the United States Army took the young teacher later that summer and posted him to Camp Upton, located near Yaphank, Long Island, with thousands of other draftees from the northeastern United States. Named after Emery Upton, a Civil War general, this encampment was constructed during the summer of 1917 and was designed to house and train forty thousand troops. They began arriving by rail in September and by December the facility was full. The trainees were issued equipment and uniforms, and assigned a bunk while military instructors— some were British and French army officers—drilled them relentlessly in basic military maneuvers and the finer points of trench, tank, and gas warfare. Rifle marksmanship, hand grenades, and machine guns received much attention as did hand-to-hand combat, the latter often taught by professional boxers. The army's famous Seventy-Seventh Division, which would go on to fame for its stalwart fighting at the Argonne Forest in August 1918, was formed at Camp Upton. One of its soldiers, Sergeant Irving Berlin, later would write *Yip, Yip, Yaphank*, a Broadway musical based on his army experience on Long Island, which included one of his most famous songs: "Oh, How I Hate to Get Up in the Morning."[34]

Disqualified from active combat because of his missing finger, Carnagey was assigned an office job at Camp Upton. Given the rank of sergeant—doubtless due to his college education—he became an assistant to an army major and took on the responsibility of organizing office work, running errands, and answering the phone. At the beck and call of his superior, he was expected to perform any task, no matter how unusual. "I had just bought a Chevrolet car, and he asked me to drive him from Camp Upton to New York City and back every weekend," Carnagey reported. "Naturally I was glad to do it because it meant a weekend away from the dull routine of the Army." The major, an attorney in civilian life, jealously protected his status. "He always had a copy of the *New York Times* on his desk every morning," Carnagey wrote. "One morning, after I sat there for hours doing nothing, I dared to open his copy of the *Times*. He was indignant because a lowly Sargent [*sic*] had dared to peep into his three-cent newspaper."[35]

During his stay at Camp Upton, Carnagey observed two incidents that left an imprint on his thinking about public speaking. One day, he attended a gathering of "unlettered Negro troops"— they were about to be shipped off to the European front—who were being addressed by an English bishop on the reasons they were being sent into the fight. In full oratorical flight, the visitor declaimed at great length on the importance of "international amity" and "Serbia's right to a place in the sun." The troops stared at him with blank looks. "Why, half of those Negroes did not know whether Serbia was a town or a disease. He might as well, as far as results were concerned, have delivered a sonorous eulogy on the Nebular Hypothesis," the young sergeant observed. Another time, while in New York for the weekend, he heard a congressman hooted from the stage at the Hippodrome. He had chosen to speak to the crowd on the American government's elaborate preparations

SELF-HELP MESSIAH

for war, when they wanted to be entertained. After droning on for twenty minutes, mounting catcalls, whistling, and shouting finally forced him to "retire in humiliation." The lesson from such occurrences was clear: Speakers needed to gauge their audience and find a fitting way to reach them on their own terms.[36]

But most of the time, the young teacher and writer found life at Camp Upton to be completely barren of interest. After trying, unsuccessfully, to procure an assignment with the government's Liberty Loan campaign in the summer of 1918, he lingered in his dull office job until the armistice in November. He was granted holiday leave to visit his parents, and then ordered to return. Finally, in late January 1919 Carnagey received his discharge from the armed forces. "Praise the Lord I got out of the army Saturday morning about 8:47," he wrote his mother. "I surely have been happy since. It is a delight to have one's freedom again."[37]

Upon returning to civilian life, Carnagey immediately jumpstarted his YMCA teaching project. He revived his courses in New York and traveled to Philadelphia to do likewise, while also creating new instructional programs for the Rotary Club and Advertising Men's Club. Within a few months he was back up and running. On May 11, 1919, he wrote to his family on letterhead stationery with an impressive description emblazoned across the top: "The Carnagey Course in Public Speaking. Dale Carnagey—Author and Director. Conducted in YMCA Schools, New York Rotary Club, Advertising Club, American Institute of Banking, Philadelphia Engineers' Club, and Commercial Organizations. Eighth Season."[38]

Carnagey's revived classes highlighted, even more strongly than before, that the ability to speak in public would produce social and economic success. A syllabus declared "The Ability to Talk Convincingly Is Worth Hard, Cold Cash," while the instructor overwhelmed students with testimonials from graduates, such as the salesman who claimed "this training has increased my yearly income by $3,000," or the realtor who "increased his yearly commissions by $4,000 as a result of this training." Carnagey also subtly underlined the New Thought dimension of his training. Each student, he claimed, would acquire enhanced "will-power, mental concentration, self-confidence, and convincing tones," precisely the qualities that would give a man "a reputation and a power out of all proportion to his capacity."[39]

But Carnagey's enthusiastic resumption of his career as a teacher of public speaking veered into excess. A few months after leaving the army, he became embroiled in a scandal involving the leading scholarly journal in the field of speech education, which accused him of deception in one of his YMCA promotional pamphlets. The resulting blow sent him reeling.

The difficulties began with Carnagey's article "My Triumph Over Fears That Cost Me $10,000 a Year," the story of an anonymous businessman whose enrollment in a public-speaking course catapulted him to the top of the business profession. After being mustered out of the army, Carnagey revised the article into a pamphlet and sent it to the editor of an academic publication, *The Quarterly Journal of Speech Education*. He urged the journal to reprint the article and noted that he would happily secure permission from *American Magazine* to do so.[40]

In fact, Carnagey's reprint made several additions to the original *American Magazine* article. Most of them were inconsequential, merely adding details or elaboration to original points, but two changes carried more weight. First, it identified the protagonist's inspiring speech teacher by name—Dale Carnagey—and added a statement from the YMCA that praised the efficacy of his courses: "they had more than four thousand students enrolled in various classes, and that more men from their public speaking classes had testified to the benefits they had derived than from all of their other classes combined." Second, the revision added a section informing readers that "the nationally known Carnagey Course in Public Speaking" was being taught at the YMCA in their city, and invited them to attend a session. Moreover, Carnagey's communication to *The Quarterly Journal of Speech Education* included a second pamphlet entitled "How to Promote Y.M.C.A. Classes in Public Speaking" with this passage:

> You ought to distribute a large number of the booklet entitled, *How I Overcame Fears That Cost Me Ten Thousand Dollars a Year* ... It is a biographical article of a man who joined a Y.M.C.A. course in public speaking and profited by it greatly. Written in a popular magazine style, it is interesting reading. The human interest story told in the article will lead men to read it who are not in the least interested in educational work. *And it is the best sales literature in Christendom for this course.* I shall be glad to send you sample copies of the reprint. You are urged to give copies of it to every man who inquires about the course or attends the opening session ... This reprint can be obtained from me at the following prices: $1.50 for a hundred, $10 for a thousand.[41]

Then the trouble began. Somewhat taken aback by Carnagey's self-promotional onslaught, the staid, scholarly *Quarterly Journal of Speech Education* decided to investigate the provenance of the man and his article. It discovered a serious problem. Professor J. M. O'Neill, from the University of Wisconsin, produced the journal's findings in an article entitled "The True Story of $10,000 Fears," published in March 1919. After confronting Carnagey about the factual basis of his article, O'Neill related, the young teacher had admitted that the piece was not about a real man but "a story of the experiences of a number of his students." But even after admitting deception, O'Neill continued, Carnagey still urged the journal to publish the article and "say that it is a true story, because it is a group of true stories." The investigation came to an indignant conclusion: "The apparent assumption that the Editor of *The Quarterly* would be willing to reprint this article and tell the readers that it was a true story, knowing the actual facts of the case, was not very pleasing or complimentary."[42]

Nor was this an isolated incident. Around the same time, in *Public Speaking: The Standard Course*, Carnagey presented a lengthy narrative of "my own story, which I hope may serve as a guidepost to the thoughtful student." This inspirational tale was, to put it mildly, a tall tale. He began by noting that during much of his career, he had remained mentally dormant until his company created a new department. Deeply disappointed when he was passed over for a promotion to manage it, Carnagey continued, he decided to change his demeanor and become "buoyant, enthusiastic, and optimistic." He forced himself to be cheerful every day, read inspirational and historical literature, and focus his willpower on becoming successful. He discovered the virtues of public speaking and pursued it to develop self-confidence. Then, according to Carnagey's account, "the general manager of our company was shot while hunting deer in Maine. I was given his position." Only two years later, his success brought him to the leadership of an even bigger company that manufactured hardware and automobile parts. This prestigious, lucrative job, Carnagey concluded, provided more "leisure to devote to the hobby of my life—public speaking." While some of the details matched aspects of Carnagey's experience, this life story was a complete fabrication in its description of corporate positions and advancement.[43]

Both the imbroglio with *The Quarterly Journal of Speech Education* and the embellished life story in his book revealed a reckless overreaching by Carnagey. It suggested a willingness, at this stage of his life, to use puffery as a tactic in climbing to success. The demobilized young soldier, straining to get his career back on track, became overzealous and allowed his enthusiasm to clearly outdistance his judgment. When the leading journal of speech teachers publicly chastised him, it must have been an embarrassment. Carnagey never addressed the controversy, either publicly or privately, but the fact that he never again engaged in such behavior suggests that he learned a lesson.

In another sense, however, Carnagey's difficulties in the aftermath of World War I help explain his unusual departure in the next few years. Hindered by the wartime interlude that disrupted his business and embarrassed by the dustup over his ethics in speech teaching circles, he was susceptible to the allure of an unusual but inviting new project that came out of the blue. It would send him on a fascinating adventure that took him far afield, both vocationally and geographically.

7

Rebellion and
the Lost Generation

The notion of personal reinvention nearly defined *How to Win Friends and Influence People*. From its opening pages, Dale Carnegie insisted that readers needed to change their approach to problems and people, move outside familiar patterns of behavior and thought, and create a new persona to face the world in order to influence people and achieve success. His own experience illustrated this need. As Carnegie had learned, the changing circumstances of life often made older values and beliefs archaic. "I believe now hardly anything that I believed twenty years ago—except the multiplication tables, and I begin to doubt even that when I read about Einstein," he admitted. "In another twenty years, I may not believe what I have said in this book. I am not so sure now of anything as I used to be." But despite the ongoing flux of life, Carnegie continued, nearly everyone sticks with comfortable habits and "lives far within his limits. He possesses powers of various sorts which he habitually fails to use."[1]

But summoning the courage to overcome life's impasses and embrace personal transformation promised enormous benefits. Carnegie described the example of one of his students, a sophisticated art dealer who spoke several languages fluently and had graduated from two foreign universities, but who had fallen into crisis when forced to confront his personal disarray and lack of effectiveness. He "was so shaken by a realization of his own mistakes, so inspired by the vista of a new and richer world opening before him, that he was unable to sleep" for days. So he decided to revamp his life and energize his career by becoming a more skilled practitioner of human relations. Carnegie believed that the ideas in his book, of course, would serve as a catalyst for change—"Incredible as it sounds, I have seen the application of these principles literally revolutionize the lives of many people"—but that personal transformation ultimately must come from within. "Do you know someone who would like to change and regulate and improve? Good! That is fine. I am all in favor of it," he exclaimed. "But why not begin with yourself? . . . 'When a man's fight begins with himself,' said 19th century poet Robert Browning, 'he is worth something.' "[2]

Carnegie's second major book, *How to Stop Worrying and Start Living*, extended the theme. Meeting traditional expectations, he suggested, might bring security but often stifled life in other ways. "Wherever did we get the idea that secure and pleasant living, the absence of difficulty, and the comfort of ease, ever of themselves made people either good or happy?" he asked. He cited the example of a woman who had turned her life around after realizing her obsession with meeting others' expectations and ignoring her own needs. "In a flash, I realized I had brought all this misery on myself by trying to fit myself into a pattern to which I did not conform," she confessed. The key, Carnegie concluded, was to find yourself and not just copy others. "You and I have such abilities, so let's not waste a second worrying because we are not like other people," he proclaimed. "You are something new in this world. Never before, since the beginning of time, has there ever been anybody exactly like you; and never again throughout all the ages to come will there ever be anybody exactly like you again."[3]

The embrace of personal reinvention had deep roots in Carnegie's own experience in the 1920s, when he overthrew just about everything that was familiar in his life. Abandoning his heritage of Midwestern Protestantism, his thriving public-speaking courses in New York, and even his native country, he embarked upon a commercial entertainment venture that sent him out of the country for the first time. While the financial rewards of his new project would prove less than he hoped for, the cultural exposure and broadened experience made it one of the most important episodes of his life. In fact, this adventure would trigger an extended hiatus abroad as Carnegie married a European woman, became a writer of fiction, and launched a stinging critique of life in the United States. In many ways, his life would never be quite the same.

In the early spring of 1917, the telephone rang in Dale Carnagey's office in the Carnegie Building in New York. When he picked up, a voice said, "This is Lowell Thomas. I'd like to come and see you." The widely traveled Thomas, then a visiting professor in the English Department at Princeton, had been invited by Secretary of the Interior Franklin K. Lane to speak on Alaska at the Smithsonian Institution in Washington, D.C., as part of the government's promotion of domestic tourism in light of the war in Europe. He had accepted, but wanted a public-speaking coach to help him shorten and sharpen his remarks. He had heard of Carnagey's successful course, so now Thomas contacted the young instructor and convinced him to help. They met several times and collaborated on revisions. Thomas delivered the revamped speech with great success a few weeks later and it helped launch his wildly successful career.[4]

Grateful for Carnagey's expert coaching and advice, Thomas wrote an endorsement letter describing the New York instructor as "one of the best public speaking teachers in America today." He reported that he had used some of Carnagey's teaching materials with his students at Princeton and enjoyed great success. "I have known many students who have had their stock of confidence increased, their personalities developed, and their earning power expanded by studying under Mr. Carnagey," he continued. "His course ought to be worth thousands of dollars to every man who profits by his suggestions and criticisms." Carnagey used the letter in advertising his YMCA courses in several eastern cities.[5]

Such was the beginning of a lifelong friendship between the two men. Each would go on to become world famous, Carnagey as a teacher, lecturer, radio host, and advice writer, and Thomas as a travel writer, media personality, and adventurer. Over the next four decades they maintained a close relationship, with Carnagey regularly visiting Thomas's farm in upstate New York, and Thomas writing glowing introductions to several of Carnagey's books. Carnagey dedicated his best-selling book *How to Stop Worrying and Start Living* "to a man who doesn't need to read it—Lowell Thomas," while Thomas inscribed a gift copy of his *Pageant of Life*: "To Dale, World's No. 1 authority on the pageant of life!"

But in 1919 the two ambitious young men came together in a joint undertaking, the origins of which lay in World War I. Thomas had dashed off to Europe as a war correspondent to prepare a series of syndicated reports for American newspapers. He not only wrote a number of dispatches but employed a cameraman, Harry Chase, to film the action. Initially focusing his efforts on France and Italy, Thomas shifted his attention to the Middle East, where the British general Edmund Allenby had just commanded the Allied takeover of Jerusalem. Journeying first to Egypt, and then flying to

Palestine to cover the Allied capture of Jericho, Thomas eventually
landed in Jerusalem, where he was introduced to Major T. E. Lawrence in February 1918. The unorthodox British officer, who had
been fighting alongside Arabian fighters in their rebellion against
the Ottoman Empire, fascinated Thomas and within a few weeks
he had received permission to join Lawrence in Arabia. He would
spend the next several months with the iconoclastic Englishman
filming war travelogues and taking numerous photographs before
returning to Europe.[6]

The Thomas came back to the United States after the armistice determined to take financial advantage of his fascinating war experiences. Utilizing hundreds of photographs and thousands of feet of
film, he put together an illustrated lecture entitled "With Allenby
in Palestine and Lawrence in Arabia" for a run at a theater in New
York City. Thomas introduced the show, then moved offstage to
serve as an invisible narrator while three projection machines offered a variety of colored slides, films, and lighting effects. Although
modestly successful, Thomas's lecture was rough and amateurish,
with the images appearing unevenly and the narration not always
matching what audiences were seeing on the screen. It didn't help
matters that he often spoke extemporaneously. Nonetheless, Percy
Burton, an English impresario, arranged to present the show at
London's Royal Opera House in Covent Garden.[7]

Realizing that his show required "a complete rewrite job,"
Thomas once again contacted Carnagey for help. He also offered
the speech instructor a position as business manager for the tour, a
job that would bring a cut of the profits. The young teacher agreed
to help and attended several of Thomas's shows "until I became
familiar with his films and material." Plans were quickly drawn up
for passage to England, since the London performance was slated
to begin shortly.[8]

Thomas, Carnagey, and cameraman Harry Chase sailed for Europe on the French ship *La Lorraine*. As they crossed the Atlantic, the trio labored frantically, usually twelve hours a day, on a new version of the show. "All day and far into the night, Dale, Chase, and I were huddled over our projector and scripts, working under the pressure of an opening less than two weeks off," Thomas said. "But by the time we docked in Southhampton, we had put together the two parts of a tight, swiftly moving show: 'The Last Crusade—With Allenby in Palestine and Lawrence in Arabia.' " In addition, the team also created advertising that would be used on billboards and in newspapers.[9]

Upon arrival, the three Americans and Percy Burton quickly joined forces to put everything into place and tidy up the last details. The show opened spectacularly. Burton arranged to rent the "Moonlight on the Nile" stage set from the opera-oratorio *Joseph and His Brethren* and hired the prestigious Band of the Welsh Guards, forty members strong, who presented an overture onstage and then moved to the orchestra pit to provide musical accompaniment throughout. The show began on a mysterious, evocative note, as Thomas related:

> The curtain opened on the Nile set, the moon faintly illuminating distant pyramids. Our dancer glided onstage in a brief Oriental dance of the seven veils. We had set to music the Mohammedan call to prayer and, from the wings, a lyric tenor sent this haunting, high-pitched melody sailing away to the farthest reaches of the theater. Two minutes later, I stepped into the spotlight and began to speak . . . "Now come with me to the lands of mystery, history and romance."

He then told the audience how he first encountered the centerpiece of the show while walking down a street in Jerusalem. "I met a

man clad in the gorgeous robes of an oriental potentate; and, at
his side, hung the curved gold sword worn only by the descendants
of the prophet Mohammed. But this man had none of the appearances of an Arab. He had blue eyes; and the Arabs' eyes are always
black or brown." It was, of course, T. E. Lawrence.[10]

The revamped show worked beautifully as the carefully crafted
narrative, tightly synchronized film and photographs, and complementary set, music, and lights melded into a seamless whole. It was
a triumph and the reaction, both popular and critical, was ecstatic.
"Afterward, the audience stood and applauded for ten minutes,"
Thomas noted, while the London newspapers—*The Times, Morning Post, Daily Mail, Lloyd's Weekly News*—ran front-page pieces
on the show. "One paper said it was the most wonderful film ever
seen in England and all London would shortly be talking of nothing else," Carnagey wrote his mother. According to *Lloyd's Weekly
News*, "For two hours great audiences sit, never moving; such is
the enthrallment of the pictures they see and the thrilling story they
hear." In fact, the success of the show was so overwhelming that
the original seven-day engagement at the Royal Opera House was
extended to nearly five months and the opera season postponed for
six weeks to compensate. As the demand for tickets skyrocketed,
the show was moved to Royal Albert Hall for six weeks, and then
to Queen's Hall for several more weeks. As *The Times* reported,
"Even Royal Albert Hall (the largest concert auditorium in the
world) is proving hardly large enough for the crowds who want to
enjoy it. It is a unique and wonderful entertainment." More than
one million eventually would attend the London performances.[11]

Carnagey played a central role in this success. All promotional
materials for *With Allenby in Palestine and Lawrence in Arabia*
noted that it was "Under the direction of Dale Carnagey," but, in
fact, his job was much bigger. He served as the general manager

for the entire operation: hiring two business managers, overseeing bookings, resolving technological issues with film, bulbs, and projectors, and dealing with a thousand and one details of this complex presentation. For such an important job, Carnagey had worked out a profit-sharing plan with Thomas, wherein he received a percentage of the weekly take after operating expenses and a special rental fee for Thomas's films were taken off the top.[12]

With the success of the London show secured beyond doubt, Carnagey recrossed the Atlantic in the late fall of 1919 to oversee a duplicate version of the show in Canada and the northeastern United States, which was completely under his management. Hopeful of gaining more profit in the long run, he had refused a salary in favor of another percentage of the take. But the organizational, logistical, and financial tasks facing him were enormous. As he explained, "I have to rehearse the talk with my machine operator, have to get advertising going in the newspapers, have to tend to bookings, have to get some films copied, slides colored, and a thousand things you never dreamed of." He also trained lecturers to replace Thomas. More pressure came when Canadian attendance proved very spotty. Carnagey gained a few additional bookings in New York and Baltimore, and by March 1920 he had wrapped things up and returned to England.[13]

While Carnagey primarily saw the Thomas show as a moneymaking venture, a more personal motivation also entered into his calculations. For the youth who had left the Midwest to study acting, but then aborted his theatrical career, this production served as a vindication. In 1920 he wrote to his parents on letterhead stationary reading "The Lowell Thomas Travelogues: 'With Allenby in Palestine and Lawrence in Arabia,' Under the Direction of Dale Carnagey." The message within was a triumphant one. "You used to be always saying to me, mother, that I had never done as well

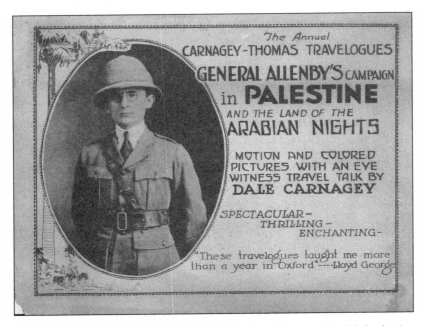

Carnagey in a poster for a version of the travelogue show in London he had helped put together with Lowell Thomas.

at anything else as I did with Armour. What do you think about it now?" he wrote. "I think both you and father thought I was making a mistake when I went to New York to go on the stage, but you see what it has led to indirectly."[14]

Back in England in May 1920, Carnagey rejoined Thomas to finish up a tour to Manchester, Liverpool, Birmingham, Glasgow, and Edinburgh. When the production's popularity elicited an invitation to bring it to Australia and New Zealand, Thomas decided to go. Carnagey stayed in England to take a second version of *With Allenby in Palestine and Lawrence in Arabia* to a succession of smaller cities throughout the country. Once again, the young American faced a mountain of work. "We have to either rent or arrange to play on a sharing basis every town in England containing more

Carnagey astride a camel in a 1919 publicity shot for Lowell Thomas' Allenby and Lawrence show.

than fifty thousand," he explained. "I have two men now out doing this work for me . . . [but] all the decisions will rest with me."[15]

Thomas sailed for Down Under in July 1920, and Carnagey took the show on the road to provincial England. But problems quickly developed. People so identified the show with Thomas that significant numbers stayed away upon hearing that a replacement lecturer would be speaking. Moreover, trouble with finding suitable venues also created a snarl of problems as profits began to drain away. Carnagey decided to deliver the lectures himself, a move that only created more difficulties. While a skilled public speaker, he had never been to the Middle East, and a notable uneasiness often became obvious as the photographs and films flew by on the screen. According to a magazine, during one of the shows, "he baffled his audience by saying simply, 'Here is a beautiful picture of the East. Let us enjoy it in silence.'"[16]

Finally Carnagey buckled under the strain of these mounting problems. "There was bad news waiting for us when we docked at Melbourne—a cable from London reporting that the Allenby-Lawrence road companies had folded; poor Dale Carnagey had suffered a nervous breakdown over it," Thomas recalled later. "In the meantime, we had lost a good deal of money and poor Dale was sick, blaming himself. There wasn't a thing in the world I could do about it at a range of ten thousand miles except to cable him my absolute confidence that he had done all anyone could expect." Thomas's memory was faulty on one point—the English show had not closed down completely but Carnagey's enthusiasm certainly had.[17]

After regaining his emotional equilibrium, Carnagey limped on with the production until the end of the year. Then in December 1920 he looked over the ledger sheets and discovered "that we had taken in about $20,000 and that our expenses had been about the same." Carnagey had had enough, and he cabled Thomas that he wanted to resign from the show. He agreed to stay on until March 1921 but at a salary.[18]

Meanwhile, in early 1921 Carnagey enjoyed greater success by helping the popular English hero Sir Ross Smith put together a public lecture. In 1918, Smith had made the first flight from England to Australia, winning both a knighthood and a prize of $10,000 offered by the Australian government. Now Thomas's organization brought him back to London and arranged for him to star in another travelogue show based on his exploits. Carnagey organized this new production, wrote the lecture, and trained Smith in delivering it. *The Ross Smith Flight: From England to Australia*, a production of "The Lowell Thomas Travelogues, Under the

Personal Direction of Dale Carnagey," enjoyed a four-month run at the Philharmonic Hall in London.[19]

In the spring of 1921, Carnagey's venture with Thomas came to a close. It might have seemed obvious that the young teacher would return to New York City and resume his lucrative teaching endeavors with the YMCA. But an unexpected development muddied the waters and made his future direction unclear. Dale Carnagey had fallen in love.

The August 4, 1921, edition of the *Belton Herald* carried a brief wedding announcement. Submitted by James and Amanda Carnagey, it noted that their son Dale had married Lolita Harris of Baltimore on July 4, 1921, in Dorking, a small town on the River Mole in Surrey County, England, about forty-five miles southwest of London. According to British records, the couple had applied for a license, registered their marriage, and received a marriage certificate from local civic authorities. "The ceremony was performed in the Congregational Church and luncheon was served at the Deepden Mansion, formerly the country home of Lord Francis Hope," the *Belton Herald* continued. It added that the newlyweds flew from London to Amsterdam two days later, spent two weeks touring Holland and Belgium, and then sailed from Antwerp for America on July 21.[20]

Carnagey's decision to marry had been rather impulsive. Having met his new bride only a few months before, he knew little about her in terms of personality, habits, and values. In fact, she had an interesting and unusual background. Born Lolita Baucaire on October 29, 1886, in Ulm, Germany, to a family of French ancestry, she had resided in Germany until 1903, when she emigrated to the United States and became an actress in a touring theatrical company. In later life, she would claim to be a countess, but that seems unlikely. In 1909, she had married Charles C. Harris, a prosperous dentist from a prominent Baltimore family of dentists. He had been president of the Maryland State Dental Association in the 1890s, while his father, James H. Harris, was on the faculty of the Baltimore College of Dental Surgery, one of the most prestigious institutions for dental training in the United States. Charles had been married before—to Grace Harris since 1888—and apparently divorced his wife to marry Lolita. Given his wealth and the fact that he had been born in 1860, thus making him twenty-six years older than his new European wife, it seems clear that she was something of a social climber.[21]

As Mrs. Charles Harris, Lolita enjoyed the 1910s as "the wife of a fashionable Baltimore doctor," in her words, who was "a member of the Baltimore Country Club, and was prominent in the social circles of that city." Speaking four languages fluently, she crossed the Atlantic more than a dozen times to travel extensively in Europe. But the marriage did not last. Lolita and her husband were divorced in 1920, and she took up with Carnagey, whom she apparently met in Baltimore when he was touring with the American version of the Lowell Thomas show. After he returned to England, she followed a few months later in September 1920.[22]

For the Missouri farm boy, the cosmopolitan figure of Lolita Baucaire must have exerted a powerful pull. Photographs from the period reveal an attractive young woman with dark eyes and wavy, bobbed brunette hair, who was habitually outfitted in fashionable attire. Letters and postcards noted her love for skiing and hiking, and a proclivity for playing poker. In other words, Lolita was the prototype of the 1920s New Woman—liberated from Victorian convention, adventurous, and displaying an added patina of European sophistication and style. More worldly in matters of

romance and sexual maneuver, and bereft of support after divorcing her rich husband, she had drawn young Carnagey in quickly
and entranced him. As a writer, teacher, and business manager
for one of the most popular entertainment ventures of the era,
he must have appeared to her as an interesting, promising, and
potentially lucrative catch. In fact, their 1921 marriage inaugurated a period of footloose living in Europe that lasted for the
next four years. With economic disarray on the Continent in the
aftermath of World War I, Europe provided an inexpensive living
environment for Americans with dollars. The Carnageys took full
advantage of the situation.[23]

Lolita Baucaire several years after marrying Carnagey in 1921.

In early 1922, after a brief trip to the United States, Dale and
Lolita Carnagey spent most of the subsequent year traveling in
the Azores, Spain, Algiers, and Italy. In the Azores, he got a crash
course in European economic deprivation, discovering that a po-
liceman there was paid a salary equivalent to $8 a month. After
some time in Cadiz, Spain, the couple crossed the Mediterranean to
Algiers, where they encountered scenes of widespread poverty and
an Islamic culture vastly different from their own. After journeying to Palermo, Sicily, they went on to Naples and several weeks of
touring through Italy before arriving in Rome in February 1922.
By June they were in Cortina, in the far north of the country in the
Dolomites. Ensconced in a beautiful but inexpensive hotel, par-
taking of delicious food, hiking and picking wildflowers, and encountering breathtaking views of the Italian Alps on a daily basis,
Carnagey exuded a palpable contentment. "This is certainly the
life," he commented to Lolita in Cortina. "Yes, who wants to live
in New York when you can live here?" she replied.[24]

The Carnageys spent much of 1923 and 1924 in central Europe,
living for varying periods in Germany, Austria, Switzerland, and
Hungary. In a September 1923 letter to his hometown newspaper,
the *Maryville Democrat-Forum,* Dale reported that he had spent the
last winter in the "Black Forests of Germany" and was now in
the Austrian Alps. He provided colorful descriptions of mountain
rivers—"not the babbling brooks that the poets sing about, but
veritable roaring torrents, foaming in cascades over thousands of
huge granite boulders"—and glaciers "200 feet thick that had been
there on the side of the mountain in the days of Belshazaar and
Babylon." The Carnageys spent much of a summer in a spa town
in the Austrian Alps near Salzburg, staying at a hotel adjoining a
beautiful old church. "We dine out in a garden under the chestnut

trees, close enough to the church to hit it with a rock," he wrote. "It is Catholic and built in 1789."[25]

They toured several other cities—Zurich and Wehrliverlag in Switzerland and Kitzbehel in the Tirol province of Austria—with Lolita's sister and her husband as companions. Dale described a stint in Vienna, visiting a palace of Franz Josef where "the haughty Hapsburgs lived until 1910." They also traveled deeper into the Continent. The Carnageys lived for six months on an island in Budapest, and Dale reported hunting wild geese "on the Hortobagy Desert down in Hungary, away out by the borders of Romania." He also noted, "I didn't get a goose, but I did get within gunshot of Russia."[26]

By September 1924, the Carnageys had settled in France, where they would spend much of the following year. "I am living just now at Versailles on the edge of Paris," he wrote to the *Maryville Democrat-Forum*. "Almost every day I spend an hour walking through what is probably the most famous park and garden in the world. Every day I walk by the Grand Palace of the most ostentatious king that ever misruled and oppressed humanity." Warming to his anti-aristocracy theme, he declared that Louis XVI "got what he needed—the guillotine, what he and all that crowd needed, and what the Russian czar needed, and Herr Wilhelm and others that I won't mention." Playing to his Missouri audience, he also contended that Marie Antoinette's gardens at Versailles paled beside the natural beauty of the countryside near Maryville, and that farming in France, in terms of efficiency and productivity, "is a joke in comparison to the farming in Nodaway county."[27]

While in France, Carnagey enjoyed a visit from Homer Croy, along with his wife and two children, and the two families spent some vacation time together on the French Riviera. The old pals from Maryville also took a six-hundred mile trip by automobile through the French countryside, where they wondered at the lack of fences, observed women washing their clothes in the creeks because they did not have money to heat water, pretended to be wine tasters, and grew astonished at the sight of grain being cut by hand with a scythe. In Paris, Carnagey found himself questioning the business values of visiting Americans. He noted that many of them came to Europe for relaxation and uplift and then talked only of "the bargains they had bought, the amount of money they had saved, or how much they had been overcharged." Carnagey defended a different standard. "I would want my child to be prepared for the appreciation of the finer things of life; to be able to come to Paris and enjoy its music and art, for there are two worlds in which a man should live: the one the world of reality, of beans and potatoes, or iron and steel . . . and another world, a greater, a finer, a nobler world, that gives to life its beauty and content and color, the world of the mind and the world of the soul," he wrote. "Therefore I would train my child for leisure, for what a man does in his leisure hours is equally as important as that which he does in his working hours."[28]

During this extended stay in Europe, Carnagey footed the bill for the couple's wandering existence. Given the weakness of European currencies and the strength of the American dollar, he was able to stretch his uncertain income to meet their needs. "In comparison to America, they are ridiculously cheap," he reported about the cost of food and lodging. He was receiving $3,000 a year from royalties on his textbooks and also procured funds from periodic bouts of teaching and lecturing. In Paris, for example, he presented a talk on public speaking at the American Library in November 1924 to an audience of "bankers, exporters, students, a diplomat, and both American and French businessmen." The response was so positive that Carnagey spent the next seventeen weeks offering his public-speaking course in the same venue. He also presented another version of the course, in his words, "with the assistance of the American Chamber of Commerce. Some of the most prominent members of the American colony here are students."[29]

Despite this, the Carnageys occasionally felt a financial pinch. This prompted a rather unlikely moneymaking scheme: raising and selling pedigree German shepherds. Using some of Lolita's German contacts, the couple established the Carnagey Shepherd Breeding and Training Farm at Dale's father's place in Belton, Missouri, with offices in the Hayes Building in Kansas City under the direction of his brother, Clifton. They purchased a grand champion German shepherd as the basis of the operation and shipped him to western Missouri along with several other dogs from Germany. They also put together a sixteen-page glossy advertising pamphlet, filling it with several dozen photographs of their German shepherds and a text written by Dale. It also noted, "Our Mr. D. B. Carnagey spends a part of each season in Europe and secures some of the famous prize winners in Europe for our breeding farm." But this venture was ill-fated. In late 1925, after losing money, in an announcement written by Dale, James Carnagey announced a "Closing Out Sale." Ever the promoter, Dale added, "This is the first time in the history of American Shepherd breeding that such a famous collection of animals have been offered for sale . . . If interested, act now."[30]

As the years in Europe passed, a corrosive element entered the picture. It became ever more apparent that Dale and Lolita were ill-suited for each other. The enthusiastic young man barely removed from the Midwestern countryside, with his religious background, self-deprecating humor, and earnest manner, stood miles apart from the worldly French-German "countess" with her sophisticated manner and demanding social standards. Actually, trouble had appeared early. Of his wedding day, Carnagey later claimed, "I was married in a church in Europe and the first words my wife uttered after the ceremony were, 'Did you tip the janitor?'" He grew increasingly resentful of his wife's attempts to curb his behavior, which she viewed as proletarian. Once, when a couple visited their house to play cards, the subject of the Russian nobility came up and Carnagey, in his words, "called them a good old virile western phrase: 'son-of-a-bitch' . . . Lolita almost passed out." He concluded ruefully, "Avoid that phrase in the future when speaking east of the Mississippi." During another card game with two Italian aristocrats, his wife grew annoyed when he forgot to say please when asking for new cards after the discard. "Lolita was ashamed of me," he recounted.[31]

In his private files, an angry Carnagey burst out in resentment, "I HERE HIGHLY RESOLVE, in the presence of my Angel of Light, to dictate a review of my mistakes until I have reached the degree of perfection approximating Lolita's and hers!!!!" After a few years together, the incompatible pair had begun to drift apart noticeably and the marriage slowly unraveled. A letter from Europe noted that in an Italian hotel, he was sleeping "in a single room on the second floor" while "Lolita has a big double room downstairs with two windows and a balcony." During one of their visits to the United States, the Carnageys stayed at Lowell Thomas's Cloverbrook Farm in Pawling, New York, and went hunting with Count Felix von Luckner and his male secretary. The foursome was photographed upon returning as they sat on a fence displaying their kill. The arrangement was telling: Dale and the secretary sat next to each other while three feet away sat the other two, with Lolita on the far side, separated from her husband but sitting quite close to the count. The tableau symbolized the state of their marriage.[32]

Dale and Lolita Carnagey, the strain between them evident, during a hunting trip with a
German count and his secretary.

Throughout his life, Carnagey refused to discuss his first marriage or its breakup. A journalist in the 1930s, for instance, squeezed
out of him the caustic admission that it had lasted "ten years and
forty days." But he also confessed, with regard to his marriage, that
his 1932 biography, *Lincoln the Unknown*, was "strictly autobiographical in every respect." Thus Carnagey's portrait of Lincoln's
miserable domestic life, with blame laid at the foot of Mary Todd
Lincoln, can be read as a thinly veiled account of his own relationship with Lolita. Mrs. Lincoln, wrote the author, had been "educated in a snobbish French school," possessed "a high and haughty
manner and an exalted opinion of her own superiority," and grew
constantly irritated by her husband's dress, manners, and behavior.

In Carnagey's words, "she wanted to make him over" and tried to pressure him into submission:

> She was always complaining, always criticizing her husband; nothing about him was ever right. He was stoop-shouldered, he walked awkwardly and lifted his feet straight up and down like an Indian. She complained that there was no spring to his step, no grace to his movements; and she mimicked his gate and nagged at him to walk with his toes pointed down, as she had been taught at Madame Mentelle's. She didn't like the way his huge ears stood out at right angles from his head. She even told him that his nose wasn't straight, that his lower lip stuck out, that he looked consumptive, that his feet and hands were too large, his head too small . . . His table manners were large and free. He didn't hold his knife right, and he didn't even lay it on his plate right . . . Once when he put chicken bones on the side dish on which his lettuce had been served, she almost fainted.[33]

Moreover, Carnagey accused, Mary Todd Lincoln spent money extravagantly, especially "in matters having to do with showing off." She bought a handsome carriage in which to be driven about town and spent money on fancy clothes, even though the Lincolns could not afford either. Gradually, her husband came to realize, in the author's words, that "he and Mary were opposites in every way: in training, in background, in temperament, in tastes, in mental outlook. They irritated each other constantly." He finally reached a breaking point when she flew into rages and attacked him physically. On one such occasion, when her physical abuse was particularly intense and long-lasting, he "lost his self-control, and seizing her by the arm, he forced her across the kitchen and pushed her toward the door, saying, 'You're ruining my life. You're making a hell of this home. Now, damn you, get out of it.'"[34]

While Lincoln took his wife back after such an episode, Carnagey did not. He and Lolita separated, apparently at his instigation, after trying to live in New York for a period in 1926 and 1927 and then traveling together in Europe once again. She stayed abroad while he returned to the United States in 1928. Lolita certainly recognized the parable of the Carnagey marriage contained in her husband's Lincoln biography. After reading it, she wrote Dale and confessed that "all the way through I felt a current, which made me feel, if Dale had never put himself into the character of Lincoln and felt that Dale's life was Lincoln's life, Dale would not have sent me away as he did, he would not have gotten rid of me as he did." Made uncomfortable by "the feeling that came over me," she asked plaintively, "Is it true? You certainly have a savage attack on Mary Todd."[35]

But Carnagey's marriage—exciting and venturesome in its early stages, despairing and painful in its latter period—provided only part of the story of his life in Europe in the early 1920s. Another aspect came from one of his recurrent attempts to make a mark in the world of the arts. Ensconced in the physical beauty and cultural riches of the Old World, Carnagey had plunged into the world of fiction writing.

In November 1919, Carnagey returned to New York for a few days during his tenure with the American version of Lowell Thomas's Allenby and Lawrence show. He tidied up some of his affairs before sailing once again for Europe. Consequently, a number of his friends, including old pal Homer Croy, gave a special dinner to send him off. The theme of the evening was surprising. As a newspaper description of the banquet noted, "it was given in honor of his giving up lecture work and taking up a career as a writer." Carnagey had decided to become a novelist.[36]

Since leaving college, the young Missourian periodically had been drawn to the creative arts. He had trained as an actor, written a number of magazine pieces, and even conducted a course on fiction writing at the Brooklyn Institute of Arts and Sciences, where he had persuaded several prominent writers in New York to make guest appearances. Now, after his experience with the Lowell Thomas project and his sudden marriage to Lolita Baucaire, the spark of creative endeavor rekindled and burst into flame. As Carnagey wrote later, "In my early thirties, I decided to spend my life writing novels. I was going to be a second Frank Norris or Jack London or Thomas Hardy."[37]

The European sojourn became the backdrop for his literary efforts. Traveling around the Continent with Lolita from 1922 to 1925, he labored steadily to produce a novel. The story was set in the small-town Missouri of his boyhood. "Mr. Carnagey expects to write of scenes in and around Maryville," reported the *Maryville Democrat-Forum* in December 1919 after receiving a dispatch from the author. He described the project as "a Nodaway County novel" and joked that "I am going to put that fountain with the gold fish back in Schumacher and Kirch's grocery, and the hitch racks back around the court house." He found the work of "hammering away on this novel every day" to be exhausting. "I have shucked corn . . . and milked and churned and cut wood . . . I have worked in the boiling sun until a sorrel mule would have fallen weak, spent, and exhausted if he had been trying to follow me," he joked to his hometown newspaper, "but all of these things put together are just child's play in comparison to writing a novel."[38]

Carnagey writing in the countryside during his 1920s sojourn in Europe.

Carnagey originally called his novel "The Blizzard" in honor of the legendary storm that marked his birth in 1888, but the title evolved to become "All That I Have." It told the story of three characters entangled in a melodramatic, triangular tale of lost love and thwarted passion. Much of the narrative centered on a young woman, who was straining to escape the bonds of Victorian propriety, and a preacher, who was struggling to present an enlightened, reformist Christianity to a stolid, suspicious rural audience. In its own way, "All That I Have" embodied the larger cultural and literary ferment in the 1920s, with Carnagey appearing as a poor man's version of the famous expatriate writers who abandoned the United States in this decade and rejected traditional middle-class conformity for the attractions of a bohemian life in Europe.

The famous Lost Generation—so termed by Gertrude Stein—fled the United States in the years after World War I to embrace a liberationist ethos on the Left Bank in Paris. Writers such as Ernest Hemingway, John Dos Passos, T. S. Eliot, Hart Crane,

F. Scott Fitzgerald, and many others joined a literary odyssey that wrenched them from their moorings in American life and sent them searching for new standards of expression and conduct. Exiled in Europe, this cadre gestured defiantly at their homeland while suffering occasional twinges of nostalgia. In the words of one participant, while they were "writing, drinking, watching bullfights, or making love, they continued to desire a Kentucky hill cabin, a farmhouse in Iowa or Wisconsin, the Michigan woods . . . [or] As Thomas Wolfe kept saying, a home to which they couldn't return." Here was a generation deeply cynical about many things in traditional America: political virtue (from the disillusioning experience of World War I), moral and emotional restraint (from the steady assault on Victorian gentility since the 1890s), religious piety (from the onrushing influence of science), and material greed (from the rapid advance, and embrace, of consumer prosperity in the early twentieth century).[39]

A related literary impulse gained traction in the "revolt against the village," as critic Carl Van Doren termed it. It featured writers such as Sherwood Anderson, in *Winesburg, Ohio* (1919), with its heartbreaking dissection of small-town "grotesques"; Sinclair Lewis, in *Main Street* (1920), with its penetrating diagnosis of America's "village virus"; and Edgar Lee Masters, in *Spoon River Anthology* (1915), with its mordant description of cozy village life as, in fact, stagnant and ruthless, complacent and apathetic, envious and mean-spirited. Unlike the Lost Generation, these denouncers of small-town life never went into physical exile, instead embarking on an internalized spiritual migration to escape the traditional American values they felt were smothering them.[40]

Somewhat haltingly, Carnagey enlisted in this cultural insurrection. Like the Lost Generation, he exiled himself to Europe for several years, far from the main currents of American life that had produced him. Like the village revolutionaries, he also rejected, often bitterly, the standards and proclivities of small-town existence. And like both groups, he periodically betrayed a subtle nostalgia for certain elements in America's village past even as he claimed to have thrown it aside. All of these elements appeared in the manuscript of the novel that he labored to finish while traversing the Old World during the first half of the 1920s.

"All That I Have" was set in 1917–18, in the region of Carnagey's boyhood, along the 102 River in northwest Missouri, with the fictional town of Carson Oaks standing as a replacement for Maryville. The plot revolved around three figures. Jean Burns, an intelligent and sensitive young woman attending college in her hometown, yearned to break away from her pinched religious background and experience the world. Forrest Croy, the wealthiest young man in northwest Missouri, a banker and large landowner whose father had been the lieutenant governor and a congressman, fell in love with Jean and convinced her to marry him just as he enlisted in the U.S. Army to serve in the war. Reverend Wendell Phillips Curnutt, a dynamic and idealistic young preacher, equally smitten by the young woman, stepped aside when she agreed to marry Croy. But in despair, he left Carson Oaks to accept a new ministerial position. Then several events overturned everyone's lives. First, before Forrest and Jean could be married, he was suddenly shipped off to the battlefront in Europe. Second, she became pregnant after a passionate interlude when visiting his training camp before his departure. Third, a few weeks later, she received a telegram saying that Forrest had been killed in action.[41]

Wendell, hearing the dreadful news, reentered the picture and appealed to the young woman to marry him. Even after hearing the shocking news that she was carrying an illegitimate child, he persisted and they became engaged. But when they returned to his

new church, the relationship triggered an enormous scandal about
"the parson's pregnant sweetheart." There were fisticuffs and angry
words, moralistic condemnations and passionate defenses. Then,
shockingly, Forrest reappeared. He had only been knocked unconscious by an artillery shell and taken prisoner by the Germans.
Nonetheless, Jean felt honor-bound to go ahead with her marriage
to Wendell. But before this could take place, Wendell was caught in
a massive blizzard on the prairie and died. At the book's end, Jean
and Forrest were finally married and provided their child with a
love-filled home.

The narrative of "All That I Have" highlighted several themes that
illuminated Carnagey's worldview in the early 1920s. They suggest
that the author, in his early thirties, had repudiated large portions of
his Midwestern, rural, pious heritage while, at the same time, harboring a profound nostalgia for certain parts of it. They also revealed
an author struggling to formulate, in some fashion, new standards of
behavior that were more realistic, fulfilling, and humane.

Carnagey's depiction of life in Carson Oaks was part affectionate remembrance. People passing through rural northwest Missouri on the train, he wrote, "imagine that it is a prosaic valley,
that nothing ever happens here, that people drag through dull and
colorless lives. And many do, just as many do in Paris and New
York and Palm Beach. Many, but not all, for there is romance here
along the 102." Carnagey fondly depicted the yearly Chautauqua
Fair as a vibrant feature of small-town life when townspeople "embraced music, oratory, and culture." He praised the community
spirit of Carson Oaks at the beginning of the war, when inhabitants
launched a Red Cross campaign and "laboring men gave a day's
wages, professional men contributed a day's fees."[42]

At the same time, Carnagey pilloried the village values of the
small-town Midwest, primarily because of its repressive, unforgiving

moral creed. Victorian restraint too easily became repressive intolerance, he argued, as illustrated by the problem of Jean's pregnancy. Carrying an illegitimate child made her a social pariah as she faced expulsion from school, ejection from her boardinghouse, and being shunned by old friends who were afraid to be seen speaking with her in public. Even worse than such meanness, in Carnagey's rendering, was the hypocrisy engrained in such attitudes. Every child was a "divine miracle," he wrote, but Jean endured attacks that made her transgression seem worse than "lying and selfishness and thieving and drunkenness all heaped together, more than almost anything she could imagine short of murder." But community outrage would evaporate the moment she married, even if her husband was vile, profane, and lazy.[43]

A defiant Wendell confronted such hypocrisy when he preached a sermon listing the accomplished famous bastards of history and calling for Christian forgiveness. But his small-town parishioners reacted badly, rushing to the library to investigate the legitimacy of famous people's births, engaging in heated arguments, and prying into the birth backgrounds of local dignitaries. In this atmosphere of hate and prejudice, Carnagey charged, had "Christ himself come to Canute City incognito, preaching and associating with Mary Magdalene, the reformed harlot, he, too, would have been chased out of town."[44]

In the author's view, religion lay at the root of this rancid, festering atmosphere of small-town intolerance. Jean's mother, Amanda Burns (a transparent stand-in for Amanda Carnagey), symbolized outdated religious standards that glorified ignorance and restriction over knowledge and possibilities. This intensely pious character worshipped an all-powerful punishing deity, studied the Bible daily, and traveled ten miles to the local church to teach a Sunday school class where she relished "jousting with the forces

of darkness." Amanda possessed a militant faith and "knew no
greater joy than attending the revival meetings held by the traveling evangelists, occupying a seat well up front, murmuring fervent
'amens.'"[45]

In contrast to such a narrow theology, Reverend Curnutt, with
whom Carnagey obviously identified, represented a reformist
impulse that sought to enhance, not cramp, the life of believers.
This handsome, ex–football star and cowboy had shaped a vigorous, manly religious creed after being converted by the evangelist
Dwight L. Moody. In fact, Curnutt embraced a radical view that
"Christianity should touch the whole gamut of life" and agitated
for the inclusion of Christlike principles in business, farming, and
community life. In the author's words, "He was a storm center
wherever he went."[46]

Carnagey's attack on the tradition of evangelical Protestantism
and Victorian moralism, like that of many in the Lost Generation,
found a particular target in the brutality of World War I. Similarly,
but much less skillfully, than novelists such as Hemingway in *A
Farewell to Arms* and *The Sun Also Rises* and Dos Passos in *Nineteen Nineteen*, he excoriated the brutal bloodbath that had swept
the Continent in the 1910s. Ordinary townspeople knew nothing about the European politics that created the vast carnage of
the war, Carnagey accused, but they nonetheless lined up to insist
that "the world must be made safe for democracy." The result was
nightmarish warfare where vast armies leapt out of their trenches
and created "slaughter, ghastly slaughter, . . . slaughter on a scale
never before conceived by the mind of man."[47]

Thus "All That I Have" represented Carnagey's sustained grap-
pling with his cultural heritage of rural piety, moral steadfastness, and cultural self-restraint. It was an authentic, heartland
expression of the revolt against the village and the evangelical

Protestantism that had sustained it. It was a plaintive cry of the Lost Generation, struggling to pull away from the stifling conformity of Victorian gentility. It was a plea for a more capacious Christianity that would encourage possibilities rather than punishment, and a more tolerant culture that would cherish relationships rather than repression.

The young writer did not plan on stopping there. During his travels through Europe in the early 1920s, he wrote rough outlines of three short stories and made plans for additional novels. He envisioned one as a fictional account of Abraham Lincoln, another set in the armistice ending World War I, and a third focused on a globe-trotting explorer. Carnagey filled his files with newspaper clippings related to the craft of writing: an instructional essay on "Making a Popular Writer," a remembrance by a British novelist that discussed style and technique, a plotline suggested by the lurid headline "Woman Missionary Admits Love Child," and a list of names from the social page of the *Maryville Democrat-Forum* to be mined for characters' names.[48]

Ultimately, however, Carnagey's plans to become a novelist were torpedoed by a relentless fact—his talent did not match his ambition. Carnagey's literary agent told him bluntly that he had no talent for writing fiction, and that his novel was "worthless." Abundant evidence supported this conclusion. "All That I Have" featured wooden characters, stilted dialogue, a contrived plot, and flights of highly sentimental language at odds with its liberationist sensibility. In nearly every way, the novel was decidedly amateurish. But the agent's critique staggered Carnagey. In his words, when he heard the report on his novel, "my heart almost stopped. I couldn't have been more stunned if he had hit me across the head with a club. I was stupefied . . . What should I do? Which way should I turn? Weeks passed before I came out of the daze."[49]

The shock of his failure as a novelist brought Carnagey to "a crisis in my life—a crisis when I stood watching my dreams and my plans for the future and my work of years vanish into thin air." And this vocational catastrophe was compounded by the fact that his marriage to Lolita was unraveling. Yet true to the practical, optimistic side of his personality, he absorbed this tremendous emotional blow and came to terms with it. After considerable pain and reflection, he was able to accept "two years of sweating over that novel for what they were—a noble experiment—and went forward from there." In later years, he even joked about his unexpected discovery that " 'All That I Have' wasn't enough."[50]

So Carnagey returned to America, both physically and emotionally. For all of his expatriate ennui, for all of his disdain for small-town values, the aspiring writer had never really abandoned his country. To be sure, he found it "very stimulating mentally" to dine on the ship with a bishop of the Anglican Church and an academic dean from the University of London while crisscrossing the Atlantic. And he quickly chastised his mother for small-mindedness when she criticized women who smoked, retorting that "it would be absurd to say that they were morally bad in other respects simply because they smoked. I presume half of the women that one sees in the restaurants here in London smoke." Carnagey clearly admired the Old World for its intellect, sophistication, and savoir faire. Yet he also complained about a lack of drive and ambition among Europeans, contending that they "lack American hustle and ginger." Ultimately, his revolt against his homeland was temporary. "Living over here is a splendid education, but I confess that the more I see of Europe, the more respect I have for America," he observed. In a dispatch to the *Maryville Democrat-Forum*, he concluded that "the average person in Nodaway is a great deal better off than he realizes. That applies to almost everyone in America."

Despite the attractions of European culture, he ultimately resisted the pull of cosmopolitanism.[51]

So unlike many in the Lost Generation, Carnagey, for all his criticism, fully reconciled with mainstream America. With a new perspective on his country's life and values gained from his stint abroad, he returned to his homeland with a vague desire to somehow throw off its provincial shackles and embrace a new creed of dynamic possibility. Having exhausted his artistic capabilities, first with acting in the early 1910s and now with fiction-writing in the early 1920s, Carnagey finally reconciled to doing that for which he was best suited—teaching and writing about public speaking. Only now he did so with a newfound sense of commitment. And over the next few years, Carnagey would begin inching toward something even bigger: the formulation of a success model for modern Americans. Shortly, his accomplishments in this area would make him more famous and widely read than he had foreseen even in his grandest dreams of novelistic glory.

8

Business and Self-Regulation

I n his lively introduction to *How to Win Friends and Influence People*, Lowell Thomas described a common characteristic among the speakers who paraded across a New York hotel stage promoting Dale Carnegie's adult-education course. They represented, in his words, "a cross section of American business life." In fact, Thomas stressed, the book's author had trained more than fifteen thousand businessmen from large organizations such as Westinghouse Electric and Manufacturing Company, McGraw-Hill Publishing Company, Brooklyn Union Gas Company, the American Institute of Electrical Engineers, and New York Telephone Company. Clearly, wrote Thomas, Carnegie's teaching and writing efforts met a need among individuals operating in the "rough-and-tumble of business and professional life. They had seen some of the most important business successes won by men who possessed, in addition to their knowledge, the ability to talk well, win people to their way of thinking, and 'sell' themselves and their ideas." Carnegie reiterated this theme in his explanation of why he had written the book. He explained that since 1912 he had conducted classes "for business and professional men and women in New York," an endeavor that taught him a critical fact: "Dealing with people is probably the biggest problem you face, especially if you are a businessman."[1]

This stress on business—both its values and opportunities, and its receptive clientele—became a hallmark of *How to Win Friends.* Carnegie constantly discussed how his rules for human relations would enable commercial success through promotions, enhanced salary, and growing influence in corporate bureaucracies. He described how "the president of an important Wall Street bank" who had taken his course devoted himself to self-improvement by setting aside every Saturday evening for "the illuminating process of self-examination and review and appraisal" where he considered the mistakes he had made, how he could rectify them, and how he could improve his performance in the future. "I have asked thousands of businessmen to smile at someone every hour of the day for a week and then come to class and talk about the results," Carnegie noted. He proudly reported a stockbroker's comment: "I find that smiles are bringing me dollars, many dollars every day." He provided a long list of businessmen who testified to the efficacy of his principles, including the famous (Henry Ford, Walter Chrysler, Charles Schwab, Andrew Carnegie, John D. Rockefeller, J. P. Morgan, Harvey Firestone) and the near famous (George Eastman, the president of Eastman Kodak Company; Cyrus H. K. Curtis, the publisher of *The Saturday Evening Post* and *Ladies' Home Journal*; Samuel Vauclain, the president of Baldwin Locomotive Works).[2]

Carnegie's immersion in early twentieth-century business culture occurred during the late 1920s, a period when he returned from Europe to embrace the vibrant commercial milieu of the era. With the launching of his adult-education courses in 1912, large numbers of low- to mid-level white-collar workers had flocked to enroll, searching for a means of advancement in the new corporate atmosphere of the early 1900s. But now, upon returning to the United States after his rebellious interlude abroad, Carnegie self-consciously connected himself to the booming business economy of the post–World War I period. With prosperity filling pockets and purses with unprecedented amounts of cash, opportunity was in the air. Determined to take advantage, the young teacher and writer aimed his appeal at a business audience. Its members, he shrewdly ascertained, provided the most likely recipients for his message of self-improvement, self-management, and success. Carnegie never regretted the decision that pushed him into the national spotlight for the first time.

In 1926, Dale Carnagey returned to the United States with a new determination to revive his career in teaching and writing about public speech. He also returned with a new name. Sometime during the previous year, he decided to change both its spelling and pronunciation. In a public letter to the *Maryville Democrat-Forum* in November 1924, he had signed his name in the traditional fashion as "Dale Carnagey," which was pronounced with an accent on the second syllable. But a year later, in October 1925, another letter to that same paper now was signed "Dale Carnegie," now pronounced with the accent placed on the first syllable. In 1926, the appearance of a new book underlined that change, proudly listing on its title page: "by Dale Carnegie."[3]

What prompted this alteration? Carnegie never fully explained it. He discussed the name change briefly with an interviewer a decade later, who reported, "Everybody in New York pronounced it Carnegie anyway, accenting the first syllable; and besides, it was against all the principles of showmanship, which were already at work within him, to rent space in Carnegie Hall, and go on doggedly

calling himself 'Carnagey.' " Then some years later, he claimed that
he had been walking with his good friend Homer Croy in a beech
forest on the outskirts of Interlaken, Switzerland, during his interlude in Europe, when Croy persuaded him "to spell his name in a
way that would be easy to remember." But these explanations seem
rather flippant, carrying insufficient emotional heft to motivate a
change of such personal and professional magnitude.[4]

   In fact, the name alteration symbolized much more than
Carnegie ever admitted (or, perhaps, even realized). In several
ways, it reflected an important transition in his life. First, changing
his name from that of his parents signified a final rejection of the
pious, provincial, repressive culture that had produced him, of the
small-town American creed that he had first snubbed in marrying
a European divorcée and then pilloried in his novel manuscript,
"All That I Have." Second, a psychological perspective (something
Carnegie himself was always eager to adopt) suggests that for a
man with an infectious devotion to positive thinking, removing the
accented "nay" at the very heart of his traditional name removed
a negative symbol and helped liberate him emotionally to acceler-
ate his pursuit of distinction. Third, by adopting the name commonly associated with the famous, powerful industrialist Andrew
Carnegie, this ambitious young man signaled a growing willingness
to identify with the expanding business culture of early twentieth-
century America and its wealth of opportunities. In a magazine
interview years later, he even suggested an occult connection with
the powerful steel magnate. Carnegie told the interviewer that as a
young man he had dreamed one night about chatting with the industrialist's wife and inquiring how her husband was getting along.
Mrs. Carnegie replied, "He's dead." The dreamer was startled to
open the following morning's paper and read its announcement of
Andrew Carnegie's death the preceding night.[5]

In other words, "Carnegie" represented a new identity for this thirty-seven-year-old ex-actor, ex-salesman, ex-journalist, ex-churchgoer, and failed novelist. It symbolized throwing off his past and embracing a new world of prosperity and possibility. It symbolized his determination to accept teaching and writing about public speaking not just as a vocation but as a calling. But most immediately, it affirmed his determination to anchor his future in the dynamic business activity of 1920s America. Back from his jaunt through Europe, Carnegie had assiduously rebuilt his network of YMCA classes in New York, Baltimore, Philadelphia, and other northeastern cities. Within a few months, students were crowding into his courses once again and most of them were businessmen, both actual and aspiring. They were not interested in delivering flowery speeches but came to his classes with a utilitarian agenda: They wanted results and wanted them quickly; they wanted practical techniques they could use immediately in business meetings with colleagues and interviews with clients.

Responding to this demand, Carnegie published his third book, *Public Speaking: A Practical Course for Business Men*. Actually, he had worked intermittently on the project during his European travels. Unsatisfied with his 1920 YMCA textbook, despite its success, he wrote to a correspondent in 1925 that it "never met with my entire approval" because of changes made by the editors at the last moment when he was departing for Europe. In addition, there had been a dispute with the YMCA over royalties. The organization's director claimed that it had borne the expense of adding additional material to the text demanded by the author, so he should accept a lesser percentage. This proposal annoyed Carnegie. "I request you to kindly hold in abeyance for the present the matter of royalties. It will not be necessary for the Association Press to send me a cheque until after this matter has been discussed with you," he wrote back, straining for tact. "United YMCA Schools can rest assured that all questions that arise will be settled, I am sure, to the entire satisfaction of all concerned."[6]

Carnegie decided that the ultimate solution to the problem lay in a new version of the book that he would compose in its entirety. So throughout the early 1920s, while traveling in England and on the Continent, he regularly took time away from writing his novel to rework the textbook to his own specifications. In 1922, while in Cortina, Italy, he wrote a letter to a Maryville newspaper describing his daily regimen as a split between writing fiction and nonfiction. "I am devoting six hours a day to writing—three to revising the public speaking course [book] and three to the story of Forrest Croy," he noted. He must have made great progress on the new textbook manuscript, because soon after his return to the United States, it was published. Although borrowing sections and concepts from his earlier writings, in nearly every respect it was a different volume that reflected its author's maturing ideas.[7]

Public Speaking: A Practical Course for Business Men, wove a number of themes into the text that reflected several of Carnegie's salient life experiences. He mentioned numerous times that the successful speaker drew upon acting, because this craft focused on the emotional dynamics of appearing before a group. "It takes practice to be natural before an audience," Carnegie observed. "Actors know that." At times, he also framed public speech as a quasi-religious impulse. He explicated "The Art of Preaching," a series of lectures by the dean of the Yale Divinity School, who insisted upon the importance of "the vital energies" of the preacher, and often cited the famous evangelist Dwight L. Moody on the need for enthusiasm and commitment in addressing listeners. "The finest thing in speaking is neither physical nor mental. It is spiritual," Carnegie added. "If you want a splendid text on public speaking, why not read your New Testament?" Finally, he frequently drew on his New Thought background to enumerate the virtues of positive thinking. "See yourself in your imagination talking in public with perfect self-control," he instructed. "It is easily in your power to do this. Believe that you will succeed. Believe it firmly and you will then do what is necessary to bring success about."[8]

The jaunty writing style of Carnegie's new book also struck the reader. Freed from earlier constraints imposed by editors, collaborators, and his own inexperience, Carnegie now developed a mode of expression that was uniquely his own. He utilized several elements: a conversational, even breezy tone; frequent dashes of inspiration; an abundance of anecdotes; and many informal asides and flashes of dry humor. An opening passage in the book, dealing with the development of confidence, illustrated the emerging Carnegie style. "Is there the faintest shadow of a reason why you should not be able to think as well in a perpendicular position before an audience as you can when sitting down? Surely, you know there is not," he wrote.

> Do not imagine that your case is unusually difficult . . . William Jennings Bryan, battle-marked veteran that he was, admitted that in his first attempts his knees fairly smote together. Mark Twain, the first time he stood up to lecture, felt as if his mouth were filled with cotton and his pulse was speeding for some prize cup. Grant took Vicksburg and led one of the greatest armies the world had ever seen, yet when he attempted to speak in public, he admitted he had something very like *locomotor ataxia* . . . So take heart.[9]

But much of the significance of *Public Speaking: A Practical Course for Business Men* lay in its subtitle. With clear intent, he shaped a volume aimed squarely at the desires, perspectives, and needs of millions of men who were trying to make their way in American business. From its sensibility to its examples, its references to its style, its techniques to its conclusions, the author envisioned his reader as an individual seeking to navigate a course through the dynamic business atmosphere of 1920s America.

This struck a chord as the pulsating commercial climate of the decade proved enormously receptive to Carnegie's efforts. The 1920s marked an era of business prosperity when, in the aftermath of World War I, the manufacture, sale, and consumption of goods reached unprecedented heights in American history. The pursuit of business became identified in the public imagination not only with the advancement of the striving individual but with the advancement of the country. Calvin Coolidge, having acceded to the presidency in 1923 after the death of Warren G. Harding, helped set the dominant tone of public discussion with his pronouncements. "The chief business of the American people is business," he declared in a much-publicized 1925 speech. Another commentary elevated business activity to the level of religion. "The man who builds a factory builds a temple. The man who works there worships there, and to each is due not scorn and blame, but reverence and praise," Coolidge intoned.[10]

Indeed, booming business expansion had become a fact of life in the United States in the 1920s and its impact appeared everywhere. Most significantly, the consumer economy that had been slowly gathering force since the 1890s reached a takeoff stage and rocketed into the economic stratosphere. With the spread of electricity to more than 60 percent of the nation's homes by 1925, and the perfection of mass-production techniques in many industries, the factory system churned out a vast array of goods ranging from canned food to ready-made clothing, furniture to washing machines, vacuum cleaners to golf clubs, all of which were eagerly consumed by the middle class. From 1922 to 1929, unemployment dropped to around 3 percent, prices held steady, and the gross national product swelled from $70 billion to $100 billion. In this bountiful atmosphere, the automobile emerged as both a leading commodity within and a larger symbol of the consumer revolution. As the pioneering automaker Henry Ford put it during the 1920s, his popular product (first the Model T, replaced by the more stylish Model A in 1927) was moving the nation closer to realizing a utopian vision of abundance. "The automobile, by enabling people to get about quickly and easily, gives them a chance to find out what is going on in the world," he wrote, "which leads them to a larger life that requires more food, more and better goods, more books, more music, more of everything."[11]

The consumer surge of the 1920s altered the American landscape. Under its influence, certain institutions and ideas achieved a newfound prominence. Department stores and grocery chains became staples of middle-class economic life in urban areas, serving as commercial conduits for the flood of goods from factories to homes. The A&P grocery stores, for instance, expanded from 5,000 sites in 1922 to 17,500 in 1928. The discipline of "domestic science"—which trained young women to become efficient managers of the consumer-centered home and masters of newfangled techniques involving electric appliances, cleaning products, and nutritious diets—emerged as a mainstay of the educational curriculum. Installment buying became ubiquitous, with consumer credit purchases rising dramatically, from $4.5 billion at the start of the decade to $7.1 billion at its conclusion. On the cultural front, the allure of material goods helped shape a new set of values, replacing Victorian self-restraint with self-fulfillment, salvation with self-realization, and scarcity with plenty. By the 1920s, as one historian has described, American society had become "preoccupied with consumption, with comforts and bodily well-being, with luxury, spending, and acquisition."[12]

A particularly telling indicator of consumer prosperity in the 1920s appeared in social and political ideology, as prominent spokesmen for corporate America articulated a business ideology often described as a "people's capitalism." This position, according to its leading historian, represented "an enhanced vision of enlightened private orders enlisting in the national service and working with public agencies to advance the public good." Figures such as Owen D. Young of General Electric, Edward A. Filene of Filene's Department Stores, and Secretary of Commerce (and then president) Herbert Hoover, rather than defending the unfettered pursuit of profit, promoted a capitalist creed that embraced rapprochement with organized labor, efficient production and management, and collaboration with government. This approach of enlightened self-interest, they argued, would overwhelm all social divisions and economic problems with a flood of prosperity. From such developments sprang a full-blown culture of consumerism that dominated 1920s America. This bountiful "land of desire," as merchant John Wanamaker once termed it, promised a heightened standard of living, sought public policies to achieve that goal, and redefined happiness in terms of material abundance.[13]

To a certain extent, of course, Carnegie had been aware of America's evolving business dynamism in his earlier career and intermittently had addressed issues emerging from the maelstrom of corporate competition and business success. In his YMCA textbook, he had praised Worthington C. Holman's *Ginger Talks: The Talks of a Sales Manager to His Men* (1905), a collection of inspiring pep talks for salesmen. "Selling goods is a battle and only fighters can win out in it," Holman had written. "Take your courage

with you when you enter the selling game." Carnegie also explicated the case of John H. Patterson, the president of the National
Cash Register Company, who had demonstrated modern management skills by clearly explaining the advantages of the company's
latest, and more expensive, cash register model "that ended with
the agents on their feet and cheering wildly." Carnegie's growing
awareness of his business clientele also informed the promotional
literature for his course. In a 1917 advertising pamphlet, he had
noted that many students profited from his course in "their business interviews, sales letters, and advertisements. This training is so
valuable for business intercourse that New York City banks have
employed Mr. Carnagey to drill their employees in public speaking." The pamphlet also included endorsement letters from several course graduates in the real estate, advertising, and insurance
fields.[14]

But now, after returning from Europe with a revived dedication
to his teaching career, Carnegie embraced America's vibrant business culture completely and enthusiastically. *Public Speaking: A
Practical Course for Business Men* presented numerous guidelines
for success in the commercial world, which were woven seamlessly
into the fabric of 1920s business boosterism. From the beginning
of the project, the author explained, he had aimed the book at a
business audience. "In my opinion, the ideal text on this subject for
businessmen must have something besides colorless knowledge,"
he wrote in a 1925 letter. "It must have sweep and scope and spirit.
It must have inspiration as well as perspiration. It must have sentences that glow and breathe and march. Such has been my ideal."[15]

Carnegie's basic argument was simple. His new book contended
that public-speaking skills would propel their holder upward in the
business structure of 1920s America. "More than eighteen thousand businessmen, since 1912, have been members of the various

public speaking courses conducted by the author," Carnegie stated in the opening sentence of his book. And most of them enrolled for the same reason. He quoted one of his students: "I want to get my thoughts together in a logical order and I want to be able to say my say clearly and convincingly before a business group or audience." Carnegie's first example was the head of a Philadelphia manufacturing establishment, who parlayed techniques learned from the Carnegie course into a high-profile position in the business and civic life of his city. "Think of what additional self-confidence and the ability to talk more convincingly in business will mean to you," Carnegie declared. "Think of what it may mean and what it ought to mean, in dollars and cents." In fact, he added, many of the country's leading business figures endorsed the value of public speaking, as quotes from the steel tycoon Andrew Carnegie, the railroad kingpin and later U.S. senator Chauncey M. Depew, and the meat-packing magnate Philip D. Armour illustrated.[16]

Upon this foundation, the book constructed an edifice that was part instruction, part inspiration. Carnegie's practical advice for businessmen centered on the techniques that he had been advancing over the past fourteen years: speaking plainly yet forcefully, preparing assiduously, briskly opening a talk, convincingly closing one, keeping an audience's attention, exuding confidence, utilizing dramatic or colorful illustrations of main points, and using natural gestures. He also included much advice on warming up and loosening the vocal cords, relaxing the throat, and improving articulation. At the same time, the author larded his text with exhortations aimed at exciting the emotions and pumping up the enthusiasm of his readers-cum-speakers. Those who successfully addressed others, Carnegie insisted, projected conviction. "Aren't you unconsciously drawn to the speaker who, you feel, has a real message in his head and heart that he zealously desires to communicate to your head and heart? That is half the secret of speaking," he contended. "People cluster around the energetic speaker, the human dynamo of energy like wild geese around a field of autumn wheat."[17]

While delineating such skills provided the structure of the book, its basic energy flowed from their application to the business world. Carnegie peppered readers with a barrage of quotations from literary figures such as William Shakespeare, William Butler Yeats, Rudyard Kipling, and Mark Twain; politicians such as Thomas Jefferson, Alexander Hamilton, Ulysses S. Grant, William Jennings Bryan, Woodrow Wilson, and, most often, Abraham Lincoln; religious figures such as Martin Luther, Dwight L. Moody, Henry Ward Beecher, and Harry Emerson Fosdick; and philosophers Herbert Spencer, Ralph Waldo Emerson, and William James. But time and time again, he brought the discussion around to the modern business world and its issues, needs, and perspectives.

From the outset, Carnegie defined businessmen as his natural audience, as the group most likely to utilize the gratifying results to be garnered from his course. "It has been the author's professional duty as well as his pleasure to listen to and criticize six thousand speeches a year each season since 1912," he explained near the beginning of the text. "These were made, not by college students, but by mature business and professional men." Observers at the closing banquet of one of his speaking classes in New Jersey were astonished to hear a series of poised, confident speeches "made by businessmen who had been tongue-tied with audience fear a few months previously. They were not incipient Ciceros, those New Jersey businessmen; they were typical of the businessmen one finds in any American city." Indeed, the author continued, his successful students were not unusually brilliant. "For the most part, they were the ordinary run of businessmen that you will find in your own home town."[18]

As he proceeded through his lessons, Carnegie consistently drew upon business situations or dilemmas to explain techniques in the art of constructing persuasive oral presentations. "Let us suppose that you have decided to speak on your business or profession" was a typical preface for an instructional point. When discussing the advantages of clear, concise organization over memorization when addressing others, he asked, "When you have an important business interview, do you sit down and memorize, verbatim, what you are going to say? Of course not. You reflect until you get your main ideas clearly in mind." Upon considering the importance of presenting a firm conclusion, he wrote, "Your problem, perhaps, will be how to close a simple talk before a group of businessmen. How shall you set about it?" The issue of putting figures and sums in the most favorable light elicited this illustration: "For example, a life insurance president, addressing the sales organization of his company, impressed his men with the low cost of insurance in this fashion. 'The man of thirty-four who smokes a quarter's worth of cigars daily can stay with his family longer, and leave them three thousand dollars more, by spending his cigar money for insurance.'"[19]

Finally, throughout *Public Speaking: A Practical Course for Business Men*, Carnegie summoned famous American businessmen as expert witnesses to buttress his arguments. At the outset of many chapters, for example, he presented their epigrammatic statements. John G. Shedd, the president of Marshall Field and Company, and Walter H. Cottingham, the president of the Sherwin-Williams Company, both testified to the value of enthusiasm at the beginning of a chapter entitled "Keeping the Audience Awake." The railroad mogul E. H. Harriman commented on the need for commitment and hard work for the chapter "Essential Elements in Successful Speaking." Eugene Grace, the president of Bethlehem Steel Corporation, prefaced "The Secret of Good Delivery" by stressing the importance of concentrated energy: "Do one thing at a time, and do that one thing as if your life depended on it."[20]

Carnegie often drew on the examples of legendary business figures to illustrate his contention that wealthy men tended to lead very simple lives and cultivate plain habits, qualities that readers should emulate. "John D. Rockefeller, Sr., had a leather couch in his office at 26 Broadway, and took a midday nap each day. The late J. Ogden Armour used to retire at nine o'clock, and get up at six," the author wrote. "The late John H. Patterson, President of the National Cash Register Company, neither smoked nor drank. Frank Vanderlip, at one time president of the largest bank in America, eats only two meals a day. Milk and old-fashioned ginger wafers constituted Harriman's midday meal . . . Andrew Carnegie's favorite dish was oatmeal and cream."[21]

One of Carnegie's deployments of legendary American businessmen, however, reached to a deeper level of analysis. Discussing the need for using concrete cases to support generalizations, he quoted from a business article that showed how leading executives were developing extensive organizations. "Woolworth once told me that his was essentially a one-man business for years. Then he ruined his health, and he awakened to the fact that if his business was to expand as he hoped, he would have to share the managerial responsibilities," wrote the author. "Eastman Kodak in its earlier stages consisted mainly of George Eastman, but he was wise enough to create an efficient organization long ago . . . Standard Oil, contrary to the popular notion, never was a one man organization after it grew to large dimensions. J. P. Morgan, although a towering giant, was an ardent believer in choosing the most capable partners and sharing the burden with them."[22]

This observation on a broader trend in modern business highlighted an important aspect of Carnegie's message. In the extensive new business structures that had evolved in 1920s America, indeed throughout the early twentieth century, an unfamiliar figure had appeared: the white-collar executive. Trying to maneuver in a strange new world, he stood badly in need of a new prescription for career advancement. Carnegie provided one.

Carnegie believed that in the modern business world a fresh requirement had emerged for moving ahead. "According to experiments conducted by the Carnegie Institute of Technology, personality has more to do with business success than has superior knowledge," he explained. "This pronouncement is as true of speaking as of business." As a result, *Public Speaking: A Practical Course for Business Men* bombarded readers with advice on how to cultivate and project attractive personal images. A compelling speech, Carnegie insisted, expressed your personality. Putting it together, in his words, meant "the assembling of *your* thoughts, *your* ideas, *your* convictions, *your* urges . . . Your whole existence has been filled with feelings and experiences. These things are lying deep in your subconscious mind as thick as pebbles on the seashore. Preparation means thinking, brooding, recalling, selecting the ones that appeal to you the most, polishing them, working them into a pattern, a mosaic of your own." In order to reach listeners—especially colleagues, clients, buyers, and consumers—the modern businessman must go beyond professional competence, mastery of facts, a determined work ethic, and commitment to quality. He must do more than sell his product; he must sell himself.[23]

Where did this growing emphasis on personality come from? In part, it stemmed from the broader culture, where the relentless process of erosion that had been under way since the late 1800s had gradually undermined the old Victorian mind-set. With the decline of a producer-oriented economy of scarcity with its attendant values of hard work, self-control, self-denial, thrift, and character, an emerging consumer economy of abundance had emerged to create a "culture of personality" that stressed self-fulfillment, self-expression, and self-gratification. Thus a changing socioeconomic structure and a redefinition of self intersected. "The older vision [of character] no longer suited personal or social needs," one historian concluded; "the newer vision [of personality] seemed particularly suited for the problems of self in a changed social order, the developing consumer mass society."[24]

But a practical development proved equally influential—a revolutionary change in the business structure. By the time *Public Speaking: A Practical Course for Business Men* appeared in 1926, a sweeping transformation from old-fashioned entrepreneurship to complex corporate bureaucracies was nearly complete. Beginning in the late 1800s, the individually owned companies, partnerships, and small businesses that had characterized the market revolution of the earlier nineteenth century were giving way to large corporations. In every important segment of the economy, huge business organizations with thousands of employees, dozens of managers, numerous stockholders, and complex divisions of authority and responsibility had achieved positions of dominance by the 1920s. In these rationalized business structures, a "managerial revolution" created complex bureaucracies where hosts of salaried, white-collar employees staffed various offices and groups whose endeavors ultimately converged to create and dispense the corporation's products. "Managers were responsible for hiring and organizing the increasingly large number of white-collar workers who processed the reams of paper the corporations used," a historian of this trend has written. These office laborers comprised "new groups of middle-class Americans who filled hierarchical corporate structures and promoted new ways of working, living, and interacting with one another." This was precisely Carnegie's audience by the 1920s, and he took the lead in defining new ways of acting, working, and striving for advancement in this bureaucratized business atmosphere.[25]

The author clearly sensed a prevailing need in his business audience. The white-collar world of corporate bureaucracy no longer valued the headstrong, self-directed entrepreneur striving diligently for his *own* profit and success. Instead, it valued the team player who could work with *others*—often many others—in a highly rationalized system for the good of the corporation. At the same time, of course, the drive for individual advancement still ran strong in this new white-collar world of modern business. Such a complex situation demanded fresh approaches at every turn—new modes of behavior, new strategies for success, new social skills attuned to bureaucracy, and new personal qualities. Carnegie repeatedly addressed such topics throughout *Public Speaking: A Practical Course for Business Men*. And he relentlessly advanced a central argument: the development of personality would smooth one's interactions with others in a modern, white-collar business setting, and thus smooth the way for upward advancement and career success.

To a certain extent, Carnegie had grasped the broad direction of this economic and cultural shift in his earlier efforts. In the late 1910s, he had begun to offer advice aimed at the enhancement of personal qualities. A 1919 syllabus for his YMCA course, for example, contained brief sections on "The Power of Personality" and "Personality Can Be Developed." Then his 1920 YMCA textbook offered tips on "Building Personality." "Most successful men radiate achievement in their tones and their manners. When you meet them you, immediately and unconsciously, feel that they are accustomed to putting things across," he wrote. The successful speaker, he urged, should address his audience with confidence, authority, and enthusiasm. "So when you speak, speak with might and sincerity," the author enjoined. "Let your tones be colored with your feelings and the power of your personality will be trebled."[26]

By 1926, however, personality development had become the centerpiece of Carnegie's program. From the beginning, *Public Speaking: A Practical Course for Business Men* bombarded the reader with instructions for mobilizing personal traits to shape effective speech. Putting together a compelling talk, he insisted, consisted largely of "digging away down deep into your own mind and heart and life, and bringing forth some convictions and enthusiasms that are essentially yours! Yours! YOURS! Dig. Dig. Dig. It is there. Never doubt it." He continued, "Always remember that *you* are the most important factor in your talk. Hear these golden words from Emerson! They contain a world of wisdom: 'Use what language you will, you can never say anything but what you are.' "[27]

Everyone's personality was unique, Carnegie insisted, and no one "will talk and express themselves just as you do when you are speaking naturally. In other words, you have an individuality. As a speaker, it is your most precious possession. Cling to it. Cherish it. Develop it. It is the spark that will put force and sincerity into your speaking." Indeed, the author maintained, instead of restraining emotion or repressing impulses one should use them in trying to reach others. "When a man is under the influence of his feelings, his real self comes to the surface," he wrote. "The bars are down. The heat of his emotions has burned all barriers away. He acts spontaneously. He talks spontaneously. He is natural."[28]

Such exhortations reached a culmination about halfway through the book in a chapter entitled "Platform Presence and Personality." Carnegie opened with an audacious statement: "Personality—with the exception of preparation—is probably the most important factor in public address." Personality was an elusive thing that almost defied analysis, he admitted, but its existence (and importance) was very real. Personality expressed "the whole combination of the man, the physical, the spiritual, the mental; his traits, his predilections, his tendencies, his temperament, his cast of mind, his vigor, his experience, his training, his life." Moreover, although many personal traits were inherited, the striving individual still could improve his natural personality and "strengthen it to some extent and make it more forceful, more attractive. We can strive to get the utmost possible out of this strange thing that nature has given us. The subject is of vast importance to every one of us."[29]

As the chapter unfolded, Carnegie explored how personal images could be shaped and projected toward others in a compelling manner. He began with the trait of enthusiasm. "Do nothing to dull your energy. It is magnetic. Vitality, aliveness, enthusiasm" are crucial, he wrote. Physical appearance also mattered, since good grooming and neat attire instilled self-confidence in the speaker and garnered respect from an audience. Other techniques helped enhance personality: displaying a winning smile, maintaining an upright posture with chest held high, sitting on the dais in a calm fashion, assuming a dignified manner. Indeed, Carnegie stressed, a convincing speaker must remember to "stand still and control yourself physically and that will give you an impression of mental control, of poise." Even gestures were an expression of personality. A person's gesture "is merely an outward expression of inward condition," Carnegie contended. "A man's gestures, like his toothbrush, should be very personal things. And, as all men are different, their gestures will be individual if they will only act natural."[30]

The power of personality, however, consisted of more than the projection of a magnetic, forceful image. As with conducting electricity, the process of personal connection required another pole—the audience—to complete the circuit and create the charge of

energy. And establishing a relationship with an audience, whether it
consisted of one person or many, Carnegie insisted, required sensitivity to others' feelings, interests, and perspectives. The three most
interesting subjects in the world were sex, property, and religion, he
proposed, because they involved creating, sustaining, and continuing life. But the important point to remember was "it is *our* sex, *our*
property, *our* religion that interests us. Our interests swarm about
our own egos . . . So remember that the people you are to talk to
spend most of their time, when they are not concerned with the
problems of business, in thinking about and justifying and glorifying themselves."[31]

This social fact had profound implications for creating an attractive personality. "Aren't you constantly trying to win people to
your way of thinking—at home, in the office, in the market place?
How do you begin?" Carnegie queried. The answer lay in "thinking about the other fellow's views and desires, trying to find a common ground of agreement." The personable businessman avoided
confronting people verbally because that made them feel defensive.
Arguing with another person, Carnegie contended, only made people more obstinate in opposition because it challenged "his opinions, and his precious, indispensable self-esteem would have been
threatened; his pride would have been at stake." Thus the shaping
of a compelling, charismatic personality involved a special sensitivity to others' feelings, a psychological awareness of the foibles of
human nature that eased one's connection with them.[32]

Indeed, psychology, one of Carnegie's keen interests since the
1910s, comprised an important part of his endorsement of the
personality paradigm. The connection was a natural one. The
cultural shift from character to personality in early twentieth-
century America was tightly intertwined with a solidifying zeitgeist

stressin; psychological understandings of human behavior. In the 1800s, historian wrote, "Inspirationalists of the old school sought to nurt ire conscience and install virtue" as a code of conduct for individ ials but by the early 1900s, "inspirationalists of the new concen rate on the cultivation of personal power and self-mastery." In Freu dian terms, he continues, through this "important shift in empha is, the new success ideology places the enhancement of ego rather han the super-ego at the center of its message." Carnegie steppe forward as a practical philosopher of the new personality-as-ego movement. As he asked rhetorically in a chapter devoted to makin; the speaker appear impressive and convincing, "Has psycholog y any suggestions that will prove useful to you in this connectio ? Emphatically, yes. Let us see what they are."[33]

Car legie's psychological techniques included having "something to say worthwhile and to say it with contagious conviction" because of the emotional impact. As he phrased it, "the stupendously impor ant thing in making a talk is the psychological aspect of it." He also accented the merits of positive thought: "Think success in this c urse. See yourself in your imagination talking in public with perfec : self-control. It is easily in your power to do this. Believe that y u will succeed. Believe it firmly and you will then do what is neces ary to bring success about." He urged the successful speaker to im ress upon listeners a central concept and, through repetition and s ggestion, negate the influence of any antithetical, distracting conce pts.[34]

In fact, modern business, the arena to which Carnegie turned time and again throughout *Public Speaking: A Practical Course for Business Men*, provided abundant opportunities for realizing the p tential of personality and psychology. Shrewdly, he focused on a pair of crucial endeavors in the maturing consumer economy:

selling and advertising. He pointed out that "salesmanship and modern advertising are based chiefly on suggestion," and plunged into books such as Arthur Dunn's *Scientific Selling and Advertising* (1919), which had laid out a scheme for attracting attention, winning confidence, and appealing to the egotism and pride of consumers and clients. The result was a plan that stressed personal appeal and psychological maneuver, a template for appealing to "the motives that made men act."[35]

Carnegie insisted that successful salesmanship, for example, often relied on suggestion rather than logic. A novice waitress at a restaurant, Carnegie explained, might say to a customer at the end of the meal "You don't want coffee, do you?," thus making it simple to answer no. A more experienced waitress might ask "Would you like coffee?" and set up arguments for and against in the customer's mind. But the best waitress always asks, "'Will you have your coffee now or later?' What happens? She has subtly assumed that there is no question about your wanting it, and she concentrates your entire attention on *when* you wished it served." This strategy of encouraging positive responses, he asserted, brought results in any kind of sales.[36]

Carnegie posed advertising as another example of the influence of personality and psychology on modern business culture. Advertising, of course, had been developing as a vital lubricant in the smooth operation of a modern consumer economy since the late 1800s. In a 1926 address to the American Association of Advertising Agencies, President Calvin Coolidge recognized its importance, describing it as "the method by which the desire is created for better things."

It is the most potent influence in adopting and changing the habits and modes of life, affecting what we eat, what we wear,

and the work and play of the whole nation ... Mass production is only possible where there is mass demand. Mass
demand has been created almost entirely through the development of advertising ... Modern business constantly requires
publicity. It is not enough that goods are made—a demand for
them must also be made.[37]

For Carnegie, however, advertising did more than simply sell
consumer goods through publicity. It involved a deeper process of
linking personal meaning, image, and self-fulfillment to the consumption of certain kinds of goods. "We are creatures of feeling,
who long for comforts and pleasures," he wrote. "We drink coffee and wear silk socks and go to the theater and sleep on the
bed instead of the floor, not because we have reasoned out that
these things are good for us, but because they are pleasant. So show
that the things you propose will add to our comforts and pleasure,
and you have touched a powerful spring of action." More often
than not, advertising utilized the psychological power of suggestion to precisely this end, subtly appealing to people's emotions
and impulses rather than to their reason. "We have come to regard
Arrow collars, Royal baking powder, Heinz pickles, Gold Medal
flour Ivory soap as among the leading, if not the best, products of
their kind. Why? Have we adequate reason for these judgments?"
he wrote. "We have come to believe things for which no proof has
been given. Prejudiced, biased, and reiterated assertions, not logic,
have formulated our beliefs. We are creatures of suggestion."[38]

The linkage of advertising, psychology, and the cult of personality was not peculiar to Carnegie in this period. Other cultural pioneers were making the same connection, including a popular writer
immersed in the business culture of the 1920s. Bruce Barton, in *The
Man Nobody Knows* (1925), authored a best-selling biography of

Jesus that presented him as a businessman, advertising genius, and fascinating personality. He described Jesus as "the founder of modern business," interpreting the Messiah as a corporate organizer who took "untrained men, simple men with elementary weaknesses and passions" and "molded them into an organization which carried on victoriously." Jesus strode from the pages of the book as a skilled salesman who understood people and human motivation; indeed, "every one of the 'principles of modern salesmanship' on which businessmen so pride themselves, are brilliantly exemplified in Jesus' talk and work," wrote Barton. Jesus was also, according to the author, a shrewd ad man who understood the value of big stories, colorful language, and spreading messages. Through trenchant parables and astounding miracles, he was, in Barton's phrase, "the great advertiser of his own day." Perhaps most important, however, Jesus became successful because of his sparkling personality. Barton described him not as a prudish moral icon but as a fascinating, charismatic figure who had "an all-embracing fondness for folks" and attracted them with his "personal magnetism" and "consuming sincerity," "manly vigor," "blazing conviction," "unwavering patience," and a "marvelous instinct for uncovering others' latent powers." Ultimately, Barton contended, Jesus carried the message that God was not a punishing, wrathful entity interested only in spiritual justice but "a great Companion, a wonderful Friend, a kindly, indulgent, joy-loving Father."[39]

Carnegie offered a less grandiose object lesson on the importance of personality and business success. Rather than expropriating Jesus of Nazareth, he told a more modest tale of two businessmen who had been classmates in college as engineering students. One was bright and hardworking but very old-fashioned and "conservative," the kind of man who bought shirts at different stores in town and then kept a chart indicating which ones "laundered best, wore longest, and gave the most service per dollar invested . . . His mind was always on pennies." Proud and confident of his own abilities, he nonetheless languished in a minor job after graduation, waiting for an advancement that never came. In contrast, his classmate was "a good mixer. Everyone liked him." He looked for opportunity, worked well with others, and moved to a different city at the request of his employer to take on a special project. "Through his agreeable personality," wrote Carnegie, this executive won the friendship of a local businessman, went into a partnership in the contracting business, and began to amass a fortune. "Today he is a multi-millionaire," observed the author, "and one of the principal owners of Western Union."[40]

Ultimately, Carnegie's appeal to businessmen in *Public Speaking: A Practical Course for Business Men* bore fruit. The book's nexus of advice on professional behavior, personal aspiration, and the social presentation of self proved well suited to white-collar workers operating in the dynamic, expanding commercial environment of 1920s America. Carnegie's practical instructions on using speech to influence others in corporate bureaucracies rang true to his students and readers. So, too, did his more abstract reflections on the need to develop personality as a means of advancing in this commercial milieu.

But Carnegie's authorial injunctions, in turn, rebounded to impact his own life. At a personal level, they prompted a shift in his code of behavior. At a broader level, they brought recognition and acclaim among the audience he cultivated as he became a trusted, widely recognized adviser in the very corporate culture he was helping to shape.

In December 1927, Carnegie began keeping a new file amid the voluminous collection of article clippings, interview transcripts, class syllabi, and speech notes that piled up in his office. Entitled "Damned Fool Things I Have Done," it was a kind of irregular diary with entries listing areas in which he could improve his personal qualities and conduct. This endeavor represented an old tradition in Protestant culture, of course, dating back centuries. In the seventeenth century the Puritans had engaged in disciplined self-examination to gauge their religious purity and, it was hoped, chart their steady progress toward salvation. In the eighteenth century, figures such as Benjamin Franklin secularized the process to measure one's "republican virtue" as both a civic responsibility and "The Way to Wealth." In the nineteenth century, Victorian "Christian Gentlemen" constantly assessed their conduct in terms of a bourgeois character ethic of self-control, hard work, thrift, and genteel manners.[41]

But Carnegie's "Damned Fool Things I Have Done" file was of a different sort. "I put in that folder, month after month, written records of the damned fool things I have been guilty of," he wrote. "I sometimes dictate these memos to my secretary, but sometimes they are so personal, so stupid that I am ashamed to dictate them, so I write them out in longhand." The exercise shared the traditional impulse to closely examine one's conduct and some of the entries listed customary concerns: wasting time, inefficient work habits, tardiness, sloth. But the great majority of Carnegie's concerns, in contrast to his predecessors, did not weigh spiritual shortcomings, lapses of virtue, or character defects. Instead, they painstakingly detailed faux pas that might have offended others and lowered the esteem in which they held him.[42]

The entries ran the gamut of social slights and professional blunders. In December 1927, he chastised himself for verbal repetitions while instructing: "Caught myself saying 'by the way' at least four times when teaching the class of dentists." Procrastination

also dr w his ire, as when he delayed contacting potential students
to whc m he had promised a course and hence offended them: "I
should have written them in the middle of October, and instead
I proc astinated until the 25th of November and some of them
felt tha t I didn't intend to fulfill my contract." Outbursts of anger
were n ted: "Wasted ten minutes in an unnecessary harangue with
the ph ne company about their shortcomings." Failure to appreciate otl ers drew a reprimand: "H. P. Gant made an extraordinary
succes as toastmaster tonight. I should have complimented him
highly but I was so absorbed in myself that I neglected to speak any
words of appreciation."

Th following year, Carnegie touched upon a recurring personal
weaki ess: bursting out with generalizations that hurt or angered
other . In an entry entitled "Don't make sweeping statements that
may ffend someone," he offered these details: "In the spring of
1928 I said, while teaching the 5–7 PM class, that 'all Tammany
politi ians are crooks,' or something very nearly that." He noted
that ' Joseph Davern, an ardent Catholic, took a feeling exception
to it. t was just at the time that the religious controversy regarding
Al Sr ith's religion was developing. Davern made a most excellent
speec h on intolerance, decrying the fact that I should make such
an u iguarded and unfounded accusation. I apologized." Then in
Augi st 1928, Carnegie lamented his failure to show patience and
appr ciation, a defect that made a "welcoming in" response from
othe s impossible. He visited an American Express office and grew
anni yed when the clerks continued a conversation and were slow
to h lp him. "I was peeved. My voice showed it," he wrote. "I ir-
ritai d the clerk and got very poor service in return . . . It effected
notl ing desirable whatever. I, who take money from people for
telli ig them how to handle human nature, was as crude and inef-
fect ve as a cave man. I was ashamed of the incident."

Carnegie regularly chastised himself for bungling interactions with others that tarnished his image. An insipid inaugural talk at one of his courses earned this rebuke: "If there's to be any enthusiasm in these meetings, Dale Carnegie and Dale Carnegie alone must supply it . . . Whatever success I have had in my work has been done more by enthusiasm than any other one thing and yet I tried to open a course without this indispensible quality." Another time, when an acquaintance complimented him on an advertisement for the course in *The New York Times*, he replied that it had produced disappointing results, and then overcompensated by suggesting that the man sign up for his course. "It looked like a whipped and defeated man grasping at straws, and I'm sure it had a very bad psychological effect," he wrote. In late 1928, Carnegie botched a presentation before the board of directors of the Elks Club by standing to talk. "I immediately noticed that it was too small a group for that. In fact, one of the men asked me to sit down and be comfortable. I should have sensed this myself," he reported. "I believe it would have been wiser for me to have seen each member of the board personally before this meeting and acquainted him with my idea."

Carnegie drew important lessons from the self-admonishments in his "Damned Fool Things I Have Done" file. "When I get out my D.F.T. folders and re-read the criticisms I have written of myself, they do more to help and direct me than anything Solomon could have written," he admitted. "They help me to deal with the biggest problem I shall ever face: the management of Dale Carnegie." This sustained effort at self-management—smoothing the rough edges of relations with others, burnishing one's personal image for maximum impact and influence—had a profound historical resonance. It represented the culture of personality's growing power in bus ness, one that the author had promoted publicly and now attempted to inculcate in his own life.

At the same time Carnegie was striving to internalize his own advice from *Public Speaking: A Practical Course for Business Men* about the necessity of shaping personality, the success of that book (and the attendant classes) dramatically raised his public profile. For the first time, Carnegie became a widely recognized authority in corporate America. A much-in-demand teacher and speaker with a growing reputation as a trusted counselor, he began to move easily in corporate circles and among business organizations.

Numerous asides in his 1926 book indicated how, just months after his return from Europe, he was emerging as a familiar figure in corporate America. Carnegie noted that he "conducted a course in public speaking for the senior officers of New York City banks," attended luncheons at the New York Rotary Club to hear talks "in which almost every New York businessman was interested," and trained men "in the New York City chapter of the American Institute of Banking to speak during a thrift campaign." Further afield, he addressed the Thirteenth Annual Convention of the National Association of Real Estate Boards, the St. Louis Chamber of Commerce, and taught a course in public speaking sponsored by that same Midwestern body.[43]

By 1930, Carnegie had lengthened his reach by establishing connections with some of America's biggest corporations. A 1930 publicity pamphlet offered a photo of the teacher-author attired in a pin-striped suit with a crisp white shirt and tie, and listed the companies and business groups for whom he had conducted classes: the Brooklyn Chamber of Commerce, the Philadelphia Chamber of Commerce, New York Credit Association, Philadelphia Association of Life Underwriters, Bell Telephone Company of Pennsylvania,

Westinghouse Electric and Manufacturing Company, Brooklyn
Union Gas Company, the Manufacturers' Club, and many others.
It also noted that his *Public Speaking: A Practical Course for Busi-
ness Men* had become the official text of the American Banking
Association and was used in educational programs in one hundred
of its chapters nationally.[44]

Testimonial letters from corporate clients also began to pour in.
A 1930 promotion for a Carnegie course sponsored by the Engineers' Club of Philadelphia contained endorsements by delighted
graduates from companies such as American Telephone and Telegraph, Westinghouse, and New York Edison Company. "It is no
exaggeration to state that this course marked a definite turning
point in my life," wrote an executive from the National Broadcasting Company. A manager from the General Electric Company
was almost worshipful: "This training has been a God-send to me.

Carnegie at a New York City newsstand around 1930, after resuming his teaching career.

Many of us here at General Electric have often said, 'Dale Carnegie will never be forgotten in our lives.' "[45]

Carnegie's growing business cachet found further confirmation in a pair of articles he published in venues directed at a corporate audience. "Public Speaking for Plant Executives" appeared in the professional journal *Factory and Industrial Management*. Then in January 1927, he published "Why a Banker Should Study Public Speaking" in the *Bulletin of the American Institute of Banking*. After assuring readers of his many contacts with highly placed bankers in New York, Philadelphia, and Baltimore, he covered many familiar bases in arguing for bankers to take a public-speaking class (preferably his): the cultivation of enthusiasm and sincerity, the assistance in overcoming fear, and the development of self-confidence. True to form, he also stressed personal qualities: "superior personality has more to do with business success than does superior knowledge .. [T]he most important questions that any bank man can ask himself is, 'How can I develop my personality?' " The qualities learned in a public-speaking class, he maintained, were precisely those required by the white-collar organizations in which most bankers worked: "Have you ever had the experience of sitting in these organizations and letting some man with perhaps less knowledge and less ability than yourself, stand up and run things simply because he had the courage and the knack of expressing his ideas clearly and with conviction?" The author knew they had.[46]

Carnegie's prominent position as an adviser to and analyst of American business also appeared clearly in a more popular venue. From 1929 to 1931, he presented a series of pieces in *American Magazine* entitled "How They Got There." Teaming with notable Kansas cartoonist Albert T. Reid—whose drawings had appeared in the *Kansas City Star*, *Chicago Record*, and *New York Herald* as well as national magazines such as *The Saturday Evening Post* and

McClure's—Carnegie composed a dozen text-and-drawing panels (they covered the top one-third of a page in the magazine) that extolled the career success of many leading American business figures. These brief, colorful sketches celebrated men such as William Durant of General Motors, George Eastman of Eastman Kodak Company, Owen D. Young of General Electric, Walter Chrysler of Chrysler Motors, James G. Harbord of the Radio Corporation of American, Adolph Zukor of Paramount Pictures, and George F. Baker, the "dean of Wall street bankers." Carnegie provided snippets of information about their private lives, brief notes on their interests and hobbies, and then tied their success to determination, a keen eye for opportunity, and a compelling personality.[47]

His sketch of Charles Schwab, the chairman of U.S. Steel, was typical. The business magnate had been raised in rural Pennsylvania where he had delighted in acting as ringmaster for small county fairs. Driving a hackney from railroad stations to various points, he studied in his spare time and gave music lessons to supplement his meager income. Schwab then started as a common laborer at the Carnegie Steel Mill, owned by Andrew Carnegie, and within fifteen years had risen to become president of the company. Schwab then tore up his contract for a million dollars a year in salary to ease the acquisition of Carnegie Steel by U.S. Steel Corporation, of which he was appointed chairman.[48]

Thus by the late 1920s, Dale Carnegie had stepped onto the national stage for the first time. Assembling a worldview attuned to a dynamic new society of consumer abundance, corporate bureaucracy, and personal fulfillment, he emerged as a skilled interpreter of modern American business culture who understood both its demands and its opportunities. Left far behind was the old "Carnagey" culture instilled by his parents, with its Victorian demands for self-denial and thrift, piety and propriety, self-control and pe sonal character. Now the new "Carnegie" program confidently ndorsed the notion that advancement depended on a twofold ab lity: first, to project a compelling personal image to others; and sec ond, to interact smoothly and skillfully with them.

Car egie's profound insights into modern America in the late 1920s culminated the first stage of his life, one that had swept him fr m rural regions of the Protestant Midwest to the dynamic consui ner-oriented, bureaucratic society of the urban northeast. These insights formed the building blocks of a new success ethic that b gan to assume a dim shape in his mind before being formulated nto a wildly popular book that would take the country by storm a few years later. But the initial setting for the second stage of Carne gie's life came in an unforeseen event. Like all Americans, he was f rced to confront an economic and social disaster of unprecedent d magnitude. This trauma, while unsettling, also provided great opportunity.

PART TWO

WINNING FRIENDS AND
INFLUENCING PEOPLE

9

"Do the Thing You Fear to Do"

n t e fall of 1929, the United States was devastated by biggest ecc nomic disaster in its history. The stock market plummeted in lat October and then crashed as investors, businessmen, and average holders of bank accounts all over the United States panicked at th : precipitous fall in prices and value. A recovery failed to materia ize over the next few months. Instead the economy spiraled stea ily downward into a calamitous economic failure. By the early 193 s, the Great Depression had settled in with millions of lost jobs and home foreclosures, thousands of bank failures and business bankruptcies, and a stunning expansion of poverty in every cori er of the country. The figures were staggering: unemployment hov red around 25 percent, investment stood nearly 90 percent belc w 1929 levels, and the gross national product and consumer pri e index remained at about 25 percent below pre-crash figures. In his context of evaporating wealth and opportunity, an atmosph ere of despair and dread settled over the United States.[1]

his economic tsunami hit Dale Carnegie hard but not fatally. He lost a substantial portion of his savings in the 1929 crash, joking grimly in a letter that "when I think of my record in the stock market, it seems a joke for me to be giving anybody financial advice about anything." But over the next few years he saved "a new though small nest egg" and managed to hold on to the house he had purchased at 27 Wendover Road in Forest Hills, Queens, in New York City. His good friend Homer Croy was not so lucky. The Missouri novelist owned a home not far from Carnegie in Forest Hills, and in 1933 the sheriff evicted the Croy family when the bank foreclosed on the mortgage for nonpayment. Several unwise investments in real estate had doomed Croy, and now, in his words, "the great depression swept down upon me like a Kansas cyclone and shook me as a tornado would shake a chicken coop."[2]

Several personal experiences made Carnegie acutely aware of the spreading poverty. When the parents of his devoted secretary, Abbie Connell, were about to lose their farm through foreclosure, he loaned them the large sum of $200 to save their property and told her to pay it back as she could. In late 1930, he raised about $120—mostly from his classes, with $25 from his own pocket—and purchased twelve hundred dimes to distribute at the "City Poor House" in New York. "I wish you and father could have been with me. You would have come away thanking Almighty God for the rest of your lives that you are situated as you are," he wrote his mother. "It was pitiful to see those people living in such poverty ... One old woman, a Negro, said to me, 'I dreamed that I had a silver coin, and now you have given me one' ... Another man broke down and wept when I gave him the money ... There were over 2500 people there. If you could have been with me on Christmas Day, Mother, you would never complain again."[3]

But ultimately for Carnegie, the Depression loomed less as an economic trauma than as a mental and emotional challenge. Neither politically inclined nor ideologically oriented, he did not see this disaster as a crisis in capitalism, a dangerous incitement to clas warfare, or a prod to rethink the regulatory role of the federa government. Instead he viewed it as a test case for the efficac of his basic principles: positive thinking, enthusiasm, and p rsonality development. In light of the joblessness, homelessne s, and economic desperation settling in during the early 1930s such a view may appear rather otherworldly to modern eyes. I ut Carnegie's attitude, in fact, highlighted a pervasive trend in De ression-era America. Millions of middle-class citizens also saw t e Depression mainly as a challenge to the resiliency of their indivi ual fiber, as an emotional trial that required courage, confidenc , and adjustment to surmount. As the historian Warren I. Susm n has explained with great insight, the middle-class in the Unite l States reacted to hard times in a conservative fashion: unsettle l and shamed by failure, either actual or threatened, they did n t embrace radicalism but sought to define and defend an "Am rican Way of Life" that was threatened by circumstances and t adjust their own efforts to sustain it. In Susman's words, the (reat Depression produced "a middle-class America frightened nd humiliated, sensing a lack of any order they understood in th world around them, and tending so often to internalize the blam for their fears, tending to feel shame at the inability to cope rath r than overt hostility to a technological and economic order they did not always understand." Americans did not seek to overthro v the system but to reform and repair it; they did not desire to al andon individualism for collectivism but to repair their battere sense of personal efficacy.[4]

C rnegie shared this middle-class reaction to the Great Depression and he responded in several ways that reflected the middle clas 's sensibilities and values. He revamped his public-speaking cou se to stress methods for overcoming the rampant anxieties and inse urities of the age. He wrote a celebratory book on an American folk hero, which captured a common impulse of the 1930s—the embrace of an unswerving, sentimental faith in common people. Finally, he hosted a radio show that highlighted another powerful cultural current in an atmosphere of looming economic failure: the escapist allure of celebrity. In all of these ways, Carnegie aligned himself with a mainstream culture seeking to rescue the American Way of Life from perhaps its greatest modern challenge. Ironically, the Great Depression, for all its privations, provided a great opportunity for Carnegie to begin forging a new creed of survival and success.

On March 4, 1933, Franklin D. Roosevelt assumed the office of the presidency after crushing the incumbent, Herbert Hoover, in the national election. He stood before a large, anxious, rather dispirited crowd of several thousand gathered at the Capitol in Washington, D.C., while millions more tuned in by radio, and faced a nation struggling during the darkest days of the Depression. Roosevelt began his inaugural address with a ringing declaration of reassurance that cut through the gloom. The problem now hindering national recovery, he insisted, was not fundamentally political, social, or economic in nature. It was emotional. In famous words that offered a rallying point for a discouraged citizenry, he proclaimed "my firm belief that the only thing we have to fear is fear itself—nameless, unreasoning, unjustified terror which paralyzes needed efforts to convert retreat into advance." Overcoming this fear, he insisted, would clear the way for the United States to solve many pressing problems and resume "a rounded and permanent national life."[5]

In many ways, Carnegie, now age forty-four, offered a cultural corollary to FDR's memorable assessment of American difficulties during the Great Depression. Even more than the president, he viewed his economic crisis as an emotional trauma that had brought fear and uncertainty, isolation and debilitating doubt in its wake. In an article entitled "Grab Your Bootstraps" in *Collier's*, a very popular middle-class magazine, he depicted the nation's economic travail as an assault on the emotions that threatened to shatter people's confidence, both in the future and in themselves. "My! My! Recessions are bad. We get in the trough of one and all we can see are black waves pounding down on us, smothering and drowning us,' he wrote in jaunty, Rooseveltian language. "Of course, fear is at the very bottom of our present worries. And what an old forktail he is! But the worst fear of all in the box of fears is fear of the unknown. To be aware of a fear and yet not to know what it is— that is the very worst terror in the world."[6]

The key, Carnegie continued, was to face fear squarely and learn to cope with it effectively. He offered old-fashioned advice with a modern twist: pull yourself up by your own bootstraps, but do so psychologically and emotionally rather than in terms of the old work ethic. For the author, "a changed mental attitude" was critical. But he was not advocating a Pollyannaish avoidance of difficulties and problems. "I am not counseling you to have no fear at all, for that would be foolish; but don't let it get the upper hand," he clarified. "Ralph Waldo Emerson had an idea on that subject: 'Act as if you are not afraid, and the death of fear is certain.' And that's the very thing for us to do in these days of doubt and uncertainty. Face the future, act unafraid, and we will, to some extent, conquer fear." Carnegie urged Americans to cultivate "hopeful thoughts" and a "bold spirit" as they faced the prospect of losing a job or a home. A positive mental attitude would ensure that "the thoughts that jump on for a free ride are helpful thoughts, and not bushwhackers." Americans needed to analyze their fears, determine a logical course of action, keep physically fit, remember that hard times always pass, and think in terms of encouragement. If the individual could conquer fear and act positively, he wrote, "I guarantee instead of being tortured and wrecked by the recession you will meet it boldly and courageously—and triumphantly."[7]

Carnegie's sanguine, optimistic view of American problems (and the potential for recovery) was deeply influenced by a foreign visit he described as "my greatest adventure in living." In the summer of 1932, he toured China for several weeks, and it had a profound impact on his thinking about the Great Depression. When he departed, in his description, "Conditions were tragic in the United States. Bread lines were a familiar sight—men roamed the streets in the thousands, begging for work—and unemployment stalked the land." Upon arriving in Shanghai by steamship and traveling throughout China, however, he realized that "America hadn't the foggiest idea of what a depression was." Shocked by the squalid living conditions and almost universal unemployment, he concluded that for centuries "China has never known anything but cruel, grinding poverty" as disease, floods, and starvation killed millions of peasants and urban laborers each year. This fact profoundly altered his perspective on American troubles and renewed his appreciation of opportunities that still existed at home. "Suppose I had lost my life savings in the stock market? So what? I was alive. I was healthy. I didn't have to sleep on the ground," he posited. "It would be a veritable Vale of Kashmir in comparison to the poverty, disease, and misery that four hundred million Chinese were enduring in the Orient."[8]

The Great Depression had an important impact on Carnegie's public-speaking course, still the main source of his income and the basis of his public stature. Continuously tweaking its shape and content, he revamped it in the early 1930s to reflect the anxieties and needs of the period. He drew upon the American self-help tradition with a new urgency and informed students, "If you have a sincere desire to improve yourself, come along. We can help you help yourself. But if you haven't a real urge to improve yourself, save your time and money, for no one can help." He also went further Convinced that the economic crisis could be overcome by teaching people to act with greater effectiveness in the complicated world of modern business by shaping enthusiasm, proper presentation of self, and, especially, positive thinking, he expanded the Carnegie Course to meet those goals.[9]

Building upon the solid foundation laid in the late 1920s, he enlarged his Dale Carnegie Course in Effective Speaking and Influencing Men in Business by taking on a number of prestigious assistants to help with its presentation. He convinced his good friend Lowell Thomas, now a best-selling travel and adventure writer and NBC radio celebrity, to conduct one of the sessions in New York. He had written Thomas a playful appeal: "think of the fun you would get . . . You could come down after your broadcast, load up your pipe, spill a little wisdom, criticize thirty three-minute talks, and make enough money to buy the carcass of a dead horse to feed the foxes for a while at least [on your upstate farm]." He also recruited two professors from New York University: Richard C. Borden, the author of three books on salesmanship and former sales supervisor for the Hearst Newspapers, and Charles A. Dwyer, an experienced teacher of public speaking. In addition, Carnegie enlisted seasoned businessmen as instructors, such as Richard Ford, the assistant manager of Rogers Peet Company in New York, and George H. Wright, an advertising manager with Jacob Reed's Sons in Philadelphia.[10]

But the content of the Carnegie Course, more than its personnel, revealed the impact of the Great Depression. It began by accepting an atmosphere of troubles. Carnegie asked his students to start their training by giving a talk on their business or profession. He offered these guidelines:

> Are you happy in your work? . . . What are your most per-
> plexing problems? Sales? Publicity? Collections? Labor? Di-
> sastrous competition? . . . In preparing this talk, remember
> that your hearers are far more interested in themselves and
> their troubles than they are in you and your problems. So if
> you want to make a talk that will hold everyone's attention,
> select some feature of your business that will help your listen-
> ers solve their problems.[11]

In the session focused on how to open and close a talk, he of-fered students one hundred potential topics to choose from, and a great many reflected the social, economic, and personal discontents brought on by the Depression. Among them:

> What do you believe have been your greatest handicaps in
> the struggle for success, and how have you tried to over-
> come them? . . . Some lessons I have learned in business,
> and what they cost me . . . What Wall Street did to me—and
> how . . . Mistakes that I have made which I want my son
> to avoid . . . The mistakes people make in applying for a
> job . . . What is wrong with our banks? . . . The greatest fears
> I have ever known and how I conquered them . . . The best
> way to commit suicide . . . Do you think America has already
> reached and passed the greatest period of prosperity she will
> ever enjoy during our lives?[12]

Indeed, in one sense the Carnegie Course became a test of nerve, where anxiety and fear of failure provided the very clay that its teacher used to mold new personalities. As was reported in *American Magazine*, he noted the profound dread that often enveloped students as they faced the prospect of speaking publicly. "I have seen them writhe in actual physical pain. I have seen them, hundreds of times, so nervous that they wildly applauded their own speeches after they sat down," Carnegie said. "I have seen their knees sag beneath them. One man, an experienced business executive, actually fainted." Heightening this natural anxiety was the infamous "heckling session"—it was also called the "breaking through" session—about halfway through the course, where the speaker was bombarded with abuse from the audience. The magazine described a company vice president as he endured this ordeal:

> The atmosphere was filled with nervous tension . . . The vice-president's face was red . . . They stamped their feet, pounded on the tables, shook their fists. The sweat poured from the vice-president's brow. His face was now white. At this unhappy moment a thin, smallish, bespectacled man [Carnegie] stepped up behind the once-honored vice president, hauled off, and hit him a staggering blow on the back with a tightly folded newspaper. "Now's your time," he grated. "Snap into it. Let loose the old enthusiasm. Dominate these yapping curs. Go after them. Make them eat out of your hand." The vice-president glared at his adviser, then turned to face his other tormentors. Timidity and nervousness vanished before his rising anger. He fought off his hecklers, made them listen to him, and finished his speech triumphantly.[13]

Career survival was at stake, Carnegie asserted. "Many men who have taken this training have become leaders in their business or community because they were able to express their ideas clearly and

Can You Think Fast
On Your Feet?

Here is one of the tumultuous heckling sessions by which Dale Carnegie trains men to dominate their hearers. Mr. Carnegie, who stands at the left of the harassed speaker, has listened to 150,000 speeches. In this article he passes along some of the helpful things he has learned while teaching executives to speak in public

By JOHN JANNEY

ONE night early this winter thirty of the executives, engineers, and sales managers of a large Philadelphia corporation were gathered in a committee-room. The atmosphere was filled with nervous tension. The senior vice president, a tall, grave, and hitherto highly respected man, rose to speak.

"Gentlemen," he said, "the first great rule of success is hard work. I want . . ."

"Booooh!" was the unanimous response.

"Boo all you want," said the vice president, with attempted calm, "but the fact remains that unless a man rolls up his sleeves . . ."

"In this weather?" demanded the sales manager for the Chicago territory, sneeringly. "Try that on the lake front and catch pneumonia."

The vice president's face was red. He mopped his brow.

"Now, listen, gentlemen," he pleaded. "Give me a chance. It's only fair play to . . ."

"Boooooh!" came the hostile roar again. "Throw him out . . . put him out of his misery . . ."

THEY stamped their feet, pounded on tables, shook their fists. The sweat poured from the vice president's brow. His face was now white. And at this un-happy moment a thin, smallish, be-spectacled man stepped up behind the once honored vice president, hauled off, and hit him a staggering blow on the back with a tightly folded newspaper.

"Now's your time," he grated. "Snap into it. Let loose the old enthusiasm. Dominate these yapping curs. Go after them. Make them eat out of your hand."

The vice president glared at his adviser, then turned to face his other tormentors. Timidity and nervousness vanished before his rising anger. He fought off his hecklers, made them listen to him, and finished his speech triumphantly.

This discordant meeting was not a business crisis. It was a class of instruction. The *(Continued on page 92)*

(Continued on page 92)

Carnegie in 1932, leading the famous, and raucous, "breaking through" session of his public-speaking course.

impressively. They got into the limelight while the inarticulate man was overlooked and forgotten," he maintained. Advertisements for the Carnegie Course stressed this same theme, depicting a business-man being choked by two hands which grip his throat from be-hind, as the caption asked, "Are You Strangled by FEAR, when you are asked to say a few words?" A long treatment of Carnegie and his enterprise in *The Saturday Evening Post* grasped the menacing atmosphere that subtly pervaded it. "Normal existence has come to be so sharply identified to Carnegie as a grim battle, that he sees the world as a place full of people struggling against fearful odds, groping in a vast darkness haunted by specters," the magazine re-ported. "A successful man, to him, is a stouthearted man who is prepared for the worst." In essence, the Carnegie Course operated as an allegorical reflection of the Great Depression where individu-als struggled to flourish while under assault.[14]

But for a practical-minded man such as Carnegie, the value of his course lay not in abstract connections to the social milieu but in concrete techniques for coping with it. Thus he created two ob-jectives for his course that, if met, would help his students survive, and perhaps even prosper, during the hard days of the Depres-sion. First, Carnegie sought to overcome fear and instill confidence among traumatized individuals. Second, he sought to increase their earning power in a threatening economic environment. These goals pervaded both the content and the tone of the Carnegie Course as hundreds of anxious businessmen flocked to its sessions in the early 1930s.

Carnegie relied on one of his favorite quotes to set the tone. "Emerson said that the way to conquer fear is to do the thing you fear to do," he declared. He labored to help students overcome their fear of audiences by requiring them to speak at each session, gently critiquing their efforts, and easing them into a comfort zone where presenting their ideas to others became a more natural endeavor. Overcoming terror about standing up before an audience, he insisted, would develop "a new courage, a new poise." He repeatedly insisted that a positive, confident attitude separated successful individuals from failed ones in the modern world. "I have been convinced by observing the experience of thousands of men that the most valuable thing they obtain from a course in public speaking is not the ability to talk in public, but an increased self-confidence," he argued. "Don't you know men in your city who are never going to get very far simply because they do not think they can—men who are whipped before they start?" He administered a heavy dose of positive thinking, telling students, "Remember, nothing is holding you back except your own thoughts." In a more practical vein, Carnegie designed his infamous "heckling session" not as an exercise in masochism but as a technique for forging confidence, resolution, and courage in "a baptism under fire." As he told a reporter from *American Magazine* in 1932, "Learning to speak in public is like swimming. The best teacher in both is practice and the greatest obstacle to both is *fear*."[15]

Carnegie consistently underscored his second goal—raising students' financial status—by promising that his training would "Increase Your Income" and "Increase Your Earning Power." In a modern economy dominated by corporations, bureaucracies, and complicated webs of human interaction, he told his students that success depended increasingly on the cultivation of personality, enthusiasm, clear communication with others, and human relations. "The prime purpose of this course is to develop that very ability in businessmen and consequently increase their earning power," Carnegie told his charges. He brought in businessmen to speak on "How to Make Money," who invariably underlined the importance of confidence, a positive attitude, and the ability to influence the actions of others. As one enthusiastic speaker told students, the Carnegie Course "will help almost any man increase his earning power. have often seen, as I am sure you have, some of the most important business successes won by men who possessed . . . the ability o talk well and win people to their way of thinking and 'sell' themselves and their ideas."[16]

Thu Carnegie deployed his course as a force for recovery, both emotional and financial, during the dark days of the Great Depression. And at least a few commentators grasped the significance of his efforts. "Dale Carnegie sells people what most of them desperately need," wrote *The Saturday Evening Post*. "He sells them hope." Another journalist noted Carnegie's "ingenious technique of chasing away the jitters that hover around the average man." Old friend Lowell Thomas, writing a new introduction for the 1935 reissue of *Public Speaking and Influencing Men in Business*, added his own shrewd observation. "Dale Carnegie will tell you that he has made a living all these years, not by teaching public speaking— that has been incidental," he wrote. "He claims his main job has been to help men conquer their fears and develop courage."[17]

But Carnegie also dealt with the Great Depression in more indirect ways in the 1930s. Like many of his fellow citizens, during this trying period he sought solace and support in the bedrock of American tradition. Probing the past, he tried to discover an inspiration for coping rooted in the democratic impulses of ordinary citizens. Operating as a writer rather than as a teacher, he discovered someone who, in his telling, personified the resilient virtues of the American people.

In the early 1920s, while working with the Lowell Thomas show in London, Carnegie had run across a newspaper column while breakfasting at his hotel. It examined the life of Abraham Lincoln, particularly his personal experiences and private makeup. In fact, the article proved to be the first in a series and subsequent pieces ran for the next several days. Carnegie had always been interested in American history and held a special fondness for the Great Emancipator, a fellow Midwesterner, but now he encountered a side of the legendary president of which he had been completely unaware. He was utterly intrigued. "I, an American, had had to come to London and read a series of articles written by an Irish-man, in an English newspaper, before I realized that the story of Lincoln's career was one of the most fascinating tales in all the annals of mankind," he joked.[18]

Carnegie began to visit the British Museum library in his spare time, soaking up every book on Lincoln that he could find. Soon, in his own words, "I caught on fire and determined to write a book about Lincoln myself." Originally aiming at a historical novel, he worked intermittently on a manuscript over the next several years during his interlude in Europe but made only modest progress. It was not until the early 1930s, after the shattering of his fiction-writing dreams and the onset of the Depression, that he resumed his Lincoln study. At first, he attempted to write what he called a "Biographical Novel" and admitted in the introduction that his story was "5% fiction." But Homer Croy convinced him merely to note, "The book is truth, as nearly as truth can be arrived at, with a small allowance for dramatization." Carnegie also described his effort as the result of "a genuine need for a short biography that would tell the most interesting facts about [Lincoln's] career briefly and tersely for the average busy and hurried citizen of today." After a couple of years of intense writing, including several months spent in the environs of his subject's home in Springfield, Illinois, the result w is *Lincoln the Unknown* (1932), Carnegie's homage to the martyre d savior of the American Union.[19]

But Carnegie's Lincoln was not the president, politician, and statesm in whose nearly every thought and policy had been examined and dissected by professional historians in the six decades since h s assassination in 1865. Instead, he was a talented and tormented man who symbolized two compelling American traits: first, as an i on of success who overcame obstacles and severe setbacks (often vith the aid of Carnegie-like principles); and second, as an icon of the common people who expressed their fundamental virtues of decency, resiliency, fairness, and democracy. In other words, Carne ie presented his famous subject rather transparently as a reflecti on of Depression-era America and its concerns.

"Lii coln the unknown" was a man who, like a host of citizens in the 930s, struggled to survive a long string of travails the world threw at him. His life consisted of recurring efforts to overcome failure and disappointment. Bankrupted as a young man when his grocei y partnership failed in the village of New Salem, Illinois, he "had o do any kind of manual labor he could find: he cut brush, pitche d hay, built fences, labored in a sawmill, and worked for a while as a blacksmith." Embarking on a legal career in Springfield a few y ars later, he struggled with being $1,100 in debt, going to his credit rs and promising "to pay them every dollar with interest, if they vould only give him time." Eventually scratching out a paltry incon e, he remained sensitive to the poverty of many of his clients and c ften undercharged them. "Once a man sent him twenty-five dolla s, and Lincoln returned ten, saying he had been too liberal." Even in politics, which became his passion, his fortunes ebbed and flowe d with a few electoral victories overshadowed by more numerc us defeats. In 1858, after losing the senatorial race to Stephen

Douglas, Carnegie's Lincoln despaired. "'With me,' he confessed, 'the race of ambition has been a failure, a flat failure.'"[20]

This litany of disappointment continued during his presidency, with a succession of Union military disasters during the early years of the Civil War. "Failure and defeat were not new experiences to Lincoln," wrote Carnegie. "He had known them all his life; they did not crush him; his faith in the ultimate triumph of his cause remained firm, his confidence unshaken." By 1864, when General Ulysses S. Grant's dogged pursuit of Robert E. Lee's Army of Northern Virginia had run up enormous casualties, many Northerners denounced him as a heartless butcher. "Year by year his laughter had grown less frequent; the furrows in his face had deepened; his shoulders had stooped," wrote Carnegie. "He said to a friend, 'I feel as though I shall never be glad again.'"[21]

Lincoln's proclivity for melancholia exacerbated such ordeals. In New Salem during the 1830s, the death of his sweetheart, Ann Rutledge, sent him plummeting into depression. "He couldn't sleep. He wouldn't eat," Carnegie related. "He repeatedly said that he didn't want to live, and he threatened to kill himself. His friends became alarmed, took his pocket-knife away, and watched to keep him from throwing himself into the river." An unhappy marriage drained him emotionally, and the death of perhaps his favorite son, Willie, sank him into a profound despair. One of his best friends, law partner William Herndon, claimed, "If Lincoln ever had a happy day in twenty years, I never knew of it. A perpetual look of sadness was his most prominent feature. Melancholy dripped from him as he walked."[22]

But Lincoln overcame the great disappointments of his life, Carnegie stressed, by means of several habits that he cultivated over the years. In early life, he imbibed a capacity for hard work. Life on the frontier demanded unceasing labor, and when his family moved to Illinois "Abe helped to fell trees, erect a cabin, cut brush, clear the land, break fifteen acres of sod with a yoke of oxen, plant it in corn, split rails and fence the property in. The next year he worked as a hired man in the neighborhood, doing odd jobs for farmers: plowing, pitching hay, mauling rails, butchering hogs." Lincoln also discovered a thirst for knowledge as he studied hard and, because of the high cost of paper, "wrote on a board, with a charcoal stick. Sometimes he ciphered on the flat sides of the hewn logs that formed the cabin walls." Lincoln devoured books by Shakespeare, Burns, Blackstone, Gibbon, and Tom Paine, often walking around with an open book in his hand. "When he struck a knotty passage, he shuffled to a standstill, and concentrated on it until he had mastered the sense," Carnegie wrote. "He kept on studying, until he had conquered twenty or thirty pages, kept on until dusk fell and he could no longer see to read."[23]

Lincoln also survived and prospered because of his devotion to several principles that Carnegie also cherished. He fought melancholy with humor and a determination to think positively about the future, whether it was his legal career or the conclusion of the Civil War. Like the author, Lincoln became a skilled public speaker as a method of gaining self-confidence and reaching people. As a youth, out working in the fields, "he would now and then drop the grub hoe or hay-fork, mount a fence, and repeat the speeches he had heard the lawyers make down at Rockport or Boonville. At other times he mimicked the shouting, hard-shell Baptist preachers who held forth in the Little Pigeon Creek church on Sundays." Upon moving to New Salem and deciding to seek political office, he learned to speak in public and "discovered that he had an unusual ability to influence other men by his speech." In the 1850s, in heated debates over the expansion of slavery, he spoke passionately as a man "stirred to the depths by a mighty wrong, a Lincoln pleading for an oppressed race, a Lincoln touched and moved and lifted up by a moral grandeur." In Carnegie's view, this rhetorical trajectory peaked in the president's second inaugural address, where he presented "an address that sounded like the speech of some great character in drama. It was like a sacred poem."[24]

Finally, Carnegie's Lincoln achieved success through an understanding of human relations. He grasped the importance of several principles that enhanced his ability to influence people: appreciating others' point of view, soliciting positive responses, handling people deftly instead of denigrating or attacking them. Once, when a subordinate carried an order to Secretary of War Edwin Stanton, the voluble, strong-willed cabinet officer burst out, "If the President gave such an order he is a damned fool." Upon hearing this, Lincoln replied mildly, "If Stanton said I was a damned fool, then I must be, for he is nearly always right. I'll just step over and see him." When Stanton convinced him the order was harmful, the president withdrew it. Lincoln explained, "I cannot add to Mr. Stanton's troubles. His position is the most difficult in the world . . . The pressure upon him is immeasurable and unending . . . I do not see how he survives, why he is not crushed and torn to pieces. Without him I would be destroyed." Another time, after the Battle of Gettysburg, when General George Meade let the Southern general Robert E. Lee escape with his army, a furious Lincoln fired off a chastising letter to the Union commander. But after pondering the situation, he never sent the missive. According to Carnegie, Lincoln concluded that "if I had been awake as many nights as he had, and had seen as much blood, I might have let Lee escape, too." Through such actions, the president won the respect and loyalty of nearly everyone in the government and army.[25]

If Carnegie's portrait of Lincoln as a modern success icon inspired an audience whose confidence had been shaken by the Great

Depression, another dimension of *Lincoln the Unknown* proved equally appealing. Throughout the text, the author presented his subject as a man of the people. Carnegie's Lincoln was a heroic figure, to be sure, but one whose triumph amid the greatest crisis in American history could be traced to his profound respect for and identification with the common man. The ability to surmount overwhelming public problems, the author suggested, lay in the virtues and decency of ordinary Americans.

Here Carnegie did not labor alone. In fact, he was part of a larger cultural crusade launched by a host of writers, artists, journalists, and public leaders during the Depression era to locate national survival in the traditions of hardworking, simple citizens who formed the backbone of the republic. As popular poet Carl Sandburg decreed in his 1936 book-length poem *The People, Yes*:

The people yes,
The people will live on.
The learning and blundering people will live on.
They will be tricked and sold and again sold
And go back to the nourishing earth for rootholds,
The people so peculiar in renewal and comeback,
You can't laugh off their capacity to take it.

The historian Warren Susman has pointed out that 1930s culture became obsessed with "finding and glorifying an American Way of Life" rooted in the practices and loyalties of common folk. This "myth of the people," as he termed it, was part of a "larger search for mythic and symbolic sources of identity." The trauma brought on by economic collapse in the 1930s, many believed, could be ameliorated by reliance on the hardy values and practices that had sustained "the folk" in the past.[26]

Indeed, evidence of Depression-era "sentimental populism" appeared everywhere in American life. A great wave of nostalgia and tradition washed over the United States as a variety of cultural detectives uncovered and investigated the sturdy elements of ordinary American life. Norman Rockwell, the people's artist, dispensed sentimental paintings of village life and middle-class rituals throughout the decade while the popular folksinger Woody Guthrie conveyed a democratic optimism in his music. Politician Huey Long's "every man a king" rhetoric invoked the virtue of the people as did composer Aaron Copland's *Fanfare for the Common Man*. Critic Van Wyck Brooks's Makers and Finders series exalted the democratic tradition of American letters while regionalist painters such as Thomas Hart Benton, Grant Wood, and John Steuart Curry depicted the workaday heroism of rural Midwesterners. Archibald MacLeish called for a new poetry in the mold of everyday public speech while Lewis Mumford promoted his agenda for reintegrating industrial technology with the "culture of the folk." Industrialist Henry Ford created Greenfield Village, a collection of historical homes, churches, public buildings, and artifacts of common life in the eighteenth and nineteenth centuries, and made it into one of the premiere tourist attractions in the nation. This sentimental populist upsurge, according to one assessment, "embodied a fascination with the folk and its culture, past and present . . . a kind of collective identification with all of America and its people."[27]

Carnegie fully embraced this culture of the folk. In fact, he immersed himself in it, destroying the few chapter drafts of his Lincoln book he had completed in Europe and, instead, traveling to rural central Illinois, where he "met, walked, talked, and dreamed with folks who knew authentic tales [about Lincoln]. He came to know the man as he was—not as he might have been, or as historians think he should have been." He came to "almost worship

Carnegie displaying his lifelong love of dogs, dating back to his boyhood days on the farm and his pet, Tippy.

Lincoln," as he admitted to one journalist, as "the simple railsplitter who made his most dramatic speeches in short-legged trousers and minus a collar." He haunted Lincoln's home and law office in Springfield, stomped through the woods and fields in areas adjacent to where Lincoln had lived as a younger man, and wrote part of the book under branches of massive oak trees at New Salem where his subject had strolled decades earlier. Indeed, Carnegie's near-mystical encounters at New Salem—"I used to go there alone on summer nights when the whip-poor-wills were crying in the woods along the bank of the Sangamon, when the moonlight outlined Rutledge's tavern against the sky; and it stirred me to realize

that on just such nights, about a hundred years ago, young Abe
Lincoln and Ann Rutledge had walked over this same ground arm
in arm in the moonlight"—unwittingly reflected the larger populist
impulses of the 1930s. The pioneer village that captured the author's imagination was, in fact, a historical reconstruction funded
by Roosevelt's New Deal and completed by the Civilian Conserva-
tion Corps in the early 1930s.[28]

Carnegie's Lincoln took shape as a product of the American folk
and their sturdy, unpretentious, and virtuous habits. He came from
a desperately poor background, born in the winter of 1809 "on a
bed of poles covered with corn husks . . . [as] the February wind
blew the snow through the cracks between the logs and drifted
it across the bearskin that covered Nancy Hanks and her baby."
He endured terrible poverty as a youth and struggled to make a
livelihood through early adulthood in the pioneer environs of rural
Illinois. But in New Salem he plunged into the democratic political
process, "going from cabin to cabin, shaking hands, telling stories,
agreeing with every one, and making speeches whenever and wherever he could find a crowd." Even after becoming a successful lawyer in Springfield, he maintained common habits and could be seen
walking about town without a coat or collar, with "only one gallus
holding up his trousers, and when a button came off he whittled a
peg and pinned things together with that."[29]

During the 1858 debates with Douglas, Lincoln's supporters drove
him about in a farm wagon pulled by mules while his opponent traveled the state in a fine carriage drawn by white horses and appeared
in fashionable suits and hats. Lincoln, in Carnegie's words, "detest-
ing what he called 'fizzlegigs and fireworks,' traveled in day coaches
and freight trains and carried a battered old carpet-bag, and green
cotton umbrella with a handle gone and a string tied around the middle to keep it from flapping open." He kept a common touch after

assumir g the presidency, frequently demonstrating great leniency to ordinar ʳ solders in the Union Army who had broken military rules and apɪ ealed to him for pardon. While Lincoln distrusted the high-handed impulses of professional military officers, "he loved the volunteers ɔn whom he had to depend for winning the war—men who, like hin self, had come from the forest and the farm."[30]

Thuɪ Carnegie's mining of a usable past as a writer paralleled his efforts ɪs a teacher in the early 1930s. Both undertakings sought to help Americans survive the travails of the Depression by providing em ɔtional sustenance and principles for coping. So, too, did anothe ʳ project. In this same era, he became involved with radio, a mediuɪ ɪ having an increasingly powerful impact on popular life in Ameriɪ a. As with President Roosevelt and his fireside chats, Carnegie usɪd it to broadcast his belief in the power of personality and to reaɪ h new heights of influence.

In the late summer of 1933, a series of newspaper stories around the Uɪ ited States announced a new radio show set to appear on the N BC network's flagship station in New York, WEAF. On Auguɪ t 20, the popular lecturer, teacher, and author Dale Carnegie v ould begin hosting a weekly half-hour program entitled *Little Known Facts About Well Known People.* Each Sunday afterno ɪn starting at five thirty, he would treat famous individuals from the past and present, and "endeavor to stress the human side c f his subjects, bringing to the microphone interesting facts abou each with which the general public is not familiar." The show sponsored by Maltex Cereal and promoted by the Samuel C. C oot Advertising Company, also featured announcer John Holb ɪook and the Harold Sanford Orchestra. This foray into radic gave a great boost to Carnegie's national stature. Not only did his entry into a wildly popular new medium support his efforts as a teacher and lecturer but it enhanced his writing career when a number of his radio stories were collected and published as a book in 1934.[31]

Lowell Thomas had given Carnegie a powerful assist in this undertaking. Already established with *Today's News*, his own daily program on NBC, Thomas had begun attracting a mass audience that would make him one of the most popular figures in American radio over the next forty years. His patented greeting ("Good evening, everybody") and sign-off ("So long until tomorrow") were already becoming hallmarks, as was his warm, resonant voice. Thomas had urged NBC to give his ex–business manager a shot. The Croot Company had convinced Thomas to appear on Carnegie's first show and introduce him to the radio audience. In return, the new radio host featured him as his first biographical subject, asserting, "Lowell Thomas is one of the most extraordinary men I have ever known."[32]

Carnegie as he launches his NBC radio show, *Little Known Facts About Well Known People*, in 1933.

Carnegie's show launched successfully, although with a shaky beginning. Initially, he was knocked off-kilter by the unfamiliar shock of the broadcasting studio's barely controlled chaos. "My first broadcast was far from satisfactory to me," he wrote; "there was a tremendous amount of confusion in the room and the orchestra leader was going around talking to all the members of the orchestra while I was speaking. It was my first time on the air and the result was that I was a bit confused. In fact, all of this noise and talking darned near drove me nuts." He derived solace from the fact, however, that the Maltex Company and the advertising agency seemed pleased with the show. A friend, J. R. Bolton of the Advertising Club of New York, also judged the initial effort successful and complimented its host on "the wonderful broadcast last Sunday afternoon, and the splendid start you have made in the series." Carnegie hit his stride in the second broadcast as he adapted to studio conditions, tightened his material, and improved his delivery. Radio success, he quickly concluded, relied on the same thing as public-speaking success. "You have got to put your own personality in it," he related. "If I had Kipling writing my speeches for me, he would probably write speeches that were a thousand times better than mine, but I couldn't get up before the microphone and put any enthusiasm in them because they wouldn't fit me any more than Kipling's clothes would fit me. The more I study the art of self-expression, the more I am convinced that each man must be himself, with all his faults, and not imitate others."[33]

Over the next two years, *Little Known Facts About Well Known People* offered radio listeners an array of biographical sketches deftly drawn and shaded with the Carnegie touch. They ranged from historical giants such as Cleopatra, Christopher Columbus, and Lenin to writers and artists such as Edgar Allan Poe, H. G. Wells, and Mozart, to contemporary figures such as Greta Garbo,

George Gershwin, and Albert Einstein. Regardless of his subject, however, Carnegie maintained a persistent focus: human-interest angles, sentimental or comical aspects, or quirks and oddities that illuminated their personalities. Focusing more on breadth than depth, he and his assistants scoured magazine articles, pored through published biographies, and occasionally conducted interviews. As he emphasized in a promotion for the show, "he spends two hours in research for every sixty seconds on the radio."[34]

Carnegie studied the medium he was seeking to master. He immediately perceived an important difference between delivering talks before a live audience, where he was tremendously experienced, and speaking into a radio microphone, where he was a novice. The latter was more difficult, he decided. "When you deliver a lecture, you know that the people are generally there because they really want to be. They've come to hear you talk and they listen attentively. But with radio, it's different. You never know whether or not you're a welcome visitor. Your audience is invisible and you have no way of gauging the reactions while you're speaking." Nonetheless, Carnegie became convinced that a common denominator linked any form of communication—delivering "a series of startling and interesting statements" with enthusiasm held the key to reaching any mass audience. "When I broadcast, I have the word 'joy' written in red ink at the top of each page of my script. That word symbolizes my own pleasure in what I am doing." The radio host attributed some of his own radio success to his training as an actor. The technique he had learned for the theater—"stage presence, diction, the power to attract and hold an audience—all these lessons proved invaluable."[35]

Carnegie's radio program reflected many concerns and proclivities—both his own and his audience's—common to the early 1930s. Some of the episodes touched upon Depression themes of hard times

and success, albeit with an unfailingly optimistic tone. One broadcast, entitled "They Spent Their Lives Keeping the Big Bad Wolf
Away,' noted how individuals such as Mark Twain, Ulysses S.
Grant, Daniel Webster, and Abraham Lincoln had struggled with
debt throughout much of their lives and "didn't have any more
sense than you or I had—back in 1929." Carnegie surveyed several
populist heroes from the era. Walt Disney appeared as a man of
the people who dreamed up Mickey Mouse while working in a
cramped office above a repair shop where "the grease and gasoline
smells of that garage gave him an idea that was worth a million
dollars," while Will Rogers, "a man who never had much education," climbed to prominence and "wears old, dilapidated clothes
and frequently drives into Hollywood without a necktie and wearing boots and old, blue denim overalls with brass rivets in them."[36]

But much more often, Carnegie pursued another theme in his
biographical radio sketches: the individual as celebrity. The development of personality had been a longtime concern, of course, but
now he elevated personal charisma into *the* predominant influence
in modern life. As he had noted in *Public Speaking: A Practical
Course for Business Men*, "You may possibly bore people if you
talk about things and ideas, but you can hardly fail to hold their
attention when you talk about people . . . [and] personalities." He
reiterated this point in the 1930s when discussing radio with a
newspaper reporter. "If you talk about an abstract subject, chances
are your listeners will begin to yawn," he remarked. "Talk about
people—personalities, human struggles, joys and tragedies—and
your audience will strain to catch every word."[37]

So on the weekly broadcast of *Little Known Facts About Well
Known People*, Carnegie spoke almost solely about the personalities of his famous subjects, their private dramas and challenges
and triumphs, while giving scant attention to their ideas or public

achievements. H. G. Wells became one of the world's most famous authors when a badly broken leg confined him to bed where "he devoured every book he could get . . . and developed a taste for books, a love for literature." Railroad magnate Cornelius Vanderbilt, an eccentric and superstitious man, "had each leg of his bed set in a dish filled with salt, to keep the evil spirits from attacking him while he slept." Gandhi appeared as a saintly eccentric who "has a set of false teeth, which he carries in a fold of his loincloth. He puts them in his mouth only when he wants to eat." Lenin, dubbed only as the instigator of an "economic experiment," was portrayed as an "expert chess player," "happily married," and a "revolutionist" who wore false whiskers, communicated by letters written in invisible ink that could only be read when dipped in water, and often "slept in a packing box." In such fashion, the radio host helped usher in a culture of celebrity in this period, where charm and personality were crucial components in the calculus of fame. In such an atmosphere, as Daniel Boorstin once quipped famously, modern celebrities became "well-known for their well-knownness."[38]

Carnegie's celebrity compulsion became especially evident in his treatment of movie stars. Homer Croy had connections in Hollywood because of several film adaptations of his novels, so the fledgling radio host hired him to conduct interviews and help write scripts on famous actors. "You are my Hollywood expert, you know," Carnegie wrote, and peppered his old friend with requests to contact various film celebrities. "I shall have only six broadcasts after the first of the year and if you send me Mickey Mouse and Mary Pickford that would mean three Hollywood people. I expect to interview Eddie Cantor here," he wrote Croy in December 1933. "How about one on Greta Garbo? . . . How about interviewing Harold Lloyd? What about Lionel and John Barrymore?" After Croy had sent him a series of write-ups on famous actors and actresses, Carnegie asked him to tailor the writing to his own style. "If you would write these broadcasts in the way that I want them so that I won't have to spend hours changing them, it would be an enormous help to me and I would appreciate it beyond words," he instructed. "The way I want them may be God-awful, but you taught me not to imitate other people but to roll up my sleeves, spit on my hands and be myself, and that is all I am trying to do."[39]

Once again, with his keen sense of the popular mood, Carnegie captured a powerful trend in the 1930s. Celebrity exerted a powerful pull in Depression-era America. In an age when many were struggling to survive, hosts of working-class and middle-class individuals clung to visions of wealth, glamour, and radiant personal ties as a ray of light in the gloom. They flocked to the movies in unprecedented numbers, for instance, to find solace in a darkened theater as film, in the words of one critic, "became the fantasy life of a nation in pain." Large popular audiences breathlessly followed the exploits of wealthy debutantes such as Barbara Hutton and the difficulties of "poor little rich girl" Gloria Vanderbilt; they devoured fan magazines such as *Photoplay* and *Motion Picture* that burnished the fantasy lives of Hollywood movie stars; they imbibed advertising that deployed high-society figures to convey attractive images of abundance to consumers. While escapist, of course, celebrity culture also served another function. It helped to reaffirm the American Dream under duress by "focusing on the endless possibilities for individual success," as one analyst has put it. Only now it was personality and charisma that moved one forward, not hard work and upright character.[40]

Carnegie's radio show proved moderately successful, running for two seasons from 1933 to 1935. It changed format and backing in its second year, switching to a daily broadcast of five minutes from 1:45 to 1:50 in the afternoon, and attracting the American

Radiator Company as a sponsor. In 1934, cashing in on publicity generated by his radio broadcasts, Carnegie collected his first
season's sketches and published them with Greenberg Press as *Little Known Facts About Well Known People*. The book generated
mixed reviews, with some critics finding it fascinating and charming while others deemed it superficial and grating. "It is written
in a colorful and anecdotal style which holds the reader's attention from beginning to end," said an Associated Press review that
appeared in many newspapers. But the *New York Herald Tribune*
disagreed, characterizing Carnegie's talks as "marred by an artificial intimacy, a straining for conversational idiom, and an assumption of an exceedingly low common denominator of information
and intelligence in the listeners to whom they were addressed . . . A
good example is the author's conjecture of what Caesar said when
he first saw Cleopatra: 'My, my! Oo la la! Why haven't we girls like
that in Rome?' "[41]

But whatever its merits, the radio show helped make Carnegie
himself a minor celebrity by 1935. In addition to the broadcasts and
the spin-off book, NBC's promotional efforts gave a great boost to
his national stature. NBC Artists Services, for example, promoted
Carnegie to business groups and organizations as "a well-known
radio speaker" whose sponsor "already renewed a contract for his
services to begin early in the fall. According to the statement which
has been made by the Maltex Company, their broadcast program,
in which Mr. Carnegie was featured, actually increased their sales
thirty per cent last season. May we suggest that you have Dale
Carnegie address your employees, sales conference, business convention, or club meeting on 'How to Win Friends and Influence
Men in Business?'" Another promotional sheet entitled "NBC
Personalities—Dale Carnegie," sent to various publicity venues, described a vigorous, fascinating chronicler of the human condition:

"He has gone to the ends of the earth to interview the great figures of today. He has spent years penetrating long-forgotten archives and memorabilia. And from his painstaking explorations into the past and his far-flung associations and intimacies, Dale Carnegie, celebrated author and lecturer, brings to the microphone new data on interesting personalities of the past and present."[42]

Carnegie's array of activities in the early years of the Great Depression set the stage for the greatest performance of his career. With a wildly successful class in public speaking, a growing career as a writer, a national radio profile, and, above all, a keen sensitivity to the feelings and values of ordinary Americans, he was poised on the edge of greater success. Even so, few would have predicted the fame, wealth, and influence that would soon come his way from writing one of the best-selling, most influential books in American history.

10

"Men and Women, Hungry for Self-Improvement"

B y the mid-1930s, Dale Carnegie's life had stabilized in every regard. Professionally, his experiments during the previous decade had given way to a steady, lucrative career combining his popular public-speaking course, nonfiction writing, and radio program. Firmly entrenched as a trusted figure in the American business community, yet sensitive to the trials and fears of ordinary people in a threatening age, he had responded to the Great Depression by reaching out to a mass audience with prescriptions for survival, escapist entertainment, and soothing populist injunctions.

Personally, Carnegie also resolved many lingering problems from the 1920s. He settled into a comfortable home in Forest Hills, Queens, after divorcing Lolita Baucaire in 1932 and ending their stormy, decade-long marriage. While the final break was a relief, Lolita played shamelessly on her ex-husband's sympathy for years to come. After receiving *Lincoln the Unknown*, for instance, she replied with a guilt-inducing letter that described how reading it "was a great treat for me, as in my loneliness I lived with you again . . . It made me think I am sitting on the sofa, and you have a chat with me and tell me interesting things." Complaining constantly about a variety of physical ailments—carbuncles, rheumatism, chronic fatigue—she elicited regular installments of money from Carnegie. "I just received your letter with cheque," she noted in one missive from a treatment facility in the Pennsylvania countryside "Thank you very much, Dale, for helping me to get well." Eventually Carnegie would purchase a house for her in New Jersey, as well as paying a generous alimony, yet she still annoyed him by appearing at his office periodically and announcing herself as "Mrs. Carnegie."[1]

Harmony prevailed in his immediate family. Initially the dissolution of Carnegie's marriage had prompted a painful encounter with his pious mother, now age seventy-four, who claimed that he had gone "against God's will" in marrying Lolita, a divorced woman, and would do so again if he tried to remarry after his divorce. But Carnegie smoothed over this difficulty, lent financial support to his parents, and was pleased to attend their golden anniversary in early 1932 As a crowd of family and old friends gathered to celebrate at their farm in Belton, a local Methodist minister read the marriage ceremony and asked James if he would take the former Amanda Harrison to love and obey. In Carnegie's words, "father spoke up and with a twinkle in his eye, said, 'I have tried to obey my wife for fifty years and I don't believe I care to promise to obey for another fifty years!'" With his footloose brother's family settled nearby in a caretaker role, Carnegie further cemented family tranquillity by taking Clifton's daughter, Josephine, into his Queens home as an assistant and secretary. The niece would become close to her uncle and remain in his employ for many years.[2]

Then a serendipitous event occurred that turned this contented life upside down. An editor from a major publisher in New York signed up for the Carnegie Course and became greatly impressed with the message and manner of its founder. After one class, he approached Carnegie and urged him to expand his presentations into a book. This simple request set into motion a chain of events that would change irrevocably the life of the author and the course of American culture.

Leon Shimkin, an intelligent, aggressive, and ambitious young man from a Russian immigrant family in Brooklyn, joined the newly formed Simon and Schuster in 1924 as a bookkeeper. Founded by Richard L. Simon and M. Lincoln "Max" Schuster, this commercial publishing firm rose to prominence by the mid-1930s and the talented Shimkin rose along with it as its business manager (and unofficial acquisitions editor). In 1934, he stumbled across a keen opportunity. He accepted an invitation to attend a gathering of junior executives in a New York suburb where Dale Carnegie, the famous teacher of public speaking, explained his course and invited attendees to join. Shimkin, intrigued by the instructor's strategy for giving people self-confidence, signed up. Fascination soon gave way to admiration. Shimkin was deeply impressed by the teacher's ideas about human relations and his practical, "down to earth" techniques for imparting them to students. He decided that "Dale Carnegie had something specific to offer to help people."[3]

So at the conclusion of one session, Shimkin approached the instructor with a proposal. He pointed out that course presentations, no matter how brilliantly done or enthusiastically received, were confined to the physical space of the classroom. But if Carnegie "wrote a book on the art of dealing with people, his voice could be heard throughout the country." Shimkin proposed that Carnegie write such a book to be published by his company. When the teacher asked whom he worked for, and the young man replied Simon and Schuster, Carnegie immediately cooled and said he would not submit a book to them "because they had rejected two of his previous manuscripts and besides, he was too busy." But Shimkin persisted. He tried another tack and suggested that a stenographer record some of the lectures and type them up as a basis for a rough manuscript and then Carnegie "could look over the material to see if he agreed that the ingredients were present for a book." The instructor reluctantly agreed. So Shimkin, along with Verna Stiles, Carnegie's secretary and researcher, worked together for several weeks on compiling a rough first draft. After seeing the promise of their work, Carnegie warmed to the project and began a serious process of rewriting, refining, and shaping the manuscript in his personal style.[4]

The burdensome task of writing a book was eased somewhat by the existence of Carnegie's keenly honed course lectures as well as principles and examples from *Public Speaking and Influencing Men in Business*. "I didn't really write *How to Win Friends*," Carnegie commented many years later. "I collected it. I merely put on paper the lectures I had been giving people to help equip them for business and social life, and the success hints they had been telling me." Especially useful—in fact, it became the thematic centerpiece of the manuscript—was a talk that Carnegie had delivered hundreds of time to students, Rotary Clubs, businessmen's groups, and even college audiences. Originally called "How to Get the Welcoming-In Response," Carnegie had changed the title by mid-decade to "How to Win Friends and Influence People."[5]

In interludes between his busy teaching schedule and radio-show obligations, Carnegie labored on the book throughout 1935 and into 1936. With plans for a late-fall publication, Simon and Schuster, in the author's words, was "hounding me daily for the manuscript" even though a final chapter was not completed. "Finally, I decided they could have it as it was," Carnegie recalled later, and decided to write the last chapter—"it would have concerned itself with the way to handle the few times where human relations would be out of place"—at a later time. The author submitted the text to the publisher in early summer and boarded a train for several weeks of vacation at Lake Louise in western Canada. When he returned to New York in September, the book was ready for publication except for one minor problem. Carnegie had suggested "How to Make Friends and Influence People" as the title, but the designers were having difficulty placing it artistically on the dust jacket. They concluded it was one letter too long. According to Carnegie, he suggested changing "make" to "win," just like his lecture title, and Shimkin "wasn't happy with it, but said it would have to do. There was no time to fuss around with it."[6]

Simon and Schuster constructed a skilled advertising campaign. In addition to utilizing traditional bookstore outlets, they launched full-page newspaper advertisements in a handful of major cities. The ad, later praised as among the "100 greatest advertisements in American history," was put together by the noted agency Schwab and Beatty. Its striking layout featured the book's title and Carnegie's photograph, and conveyed, according to one expert, "that here is something important, something well worth reading in terms of reader benefits." The vigorous text, written by famed copywriter Victor O. Schwab, covered several bases: lauding Carnegie's experience as a teacher of businessmen; telling the story of Michael O'Neill, a flop as a salesman who became one of the nation's best after implementing Carnegie principles; listing the major corporations whose executives had been trained in the Carnegie system; and including a plug from Lowell Thomas, who described his friend as "a wizard in his special field." The ad pointed to thousands of beneficiaries and insisted "What Dale Carnegie has done for them he can do for you," claiming that the book "will mean more to

you the n ANY book that you have ever read." It also included a
mail-or ler coupon. Addressed directly to Simon and Schuster, the
coupor read: "Please send me *How to Win Friends and Influence
People.* I will pay the postman only $1.96 plus a few cents postage
charge . It is understood that I may read it for 5 days and return it
for refi nd if I then feel that it does not in every way live up to the
claims nade for it."[7]

Hou to *Win Friends and Influence People* was published in No-
vembe 1936 with modestly optimistic hopes, both from the publisher ind the author, for robust popular sales. But to the shock

A 193 7 newspaper and magazine advertisement that helped make *How to Win Friends
and I fluence People* a runaway best seller.

of all concerned, a tidal wave of enthusiasm immediately overwhelmed expectations. Within the first three weeks of its appearance, the book sold seventy thousand copies. Sensing they had a hit on their hands, Simon and Schuster quickly ratcheted up the advertising effort and in January 1937 expanded it to thirty-six newspapers and magazines around the United States. The mail-order campaign turned out to be a shrewd maneuver: It helped create a public stir as purchasers talked about the book, recommended it to others, and helped create a swelling demand. Simon and Schuster announced, "We believe this book will be 1937's best-selling book of non-fiction," and events bore out the prediction. By August it had gone through seventeen editions and by the end of the year *How to Win Friends* had sold 650,000 copies, climbed to the top of the best-seller list, and made $180,000 for its author. By November 1939 it reached the one million sales mark. Over the next decade, the book would sell around five million copies and, with the advent of paperback publishing in the 1950s, would go on to become one of the great best sellers in American history, with some thirty million copies being purchased over the next eighty years.[8]

Carnegie was stunned by the public response and colossal sales. "To my utter amazement, *How to Win Friends* was an immediate success," he recalled many years later. "I knew people craved friendship, but I honestly did not realize *how much* they craved it." The whole experience was unreal, which was driven home when he received his first royalty check in early 1937. "When Abbie [Connell] opened the mail that morning, she put the check in front of me without any comment," he said. "I sat there, looking at the figure on the face of that check, completely unable to comprehend what it meant: $90,000. Twenty years before that day I hadn't known any one person on earth who had that much money." When sales figures hit a hundred thousand copies, a dumbfounded Carnegie sent

Shimkin a note that said, "Every morning I rise and face the east and think Allah that you came into my life." As the impact settled in, the author grew amazed by the breadth as well as the volume of the book's appeal. "One day my publishers received two orders in the same mail," he told a journalist with a laugh. "One was from a theological seminary, which wanted 50 copies for its ministerial students. The other came from a madame of a high-class bordello in Paris. She needed nine copies for her girls. I am the only author you ever saw who wrote a book used as a text in two such highly divergent fields."[9]

So why did *How to Win Friends and Influence People* receive such a rapturous reception from the American public? In one sense, the book synthesized all of the elements of Carnegie's life: the country boy who climbed out of poverty to success, the actor who dramatized his ideas, the salesman who sold himself as well as his products, the journalist who sought a popular audience, the author who plumbed American culture for its basic values, and the inspirational teacher who wanted to help others succeed. In another sense, the book touched a popular nerve that had been profoundly sensitized by the Great Depression. This traumatic crisis had shredded many traditional notions of personal conduct and aspiration, and threw into the water millions of floundering citizens who were desperate for a lifeline to pull them to economic safety and social success. Carnegie's optimistic advice seemed to provide it. He appeared with the right ideas at the right time.

But the nature of Carnegie's seminal popular book, and the widespread social needs it met, was more complicated than it may have appeared at first glance. While intertwined with the Great Depression, this volume also reflected the larger shift of American culture away from the genteel, pious traditions of nineteenth-century Victorianism toward the desires and demands generated by modern twentieth-century bureaucratic consumerism. The changing nature of American individualism, and the changing demands and expectations placed on it, provided the fertile soil from which Carnegie's book sprouted and flowered.

For those familiar with Carnegie's career, a striking feature of *How to Win Friends and Influence People* was its complete neglect of public speaking. Other than a brief insert inviting interested readers to sign up for the "Dale Carnegie Courses in Effective Speaking and Human Relations," any mention of speech-making and addressing audiences disappeared completely from this best-selling book. That omission spoke volumes. It revealed the most important characteristic of Carnegie's volume: He had broadened his message to make it part of that most hoary of American popular genres, the success tract. Updating what advice writers had counseled in earlier eras, Carnegie explained the modern qualities that would produce greater material wealth and rising social mobility. "Carnegie now realized that public speaking alone was not enough to make men irresistible," an astute journalist observed. "He was no longer content to teach men how to make speeches in public; he wanted to teach every man how to be a striking success in all departments of life."[10]

So Carnegie abandoned his earlier recommendations on rhetoric, instead offering a success tract for contemporary America that unfolded in a brisk, concise, folksy yet inspiring manner. Following an introduction by Lowell Thomas entitled "A Short-Cut to Distinction" that provided a biographical sketch of the author's rise from humble beginnings, Carnegie contributed a brief preface, "How This Book Was Written and Why." He explained his realization that "sorely as adults needed training in effective speaking, they needed still more training in the fine art of getting along with people in everyday business and social contacts." Research had shown, he continued, that in all fields "about 15 percent of one's financial success is due to one's technical knowledge and about 85 percent is due to skill in human engineering—to personality and the ability to lead people." So Carnegie had begun developing ideas and rules for producing success in his courses, and students, whom he described as "men and women, hungry for self-improvement," had embraced his formula with stunning results. "They work like magic," Carnegie wrote. "Incredible as it sounds, I have seen the application of these principles literally revolutionize the lives of many people."[11]

How to Win Friends was organized formally into six parts, and it was based on three large themes. The first theme, comprising parts one and two, proposed that everyone was interested, mainly, in their own problems and possibilities, and that the secret of dealing with others was to demonstrate appreciation for the other person's perspectives and desires. Carnegie explored this in "Fundamental Techniques in Handling People." He then went on to explain, in "Six Ways to Make People Like You," how readers could display sympathy by smiling, remembering people's names, being a good listener, and becoming genuinely interested in the other person's activities and beliefs.

Carnegie then proceeded to a second theme in parts three and four: how displaying sensitivity to others could be put into action and used to influence their behavior. In other words, he focused on the payoff to be gained from adopting these principles. In "Twelve Ways to Win People to Your Way of Thinking," he argued that with several maneuvers—avoiding arguments, respecting others' opinions, never telling someone he is wrong, encouraging positive rather than negative responses, and letting the other person think the idea is his—the skillful individual could nudge people in the direction he would like them to go. He elaborated in "Nine Ways to Change People Without Giving Offense or Arousing Resentment," contending that offering praise and genuine appreciation, asking questions rather than giving orders, admitting one's own mistakes and pointing out others' only indirectly, letting people save face, and using encouragement rather than criticism, would help make the other person happy to do what the reader suggests.

Finally, after laying out the nucleus of his argument, Carnegie addressed a third theme more briefly in the final two sections of the book. He offered a pair of concrete examples of how his principles could be applied to great benefit in the writing of commercial communications and in the conduct of marriage. In "Letters That Produced Miraculous Results," he showed how the skillful crafting of business letters could grant recognition to and convey sympathy for their recipients, thus enlisting their cooperation in advancing the reader's agenda. "Seven Rules for Making Your Home Life Happier" discussed use of the Carnegie method on the domestic scene. The author argued that spouses should avoid nagging and criticism, regularly express appreciation, pay "little attentions," and "read a good book on the sexual side of marriage" in order to achieve matrimonial bliss.

A compelling writing style animated *How to Win Friends and Influence People*. Carnegie had refined a perky, anecdotal, conversational manner over the course of his earlier books, but now he skillfully added elements that attracted a popular audience. Most noticeable, perhaps, was a "How could such a thing be possible? Let me tell you how!" idiom that suggested the unlocking of a treasure chest of secrets. For instance, he began his discussion of business communications in this fashion:

I'll bet I know what you are thinking now. You are probably saying to yourself something like this: *"Letters that produce miraculous results!"* Absurd! Smacks of patent-medicine advertising. If you are thinking that, I don't blame you. I would probably have thought that myself if I had picked up a book like this fifteen years ago . . .

Let's be honest. Is the title, "Letters That Produce Miraculous Results" accurate? No, to be frank with you, it isn't.

The truth is, it is a deliberate *understatement* of fact. Some of the letters produced in this chapter harvested results that were rated twice as good as miracles.

Carnegie then pointed to the successful example of one of his ex-students, Ken Dyke, now the advertising manager of the Colgate-Palmolive-Peet Company. "How did he do it? Here is the explanation in Ken Dyke's own words." [12]

Carnegie also leavened the book with numerous folksy aphorisms. In discussing the importance of avoiding criticism of others, he instructed, "If you want to gather honey, don't kick over the beehive." Advocating the quick admission of being wrong, he noted, "Any fool can try to defend his mistakes—and most fools do." Pointing out that the way to reach a person's heart lay in attentive listening elicited this comment: "A boil on his neck interests him more than forty earthquakes in Africa." Observing that successful people were motivated by "the game" of competition, Carnegie concluded, "That is what makes foot races and hog-calling and pie-eating contests. The desire to excel." Such down-to-earth phrases established a feeling of commonality between author and audience, a feeling of common people nodding approval at common sense. [13]

Frequent flashes of humor worked to lighten his message. In discussing how environment and experiences shaped people, Carnegie wryly noted, "The only reason, for example, that you are not a rattlesnake is that your mother and father were not rattlesnakes. The only reason you don't kiss cows and consider snakes holy is because you weren't born in a Hindu family on the banks of the Brahmaputra." While advocating the importance of praising others, he remarked dryly, "You don't have to wait until you are ambassador to France or chairman of the Clambake Committee of the Elk's Club before you use this philosophy of appreciation." Carnegie admonished readers to refrain from telling others they were wrong, joking that "If you can be sure of being right 55 percent of the time, you can go down to Wall Street, make a million dollars, and marry a chorus girl." Such quips wiped away any sense of pretentious preaching and bonded author and reader.[14]

Throughout *How to Win Friends and Influence People*, Carnegie drew upon celebrity examples to underline the message that people who understood his maxims had risen to the top. The famous, the prominent, the wealthy, and the accomplished littered the pages of the book from beginning to end. They included political leaders such as Abraham Lincoln and Benjamin Disraeli; generals such as Napoleon and Ulysses S. Grant; entertainers such as Florenz Ziegfeld and Douglas Fairbanks; intellectuals such as William James and John Dewey; writers such as Charles Dickens and Ralph Waldo Emerson; philosophers such as Socrates and Immanuel Kant; and legendary industrialists such as John D. Rockefeller and Harvey Firestone. Anecdotes about or pithy quotations from well-known figures became proof of the validity of Carnegie's principles—he provided readers a glimpse of the secret of their success. For example, Carnegie related how Franklin D. Roosevelt, one of the most burdened and busy individuals in the world, took time to appreci ite those around him. When representatives of the Chrysler Corpor ition delivered a special car to the White House filled with "unusu il gadgets," FDR called the project director by name and made a show of praising its special features and elegant details. Then h : subtly reinforced their feeling of importance by announcing tha he had been keeping the Federal Reserve Board waiting for thirty r iinutes and had to go back to work. A few days later, a personal r ote arrived from the president. "Franklin D. Roosevelt knew that or e of the simplest, most obvious, and most important ways of gainin; good will was by remembering names and making people feel im portant—yet how many of us do it," Carnegie concluded.[15]

Fin: lly, Carnegie utilized his own techniques in reaching out to reader ;. He assumed a tone of unwavering enthusiasm, urging his reader ; to adopt "a deep, driving desire to master the principle of huma1 conduct." He appeared solicitous of readers' desires and discer iment instead of his own, inquiring rhetorically at the outset of his book, "after I have written it, why should you be bothered to rea l it?" He established a sense of common ground, noting that "Dea ing with people is probably the biggest problem you face, espec ally if you are a businessman. Yes, and that is also true if you : re a housewife, architect, or engineer." He evinced sympathy r: ther than superiority, telling readers, "Instead of condemning peop e, let's try to understand them. Let's try to figure out why they do w 1at they do." Even when laying down rules of conduct, he proc eded in a positive rather than a negative fashion. Instead of sayin 3 don't talk about yourself, he gently enjoined, "if you want peop e to like you, Rule 3 is: 'Remember that a man's name is to him he sweetest and most important sound in any language.' "[16]

A the heart of *How to Win Friends*, however, beneath its stylistic verve and enervating principles of conduct, lay a central idea that propelled it forward. After years of teaching, observation, and reading, Carnegie had become convinced that everyone yearned, above all, for recognition, and that a firm grasp of this fact held the key to success in modern America. He insisted that human beings, beyond their animal instincts for procreation and survival, shared a powerful "desire to be important . . . the craving to be appreciated. Here is a gnawing and unfaltering human hunger." The yearning to feel important drew his attention time and again in the book. "If you tell me how you get your feeling of importance, I'll tell you what you are . . . That is the most significant thing about you," he wrote. "You want the approval of those with whom you come in contact. You want recognition of your true worth. You want a feeling that you are important in your little world," he added. "Three-fourths of the people you will meet tomorrow are hungering and thirsting for sympathy. Give it to them, and they will love you," he concluded.[17]

This overweening human need for recognition triggered nearly all of Carnegie's advice for the shrewd success seeker. The key to getting ahead lay in meeting this craving for esteem, and in Carnegie's postulation, a subtle massaging of others' need to feel important would "win people to your way of thinking," advance your agenda, and boost your success in the process. He returned to this central argument repeatedly in *How to Win Friends*:

> There is one all-important law of human conduct. If we obey that law, we shall almost never get into trouble. In fact, that law, if obeyed, will bring us countless friends and constant happiness . . . That law is this: *always make the other person feel important.*
>
> The rest of us are just like you: we are interested in what we want. So the only way on earth to influence the other fellow is to talk about what he wants and show him how to get it.

Thus the essence of Carnegie's success advice boiled down to this maxim If you consistently and sincerely made others feel important, they would adopt your ideas, accept your leadership, and follow you anywhere.[18]

The state of American life in the 1930s gave tremendous cultural purchase to Carnegie's central idea in *How to Win Friends*. Since 1929, the Great Depression had torn gaping holes in the fabric of traditional American individualism and undermined the notion that hard work would produce success. This calamity had eroded people's sense of self-worth and prospects for feeling important, particularly in the middle class. Calling into question the possibility of achievement for many, and obliterating it completely for some, the Depression had created a great wave of shame, guilt, and fear that engulfed the country.

Evidence of personal frustration and pain appeared everywhere. Studs Terkel, who interviewed scores of Depression survivors, collected numerous stories of embarrassment and humiliation. A failed businessman recounted, "Shame? You tellin' me? I would go stand on that relief line, I would look this way and that and see if there's nobody around that knows me. I would bend my head low so nobody would recognize me." A young woman who was forced to leave a boarding school when her father lost his job reported, "I was mortified beyond belief." A psychiatrist who treated middle-class patients never forgot the "internal distress" among his patients who became unemployed. "A jobless man was a lazy good-for-nothing," he explained. "In those days, everybody accepted his role, responsibility for his own fate. Everybody, more or less, blamed himself for his delinquency or lack of talent or bad luck. There was an acceptance that it was your own fault."[19]

In popular culture, many iconic attractions of the 1930s shone a light on the individual's struggles to persevere against the odds.

The popular filmmaker Walt Disney portrayed Mickey Mouse in terms of "the triumph of the little guy," while his *Three Little Pigs* appeared as a parable of common folks vanquishing the Big Bad Wolf of the Depression. Superman, the popular comic-book hero, featured Clark Kent, the witless, bespectacled underachiever who dashed into the nearest phone booth to reemerge as a superhero and save Metropolis from disaster. It was the perfect Depression-era fantasy: the disparaged individual who carried the day secretly and became an object of mass admiration. Jack Benny, perhaps the most popular radio comedian of the age, garnered huge audiences as a self-deprecating antihero who suffered various indignities before overcoming them through humor. These figures reflected an all-too-common experience in the 1930s: individuals facing ritual humiliations and struggling to endure against the worst that society could throw at them.[20]

But this widespread emotional uneasiness led not to revolutionary agitation but to reinforcement of basic institutions. It was during this period that we find, for the first time, frequent references to the "American Way of Life" and "grass roots" became a characteristic phrase, a historian of Depression-era culture has pointed out. Rather than turning against the system, ordinary people sought to define an American pattern of living and immerse themselves in it. This populist search for roots—which ranged from regionalist painters such as Thomas Hart Benton to folk-music collectors such as Alan Lomax, literary cheerleaders such as Van Wyck Brooks, and village re-creationists such as Henry Ford—sought emotional security in the tradition of the folk. It flavored radio soap operas, which reached out to embattled housewives with stories of personal crises and recovery, promoting a sense that they were not alone in their problems and that widely shared values would triumph ultimately. It even flavored the popular politics of FDR. "We

were ag iinst revolution," the president noted of his election and
the New Deal. "In America in 1933, the people did not attempt
to reme iy wrongs by overthrowing their institutions. Americans
were m ide to realize that wrongs could and would be set right
within their institutions." Under the pressure of events, Americans
launche 1 "an effort to find, characterize, and adapt to an American
Way of Life."[21]

Thus widespread personal trauma and social uncertainty during
the Gre it Depression, and the search for solutions within the American tra lition, shaped a receptive audience for *How to Win Friends
and In uence People*. Carnegie showed a way out of the morass.
Recogr izing instinctively that people were desperately yearning to
feel im ortant and find distinction in an age where socioeconomic
conditi ms seemed to crush such possibilities, he offered a new template f r effective individual action. "Men are frequently astonished
at the iew results they achieve," Carnegie wrote. "It all seems like
magic." He claimed that mastery of his principles would "aid you
in you race for richer social and financial rewards. Say to yourself
over a id over, 'My popularity, my happiness, and my income depend t no small extent on my skill in dealing with people.'" The
author also replicated two traditional features of success literature:
self-ex imination and action. He urged readers to regularly set aside
a time for review of their actions where they could evaluate "what
mistal es you have made, what improvements, what lessons you
have l arned for the future." And he insisted that his was "an action
book" for putting principles into practice. "You've been reading this
book ong enough," he declared. "Close it now, knock the dead ashes
out of your pipe, and begin to apply this philosophy of appreciation
at on e on the person nearest you—and watch the magic work."[22]

Son ie astute observers understood the book's extraordinary
appea l as a success tract. "Dale Carnegie is a major prophet to

thousands of earnest, ambitious, and industrious Americans," wrote one journalist. "To them he is a mahatma, an oracle willing to share with the faithful his revelations on the erstwhile mysteries of how to be popular and get ahead." An evaluation in *The Saturday Evening Post* came even closer to the mark. "To a detached observer, the secret of the book's success seems fairly simple. Every man or woman who buys it is instantly handed, for the sum of $1.96, the information that he or she is potentially as powerful, brilliant, rich, and successful as anybody in the world, and perhaps a good deal more so than most," it maintained. "Like the beauty doctors and the professors of charm, Dale Carnegie sells people what most of them desperately need. He sells them hope."[23]

Carnegie, of course, was not the only success writer in the 1930s. Popular books such as Dorothea Brande's *Wake Up and Live!* (1936), Napoleon Hill's *Think and Grow Rich* (1937), and Norman Vincent Peale's *The Art of Living* (1937) and *You Can Win* (1938) also attracted an audience with recipes for personal advancement that included elements of positive thought, psychology, and spirituality. But Carnegie's *How to Win Friends and Influence People* soared far above any competition in the field of success writing. It did so by offering not airy thoughts on making money, achieving emotional stability, or finding spiritual repose but a practical method for reconstituting individual agency in an age when it seemed to be threatened with extinction. Carnegie insisted that the individual *could* act effectively and succeed, and showed him how to do so. And he conveyed the advice in a hopeful, buoyant, enthusiastic style that radiated the same optimism as the president of the United States. It is, perhaps, no exaggeration to say that much as Franklin Roosevelt saved capitalism during the Great Depression, Dale Carnegie saved the culture of individualism that accompanied it.[24]

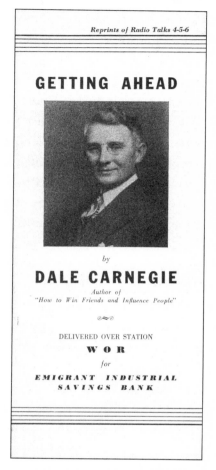

Reprints of Radio Talks 4-5-6

GETTING AHEAD

by

DALE CARNEGIE

Author of
"How to Win Friends and Influence People"

DELIVERED OVER STATION

W O R

for

EMIGRANT INDUSTRIAL
SAVINGS BANK

An advertisement for the Carnegie message of "Getting Ahead" delivered to a radio audience around 1940.

But the success message of Carnegie's book was more than a response to the crisis of individualism during the 1930s. It also reflected a longer, deeper trend. The rules given in *How to Win Friends and Influence People* for creating a sparkling personality and developing deft human relations skills reflected a sea change in American culture in the early twentieth century, one that wiped away the last vestiges of Victorian tradition and created a new institutional and personal landscape.

Charles Schwab played a starring role in *How to Win Friends and Influence People*. This influential industrialist had risen through the ranks at Carnegie Steel, from common laborer to foreman to Andrew Carnegie's right-hand man, and, finally, to the position of president of the company in 1897. Then in 1901, when J. P. Morgan bought Carnegie out and created U.S. Steel, the nation's first billion-dollar corporation, he appointed Schwab as its president. Schwab had first caught Dale Carnegie's attention in November 1916 when he published an article in *American Magazine* entitled "Succeeding with What You Have." The industrial manager wrote about the importance of a dedicated work ethic, of course, but he stressed even more the importance of motivating others, establishing partnerships, maintaining a positive attitude, and utilizing personal charm.[25]

Now the industrial magnate became a centerpiece of Carnegie's best-selling book. "Schwab's personality, his charm, his ability to make people like him were almost totally responsible for his extraordinary success; and one of the most delightful factors in his personality is his captivating smile," explained Carnegie. But there was more to it. Schwab also displayed a supple talent for negotiating difficult human situations. When one of his steel mills was under-producing and its manager could not improve things, he did not fire executives or berate workers. Instead, he ramped up the output by asking the night-shift foreman how many units it had turned out, chalking the number on the floor, and then walking away without comment. The day shift saw it and wanted to prove their ability, so they surpassed the output figure and chalked down a bigger one. The night shift responded, and shortly the mill's production improved dramatically. "The desire to excel! The challenge! Throwing down the gauntlet! An infallible way to appeal to men of spirit," gushed Carnegie. Another time Schwab was walking through one of his steel mills when he observed a group of men smoking beneath a sign that said "No Smoking." Again, he did not chastise. "He walked over to the men, handed each one a cigar, and said, 'I'll appreciate it, boys, if you will smoke these on the outside.' They knew that he knew that they had broken a rule—and they admired him because he said nothing about it and gave them a little present and made them feel important," wrote an admiring Carnegie. "Couldn't keep from loving a man like that, could you?"[26]

Such talents helped Schwab become perhaps the first person to earn a yearly salary of one million dollars, and Carnegie zeroed in on the reason. "Because Schwab is a genius? No. Because he knew more about the manufacture of steel than other people? Nonsense," the author wrote. He credited Schwab's knack for dealing with people and quoted the industrialist's own words: "I consider my ability to arouse enthusiasm among the men the greatest asset I possess . . . and the way to develop the best that is in a man is by appreciation and encouragement . . . I have yet to find the man, however great or exalted his station, who did not do better work and put forth greater effort under a spirit of approval than he would ever do under a spirit of criticism." For Carnegie, this advice became gospel, and one of Schwab's favorite phrases—"I am hearty in my approbation and lavish in my praise"—became an oft-repeated invocation.[27]

Schwab exemplified a potent ingredient in the recipe for success given in *How to Win Friends and Influence People*—becoming a compelling personality and master of human relations. In the process of rescuing American individualism from the ravages of the

Great Depression, Carnegie drew upon a decades-long transformation in the structure of personal life. As noted earlier, a shift from Victorian "character" to modern "personality" had accompanied the evolution of consumer capitalism and complex social structures in the early twentieth century. As one historian has noted, "In a society increasingly dominated by bureaucratic corporations, one dealt with people rather than things: 'personal magnetism' began to replace character as a key to advancement." In tune with this process, Carnegie had stressed the importance of personality in his earlier books and urged students to develop enthusiastic, forceful, attractive qualities to project.[28]

Now Carnegie went much further. True to form, he disparaged "the old adage that hard work alone is the magic key that will unlock our desires." But whereas, earlier, personality had served as an important factor in public speaking, now in *How to Win Friends* it became the absolute center of a larger process in seeking success. Freed from its moorings in public speech, the charismatic, compelling personality shot forward to become the very essence of the Carnegie creed of rejuvenated individualism. Readers of his book could imbibe its principles, and like Schwab, stride to success on the basis of personal charm.[29]

Carnegie skillfully pursued this theme. He laid out the qualities of the pleasing personality in "Six Ways to Make People Like You," beginning with selflessness. A subtle, sensitive persona, radiating care and concern, proved tailor-made for the impersonal, unnerving world of bureaucratic interaction that had solidified by the 1930s. Success in modern institutions, Carnegie understood, flowed not from people obeying, respecting, deferring to, or fearing you, but from *liking* you. One's personality, as he put it famously, was for "winning friends."[30]

Then Carnegie moved on to trickier but strategically critical terrain in his campaign for personality development. An attractive personality might win friends, but how exactly did it produce the "influencing people" element that was truly crucial to gaining success? Somehow, in other words, personality had to be put into practice to propel one forward. Earlier, Carnegie had claimed that displays of confidence, enthusiasm, and accomplishment automatically would attract followers because "People flock around the energetic speaker, the human dynamo of energy like wild geese around a field of autumn wheat," as he put it in 1926. But Carnegie realized that the "hearty in approbation and lavish in praise" model he now espoused was more complex and must be deployed subtly. It led him to engage the field of "human relations," as he termed it. It influenced, not forced, others to your way of thinking. So human relations, in Carnegie's innovative hands, became the emotional fulcrum upon which the modern culture of personality turned.[31]

He quickly summoned a legendary American businessman as an expert witness on this point in *How to Win Friends*. In his heyday, Carnegie claimed, John D. Rockefeller had asserted that "'the ability to deal with people is as purchasable a commodity as sugar or coffee . . . And I will pay more for that ability,' said John D., 'than for any other under the sun.'" Carnegie added his personal testimony on the importance of human relations. After encountering thousands of students over the years, "I realized that sorely as these adults needed training in effective speaking, they needed still more training in the fine art of getting along with people in everyday business and social contacts," he wrote. "I also gradually realized that I was sorely in need of such training myself. As I look back now across the years, I am appalled at my own frequent lack of finesse and understanding." In fact, he continued, "I myself had been searching for years to discover a practical, working handbook on human relations. Since no such book existed, I have tried to write one."[32]

How to Win Friends and Influence People provided a good deal of guidance on how to deal with others in a bureaucratic atmosphere. Carnegie especially focused on a central human relations maxim: The successful personality persuaded others to follow his lead without them knowing it. By not criticizing, but by showing appreciation and expressing "hearty approbation and lavish praise," he made others feel important and his pleasing personality imperceptibly assumed a position of strength as colleagues and coworkers, their self-esteem gratified, stood ready for guidance. But convincing others that they held the reins was crucial. "When we have a brilliant idea, instead of making the other person think it is ours, why not let him cook and stir the idea himself?" counseled Carnegie. "He will then regard it as his own; he will like it and maybe eat a couple of helpings of it."[33]

In the aptly entitled chapter "Making People Glad to Do What You Want," Carnegie provided illuminating examples of this human relations expertise at work. Woodrow Wilson, when asking William McAdoo to join his cabinet as Secretary of the Treasury, made it seem that acceptance of the position would be doing him an enormous favor. McAdoo agreed to do so, feeling an enhanced sense of importance and of loyalty to the president. J. A. Want, head of a large printing house in New York, was faced with a mechanic who constantly complained about the long hours and excessive work required to keep scores of typewriters and printing machines running smoothly. The company head replied by giving him a small office, lettering "Manager of the Service Department" on the door, and granting the man recognition and a feeling of importance. The complaints stopped. These gambits responded to people's needs—"such is human nature," observed Carnegie—and provided convincing evidence for his central human relations principle: "Make the other person happy about doing the thing you suggest."[34]

Once again, Carnegie gathered celebrity endorsements for his strategy of personality development and emotional maneuvering. The rich and the famous, the accomplished and the highly placed, movie stars and world leaders and billionaire businessmen and prestigious writers all lined up to testify to the efficacy of the Carnegie method. Whether it was Henry Ford on the need to see the other person's point of view, Teddy Roosevelt on enthusiastic interactions with others, Henry James on allowing everyone their own path to happiness, Harvey Firestone on giving people the opportunity to excel, Sol Hurok on the benefit of extending sympathy to others, or Dorothy Dix on the great value of praise and appreciation between spouses, the book provided a host of prominent personalities whose examples, as well as their words, reinforced the author's larger message.[35]

Thus Carnegie, in his wildly popular *How to Win Friends and Influence People*, created a dynamic success message for modern America. What Benjamin Franklin had been for the village republic of the 1700s, and Horatio Alger for the Victorian industrial society of the 1800s, Dale Carnegie now became for the dynamic consumer society of twentieth-century America. Gathering many of the earlier impulses from his life and career—an intense desire to get ahead, a belief in personality development, a keen sense of the bureaucratic context of modern life, a growing awareness of the centrality of human interaction—he presented a set of principles that promised achievement and upward mobility. With the trauma of the Great Depression serving as the catalyst, and the long-term shift from character to personality providing a vessel, a process of cultural fusion in the 1930s produced the Carnegie creed. With its stress on making others feel important and developing human relations skills, this success message addressed a thoroughly modern need: to sell *yourself* as a way to climb upward. This notion of "winning friends and influencing people" thoroughly refashioned traditional American individualism for the twentieth century.

For all of its significance as a modern success tract, however, Carnegie's best-selling book also resonated more deeply. Drawing upon its author's longtime interest in positive thought and psychology, the volume explored many of the recesses of the human psyche and analyzed the play of emotions and hidden impulses in human behavior. It emerged as a landmark text, all the more powerful for its popularity, in the advance of modern therapeutic culture in America.

11

"We Are Dealing with Creatures of Emotion"

Psychology held Dale Carnegie firmly in its grip, as *How to Win Friends and Influence People* made clear. Lowell Thomas, in his rousing introduction to the book, described his old friend's efforts as "a striking combination of public speaking, salesmanship, human relations, and applied psychology." In his own preface, Carnegie recounted his engagement with the work of Alfred Adler, William James, and Harry A. Overstreet as he spent much time "plowing through erudite tomes on psychology." Observers noted this influence. A review in *The Literary Digest* concluded that Carnegie, with his focus on "the desire for self-esteem" and the yearnings that erupted when "the ego is undernourished," certainly had paid attention to what "the psychologists tell him." Homer Croy, writing in *Esquire*, began his long piece on "Dale Carnegie's golden text" by quoting James's comment on humans "making use of only a small part of our physical and mental resources." "Whether or not modern psychologists will hold to the belief is beside the point," Croy quipped. "Dale does and that's all that matters."[1]

Indeed, the striking psychological element in *How to Win Friends* showed the book to be something more than a modern success primer for anxious Americans. The author dug deeper into human impulses, probed more searchingly in shaping his formula for advancement. Carnegie's infatuation with psychology, of course, stretched back to the 1910s, when he had first become attracted to "positive thought" and "mind cure," and it influenced his earlier teaching and writing. But now, in the heart of the Depression crisis, he moved a psychological perspective to an elevated spot in his best-selling book. At the very outset of the text, Carnegie relayed his intent to "Make the principles of psychology easy for you to apply in your daily contacts." He underscored this sensibility a bit later. "When dealing with people, let us remember that we are not dealing with creatures of logic," he reminded readers. "We are dealing with creatures of emotion."[2]

This reliance on psychological analyses, formulations, and recommendations made Carnegie a key figure in shaping a powerful new paradigm in modern American culture. Since the early 1900s, psychological discourse had emerged with growing power in many different areas. Instead of older Victorian moral certainty, a new ethos emerged that was preoccupied with personality development, personal happiness, interpersonal relations, and self-fulfillment. A form of individualism less concerned with religious salvation or overt economic profit than with emotional well-being—what Philip Rieff has termed "psychological man"—emerged visibly in the early decades of the twentieth century. Carnegie, operating in the pressurized atmosphere of the Great Depression, emerged as perhaps the greatest popularizer of psychological discourse in the middle decades of the twentieth century. He unfolded a compelling worldview where the psychological status and manipulations of the self lay at the center of both personal and social life. Such notions became a foundation for modern therapeutic culture.[3]

Carnegie's fascination with psychology, which had influenced his teaching and writing for years, burst into full flower in the 1930s. It played a major role in the Dale Carnegie Course in Public Speaking and Human Relations, where his students were "trained to use the significant discoveries of modern psychology—discoveries that increase very materially the effectiveness of their business interviews." Carnegie emphasized that the class promoted "the development of self-expression, of individuality and personality. It brings out and nurtures one's latent powers as nothing else can." Advertising described the course agenda as "Public Speaking for Business Men, Scientific Salesmanship, and Practical Psychology" and characterized it as a program "for men who realize that they must use all the discoveries of modern psychology in the fine art of getting other people to do what they want them to do."[4]

This abiding concern with psychology was strengthened by Carnegie's professional engagement with a number of psychologists, psychiatrists, therapists, and counselors in the greater New York area. When *How to Win Friends and Influence People* appeared to tremendous fanfare, newspaper and magazine stories on the Carnegie operation noted the raft of psychology-oriented teachers and writers who surrounded the course founder, either as part of the regular teaching staff or by delivering special talks. This group revealed much about Carnegie's mind-set by the mid-1930s, as well as the nature of his popular book.[5]

Harry A. Overstreet stood at the top of the list. A social psychologist and pioneer in adult education, he influenced Carnegie's thinking tremendously. Overstreet, educated at the University of California at Berkeley, taught in the Department of Philosophy and Psychology at the City University of New York and presented continuing-education courses at the New School for Social Research. He first came to Carnegie's attention, however, with his provocative and much-discussed book *Influencing Human Behavior* (1925). It had originated as a series of class lectures at the New School on "how human behavior can actually be changed in light of the new knowledge gained through psychology." The resulting book—a reviewer described it as "psychology put to work"—asserted that "the human individual is moved by a multitude of wants, of most of which he is not even conscious." Anyone seeking to influence human actions must grasp the overwhelming influence of nonrational mental life, he argued strenuously.[6]

Overstreet contended that "our chief task in life is to make our personality, and what our personality has to offer, effective in our particular environment of human beings." Life involved many things, of course—seeking food and shelter and sexual gratification; playing, fighting, aspiring, grieving—but at the center of it stood "the process of getting ourselves believed in and accepted." Thus Overstreet explored methods by which the individual could capture the attention of others, win their regard, and induce them to think and act along with him. "In this search after means, we shall find no little help in what modern psychology has to offer," he wrote. "The businessman has already discovered, in a measure, what psychological understanding can do for him; the factory manager is beginning to discover it. Education, in its more progressive aspects, is pushing vigorously into psychological fields." Overstreet focused on the importance of prompting "yes-responses" from others, a tactic that "set the psychological processes of his listener moving in the affirmative direction." He also contended, "We wish to be looked up to—by somebody, preferably by as many as possible . . . As a matter of fact, the wish to be thought well of, particularly by those of whom we think well, is quite fundamental."[7]

Those who influenced others, according to Overstreet, played to these psychological impulses. They maneuvered to get "yes-responses," granted appreciation and esteem, and understood that people acted according to their perception of a "real want," which was his phrase for "human desire." "This, perhaps, is the best piece of advice which can be given to would-be persuaders, whether in business, in the home, in school, in politics," noted Overstreet; "first arouse in the other person an eager want. He who can do this has the world with him. He who cannot walks a lonely way!" Or as he put it at another point, "The secret of all true persuasion is to induce the person to persuade himself. The chief task of the persuader, therefore, is to induce the experience. The rest will take care of itself."[8]

Overstreet's ideas had a profound impact on Carnegie. As early as 1928, in his "Damned Fool Things I Have Done" file, Carnegie wrote, "As Professor Overstreet says, 'Make the other person feel happy about becoming what you wish him to become' . . . I need to practice this rule consciously until it becomes a part of me, part of my unconscious behavior." He also noted an Overstreet article in McCall's that contained an important point. "The art of successfully influencing people consists in getting 'welcoming in' responses and never, under any circumstances, getting a 'shutting out' response," Carnegie quoted. "What now are the ways in which we can get 'welcoming in' responses? The first is the way of appreciation— the easiest of all psychological techniques and one scarcely used at all. How true. How tragically true!!" By the mid-1930s, Carnegie had introduced himself to Overstreet and persuaded him to present regular lectures on the psychology of human relations in the

Carnegie Course. Many of the social psychologist's ideas would become gospel in *How to Win Friends and Influence People*.[9]

Henry C. Link became another important figure in Carnegie's psychological circle. This versatile and accomplished psychologist had been raised in a devoutly Methodist household near Buffalo, New York, and attended a small religious college in Illinois before transferring to Yale, where he studied philosophy and psychology and earned a PhD in 1916. After graduation he supervised the psychological testing of employees at several corporations and published articles on industrial psychology and several books, including *Employment Psychology: The Application of Scientific Methods to the Selection, Training and Grading of Employees* (1919). In 1931, Link joined the Psychological Corporation, a commercial enterprise founded by the eminent psychologist James M. Cattell, which aimed to provide psychological expertise to institutions on a "business-like basis." Link became the director of its social and market research, developing a "psychological barometer" for interpreting consumer behavior, and a "personality quotient" test that purported to measure an individual's personal qualities. In 1932 Link authored *The New Psychology of Selling and Advertising*—John B. Watson, the famous behavioral psychologist, wrote the introduction—and advised the Adjustment Service of New York City, which administered psychological examinations to help fifteen thousand unemployed men and women find jobs.[10]

Link drew Carnegie's attention, however, with his best-selling 1936 book, *The Return to Religion*. This volume, which went through thirty-four printings over five years and then a "dollar edition" in 1941, explained the author's re-embrace of the religious tradition of his youth after many years of agnosticism. As he described it, however, this restoration of faith was not a case of the prodigal son's return but a move prompted by behaviorist psychology, a "mathematical and quantitative science" that was "just as precise in its methods as were chemistry and physics a hundred years ago." Rejecting the "speculative theories" of Freud and his successors, Link argued that religion performed an important utilitarian function—shaping a healthy "personality" consisting of "habits and skills which interest and serve other people." Psychological testing, he claimed, indicated that "individuals who believed in religion or attended a church had significantly better personalities than those who did not." According to Link's behaviorist viewpoint, "The mind, coupled to religion, is a stronger mind for it, and a mind not so readily swayed by the passions that parade as reason."[11]

The key to Link's argument, and the aspect that intrigued Carnegie, was his notion of a healthy personality. It was not the "introvert," who consistently turned inward to address his own concerns, but the "extrovert," looking to encourage and assist others, who should be emulated. "The introvert, or selfish person, avoids the trouble of meeting people, the extrovert goes out of his way to meet them. The introvert evades the obligations and demands of clubs and committees, the extrovert accepts them. The introvert, or selfish person, may think of doing good deeds, the extrovert does them," wrote Link. Moreover, religion played a crucial role in shaping the extrovert. "Jesus Christ, the ideal of unselfishness and the great exponent of the unselfish life, was an extrovert," he wrote. Since humans were naturally selfish and inclined to follow the dictates of impulse, "It requires religion, or something higher than the individual or even a society of individuals, to overcome the selfish impulses of the natural man and lead him to a more successful and fuller life."[12]

Link's ideal of the genial extrovert, and his endorsement of religion as a powerful tool of personal development, excited Carnegie's

admiration. As with Overstreet, he convinced Link to present special lectures in the Carnegie Course and publicized the association.
And in *How to Win Friends and Influence People*, Carnegie relied
on Link's formulations to construct his model for seeking success.
"If you want to develop a more pleasing personality, a more effective skill in human relations, let me urge you to read *The Return
to Religion*, by Dr. Henry Link," he wrote. "It was written by a
well-known psychologist who has personally interviewed and advised more than three thousand people who have come to him with
personality problems."[13]

Vash Young, while not a trained professional like Link or Overstreet, emerged as another important psychological influence on
Carnegie because of his fervent advocacy of positive thought and
mind cure. The descendant of an important Mormon family in Salt
Lake City, Young had suffered from depression, self-doubt, and debilitating fears as he struggled to find success as a salesman. After
years of spinning his wheels, he finally developed a philosophy that
catapulted him to great success as a life insurance salesman. Eager
to share his secrets with others, he authored two popular books in
the 1930s on success-seeking and personal development. This is
where Carnegie discovered him.

Young's formula rested on two primary supports: positive
thought and a resolve to help others. In his first book, *A Fortune
to Share* (1931), this advocate of mind power detailed his "victory
over my own mental processes" as he battled to eradicate negative
thoughts and cultivate "affirmative thinking." Like earlier positive
thinkers such as Elbert Hubbard, Russell Conwell, James Allen,
and Orison Swett Marden, Young concluded that happiness or
unhappiness, success or failure was largely a matter of aligning
your thoughts in an affirmative pattern that would lead irrevocably forward. Everyone owned a "thought factory," as he put it

at one point: "Nothing can go into it, neither raw materials nor partly manufactured goods, except on your permission. Nothing can come out of it except the products that you yourself design." The turning point in his life, he believed, came when he gained "dominion over my own emotions and thoughts" and banished "harmful mental habits and emotional weaknesses." He concluded, "We human beings have a lot of mental power we do not realize. The trouble is that we destroy that power by letting fear and panic dethrone the normal and proper functioning of our intellects."[14]

Young pursued his second theme—providing service to others— at length in *The Go-Giver: A Better Way of Getting Along in Life* (1934). He built upon his belief in positive thought to advocate a paradigm shift in thinking about one's career. Young contended that the old tradition of the "go-getter"—the hard-driving individual who pushes himself relentlessly in search of social advancement and profit—must give way to "a positive program of go-giving." This meant abandoning old thought habits of "self-pity," "secret doubts and fears," "false pride," and "an inferiority complex brought on by disappointment in getting." Instead, one should embrace a new mind-set of "self-confidence based on the desire to give" and "rejoicing in the success of others." This meant rising above mere selfish "acquisitiveness" and serving others: "the go-getter makes a good living. The go-giver's plan is different. He makes for himself, first of all, a good *life*."[15]

But Young gave an important twist to this message. Selflessness, in his formulation, was not just altruistic but had subtle consequences that rebounded in favor of the giver. While the go-giver sincerely strived to provide the best in service, sympathy, loyalty, and products to others, those others would return his emotional investment with interest. As Young counseled readers, "Give, asking nothing in return. And why? Because if you become a sincere go-giver, you will not need to ask a return. Success will hunt you up and ask the privilege of paying your rent." The go-giver's "good life nearly always brings along with it a good living, including financial rewards which the go-getter often misses." Young presented a formula for doing well by doing good.[16]

Such ideas powerfully attracted Carnegie. His own roots in positive thinking made Young's argument enormously compelling. For any individual who was tempted to focus on his own narrow perspective and interests, wrote Carnegie in *How to Win Friends*, "I ought to give him copies of Vash Young's excellent books, *The Go-Giver* and *A Fortune to Share*. If he read those books and practiced their philosophy, they would make him a thousand times as much profit." In fact, Carnegie adopted large parts of Young's blueprint. A list of questions for readers in *The Go-Giver* could have been found in almost any section of *How to Win Friends*: "Do people have confidence in you? Do they like you? Can you be unselfish? . . . Do you try to give the best possible return on the investment others make in you? Are you an affirmative, hopeful thinker?" As with Link and Overstreet, Young also became a featured lecturer in the Carnegie Course by the 1930s.[17]

Arthur Frank Payne, another noted psychologist, entered Carnegie's orbit in the 1930s and contributed to his thinking. Highly educated with degrees from the University of Chicago, Columbia University, and Harvard, Payne enjoyed a long teaching career at several prominent universities. During World War I, he had directed psychological surveys for the U.S. War Department and then managed the New York Guidance Clinic throughout much of the 1920s. Payne wrote on applied psychology, editing several vocational education texts and assisting with the magazine *Vocational Education*. One of his articles, "The Scientific Selection of Men," conveyed his belief in the profound possibilities opened up by psychology. A noteworthy feature of "our present civilization and particularly of our industrial and commercial development is the application of science to all phases of our everyday life," he insisted. "The new science of psychology has standardized certain scales, measures, and tests for measuring general intelligence" and this promised enormous dividends in "making a selection of certain men for certain jobs, position, and types of work."[18]

By the 1930s, Payne had reached out to the public and caught Carnegie's attention. He published *My Parents: Friends or Enemies* (1932), which argued for a psychologically informed approach to child rearing. One of his ten commandments to parents enjoined, "You shall not develop in your children that evil thing called an 'inferiority complex,' by continually making them feel inferior to yourself, to others, or to the world generally. You shall always help them build up their confidence in themselves." In another commandment, he instructed, "You shall when correcting or admonishing your children, always say something of a commendatory nature and express disappointment rather than anger, rage, or bitterness." Such advice influenced Carnegie's emphasis on the positive reinforcement of others in *How to Win Friends and Influence People*. Moreover, Payne hosted *The Psychologist Says*, a popular radio show that ran on the New York station WOR from 1929 to 1936. There he presented psychological perspectives on the issues of the day and counseled listeners on overcoming personal problems that might be damaging their daily lives. Carnegie hired him as a special lecturer in the Carnegie Course, where Payne frequently gave a talk entitled "How to Overcome an Inferiority Complex."[19]

This concern with the inferiority complex was also shared by Louis E. Bisch, the only trained psychiatrist in Carnegie's circle of colleagues in the 1930s. Bisch had received an MD and a PhD from Columbia University in 1912, after which he became a practicing psychoanalyst, consultant, and author concerned with a wide range of mental maladjustments. Over the next few years he taught educational psychology at Columbia, directed the Speyer School for Atypical Children in New York City, ran the Psychopathic Lab for the New York City Police Department, and supervised the Mental Hygiene Clinic in Norfolk, Virginia. In 1926, he took a position as a professor of neuropsychiatry at the New York Polyclinic Medical School and Hospital, where he would serve for the next four decades. In the 1920s Bisch also published several noteworthy books on psychoanalysis and personal development: *The Conquest of Self*, *Clinical Psychology*, and *Your Inner Self*. In 1925, he wrote a dramatic play entitled *The Complex*, which focused on a young woman who is led to recovery from a mental collapse by the efforts of a kindly, insightful psychoanalyst.[20]

As with these other figures, it was Bisch's endeavors in more accessible venues in the 1930s that drew Carnegie's attention. Bisch began to write widely for the popular press: a newspaper series on psychology and success; magazine articles such as "Successful Men's Sons Often Failures" and "Turn Your Sickness into an Asset"; and trade journal articles such as "Psychiatry and Advertising: Why Copy Should Appeal to Human Emotions." He even trained his expertise on Hollywood, writing "Have All Actors an Inferiority Complex?" and "Why Hollywood Scandals Fascinate Us" for *Photoplay*, and "Psycho-Analyzing the Hollywood Divorce Epidemic" for *Screen Book*. In many of these articles, Bisch examined the enervating effects of the inferiority complex. He described how it "prompts the continuous and tormenting struggle to make believe that we are other than we really are," and maintained that "Failure has more to do with the 'inferiority complex' than we realize." His most probing treatment of this theme came in, surprisingly, an address to dentists entitled "The Relationship of the

Inferiority Complex to Orthodontia." He turned to the theories of Alfred Adler to argue that "if there is an organic defect in any part of the anatomy there is likely to be a compensatory reaction in the brain." Thus many patients requiring orthodontic work were harboring "inferiority feelings" because of a physical defect and required psychologically sensitive treatment.[21]

Bisch's biggest public impact came with his chatty 1936 best seller, *Be Glad You're Neurotic*. He argued, in a perky and irreverent style, that neurosis offered a blessing in disguise for those suffering its symptoms. Bisch carefully noted that he did not mean severe neurotics with powerful obsessions requiring professional treatment. Instead, he meant milder varieties of neurosis where the individual is plagued by pangs of uncertainty, compulsion, self-doubt, frustration, discontent, and low self-esteem. This condition tormented many people, indeed almost everyone, at one time or another in life. According to Bisch, however, while these symptoms signaled "some maladjustment in the emotional life" they also revealed a keen sensitivity to the world. If successful adjustments could be made, the neurotic individual stood ready for great achievements. "When we're neurotic there is unrest inside us," he wrote. "Yet his unrest is merely the sign that we are gaited for better things; that we have not yet found ourselves."[22]

In practical terms, this meant facing and overcoming the neurosis that usually created a three-part malady. "Guilt, shame, inferiority—there's a triumvirate to conjure with!" exclaimed Bisch. "Always are they together, always do they work in unison, always do they exercise the role of the dictator to crush your spirit and make you humble." But where could the sufferer turn? For Bisch, salvation lay in a combination of psychoanalysis and positive thought. "Put your *will* to work; don't falter and you *can't* fail! All you have to do is keep at it long enough," he wrote. "What happens inside your unconscious mind is this: First you neutralize, then obliterate old reflex arcs—in other words, habits that have throttled you and prevented you from being what you want to be. Next new reflex arcs come into being to replace the old ones, new ones designed to make you efficient, that will carry you where you want to go, that will make you glad." The last sentences of his book summarized his remedy: "Analyze Yourself. Stop Feeling Guilty. Give Your Ego a Boost. Turn Your Handicaps Into Assets. Profit By Your Neurosis. Then BE GLAD!" By the mid-1930s, Bisch was making regular appearances as a lecturer in the Carnegie Course.[23]

Several other psychological experts also orbited Carnegie in the 1930s, although they did so at a greater distance than Overstreet, Link, Young, Payne, and Bisch. This secondary group included Kenneth Goode, a former editor at *The Saturday Evening Post* and *Hearst's International* who later worked for a New York advertising agency. He had a special interest in the psychology of merchandising, selling, and advertising and his popular 1929 book, *How to Turn People into Gold*, caught Carnegie's attention. "[S]uccess in dealing with people depends on a sympathetic grasp of the other man's viewpoint," Carnegie quoted Goode. Arthur Gates, a professor at Columbia University, also attracted Carnegie with his book *Psychology for Students of Education* (1933). "Sympathy the human species universally craves. The child eagerly displays his injury," Carnegie quoted Gates. "For the same purposes, adults show their bruises, relate their accidents, illnesses, details of surgical operations. 'Self-pity' for misfortunes real or imaginary is, in some measure, practically a universal practice." These men honed Carnegie's sense that making the other person feel important held the key to garnering influence and success.[24]

On marriage and family issues, Carnegie was drawn to the work of a trio of experts. Leland Foster Wood, an influential minister and writer who specialized in pastoral psychology and counseling, declared in *Growing Together in the Family* (1935), "Success in marriage is much more than finding the right person; it is a matter of *being* the right person." Dr. G. V. Hamilton, the director of psychobiological research for the Bureau of Social Hygiene, wrote in *What Is Wrong with Marriage?* (1929), "It would take a very prejudiced and very reckless psychiatrist to say that most married friction doesn't find its source in sexual maladjustment." Pastoral psychologist Reverend Oliver M. Butterfield, the director of the Family Guidance Service in New York City and author of *Sex Life in Marriage* (1936), insisted that "in spite of romance and good intentions, many couples who come to the marriage altar are matrimonial illiterates." Carnegie utilized these statements to buttress his argument for a psychologically sensitive approach to marriage and sexual relations.[25]

Thus Carnegie's psychological associates converged in their belief that insights from the new mental science could be used to solve the problems of the world. Although most were highly trained, members of his circle were far less interested in theory than in the practical application of psychology to improve human endeavor. Equally important for Carnegie, they also frequently directed their expertise to the personal struggle for achievement and advancement. Such influences proved powerful. Carnegie gathered a host of ideas from these experts, synthesized them, and created a powerful psychological dynamic at the very heart of his broader success message in his blockbuster book of the mid-1930s.

From its first pages, *How to Win Friends and Influence People* bombarded readers with psychological principles, perspectives, and recommendations. Carnegie consistently employed psychologized language to convey his ideas and drew upon an impressive array of therapeutic experts to buttress his claims. "The famous Dr. Sigmund Freud of Vienna, one of the most distinguished psychologists of the twentieth century," wrote Carnegie, "says that everything you and I do springs from two motives: the sex urge and the desire to be great." He noted another famous psychologist's stress on the human need to be valued: "William James said, 'The deepest principle in human nature is the craving to be appreciated.'" Carnegie cited the famous American behaviorist John B. Watson and his declaration that "Sex is admittedly the most important subject in life. It is admittedly the thing which causes the most shipwrecks in the happiness of men and women." But Carnegie exhibited a special fondness for Alfred Adler, the famous Viennese psychotherapist, and his book *What Life Should Mean to You* (1931). In that volume, wrote Carnegie, Adler declared, "It is the individual who is not interested in his fellow men who has the greatest difficulties in life and provides the greatest injury to others. It is from such individuals that all human failures spring." Carnegie enjoined, "You can read scores of erudite tomes on psychology without coming across a statement more significant for you and me."[26]

In a general way, psychology prompted Carnegie to consistently look for the hidden emotional, even unconscious, underpinnings of human actions. So he took a close look at human beings and their mental processes and discovered a welter of influences and impulses, many quite unpleasant, which directed their course in life. He concluded that people were "prejudiced and biased. Most of us are blighted with preconceived notions, with jealousy, suspicion, fear, envy, and pride." He offered this dictum: "When dealing with people, let us remember that we are not dealing with creatures of logic. We are dealing with creatures of emotion, creatures bristling with prejudices and motivated by pride and vanity."[27]

Studio portrait of Dale Carnegie as he became a national celebrity in the late 1930s.

Like many in his circle of associates, Carnegie held a utilitarian view of psychology, valuing it as a road map for action as much as a process for understanding. Applied psychology appeared in *How to Win Friends and Influence People* as a method for handling people deftly in one's own interest. "If we want to make friends, let's greet people with animation and enthusiasm," he instructed. "When somebody calls you on the telephone, use the same psychology. Say 'Hello' in tones that bespeak how pleased you are to have that person call." He explained that Andrew Carnegie had learned as a boy that everyone saw their own name as precious, and then as an adult "made millions by using that same psychology in business," remembering and using the names of dozens of commercial contacts. He described how President Calvin Coolidge complimented his secretary on her appearance before telling her to be more careful about her punctuation in letters. "His method was a bit obvious, but the psychology was superb," Dale Carnegie observed. "It is always easier to listen to unpleasant things after we have heard some praise of our good points." He extolled Benjamin Franklin's technique of asking help from others on some matter that utilized their talents or knowledge. Gratified by this recognition of their importance, they would eagerly assist in every way. In Carnegie's words, "Ben Franklin has been dead now for a hundred and fifty years, but the psychology that he used, the psychology of asking the other man to do you a favor, goes marching right on."[28]

As he taught others how to win friends and influence people, Carnegie frequently turned to "positive thinking," the movement that first had attracted his interest twenty years earlier. Now he continued to insist that mind power and mental transformation held the key to finding success in the modern world. Positive thought shaped several important proposals in *How to Win Friends and Influence People*. The aspiring individual, its author counseled, could shape the image he presented to others through force of mind. "You don't feel like smiling? Then what? Two things. First, force yourself to smile. If you are alone, force yourself to whistle or hum a tune or sing. Act as if you were already happy, and that will tend to make you happy," Carnegie instructed. "Everybody in the world is seeking happiness—and there is one sure way to find it. That is by controlling your thoughts." Positive thinking also could be used to subtly influence the behavior of others. In Carnegie's words, "if you want to improve a person in a certain respect, act as though that particular trait were already one of his outstanding characteristics . . . assume and state openly that the other person has the virtue you want him to develop. Give him a fine reputation to live up to, and he will make prodigious efforts rather than see you disillusioned."[29]

Carnegie's positive-thought proclivities were shared by other influential cultural figures in the 1930s. Norman Vincent Peale embraced positive thought as he launched his storied career during the Great Depression. Called to become minister of the prestigious Marble Collegiate Methodist Church in New York City, he joined forces with the psychologist Dr. Smiley Blanton to establish a therapeutic clinic. This pastoral endeavor, which combined psychological counseling with Christian religious guidance, featured a trained staff of psychologists and psychiatrists who advanced a self-described "religio-psychiatric" agenda. Eventually called the American Foundation for Religion and Psychiatry, this institution furnished the basis of Peale's message in *The Power of Positive Thinking* (1952), the massive best seller that became the centerpiece of his religious empire in the postwar era.[30]

Among advice writers, Napoleon Hill garnered a large audience with a rather airy version of positive thinking in his popular book *Think and Grow Rich* (1937). This mind-power apostle maintained that a positive mental attitude would lead automatically, if somewhat mysteriously, to the accumulation of wealth. "Whatever the mind can conceive and believe, the mind can achieve," he insisted. "Riches begin with a state of mind, with definiteness of purpose, with little or no hard work." The success seeker needed a mental transformation, according to Hill, and he offered readers "six steps to stimulate your subconscious mind." These included fixing the exact amount of money they wished to accumulate and then repeating it to themselves "once just before retiring at night and once after arising in the morning." It was Carnegie, however, embracing concepts that were circulating in 1930s culture, who created the most dynamic and practical version of success through mind power.[31]

Carnegie also drew upon adjustment psychology in formulating his principles in *How to Win Friends*. By the 1930s, a number of psychological theorists were turning away from the Freudian emphasis on the hidden, inner self to explore the individual's relationships with the larger society as the seedbed of psychological issues. Often called neo-Freudians, these thinkers deemphasized the powerful impulses of the unconscious and stressed interpersonal relations and the individual's struggle to adjust to social demands as the key factors in shaping human behavior and happiness. In many ways, they followed in the tradition of Alfred Adler, the distinguished psychotherapist who had broken with Freud, his close associate, in the 1910s. Adler had insisted that the social realm was as important to human psychology as the interior realm and began to explore notions of personality development that he outlined in books such as *The Neurotic Constitution* (1912), *The Practice and Theory of Individual Psychology* (1927), and *What Life Should Mean to You* (1931). There he focused on the inferiority complex (especially attempts to compensate for it) and the psychological importance of the individual's interactions with groups in the larger community: family, friends, work associates, society itself.[32]

By the 1930s, a number of American neo-Freudians were building on the Adlerian foundation. Karen Horney stood prominently among this group. A German immigrant, she had received her medical degree from the Humboldt University of Berlin in 1911, developed an interest in psychoanalysis, and became an associate at the Berlin Psychoanalytic Institute in 1918. Migrating to the United States in 1932, she first took a position in Chicago and then moved to the New York Psychoanalytic Institute. She also began teaching at the New School for Social Research in 1935, where she presented a popular lecture series entitled "Culture and Neurosis." Her impact spread widely with the publication of two books: *The Neurotic Personality of Our Time* (1937) and *New Ways in Psychoanalysis* (1939).[33]

Horney departed from Freudian orthodoxy in two crucial ways. First, she rejected the masculine bias of traditional psychoanalysis and insisted that women followed their own model of mental development. Second, and more broadly, she argued that "social and cultural factors, not the presumably uniform 'biological' experiences of infancy and early childhood, such as the Oedipus complex and other 'stages' of psychosexual development, were crucial to the formation of neuroses," as one scholar described. Horney believed that the individual's need for affection often clashed with hostile social and cultural factors, thus creating anxiety, insecurity, and eventually neurosis. But the culture also provided opportunities for receiving warmth, security, and appreciation and thus a pathway for escaping anxiety. Individuals who successfully adjusted to their environment could overcome "the neurotic personality of our time."[34]

Harry Stack Sullivan constructed another, self-consciously American version of adjustment psychology. After receiving a medical degree from the Chicago College of Medicine and Surgery in 1917, he became a practicing psychiatrist. By the 1930s he had moved to New York, started to publish articles and papers, and became a founder of the journal *Psychiatry* and the head of the Washington School of Psychiatry. During these years, Sullivan developed close professional ties with Horney and other like-minded intellectuals in New York, and began to move in a neo-Freudian direction.[35]

Sullivan emerged, in the phrase of one observer, as "the founder of the psychiatry of interpersonal relations." He contended that cultural factors—particularly a strict sexual morality rooted in religion—were at the source of anxiety and neurosis in modern America. A remedy lay in the improvement of interpersonal relations, which would aid the individual in adapting to parental demands, social prescriptions, and cultural expectations. The neurotic could be put on the road to recovery first by a skilled psychotherapist who could help him understand his problems, work toward self-mastery, and build self-esteem. Therapy focused on helping the individual adapt to the peer group and find a secure, nurturing place within it. "It seems beyond argument," wrote Sullivan, "that there is an improvement in personality if one changes from obvious psychoses to a considerable measure of ability to live in one's environment." Adjustments to social and cultural conditions would foster "self-esteem," a term coined by Sullivan that would become ubiquitous in modern American culture.[36]

Neo-Freudians (or more accurately, perhaps, neo-Adlerians) such as Horney and Sullivan shaped an intellectual atmosphere in the 1930s where a psychology of interpersonal relations, socially rooted personality development, adjustment mechanisms, and self-esteem assumed a central position. Horney and Sullivan stressed, in the words of one observer, "the techniques by which the individual might better adapt to his environment, the channels through which eccentric or abnormal behavior could flow into more manageable patterns of behavior." This position gained reinforcement from other intellectual directions as well. Proponents of "ego psychology," such as Heinz Hartmann, presented the ego as the most prominent factor in personality development: a powerful, resilient agent of reason and control with an "ability to adapt and thereby master the external world." The "culture and personality" school of anthropology also lent support through figures such as Ruth Benedict. "The life-history of the individual is first and foremost an accommodation to the patterns and standards traditionally handed down in his community," she wrote in her influential *Patterns of Culture* (1934). "From the moment of his birth the customs into which he is born shape his experiences and behavior." Industrial psychologists such as Elton Mayo urged corporate managers to utilize psychological techniques to help workers reconcile themselves to the demands of modern industrial organization. With a common emphasis on adjusting to social demands and cultural expectation, all of these arguments dovetailed with the neo-Freudian position.[37]

Carnegie, of course, was no intellectual and there is no evidence that he read Horney or Sullivan, Hartmann or Benedict or Mayo, although he did dip into Adler's work. As always, however, he remained remarkably sensitive to his cultural milieu, and adjustment psychology was in the air. Personifying a linkage between highbrow theory and popular expression, Carnegie became conversant with this movement through interpreters such as Overstreet, Link, and Payne and created an accessible version of it in *How to Win Friends and Influence People*. A popular psychologist par excellence, he mixed elements of adjustment psychology—adapt to your social environment, develop interpersonal relations, hone your personal skills—into a new concoction promising happiness and success to millions of Americans.[38]

Adjustment psychology provided much of the basis for Carnegie's recommendation that individuals should enhance their personalities. He approvingly cited Adler's assertion that it is "the individual who is not interested in his fellow man who has the greatest difficulties in life." He praised his associate Link as an inspiration for those who "want to develop a more pleasing personality" to deal with others. Carnegie conveyed a host of techniques for shaping an attractive personal image—smile, have a positive attitude, be interested in the other person's interests, be a good listener—that were rooted in social interaction. Clearly, the sparkling personality of Carnegie's successful striver that allowed him to fit in, make friends, maneuver skillfully through a web of social demands, and find economic success had roots in the adjustment-psychology ethos of the 1930s.[39]

Adjustment psychology also informed Carnegie's view of those upon whom the striving individual acted: discovering what they

wanted, meeting their needs, quenching their desires, and bolstering their self-esteem. He turned to Overstreet's "illuminating book,
Influencing Human Behavior," for "the best piece of advice which
can be given to would-be persuaders, whether in business, in the
home, in schools, in politics: first, arouse in the other person an
eager want. He who can do this has the whole world with him. He
who cannot walks a lonely way." He summoned associate Arthur
Gates, who declared in his *Educational Psychology*, "Sympathy the
human species universally craves." Carnegie cited Sigmund Freud,
John Dewey, and William James on the human yearning to feel
important, and concluded, "We nourish the bodies of our children
and friends and employees; but how seldom we nourish their self-
esteem. We provide them with roast beef and potatoes to build
energy; but we neglect to give them kind words of appreciation
that would sing in their memories for years to come like the music
of the morning stars."[40]

This entire panorama of needs and impulses created a process of
psychological adjustment that Carnegie labeled "human relations."
Getting along with others, winning friends, and influencing people
demanded sensitivity to the psychological yearning for self-esteem
and security, apropos of the Adler-Horney-Sullivan school. *How
to Win Friends and Influence People* was larded with psychologically tinged counseling tips on "How to Make People Like You
Instantly," "How to Get Cooperation," "A Quick Way to Make
Everybody Happy," and "the fine art of making friends out of enemies." Carnegie admonished, "We like to be consulted about our
wishes, our wants, our thoughts," and instructed, "Let the other
fellow feel that the idea is his." Carnegie's popular psychology of
human relations was summed up in his sentimental recollection
of a boyhood pet, Tippy the dog. "You never read a book on psychology, Tippy. You didn't need to," he wrote. "You knew by some

divine instinct that one can make more friends in two months by becoming genuinely interested in other people than one can in two years by trying to get other people interested in him."[41]

In the final analysis, however, Carnegie was most interested in applied psychology. Above all, he sought the practical application of psychological principles to help success seekers adapt to modern bureaucratic life, learn to manipulate it, and prosper. Thus he identified the "yes-response" as the crucial psychological technique for handling people effectively. Carnegie's entire program of praising, bolstering, and encouraging others was aimed at triggering a positive "welcoming in" response from them. As Overstreet argued in *Influencing Human Behavior*—Carnegie quoted it at length—the individual who handles others skillfully "gets at the outset a number of 'yes-responses.' He has thereby set the psychological processes of his listeners moving in the affirmative direction . . . The organism is on a forward-moving, accepting, open attitude. Hence the more 'yeses' we can, at the very outset, induce, the more likely we are to succeed in capturing attention for our ultimate proposal." Those who confront others and try to argue their way to influence and success nearly always fail. They are, Carnegie wrote, "psychologically stupid."[42]

Ultimately, of course, the adjustment psychology popularized in Carnegie's book and propounded in elevated intellectual circles by the neo-Freudians, gained much of its popular appeal from the social and economic trauma of the 1930s. Its creation of widespread personal shame and guilt among the middle class created a sympathetic audience for a psychological ethos of interpersonal relations, security and belonging, and enhanced self-esteem. One might think of this period as the "Age of Adler," historian Warren I. Susman has suggested. "[T]he effort appears to be—both in popular psychology and in the rising schools of professional analysis—to find some

way for individual adjustment, for overcoming shame and fear—
perhaps Adler's 'inferiority complex'—by adopting a life-style that
enables one to fit in, to belong, to identify."[43]

As the exploding sales of *How to Win Friends and Influence
People* clearly indicated, Carnegie had put his finger squarely on
America's psychological pulse during the painful days of the Great
Depression. The soothing allure of adjustment psychology in his
book attracted millions of anxiety-ridden readers struggling to survive, both financially and emotionally. But the psychological qualities of this best-selling text also had a longer-term impact. They
made it a key development in the creation of America's modern
therapeutic culture.

By the 1930s, the Dale Carnegie Course in Effective Speaking was
promising a challenging emotional experience for its participants.
Interactions with and criticisms from one's fellow students would
aid in learning to project a compelling personality to others. According to a promotional pamphlet, Session Eleven, for example,
would help students see themselves through others' eyes. "When
your turn comes, you will stand up before the audience, but you
won't make a talk—you will listen while other people talk about
you and the impression you make on them. They will praise your
good points and they will tell you very gently but honestly of faults
you ought to eradicate and how to make your personality more
appealing," it explained. "Everyone will be urged to be absolutely
frank, and to reveal his innermost thoughts about you."[44]

Ultimately, happy results awaited those who completed the
journey, as copious testimonials from Carnegie Course graduates
attested. Throughout the 1930s, Carnegie hosted promotional
meetings for his courses that featured fifteen to twenty recent

graduates who followed one another across the stage and testified to the life-changing impact of the principles they learned. "Their speeches suggested the 'confessions' that sinners give at revival meetings after they have been saved," reported one newspaper. A typical testimonial came from a forty-year-old salesman with a family who, by his own account, was "suffering from an inferiority complex" that was "eating his heart out." Frightened of dealing with others, he walked up and down in front of an office half a dozen times before he could summon enough courage to open the door. He had become so discouraged that he was thinking of working in a machine shop. But after taking the Carnegie Course, "he lost all fear of audiences and individuals," his income began to soar, and he became "one of the star salesmen in New York City."[45]

A writer from *The New Yorker* heard similar sentiments when he visited a Carnegie course for a feature story in 1937. Students were asked to explain why they had taken the course, and feelings of emotional inadequacy often surfaced. One man confessed, "when I went to college something terrible got hold of me—an inferiority complex. I still got it, too. I can't go out with a crowd of folks without getting scared." Another student spoke similarly: "I've got an awful inferiority complex, really, and I want to overcome it." Once again, however, according to *The New Yorker*, course graduates promised success in surmounting such psychological hurdles. "Mr. Carnegie infuses courage into the most timid and backward men so that they undertake and achieve things that surprise them," wrote one. Said another, "It is not exaggeration to state that this course marked a definite turning point in my life." One student said simply, "I owe everything that I count as a success in my entire life to Dale Carnegie's teachings in human relations." For a middle-aged man who read *How to Win Friends and Influence People* and then took the course, the only regret was that he came to the program so late. In his rueful words, "If I had read this book ten years ago I would be better off today, mentally, physically, and financially."[46]

The emotional process at work in the Carnegie course—confessing vulnerability, confronting weakness, seeking emotional growth, pursuing personal self-improvement—displayed all the hallmarks of a new therapeutic mind-set taking shape in modern America. In the aftermath of an older Victorian creed of tight-lipped self-control and upright moral character, modern Americans increasingly embraced a new value system dedicated to emotional self-fulfillment and sparkling personality. And a key part of this new orientation, as historian T. J. Jackson Lears has described, was a worldview emphasizing "self-realization in the world—an ethos characterized by an almost obsessive concern with psychic and physical health defined in sweeping terms."[47]

In this powerful new cultural paradigm, several concerns predominated. Psychologized readings of human nature led modern individuals to develop an "intense preoccupation with the self," as Christopher Lasch termed this tendency. Mental health, "the modern equivalent of salvation," became the overarching goal as therapists and counselors took their stations as new guides to happiness, peace of mind, and success. In fact, the pursuit of psychological well-being became a way of life as ideals of "personal growth" and an "abundant life" permeated the culture, influencing everything from religion to child rearing, education to marriage. This therapeutic ethos gave rise to novel mechanisms such as therapy sessions, encounter groups, personal counseling, and self-help books that proclaimed the promise of personal transformation. "Psychotherapy became directed, in a more general way, to the total enhancement of living," historian Richard Weiss observed. "Indeed, psychology was changing from a discipline of study into a way of life. Health, always the aim of therapy, began to take on a vastly expanded meaning."[48]

The new therapeutic mind-set appeared full-blown in *How to Win Friends and Influence People*. Carnegie presented human problems as primarily psychological ones and counseled readers to approach others without making moral judgments. "Instead of condemning people, let's try to understand them. Let's try to figure out why they do what they do," he counseled. "As Dr. Johnson said, 'God himself, sir, does not propose to judge man until the end of his days.' Why should you and I?" Developing sensitivity to others involved an effort to implant certain attitudes in your psyche, Carnegie contended. "Keep it on the desk in front of you every day. Glance through it often," he recommended of his book. "Keep constantly impressing yourself with the rich possibilities for improvement that still lie in the offing. Remember that the use of these principles can be made habitual and unconscious only by a constant and vigorous campaign of review and application. There is no other way." He even urged a mental drill to aid in the process of internalizing psychological adroitness: "Say to yourself over and over: 'My popularity, my happiness, and my income depend to no small extent upon my skill in dealing with people.'"[49]

Carnegie's bright promises of personal transformation cemented the therapeutic worldview. Appearing as a folksy yet inspirational popular therapist, he claimed that his surefire methods for dealing with others would "literally revolutionize the lives of many people." He proudly quoted from students and readers thrilled with the changes in their lives, both economically and emotionally. "I find that smiles are bringing me dollars, many dollars every day," reported one. "And these things have literally revolutionized my life. I am a totally different man, a happier man, a richer man, richer in friendships and happiness—the only thing that matters much, after all." Said another, "It all seems like magic." For Carnegie, these personal transformations were the inevitable result of psychological adjustments in dealing with others. "I am talking about a new way of life," he declared. "Let me repeat. *I am talking about a new way of life.*"[50]

Ultimately, as Philip Rieff has observed, such therapeutic formulations produced "psychological man" as the ideal type of modern individualism. "As cultures change, so do the modal types of personality that are their bearers," he has written, and in the twentieth century the "psychologizers" have created the individual whose main commitment is to the self. Unlike "religious man," for whom moral uprightness and salvation were the ultimate goals, or even "economic man," who doggedly pursued his self-interest in the competitive race for profit, psychological man turned inward to cultivate psychological and physical well-being as the essence of happiness. Preaching "the gospel of self-fulfillment," Rieff has noted, "psychological man has constituted his own careful economy of the inner life. The psychological man lives neither by the ideal of might nor by the ideal of right, which confused his ancestors . . . Psychological man lives by the ideal of insight— practical, experimental insight leading to the mastery of his own personality . . . [P]sychological man has espoused the ideal of salvation through self-contemplative manipulation."[51]

Carnegie's *How to Win Friends and Influence People*, drawing from an array of psychological influences in the early twentieth century, became a founding text of modern therapeutic culture. This great popularizer disseminated psychologized values to every nook and cranny of middle-class America beginning in late 1936, and in so doing emerged as the father of the modern self-help movement. In his wake would come a long line of personal-growth disciples and self-improvement publications that would become ubiquitous within a few decades. Under his influence, "psychological man" (and shortly, "psychological woman") became a cultural goal toward which countless citizens bent their efforts.

But despite the vast popularity and influence of *How to Win Friends and Influence People* as a how-to success tract, a guidebook for personality development and human relations, and a crucial event in the establishment of modern therapeutic culture, not everyone was enamored of it. Within weeks of its initial publication, the book triggered an outburst of criticism and debate. As with its popularity, the controversy surrounding the book would linger for decades.

12

"Every Act You Ever Performed Is Because You Wanted Something"

Within a few weeks of publication in early 1937, Dale Carnegie's *How to Win Friends and Influence People* shot to the top of the best-seller list for nonfiction. A great wave of acclaim and vast sales carried the book to a pinnacle of popularity, and testimonials to its life-changing impact began pouring in. "If I couldn't replace this book I wouldn't sell it at any price. The contents are priceless," wrote one delighted reader. "Have never read anything that so stirred my ambition. Will read it many times," testified another. Sales would continue nearly unabated, and over the next ten years the book would go through more than ninety reprintings and sell millions of copies.

But critical acclaim lagged far behind popular approval. Many newspapers, magazines, and journals of opinion ignored the book completely, and those that did pay notice usually offered lukewarm assessments. "You may snicker at the advice to make the other fellow feel important ... You may scorn the 'yes man' implication, the syrupy drooling. But you can't laugh off the fact that the folks we like best, those with whom we like best to spend our time, are those who endow us with the warm glow of being recognized for

what we like to think we are," admitted one reviewer rather grudgingly. Most assessments were much harsher. *The Nation* sneered
that Carnegie "has given us the best outline of the science of tail-
wagging and hand-licking ever written." *The New York Times* substituted condescension for disdain, describing the best seller as a
banal how-to book peddling hope to a pathetic audience of "wish-
ful millions who have never been able to influence other people
much, who would like to begin life all over again even though they
are past 40, who long to be told how they can think for themselves,
who live alone and hate it." *How to Win Friends and Influence
People* became an object of controversy as the intellectual establishment largely dismissed its principles and denounced its human
relations strategies.[1]

Carnegie brushed off such scornful evaluations. He dismissed his
critics as elitists who were jealous of his popular appeal and insu-
lated from the demands facing ordinary people who sought success
in the real world of business competition. In 1938, he described a
recent appearance before the Dutch Treat Club in New York where
its president introduced him rather ungraciously by noting that
most of his listeners were antagonistic to the principles in his book.
Taking it in stride, Carnegie made a charming presentation. In private, however, he described the club as a gathering of the "intelli-
gentsia who would sneer at any popular book . . . If a man can take
a book that has been rather popular and attack it—it gives him a
feeling of importance." Another time, when a prominent minister
denounced *How to Win Friends* as "the most immoral book of this
generation," Carnegie retorted that the attack merely gave the at-
tacker "an opportunity to get in the limelight himself."[2]

But in fact, Carnegie often struggled noticeably with certain
aspects or implications of his own creed. As critical controversy
unfolded, discussion highlighted several important moral, social,

and political ambiguities embedded in the book. The author, for example, insisted that readers not see his recommendations as a cynical strategy for flattering your way to the top, but then instructed, "Three-fourths of the people you will meet tomorrow are hungering and thirsting for sympathy. Give it to them and they will love you." He urged the reader to "Make the other person feel important—and do it sincerely," but then advised them to promote their own agendas by taking advantage of this malleability in others. In his words, "every act you ever performed since the day you were born is because you wanted something." Carnegie confronted the old dilemma of the Protestant Ethic—how to square virtue with wealth—and reacted uncomfortably. He liked to declare, "Don't get the foolish idea that happiness depends on money," but then repeatedly assured readers that his book would enhance their "earning power" and produce "increased sales" and "increased pay," and he filled the text with admiring references to the wealthy tycoons.[3]

Such issues generated considerable contention. As controversy enveloped *How to Win Friends*, critics zeroed in on several conundrums in the Carnegie creed. Even as the book took the country by storm, and skyrocketing sales made its author one of the most famous and influential people in the country, larger questions arose about the accuracy of Carnegie's portrait of modern America and his method for achieving success in it. Easy answers proved elusive.

Imitation is the sincerest form of flattery. Never did this old dictum appear truer than seven months after the publication of *How to Win Friends and Influence People*, when Irving Tressler presented a very funny parody of it entitled *How to Lose Friends and Alienate People*. Turning the Carnegie volume on its head, Tressler satirized it chapter for chapter, theme for theme, illustration for illustration, sometimes word for word. As *Time* magazine quipped, this cranky volume was "the only book which is today offsetting the 20-year drive by American advertisers to make everyone in this country popular with everyone else."[4]

Tressler began with a dedication mocking Carnegie's perky, positive thinking: "This Book Is Dedicated to a Man Who Doesn't Need to Read It: Adolf Hitler." It continued with an introduction by "Thomas Lowell" entitled "A Short Cut to Indistinction," which related the excitement surrounding a recent fictitious gathering at a New York hotel of several hundred people who had come to hear a lecture by Irving K. Tressler, head of the "Institute of Human Relations Up to a Certain Point and How to Keep Them at that Point." This meeting exemplified "the new movement stampeding across the country today—a movement to help people gain the privacy and seclusion they have wanted all their lives, and leave them unpestered by 'friends.'" Tressler's teachings were becoming legendary, the introduction claimed facetiously. He had helped thousands learn that "some of us are born with the ability to make others peeved, but most of us aren't . . . The trouble with most of us is that we don't talk enough. We let the other person get in his views and opinions and permit him to think that we are interested in what he has to say. As a result, we have 'friends' who drop in to say hello, corner us on streets to point out what we already know about the weather, invite us to boring dinners." This great teacher counted "each course lost which doesn't end in a free-for-all fist fight. He is proud that today he is unable to travel anywhere without a bodyguard, proud that thousands of ex-pupils have sworn to 'get that son of a - - - -!'"[5]

Tressler had an impressive background in journalism. Born in 1908 and a graduate of the University of Wisconsin, he had worked in the Washington bureau of the *Minneapolis Journal* in the early

1930s before becoming an associate editor of *Life* magazine. A humorist and commentator on social affairs, Tressler contributed many articles to magazines such as *Look*, *Scribner's*, *Coronet*, *Esquire*, *Mademoiselle*, and *Parent's Magazine*. He wrote several books that pilloried American foibles, including *With Malice Toward All* (1939), *Horse and Buggy Daze* (1940), and *Readers Digest Very Little* (1941). Sadly, he would commit suicide in 1944. Suffering from a severe form of epilepsy, which at the time was still misunderstood as a mental disorder, he had been dismissed from a number of positions in the magazine world. After psychiatrists were unable to help him understand, or cure, his uncontrollable fits, he finally fell victim to depression and ended his life.[6]

In *How to Lose Friends and Alienate People*, however, Tressler's satirical talents emerged full-blown. He gleefully mocked Carnegie's principles, cultural style, and goals. "This book is the outgrowth of years of experience in being bored," he declared at the outset. "It is the result of thousands of statements commencing, 'We know you're terribly busy, so we're only staying a minute—!'" He granted Carnegie's assumption that everyone wanted to feel important but drew a different conclusion: "It is this feeling of importance that must be deflated in every person we meet and don't want to meet again." He offered a warped version of human relations: "Be generous with your acid and lavish with your contempt. If you do, people will remember your words—remember them long after they have ceased speaking with you." A jovial, if caustic, critic of everything Carnegie stood for, he unfolded a friend-destroying strategy in chapters entitled "Always Turn a Conversation into an Argument," "How to Make People Dislike You Instantly," and "How to Discourage Overnight Guests."[7]

Other critics eschewed the jokes and mockery but followed Tressler's lead in attacking *How to Win Friends* for its principles of human conduct. The targets were there. Beneath Carnegie's breezy, anecdotal style and enthusiastic recommendations for success lay several disturbing tendencies that made the book a troubling, occasionally treacherous guide to social behavior in the modern world. Foremost among them was the issue of sincerity.

A central theme of Carnegie's best seller, of course, was the message of appreciation and sincerity. Repeatedly he instructed readers to "Give honest, sincere appreciation. Be 'hearty in your approbation and lavish in your praise,' and people will cherish your words and treasure them and repeat them over a lifetime." Developing sensitivity to the concerns of acquaintances and associates—let a person know that "you recognize his importance in his little world, and recognize it sincerely"—became a mantra throughout the text. But Carnegie subtly suggested that the real object of such concern was priming others to act to your advantage. In an almost symmetrical pattern, instructions on how to make others receptive to your agenda appeared side by side with appeals for sensitivity. In other words, calculation often appeared to be the driving force behind empathy. "Tomorrow you will want to persuade somebody to do something. Before you speak, pause and ask: How can I make him *want* to do it?" Carnegie noted at one point. At another, he observed, "if a salesman can show us how his services or his merchandise will help us solve our problems, he won't need to sell us. We'll buy."[8]

Indeed, Carnegie sometimes exhibited outright cynicism about human relations in *How to Win Friends*. While explaining how to become a good conversationalist by encouraging others to talk about themselves, he recounted a recent experience at a cocktail party. After discussing travel with a woman and listening intently, he concluded tartly, "All she wanted was an interested listener, so she could expand her ego and tell about where she had been." While urging the male reader to improve his home life by complimenting his wife, praising her fashion sense, and offering appreciation of her cooking and housecleaning, he gave the game away by cautioning, "Don't begin too suddenly—or she'll be suspicious." Carnegie frequently endorsed a method of strategic losing on small matters in order to conquer on large matters: "Let's let our customers and sweethearts and husbands and wives beat us in the little discussions that may arise"—thus giving in to another viewpoint was not so much a technique for humility as a ploy for gaining ultimate advantage by letting others feel superior. "I have quit telling people they are wrong," he wrote. "And I find that it pays." In Carnegie's view of society, every individual has two reasons for taking an action, "one that sounds good and a real one." While in our hearts we know the real reason for our actions, we "like to think of the motives that sound good."[9]

Carnegie even admitted that his central principle—making others feel important—was at bottom a tactic of emotional one-upsmanship. After telling a story about how he had complimented someone on their appearance to make them feel good, he explained that the maneuver put him in a superior position: "I got the feeling that I had done something for him without his being able to do anything whatever in return for me. That is a feeling that glows and sings in your memory long after the incident is passed." He related another tale of how a mistake on his radio show solicited a scorching rebuke from a member of the Colonial Dames. Although angry at the woman's rudeness, he controlled his emotions, called her, admitted his unforgiveable blunder, thanked her profusely for pointing it out, and begged her forgiveness. Soon he had her apologizing for her rashness and complimenting him for being so gracious. "I had the satisfaction of controlling my temper, the satisfaction of returning kindness for an insult," he smugly related of this ploy. "I got infinitely more real fun out of making her like me than I could ever have gotten out of telling her to go and take a jump in the Schuylkill River."[10]

Carnegie's ambiguous treatment of sincerity caused many critics to pan *How to Win Friends* as a primer on the cynical, self-regarding manipulation of others. In a scathing evaluation, Dr. John Haynes Holmes, the pastor of the Community Church in New York City, assailed Carnegie's principles as "mockeries of friendship, insults to virtue, and conspiracies of scorn for human kind." He summarized the book's strategy as "Play up to your friend's weaknesses, and you'll trap them . . . He tells us people want just two things—praise and feeling of importance. Therefore, he says, give them praise. They want it, so lay it on thick. Then you'll be able to do anything you want with them. What could be simpler?" As Holmes contemptuously concluded, "the thought that one should flatter, cajole, and lie to win a friend is disreputable."[11]

Others expressed similar complaints. "There is a subtle cynicism, to be sure, in directions which depend so largely upon flattering the other man's egotism," observed a reviewer for *The New York Times*. He complained that Carnegie had substituted smoothness for substance with his notion that "the superficial cultivation of 'personality' may take the place of—or even be more important than—a sound foundation of knowledge, intelligence, and ability." In the *New York Daily News*, Doris Blake contended that Carnegie was teaching people how to "sell a bill of goods . . . whether an egg beater or a suburban estate" with instructions to "sneak up on your victim with a spoken tribute to the importance of his or her position in the world." A reviewer for the *Paterson Morning Call*, a New Jersey paper, warned that the book advocated "the constant application of a cagey brand of soft-soap." But papering over differences of opinion created a toxic atmosphere of dishonesty in

social intercourse. "I think there are times when it is in order to
snarl, show your teeth, and keep full sail ahead . . . When I hear a
man loudly championing all the philosophies which seem to me
hollow and preposterous, I am likely to get my five cents into the
pot sooner or later," he wrote. "I am for the man who speaks his
mind when there is any occasion for him to speak his mind, and
lets the chips fall and the eyebrows rise where they may."[12]

James Thurber, the popular author and humorist, focused on
the vexed issue of sincerity in a review in the *Saturday Review of
Literature*. Noting the author's profound ambivalence regarding
the crucial matter of genuine regard for others versus the use of
praise to find their soft spot, Thurber decided that manipulation
overrode authenticity in the book. "Mr. Carnegie loudly protests
that one can be sincere and at the same time versed in the tricks of
influencing people," he wrote. "Unfortunately, the disingenuities in
his set of rules and in his case histories stand out like ghosts at a
banquet." Carnegie's emotional insistence that he was not urging
people to get something out of others—"What was I trying to get
out of him!!!" he exploded in exasperation at one point—did not
sway Thurber from this conclusion. As he acerbically concluded,
"exclamation points, even three in a row, do not successfully convey depth of sincerity or intensity of feeling."[13]

Attacks on Carnegie for promoting an ethic of social deception also
came in private venues. In a letter to the popular author, W. W. Woodruff of Chattanooga, Tennessee, denounced *How to Win Friends*
as a reflection of the same "philosophy of dishonesty" that had
taken over the advertising industry and the legal profession. The
notion of playing to people's weaknesses and flattering their sense
of self-importance was a kind of trickery that "is reflected throughout your entire scheme of influencing people . . . We don't need to
inflate personal egotism; it needs deflation. We don't need 'smart'

businessmen; we need honest ones with guts and some sense of humanity and responsibility." This rather cranky old-fashioned moralist advised Carnegie to in the future "use your talents toward influencing people against intellectual dishonesty rather than toward it, and . . . help to abate this flood of infectious poison [flowing] into the intellectual bloodstream of our nation."[14]

For some commentators, Carnegie's take on sincerity prompted surrealistic humor. They envisioned a bizarre scene where acolytes of *How to Win Friends* would gather in a cacophony of mutual praise where everyone's build-up of others would ultimately cancel each other out. In Carnegie's world, wrote columnist Heywood Broun, the good salesman never talks about himself, and the good customer highlights the virtues of the salesman, so finally "the whole thing comes out just the same as if each had talked about himself in the normal manner." Similarly, the *New York World-Telegram* questioned the value of an encounter between ardent disciples where "two people kept on agreeing with each other, congratulating each other, and insisting that the other talk about himself."[15]

In many ways, however, the Carnegie ethic was no laughing matter. Fears of deception grew especially intense when he urged the use of psychological manipulation in even the most intimate of relationships. The final section of *How to Win Friends* provided readers with a formula for domestic tranquillity. It was vintage Carnegie but left a sour aftertaste. He told women readers to become adept in "the art of handling men," the first rule of which was to realize that males "are not looking for executives but for someone with allure and willingness to flatter their vanity and make them feel superior." The ideal was not the female office manager who wanted to talk about modern philosophy and insisted on paying her own bill, for "she thereafter lunches alone." Instead, men preferred the company of "the non-collegiate typist [who], when invited to luncheon, fixes an incandescent gaze on her escort, and says yearningly, 'Now tell me more about yourself.' "[16]

Similarly, Carnegie instructed husbands to consistently compliment their wives on housekeeping skills, attractive appearance, and fashion sense. He argued that women had provided men, or at least those who were alert enough to notice, "a complete book on how to work her." "Every man knows that he can jolly his wife into doing anything, and doing without anything. He knows that if he hands her a few cheap compliments about what a wonderful manager she is, and how she helps him, she will squeeze every nickel," he maintained. "Every man knows that he can kiss his wife's eyes shut until she will be blind as a bat, and that he has only to give her a warm smack on the lips to make her dumb as an oyster."[17]

In both cases, the problem was less sexism—in fairness, only a tiny minority of men in the mid-1930s would *not* have believed in innate male superiority—than manipulation. Carnegie's images— of a female approaching a male armed with "incandescent gazes" and techniques for "flattering their vanity," and a man approaching his wife dispensing cheap compliments and a few kisses to make her "dumb as an oyster"—paints an unsettling portrait of love and personal relationships. Tact, affection, and appreciation are one thing; techniques for how to "work" your spouse are something quite different.

Perhaps the most unsettling implication of Carnegie's ethic of sincerity, however, concerned the success seeker himself. Suspicions about manipulating others—colleagues, associates, friends, even spouses—ultimately turned inward to raise questions about self-manipulation. *How to Win Friends* seemed to advocate a program where the individual constantly remade himself into whatever he sensed other people wanted to see. The sensitive, insightful person, in Carnegie's rendering, put on and took off a series of masks that allowed him to advance his own agenda according to the singular demands of any situation. He tightly managed himself, in addition to reading the weaknesses of others, in the interest of what Carnegie termed "human engineering." This species of self-manipulation proposed playing a part, if necessary, to get the desired result.[18]

Carnegie's blueprint for self-shaping also explained how to deliberately, conscientiously make yourself appealing to others. Whenever confronting a problem in human relations, he recommended, "hesitate about doing the natural thing, the impulsive thing. That is usually wrong. Instead, turn to these pages and . . . try these new ways and watch them achieve magic for you." He praised a Carnegie Course graduate who devoted every Saturday evening to "the illuminating process of self-examination and review and appraisal" where he would "think over all the interviews, discussions, and meetings that have taken place during the week. I ask myself, 'What mistakes did I make that time?' 'What did I do that was right, and in what way could I have improved my performance?' " Carnegie's engineering of the self constructed a model of modern individualism composed entirely of serial images, with no sturdy commitments or beliefs, no firm moral standards, no authentic and rooted core of self. It consisted only of a pliable personality eager to please others and to advance socially and economically.[19]

On some level, Carnegie recognized that his creed of sincerity provided the keystone for his entire program, and when it was challenged he reacted defensively. In *How to Win Friends*, he acknowledged, "Some readers are saying right now as they read these lines, 'Soft soap! Bear Oil! Flattery! I've tried that stuff. It doesn't work, not with intelligent people.' " He went on, "Of course, flattery seldom works with discerning people. It is shallow, selfish, insincere . . . The difference between appreciation and flattery? That is simple. One is sincere and the other insincere. One comes from the heart out; the other from the teeth out." He declared indignantly, "The principles taught in this book will work only when they come from the heart. I am not advocating a bag of tricks. I am talking about a new way of life."[20]

In fact, Carnegie could become emotional in responding to accusations of insincerity. Answering one such critic, he burst out, "No! No! No! I am not suggesting flattery! Far from it. I am talking about a new way of life. Let me repeat. *I am talking about a new way of life.*" He reported an incident where a listener responded to his advocacy of making the other person feel important by asking what he wanted to get out of the other person. "What was I trying to get out of him!!! What was I trying to get out of him!!!" Carnegie exploded. "If we are so contemptibly selfish that we can't radiate a little happiness and pass on a bit of honest appreciation without trying to screw something out of the other person in return—if our souls are no bigger than sour crab apples, we shall meet with the failure we so richly deserve." These outbursts revealed his recognition of the seriousness of this issue.[21]

For all of these vehement protestations, however, Carnegie harbored less idealism than he usually admitted publicly. While conducting a question-and-answer session for course instructors in 1938, he was asked what to do if a student was applying his principles in an insincere manner. Carnegie's answer conveyed a deep-rooted pragmatism bordering on cynicism. "Well, in the first place, let's not moralize," he said. "Let's put it on a practical basis only. In fact, I sometimes tell audiences I might as well call this talk, 'What You Want and How to Get It.' All I am interested in is what *you* want and the best way to get what *you* want. Will insincerity get it? . . . If insincerity would get it, then let's use insincerity." When another trainee asked about a student who wanted to be truthful rather than displaying tact, Carnegie replied similarly. "Anything that works best—use it!" he declared. "Oh, of course we must tell people the truth occasionally . . . But all I'm saying is this. Let's do it in a way that will get us the result we want, instead of getting the very opposite of what we want." Carnegie viewed success and advancement, in other words, as far more important than one's sincerity in achieving those goals.[22]

Ultimately, the strategies in *How to Win Friends* raised old fears about a legendary culprit in American culture: the confidence man. The con man, first arising with the market revolution in early nineteenth-century America, was a charming, glib, conniving figure who assumed any appearance, told any story, bent any rule to separate people from their money and advance upward. He deployed tricks, deception, and insincerity in pursuit of the main chance. James Fenimore Cooper had described the emergence of the con man as "the age of Dodge and Bragg" in his novel *Home as Found*. P. T. Barnum had incorporated many of the wiles of the con man in his career as a showman, while Herman Melville had made him a representative American in his book *The Confidence-Man: His Masquerade*. Mark Twain, memorably, had satirized the con man in his novel *The Gilded Age*, through the character of Colonel Sellers.[23]

Many critics saw Carnegie as a modern manifestation of this figure, only now operating openly in the mainstream of society as an ideal rather than lurking in the shadows as a villain. In the words of Sinclair Lewis, Carnegie, using sincerity as a ploy, had risen to fame by "telling people how to smile and bob and pretend to be interested in people's hobbies precisely so that you may screw things out of them."[24]

Carnegie long feared this image and did his best to avoid it. As early as 1915, in his first book, *The Art of Public Speaking*, he reported seeing a "faker" selling a magical hair tonic on the street. He denounced the false information from this trickster but marveled at the impact of his "wonderful, persuasive powers of enthusiasm" when eager customers had showered him with money. Persuasiveness was a powerful tool, he reflected, but one must be careful: "How to do this honestly is our problem—to do it dishonestly and trickily . . . is to assume the terrible responsibility that must fall on the champion of error." Twenty years later, he faced the same conundrum. In a 1937 interview, Carnegie expressed concern that some people used his book inappropriately. "I suppose lots of people read my book and say to themselves, 'Here's a new way to gyp people,'" he reflected. "Of course, a reader will succeed to some extent if he takes that attitude—the letters I've received prove that—but by the Almighty Harry, that wasn't my idea in writing the book." But Carnegie's indignant explanations did not reassure everyone. For some, his book represented a fearful world where moral standards and authentic character had vanished, where one stood defenseless before the charming wiles of the human relations disciple.[25]

But nervous attempts to gauge sincerity, and fearful glances at the specter of the con man, comprised only one contentious issue regarding *How to Win Friends and Influence People*. Another lay in discerning the ultimate object of Carnegie's program.

Fears of collapsing social morality prefaced concern about another troubling issue in Carnegie's popular book. Some accused it of having an objectionable central goal: the unencumbered pursuit of material wealth. Since the early 1900s, the growth of a consumer economy had made material abundance and middle-class security the defining characteristic of the American Way of Life. By the

1920s, however, detractors of middle-class comfort had emerged, such as Sinclair Lewis, whose novel *Babbitt* had ridiculed the banality of a life defined by shallow materialism, business boosterism, glad-handing luncheon clubs, glib salesmen, and advertising jingles. Then the Depression had undercut prosperity among great swaths of the middle and working classes. Thus the consumer vision of the good life remained strong for some, elusive for others, and undesirable for a few. *How to Win Friends and Influence People*, in the eyes of many commentators, stepped clumsily into the middle of this discussion with its unabashed endorsement of material possessions as the standard of American value and achievement.

Irving Tressler's *How to Lose Friends and Alienate People*, for example, beneath the jokes and smart-aleck commentary, had a serious subtext of social criticism. His satire exhibited impatience with the bromides of business boosters, the religious platitudes of middle-class society, and a lack of intellectual sophistication among chamber of commerce types. Tressler poked fun at Carnegie's business idols by asserting, "Rockefeller and Dillinger both wanted money and both wanted the feeling that they were somebody. The chief difference between the two is that Rockefeller never used a gun." Parodying Carnegie's habit of glorifying certain consumer items, Tressler sardonically suggested that ignoring brand products provided a shortcut for those wishing to alienate people. "Get rid of people by throwing away your Pepsodent toothpaste and leaving the ugly, dingy film on your teeth which is so unpleasant," he smirked. "Discourage further visits by overnight guests by failing to give them the sleep producing restfulness of Pequot Sheets or the absorbent friendliness of Cannon Towels."[26]

Tressler spoofed the comfortable consumerism of white-collar America by recommending preposterous strategies for undermining social respectability. He urged prosperous readers to use the golf course as a place "to nip the buds of young friendships" by giving clients weighted golf balls that veered erratically or drivers that split apart on contact. For business acquaintances who were proud of their new car, he recommended attaching the "Auto Whiz Bang" so that when the proud owner turned on the starter, an ear-splitting whine would occur, followed by a tremendous bang and a dense cloud of dark smoke from under the hood. For those moving into a beautiful new suburb, Tressler offered a foolproof method for alienating neighbors: "remark upon the terrible conditions of the street and how sloppy the homes and yards all look" compared with your last residence. Finally, when the local minister dropped by for a welcoming chat, he recommended greeting him at the door down on all fours, barking like a dog, and explaining yourself as a disciple of the "Going to the Dogs Movement" that was sweeping the country to honor our primordial ancestors. In other words, *How to Lose Friends and Alienate People*, in the manner of H. L. Mencken, made mockery of a banal American "booboisie" a cultural blood sport.[27]

Sinclair Lewis was as biting a critic of Carnegie's formulas. In two columns written for *Newsweek* in 1937, he sarcastically described *How to Win Friends* as "this new *Origin of Species*, this streamlined *Bible*" that sought to fulfill "the mission of making Big Business safe for God, and vice versa." He scoffed at Carnegie's penchant for positive thinking as "the grin that wins." He derided Carnegie's claim that in the literary world, "if the author doesn't like people, people won't like his stories," noting sarcastically, "This explains why Tolstoy, Flaubert, Sam Butler and Dean Swift have, as compared with Dr. Carnegie, been so ignored." Lewis deplored Carnegie's worship of wealth, observing that in his book "the magic expression 'million dollars' is used as in more old-fashioned, less air-conditioned volumes of inspiration where the authors used such words as Austerity, Nobility, Faith, and Honor."[28]

Lewis contemptuously deemed Carnegie the "Bard of Babbittry." Like George Babbitt, the famous protagonist from Lewis's 1922 novel, Carnegie glibly promoted a narrow life of material striving and social conformity, a life defined by "married couples envious of their friends' automobiles." Lewis turned to Henry David Thoreau, the famous Transcendentalist writer, for a nobler ideal. When Concord neighbors criticized his experiment in simple living at Walden Pond, Thoreau had replied, "It is very evident what mean and sneaking lives many of you live . . . lying, flattering, contracting yourselves into a nutshell of civility or dilating into an atmosphere of thin and vaporous generosity, that you may persuade your neighbor to let you make his shirt or his hat." In Lewis's eyes, Thoreau, not Carnegie with his bromides and deceptions, deserved to be honored as a "captain of American freedom."[29]

Carnegie had provided much fodder for these critiques in *How to Win Friends*. Granted, he talked about the importance of happiness and good relationships with others as intrinsically valuable, but even more often he enshrined material accumulation as the final goal. Those who mastered his program were "headed for higher earning power," he enthused. "Countless numbers of salesmen have sharply increased their sales by use of these principles . . . Executives have been given increased authority, increased pay." He urged readers to imagine the payoff: "Picture to yourself how their mastery will aid you in your race for richer social and financial rewards. Say to yourself over and over, 'My popularity, my happiness, and my income depend to no small extent upon my skill in dealing with people.'" Carnegie stressed that thinking about others and ignoring money, ironically, would prove profitable. He offered the example of a physician who had decided "to forget about money entirely, and to think only in terms of how much service he could render. And now, note the boomerang! This doctor declares that in a short while his average income increased more than three hundred dollars a month."[30]

Such sentiments aroused Carnegie's critics. "I regard it as an unpardonable offense to seek to reduce all human life to the standard of a drummer trying to sell a bill of goods," declared the minister John Haynes Holmes. "Next to Abraham Lincoln, apparently the greatest man who ever lived to Mr. Carnegie's way of thinking is Charles M. Schwab. And why? Because Schwab was the only man in the world who ever was given a salary of one million dollars a year." *How to Win Friends*, he claimed, was little more than a skillful how-to book on "beating your competitor" and "bringing home the bacon." Carnegie's claim that Christianity provided the foundation for many of his ideas was laughably false. In fact, according to Holmes, his popular book idealized a contrary set of values: "These three—popularity, happiness, and money—[not] faith, hope, and charity—and the greatest of these is money."[31]

Fillmore Hyde, a journalist who wrote for many New York journals of opinion, also bridled at Carnegie's establishment of money as the ultimate yardstick of worth. He wrote in *Cue*, "In Mr. Carnegie's philosophy . . . all friends become 'contacts,' and all such kindnesses as we offer our fellow creatures become stepping-stones in the business of 'getting ahead.'" Put off by Carnegie's appeals to Christianity, he accused the author of twisting Jesus's "precepts, which were first uttered as a revolt against the materialism of the ancient world, into the language of materialism in America." For Hyde, a notion of friendship that sees a friend as someone from whom we can extract a reward was all too reflective of "America today, where money and success are so much the criteria on which we judge a well-rounded life."[32]

The accusation that Carnegie was concerned only with money, however, spilled over into the political world. His book raised political hackles, with some reading it as an artfully constructed apology for existing social and political power. The implications, it was argued, were disturbing.

In *How to Win Friends*, Carnegie told the story of how in 1915 John D. Rockefeller Jr., son of the great oil tycoon, faced a rapidly deteriorating situation. His Colorado Fuel and Iron Company had been subject to a strike by angry miners, who were demanding higher wages and better working conditions. A series of failed negotiations had led to a tense standoff with property destruction and bloodshed as the crisis escalated. The atmosphere was polluted by hatred.

Then the young Rockefeller decided "to win the strikers to his way of thinking." He succeeded brilliantly. This business magnate spent weeks making friends among the striking miners and finally made a masterful address to their assembly. Carnegie listed the solicitous and generous phrases that Rockefeller employed: "I am *proud* to be here, having *visited* in your homes, met many of your wives and children, we meet here not as strangers, but as *friends*, spirit of *mutual friendship*, our *common interests*." The speech illustrated admirably how to make friends out of enemies, wrote Carnegie, and "produced astonishing results . . . It presented facts in such a friendly manner that the strikers went back to work without saying another word about the increase in wages for which they had fought so violently."[33]

Carnegie's version of this episode revealed much, not only for what it said but for what it did not say. What he recounted, of course, was the Great Coalfield War and the Ludlow Massacre, a headline-making event that was far more complex and rooted in economic interests than he explained. In fact, tensions in the

Colorado mines stemmed from the miners' attempt to join the United Mine Workers of America, which the Rockefellers had opposed intractably through mass firings and employment of armed guards to quell disturbances. Violence erupted when the Colorado National Guard, brought in to protect company property, strafed the miners' tent encampment with machine-gun fire and then set it ablaze, killing some twenty inhabitants, including women and children. A subsequent guerrilla war between armed miners and the National Guard killed between one and two hundred people before President Woodrow Wilson sent in federal troops to disarm both sides and restore order.

So John D. Rockefeller Jr.'s concern involved far more than "winning opponents to his way of thinking." And Carnegie's account of how "Junior" (as he was popularly known) completely won over the striking miners was equally oversimplified. Horrified by the violence and fearful for the future destruction of his company, Junior had come to Colorado and genuinely sought to implement labor reforms. His conciliatory speech on the need for cooperation was politely received by the miners, but their reaction was mixed. The union had run out of money and the strike had been broken, so his proposals for company grievance committees, safety codes, and improved housing and schools appeared attractive. Twenty-four hundred miners approved his program and four hundred and fifty opposed it, although two thousand miners boycotted the vote completely out of disdain for the "paternalism" of the Rockefeller plan. Moreover, the company would suffer four additional strikes in subsequent years before the United Mine Workers would gain recognition. The Wagner Act outlawed Junior's "company union" in 1935.[34]

Carnegie's simplistic rendering of this traumatic event in American industrial history epitomized a larger difficulty in *How to Win*

Friends and Influence People: a startlingly naïve view of social, economic, and political issues that reduced them to matters of personality, human relations, and psychological adjustment. Moreover, in pondering public affairs or historical issues, Carnegie invariably came down on the side of wealthy business owners, powerful managers, industrial magnates, and financiers while shortchanging the claims of the less prosperous, who usually appeared as pawns to befriend or influence to implement the agenda of the successful. This tendency got him into trouble.

Carnegie made clear his own preferences from early on in his popular book. Readers encountered a long string of anecdotes and illustrations glorifying the wealthy, powerful businessmen who had pushed their way to prominence in the late 1800s and early 1900s in the United States. John D. Rockefeller declared, "the ability to deal with people is as purchasable a commodity as sugar or coffee. And I will pay more for that ability than for any other under the sun." Andrew Carnegie appeared as a case study for the necessity of making others feel important. "He knew how to handle men—and that is what made him rich."[35]

Dale Carnegie drew upon many other businessmen to illustrate his advice on dealing with human problems, and they did so in ways that suggested the author's attraction to privilege. For instance, he explained that every affluent individual, at one time or another, faced "the distasteful necessity of discharging a servant or an employee." Let them down easy, he recommended, with words aimed at easing resentment and bolstering your chances of using them in the future. Tell the fired employee he had done a fine job, displayed much talent and commitment, and that you were rooting for his success. Thus "the men go away feeling a lot better about being fired. They don't feel let down . . . And when we need them again, they come to us with a keen personal affection." Another

time, Carnegie praised a clever tactic discovered by the owner of
company struggling with a dissatisfied mechanic. This employee
complained constantly that his work hours were too long and that
he needed an assistant. The exasperated owner finally responded
by giving him an office and painting on the door a new title: "Manager of the Service Department." By granting the employee a sense
of "dignity, recognition, and a feeling of importance"—but, significantly, no more money and no more help—the businessman
succeeded in reconciling the man to his job. While never explicitly discussing social and economic position, Carnegie clearly suggested that human relations provided a tool for those at the top to
manipulate those at the bottom. Soft power worked better than
ultimatums and force.[36]

Carnegie's sweeping view of the power of human relations influenced his understanding of politics. He blithely ignored interests of
all kinds—economic, regional, racial, religious, ethnic, ideological—
to insist that political success was largely a matter of personality
and handling others. Carnegie claimed that Theodore Roosevelt's
intense interest in other people was "the secret of his astonishing
popularity." He argued that James Farley, Franklin D. Roosevelt's
key political manager, helped sweep his boss into the White House
(never mind the Great Depression) because he had memorized the
names of, and family information about, fifty thousand people, and
upon meeting one of them "he was able to slap him on the back,
inquire after the wife and kids, and ask him about the hollyhocks
in the backyard. No wonder he developed a following!" Even at the
highest levels of political operation, Carnegie contended, personal
interactions trumped everything. When Woodrow Wilson was unable to win American cooperation with the League of Nations at
the end of World War I, it was because "he failed to use human
relations skills." Congress rejected his proposals, Carnegie argued,

because Wilson mishandled prominent Republicans. "[He] refused to let them feel that the League was their idea as well as his." Unable to comprehend that ideological differences, clashing political strategies, and party loyalties might have influenced this crisis, Carnegie insisted that the president's "crude handling of human relations" wrecked his career, ruined his health, and "altered the history of the world."[37]

Critics pounced on Carnegie's naïve approach to economic and political disputes and described it as a shallow, disingenuous cover for advancing the interests of the wealthy and powerful. This popular author, said one, was no more than "the medicine man among the commercial warriors struggling for gain in America's jungle world," offering "magic tricks" to help them move ahead in the brutal world of competition. *The Nation* claimed that *How to Win Friends* thrived "on the desperate desire for success in the land of opportunity," a desperation particularly evident among the lower echelons of the business world where white-collar clerks and mid-level managers aspired to the success of great business tycoons. Carnegie appealed to "the junior executives and salesmen, who write him stories of how they sold themselves to the boss," the journal contended. His principles kept these figures striding on the treadmill of corporate success.[38]

For some, Carnegie's sin lay in a profound disregard for working people and their interests. Sinclair Lewis mocked his hero-worship of Charles Schwab, whose million-dollar-a-year salary stemmed from his skill in inspiring workers to produce. Carnegie failed to note, Lewis observed acidly, that "this business of Mr. Schwab's getting the million and the workers getting the incentive explains the steel strikes now terminating in the C.I.O." Another critic contended that Carnegie always "slights the underdog." In one of his newspaper columns, for example, Carnegie evinced a blasé attitude toward unemployed workers haunting factory gates or the desperately poor pawing through garbage cans for scraps of food during the Great Depression. Instead, he urged the downtrodden to understand that wealth did not bring happiness and that poverty had its virtues. "I stop to realize that in certain respects no multimillionaire has anything on me. For instance, John D. Rockefeller can't enjoy a good book any more than I can. Andrew Mellon couldn't see his wonderful collection of oil paintings with any better vision than mine," he wrote. "Yes, when I think of all the joys I can have at so little cost, I might, if I didn't really enjoy my work and had no responsibility, even drop back and apply for a place on the relief role." Such a perspective, in the words of one observer, taught a simple lesson to working men and women: "Maybe you'd better hang on to your union card after all."[39]

Thus *How to Win Friends and Influence People* cut a wide swath through American culture in the mid-1930s. Carnegie's formulations regarding interactions with others created a new success ideology based on personality, one well suited to a white-collar world of modern bureaucracy. His principles regarding human happiness and motivation helped create the modern therapeutic culture, where self-fulfillment emerged from a matrix of psychology, self-esteem, emotional adjustment, and positive thinking. Finally, his defense of social stability, middle-class abundance, and economic privilege helped shore up the dominance of a corporate, consumerist ethos in modern America.

On nearly every front, moreover, Carnegie got the best of his detractors. The massive popularity of *How to Win Friends* revealed that its author, more than his critics, understood the aspirations and fears of ordinary people, especially among a middle class and working class for whom upward social mobility and material accumulation was still a cherished goal. His rules and recommendations, injunctions and inspirations responded to what Americans defined as a valuable destination, helped them define it, and showed them a way to get there. This modern mind-set became so compelling that it overwhelmed all opposition. In the process, millions of readers, students, and fans made Dale Carnegie into one of the most influential figures in the country.

13

"Give a Man a Fine Reputation to Live Up To"

As Dale Carnegie's *How to Win Friends and Influence People* surged to the top of the best-seller list in 1937, the author, now age forty-nine, advertised a demonstration meeting for his course at the Hotel Astor in New York City. The response was overwhelming. More than twenty-five hundred people showed up and pushed their way into the ballroom until they were standing shoulder to shoulder. Percy Whiting, one of Carnegie's lieutenants, left the hotel well before the starting time to run an errand but then found himself blocked from returning. "The fire department closed the doors and refused to allow anyone else to go in," he explained. "So many people were outside the hotel trying to get in that a detail of policemen was sent to the Astor to keep the sidewalk open." After this raucous episode, Carnegie moved his next meeting to a larger venue, the Hippodrome Theater on Sixth Avenue. It filled to near capacity as, in Whiting's estimation, "somewhat over six thousand people attended."[1]

Such events became commonplace for Carnegie. The enormous success of *How to Win Friends* had made him a national figure. He seemed to be everywhere on the American landscape over the next few years—traveling the country promoting his book, presenting his courses, giving lectures, receiving awards, and commenting on the issues of the day. Local newspapers fawned over him while big-circulation magazines made him the object of feature stories. Carnegie's publishing triumph opened new doors for him as a radio host and syndicated columnist. As acclaim poured in from every corner of American popular culture, the transplanted country boy from Missouri became one of the most famous people in the United States.

Perched atop this mountain of publicity, Carnegie felt simultaneously exhilarated and trapped. On the one hand, he appreciated the sudden fame and wealth accompanying this phenomenal rise to success, telling a reporter, "Nobody was more amazed than I was." On the other hand, the pressures attending his newfound status wore heavily on his psyche. The never-ending round of travel, lectures, book signings, ceremonies, and banquets caused him to complain, "From the early months of 1937 until the spring of 1940, I was so busy I could scarcely find the time to breathe."[2]

But whatever the benefits and costs may have been, one thing was clear: The life of this author and teacher changed irrevocably after the appearance of *How to Win Friends*. He became a public figure, someone whose perspective counted and whose words were heeded. Dale Carnegie was a celebrity.

In the years following the publication of his blockbuster book, Carnegie became a kind of American folk hero as he traveled around the country lecturing and teaching. Wherever he went, outlandish praise greeted him. Upon arriving in Wichita, Kansas, to teach his class, he was proclaimed "A Business Messiah" by the *Wichita Beacon*. A visit to Akron, Ohio, earned him the title of

"America's No. 1 prophet of personality." A round of lectures in Memphis prompted headlines in the *Commercial Appeal*—"Friend Maker Arrives" and "A Magnetic Personality"—and glowing descriptions of "a preacher who practices his own doctrine, a teacher who learned well the social graces before he started imparting his knowledge to others."[3]

A visit to Asheville, North Carolina, in 1939 saw Carnegie-mania engulf the town as local businessmen rushed to take advantage of his lecture at the local high school. They flooded the *Asheville Citizen* with advertisements connecting their products to his famous book. "The makers of Butter-Krust Bread are constantly winning friends daily because every loaf is made for YOU!" said one. "Pollock's Florsheim Shoes, essential to the well-dressed person in all walks of life, will help you win friends and influence people," proclaimed another. A local trucking company declared, "Like

A packed Carnegie Institute meeting at Carnegie Hall in November 1937. Carnegie is seated in the front row along aisle.

Dale Carnegie, we, too, know how to win friends by giving them service." The town's only bank adopted the Carnegie touch: "First National Bank, Service That Makes Friends and Keeps Them."[4]

The author's fame, however, went far beyond small provincial towns and local chambers of commerce. National magazines lined up to feature stories on his life and career, and in 1937 they began to appear. *The Saturday Evening Post* published a long article entitled "He Sells Hope" that was part biography and part analysis of the Carnegie phenomenon. *Esquire* offered "The Success Factory," a similar piece written by old friend Homer Croy, which had the additional attraction of the author's personal reminiscences about their boyhoods in northwest Missouri. *Look* contributed three photo-and-text stories on Carnegie: a pictorial book review in April entitled "How to Win Friends . . . and Influence People"; "One Minute Biographies," a condensation of his biographical sketches of famous figures, in June; and in December, "Dale Carnegie: The Man Who Succeeded by Preaching Success," a pictorial biography that highlighted his childhood, teaching career, and stunning authorial success.[5]

Not long after the publication of *How to Win Friends*, Carnegie was invited to the White House for dinner. He was thrilled. The meal featured wild game, he reported, a fact that left Mrs. Roosevelt unenthusiastic. As she told Carnegie, "people continually send us these gifts of game and fowl, and we have to eat them, don't we?" The president was gregarious, the author reported, and made an impression with his ability to simplify complex issues. When the First Lady inquired about the meaning of "flat money," FDR replied with a direct, pithy clarification that cut to the heart of the matter: It was "phony money." Carnegie thought, "what a simple explanation—and what a contrast to how Hoover might have answered the question." He also was struck by the president's down-to-earth sensibility, noting that while FDR had just signed one of the largest national budgets in American history, he maintained an admirable concern for the everyday costs of government. "You know what they're getting now for hospital lamps?" Carnegie quoted the president as saying to his guests. " 'Twenty-seven dollars!' He was indignant."[6]

A steady influx of Carnegie items inundated popular culture. F. S. Lincoln, a New York photographer and physician, and a Carnegie Course graduate, composed the "Dale Carnegie March," which included these stanzas:

> Oh, what a change in life has come to me
> Since I have joined this course by Dale Car-ne-gie.
> I've gotten rid of that old bluff called fear
> Now I know the goal is near.
> I'm not the same person that you used to know
> Because of Pep and Push and Go!
> You ought to take this course and profit too
> Oh, how 'twill change that self called you.

Cartoon strips, a popular feature of 1930s newspapers, drew upon Carnegie's book for punch lines. *Henry*, for instance, the cartoon about "America's Funniest Youngster," showed the boy diligently reading *How to Win Friends* after being chastised by his mother for misbehaving.[7]

Carnegie even became the centerpiece of an advertising campaign for Turret Cigarettes. Manufactured in Canada by the Imperial Tobacco Company and popular in the northern United States, the brand launched a series of print ads for magazines and newspapers. They featured a pictorial sketch of Carnegie along with quotes explaining key principles from *How to Win Friends*. In one,

Carnegie's famous insistence, "Let the other fellow think the idea is his," prompted the commercial message, "Every smoker has his own idea about which cigarette suits him best. We do not say that Turrets will appeal to everyone, but we do think that in his own interest, everyone ought to give them a trial." Another ad illustrated his maxim with "The offer of a Turret cigarette is one sure way to start a smoker saying 'yes!'" The ad campaign even drew upon the author's domestic advice that urged appreciation between spouses: "If every nagging wife, and every fault-finding husband would make it a point to 'cool off' by smoking a Turret in silence, before saying a single word, many a home might be a pleasanter place in which to live."[8]

As the volume of publicity mounted, Carnegie seized new opportunities. The clamor surrounding the success of *How to Win Friends* produced dozens of lecture invitations, and he scrambled to take advantage. "I was surprised at the number of men who were suddenly eager to be my lecture manager," he noted, and he went through two managers before finally finding Clark Gettis, who would stay with him for the rest of his career. He also took on a full-time administrative assistant: Abigail Connell, who had been working only part-time before the great popularity of *How to Win Friends* submerged his office with hundreds of letters, invitations, and requests, would become Carnegie's right-hand woman in subsequent years and a good friend to boot.[9]

Carnegie became even more of a household name through several media ventures. In 1938, at the request of NBC, he again hosted a radio show entitled simply *Dale Carnegie*. Focusing on biographical vignettes of successful people—it drew heavily from *Little Known Facts About Well-Known People* and *How to Win Friends*—it offered a series of dramatic sketches of inspiring lives. Broadcast on Monday evenings, it aimed to lift up Depression-era audiences with a recurring, reassuring message: "Success is a matter of the approach. You can do it, too." In a similar vein, Carnegie ventured into the world of newspaper writing. Impressed by Carnegie's book, Charles Vincent McAdam of the McNaught Syndicate approached the author about writing a syndicated newspaper column. It would join other McNaught columns by Will Rogers, Walter Winchell, and Al Smith. Intrigued, Carnegie invited McAdam to his house for dinner, and within two hours they had reached a verbal agreement. The column, which appeared for several years in the late 1930s and early 1940s in seventy-one newspapers around the United States, recycled inspirational material from his books, broadcasts, and teaching materials.[10]

Perhaps the clearest indication of Carnegie's newfound celebrity status, however, appeared with his participation in a prestigious frolic hosted by his old friend Lowell Thomas. In the mid-1930s, Thomas, by now a world-famous radio broadcaster, newsreel narrator, and globe-trotting travel writer, organized a summer softball team at Cloverbrook Farm, his three-hundred-acre estate in Dutchess County about seventy miles north of New York City. But this was no ordinary recreational endeavor featuring local amateur athletes. Thomas's team, the Nine Old Men, enlisted some of the biggest celebrities in the United States. Casey Hogate, the editor of *The Wall Street Journal*, manned first base, while other infielders included Secretary of the Treasury Henry Morgenthau and New York governor, and future presidential candidate, Thomas Dewey. Thomas's roster also featured heavyweight boxing champion Eddie Eagan, Congressman Hamilton Fish, actor John Barclay, singer Lanny Ross—and author Dale Carnegie.[11]

Other teams in the makeshift league offered similar lineups. The Ostervelts of Roose Bay, captained by Colonel Ted Roosevelt, son of the late president, fielded a team composed of figures such as cartoonist Rube Goldberg, baseball legend Babe Ruth, sportswriter Grantland Rice, and Broadway composer Richard Rodgers. The Nutmegs, hailing from Connecticut, featured boxer Gene Tunney, journalist Heywood Broun, *New Yorker* editor Harold Ross, columnist Westbrook Pegler, and composer Deems Taylor. But the Nine Old Men's most consistent opponent was the Summer White House Team, based out of Franklin D. Roosevelt's summer home of Hyde Park, about thirty miles away, and managed by the president himself when he was in residence. The team included John Roosevelt, the president's son; Rexford Tugwell, a key member of his Brain Trust; a few cabinet members; and several athletic, burly Secret Service men as ringers. FDR managed his team from the backseat of his presidential car, which was parked near his team's bench. According to Thomas's humorous jab, "The President is a born softball manager. Were he to put his team into professional competition, we are sure he would make money out of it, something that has thus far evaded him in governmental business."[12]

Not surprisingly, these celebrity softball contests attracted hundreds of spectators who crowded into the crude bleachers set up around the field at Thomas's farm. Good-humored banter, clever ribbing, and sharp repartee colored the proceedings more than athletic skill. When Hogate, who weighed around three hundred pounds, dropped by the president's automobile to exchange pleasantries, FDR quipped, "They tell me, Mr. Hogate, that you have to make a home run to get to first base." Hogate replied with a twinkle in his eye, "Under the New Deal, American business has to make a home run to get to first base, too." In another game, Morgenthau retired from the field in favor of a substitute, inspiring one of the Nine Old Men to loudly demand that the secretary be ensconced at the scorer's table because "anyone who can keep the Government's books could win any ball game as a scorekeeper."

On a particularly hot summer day, a heavily sweating opponent came out of the game complaining that he had lost twenty pounds, whereupon Broun rose to his feet on the bench, pointed dramatically toward the stands, and proclaimed in stentorian tones, "Go and thin no more!" In a game played at Madison Square Garden in 1939 to raise money for charity, the good-natured humor of the softball competition surfaced in the sham introduction of the competitors. Before thirteen thousand people in attendance, Thomas reported that the teams featured a number of prominent celebrities, including Florence Nightingale, Hannibal, Charles Dickens, Leonardo da Vinci, James G. Blaine, the Warner Brothers, and Zeus.[13]

Carnegie became a regular member of this elite group. He traveled regularly to Cloverbrook Farm during the warm months and participated eagerly, if clumsily, as an outfielder for Thomas's Nine Old Men. Having little athletic acumen, he became the subject of much teasing for his stiff maneuvers at bat and in the field. "Carnegie can't hit, run, or throw, but he loves the game passionately," Thomas reported. He "has been placed in right field because few hitters will ever hit to him and he is a lonely soul who likes to be alone." At bat, Carnegie stood awkwardly at the plate, leaning back with the bat perched at a peculiar angle, jaw agape, peering at the pitcher with a desperate hope that he would actually make contact with the ball. After giving way to a substitute, he sat on the bench joking with teammates or wandered genially among the crowd.[14]

Carnegie's attire became a subject of mock controversy. While the Nine Old Men featured uniforms of T-shirts and farmer's overalls, the success author insisted on playing in his overcoat. "That was a history making moment, although we did not recognize it at the time," joked Homer Croy, another participant, when first spying this odd attire. "But how often do we recognize great events

Carnegie and Lowell Thomas at the latter's upstate New York farm in the 1930s.

when they are happening?" Carnegie's teammates jokingly complained about his clothes, causing manager Thomas to rejoin that
they should be happy with the situation because he "had seen Dale
play *with* the overcoat and *without* the overcoat, and he was much
better *with* the overcoat." A team spokesman replied that he had
been misunderstood—what he wanted was "the overcoat to play
without Dale Carnegie." Finally, the author folded under the pressure and jettisoned the overcoat for a uniform of pleated pants,
suspenders, and a panama hat festooned with some daisies that
usually drooped beside his head in a short time. Even that brought

An enthusiastic but unathletic Carnegie at bat in one of the celebrity softball games at Lowell Thomas's farm.

no mercy, as a teammate quipped, upon seeing the daisies, "Are your brains dead only on one side?"[15]

Carnegie's recent book earned him a torrent of friendly abuse. Thomas joked that the real Dale Carnegie was "a charming, utterly business-like gentleman who is obviously a repressed insurance salesman. Frustrated in his efforts to peddle policies and cast out into a world which despises insurance sellers, Dale wrote *How to Win Friends and Influence People*. This was, as the Freud boys say, sheer compensation." Far from being a charismatic personality, Thomas continued, Carnegie was a "natty, eye-glassed businessman, absolutely timid and lonely, standing off by himself at the edge of the crowd, utterly disregarded by everyone." While his book made him a fortune, Thomas concluded, "it had failed to net him any friends. Softball, he hoped, would succeed where the book had failed."[16]

From early in his career, Carnegie had recognized that the power of personality was creating a celebrity culture in modern America. The country was obsessed with the personal lives of famous figures, he told his students in 1926, and the dividends could be enormous. In Carnegie's words, "Tomorrow there will be millions of conversations floating over fences in the backyards of America, over tea tables and dinner tables—and what will be the predominating note in most of them? Personalities. He said this. So-and-so did that. He is making a 'killing,' and so on." With *How to Win Friends*, Carnegie again stressed the significance of celebrity in modern life. In the preface, he claimed that he had interviewed "scores of successful people, some of them world famous—Marconi, Franklin D. Roosevelt, Owen D. Young, Clark Gable, Mary Pickford, Martin Johnson—and tried to discover the technique they used in human relations." Then throughout the text he lionized a host of rich and famous individuals, using their lives as inspiring examples of success. Now Carnegie himself, cavorting with presidents, cabinet officers, media magnates, sports legends, entertainment icons, and the giants of journalism, had become just such a figure. Things would never be the same.[17]

Carnegie's newfound celebrity status changed nearly everything about his life in the late 1930s. Irrevocably, it altered his daily endeavors as new opportunities and demands came cascading into the heretofore relatively calm existence of a teacher of public speaking and occasional author. With the astonishing success of *How to Win Friends*, Carnegie found his professional activities, his interactions with others, and his relationship with his work pushed in new directions by unfamiliar pressures. Enjoying the benefits of fame, he gradually realized that they demanded a significant price.

The cost of celebrity appeared first in a new round of activity that simply dwarfed anything he had ever experienced. "*How to Win Friends* succeeded in a way that seems incredible," he noted, "[and] after the book came out, I found myself living under a strain I had never dreamed of before: radio, lecture institute expanding, many people wanting to see me about this or that. I never want to live through another year like 1937–38. Hurried, rushed, tired." His schedule of speeches, appearances, and teaching became so hectic that even the smallest opportunity for respite was cherished. "Worked in garden today for two hours. Seemed like a real luxury just to be able to do for two hours what I wanted to do," he wrote. "Spent the evening reading *Reader's Digest*. This is perhaps the third time in six months that I have sat at home by myself reading. Always rushing here and there. 'To what end?'"[18]

Facing these unfamiliar pressures, Carnegie found himself rushing madly about the country for appearances in various cities and towns, where he would do book signings or speak about his magic formula for success outlined in *How to Win Friends*, or often both.

> I would arrive in the early morning, after a night's sleep in the Pullman car of some railroad, to be met by a deputation from a bookstore, whisked to my hotel to change into fresh clothing, and then hurried to the store. I would sit from ten until twelve, autographing copies of *How to Win Friends* for the people attending the sale. Another car would pick me up at the bookstore and take me to a Rotary luncheon at a nearby

hotel. I would barely have time to finish my talk before another car and driver would be ready to take me over to the Women's Club where I would lecture on *How to Win Friends* for an hour. If I was lucky, I would have time for a short nap before attending a banquet of some sort in my honor, and then I would be running for the train.[19]

Increasingly, Carnegie found this schedule overwhelming. Abbie Connell became responsible for organizing his schedule and, the picture of conscientiousness and efficiency, would provide her boss with elaborate itineraries listing every detail of his comings and goings. "But even with these to follow, I sometimes lost track of myself," Carnegie noted ruefully. Once, leaving New York City, Connell accompanied him in a taxi as they rushed toward the bus station on East Fiftieth Street. They barely made it as the author dashed from the car and toward the bus, which was about to pull out. "I started up the steps automatically and then realized that I had no idea where I was going," he reported. "I reached the top step and turned, in near panic. 'Where am I going?' I called down just as the door started to close. Abbie yelled back, 'Look in your pocket. It is all there.' I was already on my way across New York City before I even knew where I was going." Such frantic activity gradually took its toll. "I had been on this merry-go-round for months," Carnegie recalled later. "I began to lose weight and energy. And more important than that, my health."[20]

Another, more subtle problem also began to torment the beleaguered author. The hype surrounding his creation of the charismatic, confident, sympathetic personality who could win friends and influence people with ease began to weigh heavily. Increasingly people expected him to personify this ideal type, and such expectations proved impossible to meet. While friendly, sympathetic, and naturally drawn to people, Carnegie also maintained a considerable portion of his native Midwestern reticence. As someone who never graduated college but was now moving among national elites, he also harbored some embarrassment about his minimal education. Feeling increasingly insecure about his celebrity, he wrote a poignant memo in the late 1930s asking his staff to carefully screen the hundreds of invitations that were pouring into his office. "Before I wrote the book, *How to Win Friends*, people did not seek my company. I was just Dale Carnegie, teacher of adult education classes, and in no way sought after," he explained. "Now that I have written the book and it had such a phenomenal sale, people expect me to be something 'out of this world,' someone different. But when strangers meet me and begin to get acquainted, they find that I am just like their next door neighbor, that I am not someone with a dynamic personality. Then they feel let down. I sense that feeling and then I am embarrassed."[21]

Despite such emotional difficulties, Carnegie's newfound fame and affluence brought many practical boons to his life. He was able to lend financial assistance to old friends who had struggled during the Great Depression, such as Homer Croy, hiring him to do research for his radio broadcasts and sending him a check for $125 with the joking aside, "This is all in the world that I owe you, except a debt of gratitude." He refurnished and remodeled his two-and-a-half-story house in Forest Hills, filling it with elegant French and Queen Anne furniture, antique furnishings, Oriental porcelains, and lush Persian rugs. He expanded the scenic backyard garden and installed a patio with lovely wrought-iron furniture, a rose garden, bushes, and a small cement pond with koi and lily pads. A special project involved refurbishing both his and Connell's offices, which sat in a converted attic suite that ran the length of the house, with antique office furniture and fashionable Japanese wallpaper. Connell described the results as "breathtaking." She recalled an incident not long after the remodeling when one of her fountain pens malfunctioned, sending a squirt of ink onto the new wallpaper. Horrified by the large, ugly splotch, she went home for the night uncertain what to tell her boss. To her immense relief, there was a gracious note from Carnegie sitting atop her typewriter when she returned the next morning. "Martin Luther once hurled an ink well at the devil," it read. "If there have been any little devils hovering around here bothering you—let 'em have it. Meanwhile, let's get another roll of the Japanese wallpaper."[22]

Carnegie's celebrity also prompted an expansion of his social life. Always interested in the vast cultural offerings available in Gotham, he now became something of a man-about-town in the late 1930s. "He loved the city for its plays, museums, businesses, and restaurants," one observer explained. "He felt that New York City had made room for Dale Carnegie lovingly." Traveling into the city by subway or train, he attended numerous plays, musicals, films, art shows, receptions, and eateries, usually accompanied by a good-looking woman. As an eligible bachelor standing prominently in the national spotlight, he had little trouble attracting a number of comely females and he relished the opportunity to squire them about the vibrant city he had come to love. As he wrote to Thomas, "We are looking forward with great pleasure to seeing *Dead End* [a popular, long-running play about gangsters and slum life, by Sidney Kingsley] with you soon." Carnegie noted that he planned to bring his two nieces to the event, because they both wanted to be able to tell their families "that they went to the theatre with Lowell Thomas."[23]

On the family front, Carnegie's affluence proved to be a mixed blessing. His parents had led quiet lives in Belton, Missouri, where his father did some farming and his mother devoted herself to church work. By the 1930s, however, they were growing elderly and frail and struggled increasingly to live on their own. Dale provided generous monetary assistance, sending his parents a monthly stipend and additional injections of funds as needed. Brother Clifton, along with his wife, Carrie, moved into the parental home to help care for them. This situation seemed to work well, and in early 1938 Dale wrote a heartfelt letter to his "Darling Mother." He thanked her for her loving care during his childhood and declared, "you have been a great, grand mother. I thank God for giving me such wonderful parents." He also expressed his happiness at their comfortable situation, noting that "you now have excellent care with Mrs. Bidwell [a housekeeper], Carrie, and Clifton."[24]

But this harmonious situation fell into discord over long-standing tensions between the brothers that now were exacerbated by the younger sibling's great success. For many years, while Dale had moved forward slowly but surely as a teacher and author, Clifton had flailed about in search of a career. Flitting from job to job, he ended up back home caring for his parents while Dale became a national celebrity in New York. Gradually, Clifton's jealousy grew. Due to his brother's sporadic inability to support his family, Dale spent generously on his nieces and nephews, taking Clifton's daughter, Josephine, into his Forest Hills home and hiring her as one of his staff, while also paying for her two brothers' college educations. In addition, he also paid Clifton and his wife, as well as the housekeeper, a monthly salary as caregivers.

This unequal status eventually caused a strain. Dale, believing that money had been left over in November 1939 from his various checks, asked Carrie to use the surplus for expenses in December. Subsequently, he sent smaller amounts that month. This reduction triggered an angry letter from Clifton that, somewhat illogically, accused Dale of being a wealthy cheapskate, on the one hand, and an absentee bigwig who thought he could cover his lack of care with money, on the other. Dale replied artfully. He granted that it was "easy to understand how disturbed you were when you wrote me on Dec. 22" and expressed sympathy for his brother's frustrations in dealing with elderly parents. But then he vented his own impatience. "Your letter especially hurt me, Clifton, because of what I have done in the past," he wrote. Dale noted that he had given Clifton several thousand dollars during a crisis many years ago; that he had responded to a later missive claiming that his family would be living on public charity with a monthly stipend of $100; that he had spent thousands trying unsuccessfully to establish Clifton as a teacher of public speaking; that he had then used connections to get him a supervisory job with the Civilian Conservation Corps; that he even sent Carrie's mother a monthly check for $15 to help her. "Does a brother who has done that deserve a letter like you wrote?" he asked. But then Dale, trying to follow his own principles, concluded by offering an olive branch. He sent Carrie a string of pearls and told Clifton, "If I have hurt your feelings, I am sorry and ask you for forgiveness. Won't you please tell me what you want me to do? How much money do you need and for what?"[25]

The crisis abated as Clifton and Carrie settled into caring for the elderly Carnageys and Dale underwrote the entire operation. In a generally peaceful and supportive atmosphere, Amanda Carnagey died in her Belton home at age eighty-one on December 4, 1939. Dale had rushed to her bedside and the passing of the woman who had inspired him since boyhood left a deep emotional wound. "My mother died at daybreak last Monday. She passed away without pain or sickness a few months before her 82nd birthday," he wrote to a friend.

I had one of the noblest mothers a boy was ever blessed with. If she had not insisted on giving her sons an education in spite of poverty and hardship, I would probably still be a Missouri farmer . . . She not only made my clothes, she made the soap we used. She worked from morning until late at night, yet she often sang at her work. She sang because her religion gave her a faith and a joy that glorified her life. How I wish I had such a faith.

James lingered for another year and a half, undergoing hospitalization for "an acute internal ailment" and then from a fall. He passed away at age eighty-nine in Belton on May 18, 1941, from complications following a stroke.[26]

On another front, the financial bounty from *How to Win Friends* allowed Carnegie to indulge in one of his favorite pastimes: travel. As he gradually gained control over his pressing schedule, he was able to take regular vacations both in the United States and abroad. In 1938, Carnegie returned to Europe for several weeks, noting in a newspaper column that it was being written aboard a French ocean liner. "The *DeGrasse* is a slow boat, taking nine days to churn across the Atlantic," he wrote. "But I like slow boats. I hurry too much when I am on land. So I want to loaf across the ocean and tear off my necktie and open my collar to the sun and savor the tang of the salt air." The following year, he made an extended visit to Japan at the invitation of the Japanese Board of Tourist Industry. As part of an effort to improve communications and cultural understanding between America and Japan, he traveled throughout the entire country, visiting every region and most major cities, and giving talks on human relations as he was feted by his hosts. Near the end of the trip, he spent a few days in Korea along with a quick sojourn to Shanghai and Beijing.[27]

Carnegie also took more modest trips. In 1939, he snuck away for a brief vacation at the home of friends in Florence, on the coast of South Carolina. After a vigorous day of bass fishing, a group drove down to the beach after sunset to enjoy a majestic scene of open ocean and sky. It inspired melancholy in the author, who noted in his diary that he had spent quite a while looking up "at the star-sprinkled sky while the breakers from the Atlantic broke at our feet. Very impressive. Made me realize how unimportant man is, how tragically short life is." The next day inspired happier thoughts. While the fishing was mediocre, this transplanted farm boy who never quite lost his country tastes found another activity. "I had a grand time shooting water moccasins off stumps and tree branches," he reported in his diary. "Shot eight during the afternoon. I got a lot of savage satisfaction blowing those babies to bits."[28]

One of Carnegie's trips, however, paid a much larger emotional dividend. On a cruise to Cuba in the summer of 1937 he met someone who would become one of the most important figures in his life.

On a Friday evening in 1943, a five-year-old girl arrived at Penn Station, the huge railroad hub in the heart of New York City. She had traveled alone from New Haven, Connecticut, on a first-class ticket as a porter hovered about looking after her safety and needs. While thrilled to see the bright lights, scurrying people, and frenetic activity of America's largest city, she also remained somewhat puzzled about these trips, which occurred every few months beginning the year before. Her mother had insisted that she spend time with "Uncle Dale," and when he visited their house in New Haven she likewise urged her daughter to spend time with their guest, playing, conversing, and taking long walks in the local park.

Now, in New York, the usual routine unfolded. Uncle Dale met her at the station and escorted her to a cab for the drive to his home. Unfailingly, the cabbie would peer at Carnegie and try to place him, causing the author to ask, "You recognize me, don't you?" The driver would reply, "You're the guy that wrote that book, aren't you?" Carnegie would then introduce himself, chat briefly, and preen a bit, obviously enjoying the attention. After arriving at the house on Wendover Road, a housekeeper would get the child settled in a guest bedroom on the second floor. The rest of the weekend would be a whir of activities as Uncle Dale took her to an array of amusements—plays, musicals, the circus, the museum of natural history, the rodeo—and spun stories about his life and adventures. After she got a bit older, he would launch into soliloquies about how to get ahead and succeed in life. On Sunday evening, he would transport her back to the station to return home, a rite that again left her pondering the meaning of these special weekends.[29]

The little girl, Linda Dale Offenbach, had every right to be confused. In fact, she stood precariously in the middle of a highly unusual relationship between her mother, Frieda Offenbach, and Dale Carnegie, which had first flowered in the aftermath of his great publishing success with *How to Win Friends*. The two had met on a cruise to Cuba in the late summer of 1937—they were each traveling alone—and felt an immediate attraction. In fact, after spending much time together, they fell in love. When they returned to the United States, Carnegie sent her a copy of his book *Little Known Facts About Well Known People* and inscribed it, "My dear Frieda: I hope you enjoy reading this book one tenth as much as I enjoyed meeting you. Happy Birthday, Aug. 26, 1937, Dale Carnegie."

There was a problem, however: Frieda was married. Her husband, after initial opposition, soon adopted a complicated, even bizarre attitude about the relationship. What unfolded was one of those peculiar situations where everyone knows what is going on but no one ever addresses it forthrightly or admits to their role. Behind a veneer of polite, even friendly interchange existed a murky mixture of yearning and vulnerability, and it involved at least three adults and one child. This complex emotional scene often turned poignant, and it would continue for the rest of Carnegie's life.[30]

Frieda Offenbach, a very attractive young woman, both physically and intellectually, came from a background markedly different from that of the famous author. Born Frieda Berkowitz in Baltimore on August 26, 1910, to Max and Rose Berkowitz—they would shorten the name to Burke in subsequent years—she had grown up in a family of Jewish immigrants. Her father and mother were both born in Russia in the 1870s and came to the United States in the 1890s. They settled in Baltimore and raised a family of six children—Frieda was the second youngest—which Max supported as a shopkeeper, owning successively a grocery store, a dry goods store, and a secondhand furniture store. But Max treated his wife and children harshly. Frieda, an intelligent and sensitive girl, grew depressed over the tense domestic situation and threw herself into her studies. She was admitted into Goucher College in Baltimore, where she studied the classics and science, played tennis, and graduated Phi Beta Kappa at age nineteen.[31]

At the same time, Frieda flowered into a tall, angular, dark-haired young woman with high cheekbones and large, sensitive dark eyes. Growing up in Baltimore, she had adopted a Southern manner of soft-spoken, female gentility, listening intently to others and exuding wittiness, intelligence, and charm, particularly in the company of men. She was "very big on being ladylike," noted one observer, and seldom left the house without wearing makeup. Always dressed properly and attractively, she often wore white gloves when going out and about.[32]

After graduating from college, Frieda was admitted into the University of Chicago, one of the premiere institutions of higher learning in the United States, where she studied bacteriology in pursuit of an advanced degree. She made a rash decision to leave the program, however, after attending a party with a handsome young man with whom she had become involved. When someone at the gathering made a crude anti-Semitic remark and the young man failed to speak up in opposition, she grew quietly angry, left the party, and ended the relationship. More important, she packed her bags, left school, and returned to Baltimore. This precipitous action, which displayed a self-destructive streak, left her somewhat adrift, however, and she eventually found a job in the field of so-cial work. Soon she met another social worker, Isador Offenbach, and—obviously on the rebound from her abandoned university re-lationship—quickly agreed to marry him. The ceremony was held in Baltimore on November 29, 1933.[33]

Isador Edmond Offenbach had been born in Lodz, Poland, in 1905 and migrated to the United States two years later with his mother, Jennie. His father, Solomon, had arrived earlier and found employment as a machinist, tinsmith, and coppersmith in Bradford, Pennsylvania, in the extreme northern part of the state. Four more children would arrive in the following ten years. As an adolescent, Isador studied to be a rabbi. But rapidly failing eyesight forced him from this path—he had suffered serious injury to one eye in a boyhood accident, while the other eye seems to have deteriorated under the subsequent strain; problems with detached retinas would exacerbate the condition in adulthood and, eventually, he would be declared legally blind. Intensely intelligent and determined to suc-ceed despite his handicap, he graduated from Hebrew Union Col-lege in Cincinnati, Ohio, before going on to earn a master's degree in social work from Columbia University in New York. Gaining a job at the Jewish Social Service Bureau in Baltimore, he soon met and wooed Frieda, and within a couple of years after marrying, the couple moved to New Haven, Connecticut, where Isador had procured a position as the executive director of the Jewish Family Service.[34]

It soon became evident that the marriage was destined for unhappiness. Isador, intellectually imposing and occasionally charming, loved his young wife and wanted to please her. He readily agreed, for example, that they would not have to keep a kosher household and acted in an affectionate manner, giving Frieda numerous pats and hugs. At the same time, Isador suffered his own demons. Deeply resentful of the blindness that he believed had blighted his life, he often appeared angry at the world. Bitter about his disability, he would push to the front of lines in stores and restaurants and loudly demand special service. Difficult to work with, he alienated many of those he supervised at the Jewish Family Service.

At home, Isador's domineering tendencies made him into a stern patriarchal figure. Sitting in his overstuffed chair in the living room, he would spend hours listening to recorded books, devouring books and magazines read to him by his wife, or sometimes even holding them close to his face under bright lights where he could dimly make out the words. Everything in the household revolved around his needs and desires, and he could be harsh and dogmatic in expressing them. He regularly vented his anger, becoming an authoritarian who always had to have the upper hand. This same combination of brilliance, resentment, and domination could flare up in public, as when he scornfully corrected the rabbi when he read the Torah at temple.[35]

Frieda, for her part, succumbed and tried hard to create a tranquil household. In a graceful style she met her husband's needs— she presented his dinner every evening at the head of the table and quietly told him the arrangement of the food on the plate so he could eat and maintain his dignity, and she devotedly drove him around New Haven to every appointment or on every errand. She steadfastly attempted to make the best of an unhappy situation. Gradually, however, Frieda seemed to be maintaining a façade. Others noticed an underlying frustration, as when she rolled her eyes in scrambling to meet her husband's demands, or when she lapsed into a withdrawn state. More reticent than her intimidating husband, she steadily shrank before Isador's assertive personality while dutifully enduring his outbursts and cringing at his displays of affection. Frieda developed several physical habits aimed at soothing her frayed psyche: smoking heavily, eating little, and drinking excessively on occasion, which loosened her reserved temperament and allowed her to be sentimental and affectionate. She also tended to blossom in the presence of men who treated her respectfully. For example, Frieda grew very fond of Isador's youngest brother and when he visited they would spend hours talking and laughing. But in the normal run of life, she grew emotionally distant and morose—a classic case of someone trapped in an unhappy marriage.[36]

Thus the stage was set for the liaison between Dale Carnegie and Frieda Offenbach in 1937. Frieda was swept away by this older, accomplished teacher and author whose attractive personality, friendly low-key manner, sensitivity to human interactions, and national celebrity represented everything that her husband was not. While her self-destructive tendencies may have led her into the relationship, Carnegie also pulled her from the gloom that had enveloped her daily life. In a letter to Carnegie carrying the salutation "Dearest," she explained that she had been feeling "low, depressed . . . when along came your letter and presto! My blood started circulating again, my blood pressure went up, my pep returned." She joked, "I still insist that it would be a great scientific achievement if the affect you have could be bottled and preserved for application when one reaches a low ebb." Through Carnegie, Frieda created a kind of fantasy world where she could relax, express herself freely, and periodically escape from the strictures of her unpleasant life and find happiness.[37]

Frieda's allure for Carnegie was undeniable, if more complex. There was little doubt of his strong feelings for her. When resuming his diary in 1939 after a six-year lapse, the first thing he wrote was, "My, how much has happened in the last six years!!! Met F.O." Significantly, this appeared *before* any mention of the "incredible" success of *How to Win Friends*. He addressed her as "Dearest, Dearest Frieda" in letters and opened a charge account for her at a dress shop in New York. Her youthful looks and understated elegance certainly attracted him, of course—she was only twenty-seven and he forty-nine when they first met—but so did her obvious intelligence. Frieda's extensive college training, her knowledge of the classics, and her scientific expertise undoubtedly had an impact on this former farm boy with the limited education. Despite laboring as a social worker, she managed to keep a hand in microbiology, publishing in 1936 a brief article in *Proceedings of the Society for Experimental Biology and Medicine* entitled "Virulence in Relation to Early Phases of the Culture Cycle," which attempted to measure the virulence of bacterial growth in animal hosts. The journal identified her as affiliated with "the Department of Public Health, Yale School of Medicine." Because she wore her learning so lightly, however, and melded it with a soft-spoken manner and deferential attitude toward men, Carnegie was fascinated rather than threatened. Indeed, he even bantered about struggling to "learn the difference between the virulence and pathogenicity of e pluribus unum in white rats."[38]

But Frieda also attracted Carnegie for more complicated, even unconscious reasons. As an urban Jew, a married woman, and a female intellectual, she represented the ultimate alluring, exotic transgression—"the other"—for a man who had spent much of his adult life chafing under the repressions of a Protestant, Midwestern, rural heritage. Moreover, the unhappiness of her situation, made only more sorrowful by her adamant refusal to leave a disabled husband—once, when asked why she didn't end her marriage with Isador, she replied simply, "You can't leave a blind man"—appealed to his sensitive, solicitous nature. Unquestionably, Frieda endeared herself to Carnegie. On her birthday, while traveling, he sent a charming telegram that read, "Big excitement here in the Canadian Rockies. The news has got around. The marmots are whistling, the avalanches are roaring, the moose are calling. And all are saying, happy birthday to you, dear Frieda, happy birthday to you." On another trip, he noted that he was on a boat headed toward Alaska, before adding, "That is, my body will be on the ship, but my spirit will be at 58 Gordon St. with you . . . Wish you were going to Alaska with me."[39]

Likewise, Frieda filled her letters to Carnegie with outbursts of affection. Using the salutation "Dearest" or "My Darling," she often expressed a yearning to spend more time with him. "I want you to have a complete rest, but still I wish the Canadian Rockies were a few thousand miles closer," she wrote in one letter. "It must be heavenly where you are—I wish I were there with you," said another. When Carnegie returned to western Missouri when his father fell ill and died in the summer of 1941, she wrote, "this must be a very sad time for you when your loss is still so close—and God knows how much I want to be with you—if I could only function without regard to other responsibilities I would have taken a plane out to Belton to be at your side."[40]

As their relationship deepened, Dale and Frieda struggled to find private time together while remaining publicly discreet. Their liaisons took many forms. While traveling with her family, for instance, she maneuvered to get away for a couple of days, informing Carnegie, "about the only time there would be is for me to stop off on my way back to New Haven for a few hours, or for over night, around the 16th or 17th of June." For his part, Carnegie worked to arrange weekend visits at his home when she was free. In late December 1939, he wrote that a lecture engagement would keep him away until Saturday morning but "this need not prevent you from coming down Friday and doing some shopping and looking around and then coming out to spend the night at the house." Then he urged her to stay over for New Year's when "we will sit in front of the fireplace and watch the old year out and the new year in." The following year, another letter to Frieda noted that his recent remarks about the war in Europe had made the newspapers, and he scrawled on the clipping, "Little did you dream when you started for Peggy's Cove that you were riding with an authority on international affairs." Peggy's Cove was a tourist town on the southeastern coast of Nova Scotia, featuring a quaint fishing village and a lighthouse, which the lovers obviously had visited not long before.[41]

A surviving photograph of Dale and Frieda captured the richness of the bond between them. An accomplished photographer, she had staged (apparently in one of their homes) an artsy arrangement for the picture. A camera with a timer was aimed at a chaise lounge, with strong front lighting that illuminated their faces against a shadowy background. This produced a striking image of the pair. Carnegie, nattily attired in a pin-striped suit with a gold pin on the collar beneath the tie knot, grinned boyishly, somewhat sheepishly, as he leaned back against her chest and shoulder. Frieda, in a light blue dress with her dark hair pulled back, had both arms around him with her cheek laying atop his head, displaying a radiant smile. The photograph depicted two people in love.[42]

Dale Carnegie and Frieda Offenbach around 1940.

The greatest mystery in this affair, of course, came in the attitude of Frieda's husband, Isador. At some point early on, he stumbled across evidence of his wife's relationship with Carnegie when
she asked him to retrieve a pack of cigarettes from her purse. She
had forgotten, however, that a love letter from Carnegie also lay
within—a psychologist might question the unconscious aspect of
her "forgetting"—and Isador stumbled across it, holding it up close
to his face and making out enough to get the gist of things. He exploded in anger, demanded an explanation, and insisted that Frieda
break things off. But he soon cooled down and became accepting
of, even complicit in, the arrangement. Indeed, within two years
of becoming involved with Frieda, Carnegie met Isador, visited the
Offenbach house, and began writing an occasional letter to him.
There are several possibilities for explaining Isador's accommodat-
ing, indeed astonishing, attitude. Frieda may have dissembled, admitting only a close friendship with Carnegie, thus allowing her

husband to save face while she successfully utilized his blindness to meet the author surreptitiously. Isador may have swallowed his pride about the affair and looked the other way because of the attention and respect that this famous man began showering on him, an action that fed his considerable ego. Or Isador may have accepted Carnegie's presence for economic reasons. He had always been insecure about his ability to support his family due to his blindness, and he may have become reconciled to the relationship because of the steady flow of money that Carnegie soon channeled into the Offenbach household. Most likely, Isador's acquiescence resulted from some combination of all these motivations.[43]

But whatever the case, by late 1939 Carnegie was openly ex-pressing great admiration for the man whose wife he had fallen in love with. In a letter to "My Dear Isador," dated December 20, Carnegie laid it on thickly. "[A]nyone who can meet the slings and arrows of outrageous fortune as you have—anyone who can do that will always be the master of his fate and the captain of his soul," he wrote. "Knowing you, Isador, has been a rare privilege for me. Your heroic example has given me a real spiritual uplift." He added, regarding a recent operation on Isador's eyes, "please allow me to make a small contribution that will help a tiny bit in reducing the oppressive hospital bill that must still hang heavy about your neck like a log chain." Then came a clever sleight of hand. On a recent trip to Japan, Carnegie concluded, he had met an enterprising jeweler of great repute. "He gave me a present of some pearls. I thought Frieda might enjoy a string of them."[44]

Another strand was woven into this complicated emotional web on July 8, 1938, when Frieda gave birth to a daughter at Grace Hospital in New Haven, about ten months after first meeting Carn-egie. The delighted author immediately sent a telegram to Frieda's hospital room. "Welcome Miss Offenbach into this feverish and fascinating episode called life. I hope you have inherited your daddy's brains and character and your mother's sweetness and ineffable charm and knowledge of white rats. When you get a littler bigger please come down to Forest Hills and play with me and Rex." A short time later, he grew positively ecstatic upon learning that the baby's parents had named her Linda *Dale* Offenbach. "My dear Dale Offenbach," he wrote, "You are the only little girl who was ever named for me, so naturally I am flattered." He wished her a thrilling life and hoped that they would spend time together in the future so that he could pass along "some of the truths that I have had to learn by heart-crushing experience." Since she was sure to be very smart like her mother and want to attend Goucher College, Carnegie explained, "I am starting a little savings account for you in the Bowery Savings Bank in New York City." He signed off, "With Love, from Dale to Dale."[45]

Clearly Carnegie believed he was the father of the child and acted accordingly, as far as the peculiar circumstances would permit, over the next few years. He wrote numerous letters to "My dear little namesake" as he traveled about the country lecturing and teaching and showered her with money, gifts, and attention. He sent birthday checks, informed her of upcoming radio appearances ("I will be on the Vitalis Program on Friday night with George Jessel as M.C."), and mailed a large number of "play suits for little girls" that were made in a facility near his parents' home. He expressed great pleasure upon hearing that "you have named your doll 'Uncle Dale.'" After witnessing her rapid progress in talking, Carnegie admitted that he was "delighted with the progress you have made. You can talk clearly now and are using entire sentences." He was pleased to observe that she was "good-natured" and already displaying "what the French call *la joie de vivre*," adding jokingly, "I put that in to impress your mother." Impatient with the photographs he received of the child, he pleaded for more "colored still pictures of you" and promised to buy a projection machine and screen for Linda so in future days she could view "the kind of pictures that your mother and I enjoyed at the Kodak Exhibit in the New York World's Fair of 1940."[46]

Significantly, throughout his lengthy correspondence with the Offenbachs, Carnegie employed crafty language in referring to Linda Dale's paternity. He found numerous ways to describe Isador, calling him variously "dad," "pater," "parent," and "progenitor." However, he used the more biological word "father" very carefully, employing it only vaguely or ambiguously so that it could apply as easily to himself as to Isador. For example, writing the toddler on July 8, 1939, Carnegie said, "God was good to you, Linda Dale, when he gave you Isador and Frieda for your progenitors. I hope you grow up to possess your father's brains and character and your

Carnegie with Linda Offenbach, the girl he believed to be his daughter, at the Offenbach home.

mother's charm." Another revealing action came years later. In the last letter he ever wrote to the adolescent girl, only a few months before his death, Carnegie did not sign off simply as Uncle Dale as usual. Instead, he daringly enclosed the word uncle in quotation marks, as in "Uncle" Dale. It was, perhaps, a last subtle signal to Linda Dale that he believed she was his flesh and blood.[47]

The whole issue of paternity, of course, remained vexingly unclear because no one ever addressed it directly. For their part, Frieda and Isador deliberately, if ambiguously, sought to draw Carnegie into their daughter's life, not only making "Dale" her middle name but officially appointing him as her godfather, an unusual practice for a Jewish family. On his part, Carnegie not only sent toys, gifts, and clothes and arranged regular visits to his home within a few years, but he established a trust fund for Linda Dale. The child, of course, bore perhaps the greatest emotional burden of the issue that nobody talked about. When reaching early adolescence and entertaining questions about these peculiar circumstances, she occasionally asked her mother pointed questions about Carnegie, her family, and herself. Frieda, who tended to be emotionally distant, evaded direct answers and never opened up. Many years later, when Linda had reached adulthood and settled in with her own family, Isador, by then a cantankerous and difficult old man, sent her a letter that began, "I know you think I am not your real father. But that is not true. Let me tell you about the night I believe you were conceived." The shocked, upset daughter, who had become estranged from her father, wadded up the letter and threw it into the trash unread. The truth never came out.[48]

But ultimately, in terms of Carnegie's life, the question of Linda Dale's actual paternity was almost beside the point. He *believed* he was her father. Knowing that Frieda would never leave Isador, he nonetheless did everything he could to maintain a loving relationship with the mother and to support, as best he could, both materially and emotionally, the daughter he believed they had produced together. He dutifully maintained the façade of being "Uncle Dale" to the Offenbach family, all the while writing love letters to Frieda in which he occasionally referred snidely to her husband as "The Sheik of 58 [Street]." Or he penned letters to both Frieda and Isador in which he occasionally let slip the real objects of his love, as in "I am leaving tonight for New York. Hope to see you both before Christmas. 'Both' did I say? I meant 'you all,' all three of you." Perhaps most revealing, however, was a habitual closing in his letters to Linda Dale. He usually asked, "Is your mother keeping all these letters for you?" or enjoined, "You won't appreciate this letter now, Linda, but if your mother keeps it for you, you may prize it in 1975." Carnegie hoped that someday the girl would come to understand the true nature of their relationship.[49]

Thus by 1940, Carnegie had crossed a great divide in his life. A best-selling book with a vibrant success formula had tapped into an important vein of values in modern American culture, an achievement that made him a celebrity for millions. His subsequent fame produced both wild acclaim and hectic pressure, forcing him to present a public persona of confident success behind which lingered a private sense of insecurity. In addition, the death of his parents, especially his mother, closed a chapter in his life. Their passing prompted bereavement, appreciation for their sacrifices during his boyhood, envy for the security provided by their religious faith, and a subtle gratitude for his final liberation from stern Protestant traditions.

Finally, when Carnegie fell in love with a married woman—a relationship accompanied by an unconventional friendship with her husband and a deep affection for a child he believed to be his—it created a new level of intense emotional involvement in his life. Searching for the right pathway to success since adolescence, Carnegie had finally climbed to a lofty pinnacle of achievement. But as with so many others in various places and times, he discovered the wages of accomplishment brought unfamiliar quandaries as well as great happiness.

14

"Find Work That You Enjoy"

B y the early 1940s, Dale Carnegie had become an American institution. *The American Mercury* described him as "a king-pin in American culture," explaining that "like Benny Goodman, Duke Ellington, and other artists he has exhibited his magic at Carnegie Hall." Noting his enormous public appeal, *Collier's* concluded that "his personality has been stretched to such a point over the years that he has acquired, by osmosis, all the zeal of a crusader and the bravado of a bandit . . . These two characteristics, plus a magnificent grasp of the obvious, have enabled Carnegie to establish himself as a man with a message." At mid-decade, *Look* magazine compared him favorably to the new president Harry S. Truman. Not only did the pair come from nearby spots in western Missouri but they shared a physical resemblance and a flat, Midwestern speaking voice with the hint of a twang. More important, they shared an attitude and demeanor. Americans had been saying of Truman, noted *Look*, that "he looks and behaves like 'an average American.' So does Dale Carnegie."[1]

Carnegie's growing reputation often preceded him as he traveled the country. Local newspapers lauded him as "a noted personality

psychologist" or a "noted business psychologist." The Junior
Chamber of Commerce of Kansas City took out a full-page newspaper ad to promote Carnegie's upcoming lecture "How to Sell
Your Ideas," describing him as an "author, radio personality, and
newspaper columnist . . . a master lecturer, animated, pleasing of
voice, and with great charm of manner." Carnegie's teachings and
writings had found a broad audience, it continued, as letters "have
poured in by the thousands as testimony of the phenomenal influence his work has had on the American public."[2]

Riding this crest of popularity in the early 1940s, Carnegie embraced his enlarged public stature. He confidently wrote to President Roosevelt and recommended a new running mate in the 1940
election, Missouri governor Lloyd C. Stark. Average citizens stood
in awe of the Carnegie image. When he was in a Los Angeles store
shopping for a jacket, the clerk recognized him and insisted upon
escorting him into a special fitting room called the "Hall of Fame."
He had Carnegie write his name on the wall alongside other signa-
tures such as Spencer Tracy, Clark Gable, Mary Pickford, Douglas
Fairbanks, and many others.[3]

Carnegie even made a foray into Hollywood films, appearing in
the popular comedy *Jiggs and Maggie in Society*, where he was cast
as himself. Part of a popular movie series based on the long-running
comic strip *Bringing Up Father*, the movie detailed the efforts of
Maggie to break into Manhattan's upper crust, while her irascible
husband, Jiggs, continued to mingle with his working-class cronies
at a corner bar. Carnegie appeared in several scenes when Maggie
hired him to tutor, unsuccessfully, the wayward Jiggs.[4]

Carnegie himself became the subject of Hollywood satire when
Twentieth Century-Fox released *The Magnificent Dope*, directed
by Walter Lang, a romantic comedy that poked fun at his success

Carnegie persuading Jiggs to take his course in the 1947 movie *Jiggs and Maggie in Society.*

principles. The plot featured a Carnegie-like character, played by Don Ameche, whose success enterprise had stalled until he ran a much-publicized contest to find the biggest failure in the United States and then reform him with his human relations principles. Henry Fonda portrayed the winner of the contest, a wayward hayseed who was brought to New York, took the class, and attracted national attention with his progress. However, he soon rebelled against the pressure to succeed. After a series of comedic and romantic entanglements, Fonda ran off with Ameche's girl and became the instructor of a class on relaxation techniques.[5]

Another testament to Carnegie's popularity came when another long-standing cultural institution in middle-class America— Sears, Roebuck and Company—joined forces with him. Its annual

Carnegie broadcasting his 1943–1944 radio show, *Interesting People*, on the Mutual Network.

catalogue offered a new slogan to customers, "Prepare for Leadership, Wear the Right Clothes." The clothing best tailored for success, the catalogue proclaimed, came in the form of its "Staunton Suit." This stylish, yet modest wool ensemble projected Carnegie's principles of personal confidence and a solicitous attitude toward others. Sears promised that the aspiring individual, outfitted in this garment, would "Win More Friends, Influence More People."[6]

As his fame and influence soared, however, Carnegie confronted an unexpected situation. He nearly ran aground financially. The Carnegie Course had always been the backbone of his enterprise, the primary activity to which he had devoted himself for decades while occasionally turning to writing. But then he discovered that mismanagement had brought the Dale Carnegie Institute to the brink of ruin. While he was traveling the country giving talks and teaching, several trusted associates had created a bloated office staff in New York that was running up huge, crippling expenses.

Stunned, he retreated to New York in a desperate attempt to save his enterprise.

The New Yorker, a favorite magazine of the discerning classes in the urban northeast, was famous for its leisurely, lengthy, often droll examinations of contemporary life. Occasionally it stooped to examine ripples in the popular culture, especially when they provided eccentricities ripe for subtle ridicule, or when they became tidal waves that threatened to overwhelm the bastions of respectability. Both motivations came into play in late 1937 when Jack Alexander, one of the magazine's regular contributors, took a look at the Dale Carnegie phenomenon. He focused on the course rather than on *How to Win Friends and Influence People*. "Long before Dale Carnegie wrote his famous book," he explained, "he was one of the world's most successful teachers of public speaking." Alexander was determined to find out why.[7]

Appearing at the offices of the Dale Carnegie Institute on East Forty-Second Street, Alexander found it to be "as brisk a place of business as I have ever seen." He was turned over to "the Dean, a Mr. Nelson, who instantly showed me some letters on his desk from Carlsbad and Stockholm asking when the gospel could be translated and carried overseas." The demand for Carnegie courses had skyrocketed, both domestically and internationally, and the institute was scrambling to train instructors, Nelson told Alexander. This was a daunting task, however, because while colleges could hire instructors merely on the basis of credentials or publications, the Carnegie Institute "must get men who are experts in educating the emotions, besides being teachers of public speaking—men who can help a pupil to develop his Entire Self." The teacher must be prepared to help each student face his fears and overcome them.

For each enrollee, "His Desire to Be Important, as Mr. Carnegie calls it in his book, has started him on the high road to a new and potent personality," wrote Alexander. With the capital letters subtly signaling his disdain, the magazine writer set off to see how the course actually worked.[8]

Alexander entitled his article "The Green Pencil." This referred to, and deftly derided, the Carnegie Course's coveted award that was reverently displayed to students at the introductory session "in a small, oblong box wrapped in silver paper." Inside this receptacle, the instructor explained, was "a green mechanical pencil inscribed 'First Prize for Best Speech, Dale Carnegie Course in Effective Speaking.'" Voted upon by the students themselves, it would be given to the most compelling speaker after each meeting. "Let me tell you that the first night you go home with one of these," the teacher said earnestly, "as Dale Carnegie says in his book, you will wake up your wife and show it to her. And if you feel the way I did, you will stop strangers on the street and say to them, 'Look what I won,' don't you know."[9]

For Alexander, the importance attached to this trifling trophy captured the course's essential appeal to bedraggled, untutored, emotionally shallow people who paraded before their classmates to stammer out a few words as they desperately searched for confidence and upward mobility. There was the nervous sportswear salesman who had trouble closing sales who reported, "I—uh—came here tonight to see if I couldn't be helped." There was a "squat man" who sold vegetables in Brooklyn and wanted to make a stronger appeal to his customers. He explained, "I think if I can come here and make a little speech, I can maybe—maybe I can . . ." before trailing off. There was the "middle-aged woman with the whimpering voice" who had applied unsuccessfully for a loan from a local bank and then enrolled to see if "Dale Carnegie could show me how to get the three thousand dollars." There was the "great lump of a man" from Indiana who confessed that, years earlier, "something terrible got hold of me—an inferiority complex" but now "when I read about Dale Carnegie, I said to myself, 'Maybe he's got something there.' Well, here I am." These rambling, skittish confessions brought an exhortation from the instructor: "a Dale Carnegie course [is valuable] not only in teaching people to speak in public but in improving them in other ways . . . They get a mental stimulation, don't you know. And what is public speaking but selling—selling yourself." In Alexander's view, the Carnegie course, with its agenda of confidence-boosting and a formula for "Making the Other Person Happy About Doing the Thing You Suggest," aimed at this gallery of needy, rather dim types.[10]

Despite its condescending, sometimes sneering, tone, *The New Yorker* article captured an essential truth: the Carnegie Course was, indeed, the engine propelling the founder's operation, and by the late 1930s it was humming along on all cylinders. Ordinary people, eager to overcome their problems and find success, were flocking to enroll in ever-larger numbers. In fact, this popularity overwhelmed the original structure of the course established in the 1910s, where Carnegie had presented the course with the assistance of a few colleagues and guest lecturers. Now he began to build a more extensive, complex organization. Encouraged by the growing crowds of students, and bolstered by abundant funds from his best-selling book, Carnegie extended his reach with more offerings and a larger staff of teachers.

He had renamed his operation the Carnegie Institute of Effective Speaking and Human Relations in 1935, and the immense success of *How to Win Friends* prompted him to add "Dale" to its title to set it apart from projects endowed by Andrew Carnegie. As *The New Yorker* put it, "The friends-winning movement has grown so

STEVEN WATTS

fast that Carnegie has been unable to keep up with it. He has had to give up conducting classes himself in order to devote his time to duties of administration." The last point was only partly true. While the growth of the course forced more administrative duties on Carnegie, he never abandoned teaching; he still loved to step in and conduct a session at every opportunity. As his close friend Homer Croy pointed out, "The success of the book does not mean much to him, for privately he regards it as a fluke. His real interest is in the classes."[11]

The famous course underwent other changes as well. Because the broad success message of *How to Win Friends* transcended public speaking, the author altered the course's title to the Dale Carnegie Leadership Course. "If you can get on your feet and make a speech which will impress other people, you will get ahead much faster than if you are a tongue-tied seatwarmer," a journalist described of its success ethos. Carnegie also broadened the base by granting sponsorships to individuals around the United States. They were licensed to begin offering the Carnegie courses in their region with instructors who had successfully completed training. In addition, sponsors were allowed to procure enrollments through direct-selling initiatives as well as demonstration meetings.[12]

With such modifications, the Carnegie Course thrived as never before. Croy, who attended a class in New York and wrote a long article for *Esquire*, noted that there were twenty-two colleges and universities in the city offering public-speaking courses, but that Carnegie had more students than all of these institutions combined. He described the course as a "success factory" where "students were handled with machine-like precision." A newspaper story listed some of the typical course sessions—Overcoming Fear, Developing Courage, Acquiring Ease and Confidence, How to Improve Your Personal Appearance, Personality Improvement—and described how the instructor encouraged everyone to give a "rousing, rip-snorting speech." It noted that students addressed a wide variety of topics: bar examinations, chicken incubation, flood relief, life insurance, deep-sea fishing, photography, investment banking, the problems facing a minister, and the problem of syphilis, the last of which caused the instructor to lean over and whisper, "Gee willikers."[13]

For the first time, the Carnegie Institute also branched out to offer a special sales course. For several years, Carnegie had been deluged with requests from salesmen around the country to offer a class specifically tailored to their needs. In 1939, he finally succumbed. Working with Abbie Connell and several teaching associates, he created a five-night course that moved from city to city, combining his human relations principles with specific instruction on sales tips and techniques. "On Monday night our school would begin. I would lecture for an hour on *How to Win Friends*, and my associates would lecture on selling for another hour," Carnegie described. "Then I'd come back with more human relations for another hour, and then the last hour would be on selling. Monday through Friday, and then on to the next city."[14]

The Carnegie Course had become everything its creator envisioned—popular, influential, profitable, and effective in conveying his human relations principles. Then its founder received an enormous shock. In 1941, he discovered that all was not well; in fact, the institute was teetering on the edge of financial collapse. "I was making a lot of money. Royalties from the book were still pouring in, money from the sponsors was coming in regularly, and the money from the sales schools was good. But my New York manager was constantly needing money for expenses. What expenses? I learned that he had hired assistants to the assistants to the assistants," he related. "I returned to New York to find that my business was almost in bankruptcy." So Carnegie and Abbie Connell spent several days at his home poring over the books and spreadsheets for his company. He discovered that the central office, which he intended to house a handful of employees, had swollen to include thirty-seven in "the penthouse offices" and another ten in the publishing and distribution operation. They had run up overhead expenses that were sapping nearly all of the institute's profits.[15]

In truth, Carnegie had played a larger role in this crisis than he ever admitted. Swept away by the profits rolling in from his expanding courses and sales from *How to Win Friends*, he purchased an uptown building in New York and spent a large amount of money putting in air conditioning and classrooms. Then he sank even more funds into advertising and promotion to fill the space. It was a classic mistake of overexpansion, and the building proved to be a costly drain. "When it went bankrupt all of that money went down," wrote an institute insider. "I was on the Board [of Directors] when we voted to let it go." Carnegie referred to this situation only obliquely, noting several years later,

> I let more than three hundred thousand dollars slip through my fingers without making a penny's profit . . . I launched a large-scale enterprise in adult education, opened branches in various cities, and spent money lavishly in overhead and advertising. I was so busy with teaching that I had neither the time nor the desire to look after finances. I was too naïve to realize that I needed an astute business manager to watch expenses.[16]

But whatever the causes of his business troubles, Carnegie decided on a drastic remedy. He informed his manager at the central office in New York that the entire institute staff needed to be let go. Henceforth, the operation would be run out of his home, with publishing supplies stored in his basement while Carnegie himself, along with Connell and his niece, Josephine, fulfilled the administrative duties. This move, of course, dramatically slashed expenses and allowed the Dale Carnegie Institute of Effective Speaking and Human Relations to regain its financial footing. Three years of operation with this skeletal organization revived the enterprise's fortunes, and the founder cautiously looked to expand once again.[17]

On October 1, 1944, Carnegie solidified the organization's structure by incorporating as Dale Carnegie Courses, Inc. Under this arrangement, the sponsors of the course around the United States became legally licensed franchises that were responsible to Carnegie. The following year, he established a parent company for all of his endeavors called Dale Carnegie and Associates, Inc., a private-stock company with himself as president. The company opened its first distribution center for printed material and in 1945 held its first national convention, a gathering that was a combined sales meeting and "instructor refresher."[18]

This process of corporate consolidation continued throughout the 1940s. In 1947, Carnegie published the first in-house manual for training instructors of the Carnegie Course. He also continued to expand the network of licensed sponsors, and by 1948 he supervised licensed sponsors in 168 cities, collecting a royalty fee for each of the 16,000 students taking the courses every year. Carnegie also tinkered with the structure of the course, varying the number of sessions from fifteen to twenty-one. Percy Whiting emerged as a key player in this process. Alexander, in his *New Yorker* piece, caught something of his personal dynamism, describing Whiting as "a well-groomed, white-haired man with a facile smile . . . [and] a slightly aggressive fatherliness," who could be, in quick succession, jovial, self-deprecating, enthusiastic, and inspirational. In 1947

Whiting wrote *The Five Great Rules of Selling*, which would serve as the textbook for the sales course for the next fifty years. Other longtime Carnegie associates—Frank Bettger, Richard C. Borden, Charles A. Dwyer—remained part of the teaching team while the national organization took on a number of people who would become mainstays in teaching the course over the next three decades, including Brick Brickell, Arthur Secord, Stewart McClelland, Pat Evans, Harry Hamm, Wes Westrom, and Ormond Drake.[19]

Despite its expanding bureaucratic form and national focus, the Carnegie Course continued to derive most of its energy and focus from Dale Carnegie himself. He cherished the educational undertaking he had inaugurated thirty years earlier and, indeed, made it a key part of his identity. Traveling around the country on a regular basis, he visited classes, consulted with instructors, and labored to maintain a high standard of training to effectively impart the principles in which he deeply believed. His impact was indelible.

When talking with reporters, Carnegie loved to tell stories about his teaching experiences. He passed along a wisecrack he often shared with students: "Y'know, the real disadvantage of this course is that you'll never again be able to hear a public speaker without thinking how lousy he is." He recounted how he overcame daunting challenges, as when a frightened young man tried to make a speech but crumbled to the ground in a dead faint. As he fell, Carnegie grabbed his limp body, supported it, and announced dramatically to the class, "One month from today this man will make a speech from this platform!" And he did. He told the tale of the new chairman of a large company who, frantic at the prospect of speaking to shareholders, rushed to Carnegie and promised that if his course would cure his fright he would give him half of his earthly possessions. Several weeks later, Carnegie reported triumphantly, the man spoke successfully before an audience of four thousand. When asked if he laid claim to the earthly possessions, Carnegie replied with a smile, "You'll go to your grave wondering."[20]

In a long interview for the magazine *Your Life*, Carnegie related how a prominent Wall Street broker enrolled in the course but was so terrified that he fled from the first session. He then sheepishly returned after accepting the offer of an ambassadorship, a position that demanded regular public speeches. He was soon giving successful talks to his fellow students, and grew so enamored of public speaking that one Sunday morning he awoke and asked his wife if there was any place in New York where he could make a talk that day. When reminded that anyone could speak at a Quaker Meeting House, he found one in Brooklyn and rose to offer some remarks on how to prevent war. There was the head of a business who shrank from public speeches, but noticed one day that his accountant, usually a timid man, now entered the office with head held high, a confident look, and a booming "good morning." When the businessman asked, "Who has been feeding you meat?" the accountant replied that he had completed the Carnegie Course. So the boss took the training and four months later, according to Carnegie, "he talked to a mass meeting and was tireless. Asked to talk for three minutes, he talked nine; and if the chairman hadn't shut him up he would have talked ninety."[21]

Carnegie's teaching prowess became legendary. A host of course instructors testified to the founder's profound influence and inspiration in the years after the enormous success of *How to Win Friends*. His attention to detail was conspicuous. An instructor in Birmingham, Alabama, who arrived a few minutes before class, was startled to find the visiting Carnegie lying on a table. When the anxious young teacher asked if he was feeling all right, Carnegie replied that "he was just resting a bit, after coming down to check on how the room had been set up." Imagine, recalled the teacher, "he owned the course, but he checked on such small details." Another time, Carnegie demonstrated the wisdom of his experience. He observed a young woman in a class who was struggling with her talk as mounting fear caused her to lower her voice until she could barely be heard. Carnegie quietly went to the front of the room, tactfully asked the instructor to step aside, stopped the woman, and then placed two chairs facing each other a few feet apart. In an earnest and interested manner, after they both took a seat, he began to ask her questions about the topic of her talk. As he drew her out, she started to relax and gain confidence, spoke animatedly, and ended up having "a successful experience during the two-minute talk."[22]

Carnegie supporting a nervous student as she struggles to speak publicly into a microphone.

Carnegie's prowess in helping students overcome their fears impressed all who witnessed it. Years of experience had provided him a variety of techniques that he shared willingly. Encountering a timid student during one of his class visits, Carnegie loosened things up by asking him "to skip to the candy store with him, and they skipped completely around the room." The image of the distinguished founder of the course romping about in his tweed suit engulfed the entire class in laughter and lightened the environment so that the tongue-tied student could speak comfortably.[23]

Carnegie once aided a student paralyzed with fear because of his foreign accent. After listening to his disjointed, fumbling talk to the class, Carnegie said simply, "You should get down on your knees every morning and thank God that you are different. Your accent adds color and emphasis to what you say. It gives you a power possessed by no one else in this room." His words had an almost miraculous impact. "This comment and the manner in which it was made had an instant and transforming effect," reported the instructor. "The man seemed to stand taller. His eyes glowed with new hope. His desperation was changed to aspiration." Such interventions awed instructors and students alike.[24]

As Carnegie monitored his course and encouraged his instructors, he insisted upon the importance of "enthusiasm." In training sessions for instructors, he listened closely and evaluated their performances, often taking notes on a yellow legal pad. Ken Bowton, who would have a long career with the Carnegie Institute, never forgot how his boss critiqued one of his early teaching efforts. "He mentioned a couple of things I had done well, and then said, 'Ken, you were about as enthusiastic tonight as the turnstile down at the subway—when it's not turning.'" Bowton, hearing this comment delivered in a jovial, friendly manner, "considered this to be a challenge. I needed to relax and teach with excitement. Since that time I have realized that when instructing the class I had better turn up the level of excitement." Another time, however, Carnegie's demand for enthusiasm brought comical results. Sitting in on a class taught by Brick Brickell, he pushed the instructor to generate a higher level of enthusiasm among his students. So Brickell urged on a female student, who proved somewhat volatile during her speech. She "became so excited and angry that she took off her shoe and pounded on the table," the instructor reported. "I continued to heckle her and she started striking out at me with her shoe. In fact, she ran me down the aisle and all but out of the room. I felt I had completely failed but Mr. Carnegie thought it was great because the lady had truly come out of her shell and enthusiastically so."[25]

For all his seriousness, however, Carnegie allowed no pretense in his course. At a postwar course meeting where he was sitting in, a veteran "gave a talk about his memory of seeing natives eating garbage on an island in the Pacific." The instructor, a professor of speech at Notre Dame, remarked that the talk would have been better if he had used the word "refuse" instead of "garbage." But Carnegie jumped to his feet and said emphatically, "In the Dale Carnegie Course, garbage is garbage!" In Kansas City, he attended a special instructor-training course established by the local sponsor at the federal prison in Leavenworth, Kansas. Carnegie was enthusiastic about seeing the class, and was monitoring the proceedings when one of the students, a mobster, gave a talk on an experience that had changed his life. "He was telling of the gun battle that caused his incarceration. Just as he and a rival gangster were in a narrow alley, head to head with one another, they drew their pistols simultaneously and . . . the bell rang" to cut off the talk, reported the instructor. "Dale Carnegie jumped to his feet and said, 'I have to hear the rest of that story. Go ahead and finish it, take five more minutes if you need it.'" The audience was gratified, of course, but thereafter the prisoner-students badgered their teachers at every session and demanded five extra minutes since Carnegie had done it for the mobster.[26]

Carnegie often made a greater impact with his personal style than with his pedagogical injunctions. His genuine demeanor and encouraging tone left a lasting impression on many course instructors. During one training class, he discussed his mother's great influence on his life to illustrate a point and, according to one participant, "he was so sincere and immersed in his thoughts that he openly wept and had to stop and compose himself. We all felt that part of his secret was his total sincerity and that he cared so very much for others." One instructor, Arthur Secord, never forgot when Carnegie visited one of his classes in 1948, sat in the back row, and then left at the break without saying a word. In a couple of days, however, he received a copy of *How to Win Friends* with an autographed inscription in the front: "Hi, there, Art. There may be a better teacher of speech than you somewhere in captivity. If there is—we have never been able to find him."[27]

But Carnegie could be stern when necessary. At one location, he visited a class and noticed that the instructor was slow in ringing the bell, thus allowing speakers to add an extra thirty seconds to their two-minute time limits. At the break, he called over the young man. "Under no condition should any speaker be allowed to speak beyond the allotted time. This is an ironclad rule and it must never be broken because it corrupts the rhythm of the class," he insisted. "The Dale Carnegie classes must start on time and must stop on time—each and every session!" In another city, an instructor, obviously full of himself, went about saying that teaching the Carnegie course "is like taking candy from a baby." When the founder overheard the snide remark, he dismissed the young man the next day. Carnegie firmly handled a difficult situation that arose when he was a guest teacher and a small group of salesmen, all from the same company, came to the session intoxicated and disrupted the proceedings. He stopped the class, announced that there would be a five-minute break, and strode to the back of the room. He told the miscreants to get out and stay out. When one of them protested that they had paid their tuition and had a right to stay, Carnegie replied, "It's my course and I will not permit this behavior. You must leave." They did.[28]

Ultimately, Carnegie sought one goal: to maintain the quality of his course and ensure that its human relations principles were being inculcated in students. He took pains to maintain standards and encourage excellence. At instructor refresher courses in the 1940s, Carnegie, often in concert with Whiting, would lead the demanding and invigorating sessions. A set of "guinea pig" students would give talks, and then "instructors sitting around the room would wait for a name to be called after being drawn out of a hat to see who would comment on the students' efforts. Following this, other instructors would comment on the instructors as they did their work," one participant described. "Mr. Carnegie and Mr. Whiting would supervise rather spontaneously this whole effort and I can remember they did not always see eye to eye with the instructors, or with each other. The result was that we had some very spirited discussions right in front of the students about what could have been done, what should have been done, and how it could have been better."[29]

As the result of such rigorous efforts, the Carnegie Course met its mission with great success. With huge numbers of students and successful training methods, it even began to win grudging acceptance from the academic world. At the convention of the National Association of Teachers of Speech, Ray K. Immel, the dean of the

School of Speech at the University of Southern California, startled his audience by announcing, "The best public speaking in America today—and the best teaching—is found in the classes of the Dale Carnegie Institute." Skeptical of this assertion, Professor William A. D. Millison undertook to appraise the Carnegie Course in comparison to standard university offerings. After two years of research, he published his findings in the *Quarterly Journal of Speech* in early 1941 and came to the same conclusion. After examining the structure, methods, and instructors in the Carnegie Course, he marveled at their success "in stirring their students to an unusual amount of speaking activity and improvement." The reason, he concluded, was Carnegie's emphasis on improving the whole person, an approach that called into question academic pedagogy. "[I]t suggests that we have too long neglected the opportunity through speech to strengthen and develop the emotional life and attitudes of our students," he wrote. "We have been so concerned with the *practical* side of speech—so determined to develop technical skill or artistic expression—we may have over-looked its *social* significance and its possible meaning to the individual student in terms of social adaptation and emotional adjustment. Perhaps we have yet to discover that our students have emotions as well as a brain, voice, and body."[30]

The course, in concert with the tremendous popularity of *How to Win Friends* and his regular lecturing on its principles, sent Carnegie's public stock soaring to a new high. In fact, his reputation grew so elevated by the 1940s that it transcended the confines of public speaking and self-improvement. People began to seek his opinion on the issues of the day. This disciple of modern success, many believed, could offer shrewd insights into and effective prescriptions for not only personal life but public affairs. Flattered, Carnegie took on the role of sage and pondered how his human relations principles could resolve social, cultural, and political problems. The results would be decidedly mixed.

In the late 1930s and early 1940s, as the rise of fascism triggered growing world tensions that finally exploded in war in Europe and portions of Asia, Carnegie increasingly encountered new questions. Traversing the country lecturing and teaching, he spoke with reporters who wondered how his human relations principles might help resolve the frightening global situation. His formula for human interaction, they suggested, might somehow be adapted by nations to find world peace. This novel situation created new pressures for the success writer.

Sometimes, admirers made Carnegie into an inspirational symbol of American values in a troubled world, an icon who melded individual effort, grit and determination, optimism, and concern for others into a creed that stood in stark contrast to fascist doctrine. "Almost as interesting as Mr. Dale Carnegie's very American lecture the other evening was the very American audience which listened to the speaker with such vast interest," observed one newspaper. "The easy-going, shrewd, optimistic and kindly philosophy of Mr. Carnegie—so evidently approved by his hearers—is as typical of the youthful, warm-hearted and utilitarian viewpoint of the United States as the Nietzschean philosophy is typical of the crowded Germany or the Machiavellian philosophy of old and disillusioned Italy." One journalist suggested that the Nazis learn to avoid arguments, respect the other man's opinion, and approach others in a friendly way. "Now, if Dr. Goebbels would only discover Mr. Carnegie's immortal work! There, if you like, is a picture. Goebbels, seated cozily beside the fire, reading aloud while the Reichskanzler and Minister Goering listen in rapt attention.

Such an event might make a new and much pleasanter man out of Hitler, not to mention his two pals," he exclaimed. "It would lead to smiles and friendliness and cordial greetings. Then there might be an international kaffee-clatsch or a tea party completely unlike the grim meeting in Munich last September."[31]

Reporters sometimes asked Carnegie directly how his principles might be applied to rectify the global crisis. He often demurred, wisely claiming that political matters were beyond his reach. In 1941, he was asked about world politics and his choice for president in the last election. "I didn't vote," he replied frankly. "I didn't feel that I had enough information on the bewildering, complex problems at stake to make an intelligent choice. I don't think there were 10,000 people in the country who did." When questioned about his views on the United States's Good Neighbor policy toward Latin America, he again refused to take a position, quipping, "my opinions have decreased in inverse proportion to my years." The newspaper concluded that this expert on human relations "would not wade off into the topic of improving relations between nations."[32]

At other times, Carnegie took the bait and ventured into the political arena. In the years before the Pearl Harbor attack, he assured audiences that "Americans are opposed to dictators," observing that the United States was sending a significant portion of its war supplies to Britain and opining "it will not be long before they are sending very much more." He spoke often about the Nazis. While granting that *How to Win Friends* was a best seller in Germany, Carnegie thought the book would have little impact on Hitler and his minions. "Suppose some of them do read it and believe it, that might affect the thinking of a few—but the propaganda of the government, the bombs and the concentration camps are the things that affect the people of Germany," he ventured. "A book on friendliness would not have much chance."[33]

By 1941, Carnegie had concluded that the Nazis were immune to the influence of human relations. "Hitler already can influence people, all right, but not with friendship. He has influenced Stalin and Mussolini, but I believe there isn't a shred of friendship mixed up in it," he told one newspaper. "I talked not long ago with a man who had ridden in an airplane with Hitler and his aides since the European conflict began. This man told me even his closest advisors rarely spoke to Hitler. There was, apparently, no friendliness in his makeup. I wouldn't wish to tackle Hitler's personality. It isn't normal." The Führer's dark, abnormal tendencies made him unsusceptible to the advice in *How to Win Friends*. "You can't deal with those fellows like Hitler, except with a gun. Primarily, Hitler is a gangster out to lick the world and the only thing that will stop him is guns," Carnegie contended. "Even Jesus with his great Christian teachings of brotherly love finally saw fit to take the whip in order to drive the money lenders from the temple."[34]

Carnegie's rather banal comments on the Nazi threat were matched by a muddled assessment of rising tensions in Asia. Following a trip to East Asia in 1939, he was asked for his assessment of Japan in light of its brutal invasion of China. His reply shed little light. "The Japanese people follow very much the sort of principles expounded in my book. They are extremely gracious, friendly, and courteous and they are taught to be that way from childhood," he explained. "It seems difficult, therefore, to account for their savagery in China. But we must remember that wars are dictated by the few who are in power." He also noted that the Japanese had been shocked by the recent nonaggression pact between Nazi Germany and the Soviet Union, and promptly removed all German flags from public buildings.[35]

More significantly, Carnegie suggested that Westerners had exaggerated the scope and intensity of the Japanese invasion of China in

1937, as well as its earlier occupation of Manchuria in 1931. Press reports had recounted the brutal massacre of tens of thousands of Chinese civilians by soldiers of the Japanese Imperial Army along with thousands of rapes and other atrocities. But Carnegie detected no evidence of such horrors. "I never heard a shot during the time I was over there," he told the *New York Daily Mirror*. "In my opinion, an automobile trip from New York to San Francisco would be more dangerous than traveling to Harbin, Peking, Shanghai, and the distant borders of Tibet." This benign assessment of Japanese intentions was reflected in a cartoon that appeared in that same newspaper along with Carnegie's report. It showed a Japanese soldier sitting on a rock in the ocean, with two sharks circling about him displaying the Nazi swastika on one fin and the Soviet hammer and sickle on the other, as he frantically read *How to Win Friends and Influence People*.[36]

Eventually, despite the brutal invasions and political terror launched by Hitler, Tojo, and Mussolini, Carnegie insisted that the ideas in *How to Win Friends*, if given the chance, *could* shape international relations in a benevolent way. "If a friendly spirit and a determined desire to influence people peacefully were followed faithfully and intelligently by diplomats at their conference tables, there would be no war," he told the *Los Angeles Evening Herald-Express*. When an interviewer asked about the root causes of the global crisis, Carnegie avoided mention of political ideologies, power politics, economic interests, or even clashing national goals. Instead, he pointed rather naïvely to personal traits and misfires in human relations. "Selfishness, that is what is causing most of the world's troubles. I think practically all of our problems could be solved if everyone would follow the Golden Rule," he claimed. "This war in Europe was caused by two egomaniacs who want to go down in history as the world's greatest conquerors. Their desire to feel important caused them to plunge their nations into war. Greed and the desire to feel important cause all wars."[37]

Such simplistic analysis reflected the limitations of Carnegie's worldview. While the directives in *How to Win Friends* might bring miraculous results at the personal level, this did not translate automatically into the complex world of international politics. Analyzing Hitler as someone who "wanted to feel important" and recommending adherence to the Golden Rule offered little more than bromides in the dangerous world of the early 1940s.

This wobbly venture into international politics sometimes sent Carnegie falling flat on his face. In a long 1941 newspaper interview, he tried to apply Franklin Roosevelt's famous declaration— "All we have to fear is fear itself"—to the looming threat of the Nazis. The result was embarrassing. "Dale Carnegie is not afraid of the big bad wolf, even if its name is Adolf Hitler, and he doesn't think that any American is helping the situation by lying awake nights worrying," the interviewer observed. "Fear, he believes, is the greatest destructive psychological force known. Even in the present world crisis, he thinks that the average American can do more for his country by conquering his fear of the uncertain future than in any other way." Then the article quoted Carnegie's own words. "How many of the things you worry about never even happen? Of course, we should not go blindly along doing nothing, but after we give aid to Britain and do everything we can to help America prepare for its defense, the best thing we can do is to be happy and normal, take things as they come, and cease to worry about the future," he declared. "What if the very worst should happen, and we should be conquered by a dictator? Since history began, nations have existed under dictatorships and come out from under them. Don't worry; think of the good things in life we have instead of the bad ones." Such blind optimism appeared heedless, bizarre, even dangerous if taken seriously. Thinking happy thoughts while succumbing to dictatorship offered little guidance for navigating the dangerous waters of the early 1940s.[38]

After Pearl Harbor and the subsequent American entry into World War II, however, Carnegie thankfully abandoned his therapeutic nostrums regarding world affairs and embraced the war effort. He became an enthusiastic participant in war bond drives, appearing at shows around the country and urging citizens to financially support the nation's military enterprises around the globe. In 1943, he participated in a war bond event in the nation's capital. A full-page advertisement in *The Washington Post* announced the opportunity to meet this "brilliant author whose writings have influenced the lives of countless Americans at the WAR BOND SHOW, today, Monday, at 1:00 and 4:00."[39]

Carnegie made a point of endorsing the draft, arguing that it would have a good effect on most young men. "Especially the spoiled whelps," he added. "A year in the army, ten years in the army will do them good. For the majority of men, it would be an excellent thing. Good for them mentally and physically." The adoption of *How to Win Friends* by certain elements in the American military especially delighted him. Upon hearing that it served as a textbook at the Army Air Forces officer-candidate school in Miami Beach, he said, "That's the smartest thing I have yet heard about the Army. I read an article in *Time* that said that in Germany the officers are kind to their men and find out their sisters' names and when their birthdays come. When every officer in our army knows the birthdays of his men's sisters, then we will really be fighting the war. That is real leadership." After the war ended, Carnegie proudly advertised that his course had been officially approved for "training veterans" under the GI Bill.[40]

Carnegie had somewhat better luck commenting on public affairs when he avoided callow assessments of international politics
and addressed a topic about which he was qualified to speak: education. The curriculum in American public schools became a great
concern to him in the 1940s, one that flowed out of his experience
as a teacher and his formulations in *How to Win Friends*. Throughout the decade, he frequently spoke on the need to reform American teaching by moving it in a more practical direction. The theme
aroused his passion.

Carnegie had become convinced that standard course offerings
in American high schools and colleges were archaic. Decrying the
existing system as "medieval" and "silly, ineffectual and benighted,"
he told audiences that the modern world demanded a more "practical" curriculum. Instead of wasting time on subjects that had no
practical use, schools should focus on preparing students to get
jobs in the workaday world. In 1941, he denounced high schools
for preparing students to take college entrance exams when they
should be teaching them how to sell themselves to prospective em-
ployers. "The youth of today don't even know how to apply for a
job, and if they found one many of them couldn't hold it," Carnegie complained. Most students learned nothing about the personal
qualities necessary to succeed in the modern world, he continued,
but they knew all too much about "such subjects as French grammar, trigonometry, algebra, and Latin."[41]

Warming to this theme in lectures and interviews, Carnegie insisted that one of the two big questions asked by young people was
"What shall I do in life?" and that schools needed to address it
squarely. (The other was "Who will be my mate?") That meant less
emphasis on arcane knowledge and more on vocational training.
Schools should "throw out its algebra or geometry teacher and get
a man to instruct vocational guidance. Give vocational guidance

tests to students. Save hundreds and thousands of students the trouble of going to high school or college. Direct their energies along suited paths," he insisted. This emphasis on practical training and tracking students according to abilities or interests would bring great benefits, Carnegie argued: suitable jobs, useful study programs, happier children.[42]

Carnegie went even further. In his view, success in the modern world may not require college training. "I have been surprised and shocked at the distressingly large number of adults who are ashamed of their lack of formal education, and who go through life burdened with a sense of insecurity and inferiority," he related. This attitude was destructive and wrong, Carnegie contended. Many of the most intelligent and highest achieving individuals in American history had been largely self-educated, he noted, and pointed to the examples of Benjamin Franklin, Abraham Lincoln, Thomas Edison, and Mark Twain, among many others. Moreover, in modern America the opportunities for education had multiplied dramatically. Now "free public libraries, low-cost night schools, and books, newspapers, and magazines are within easy reach," he wrote. "The time is past when we can get away with whining that we never had a chance to go to college. So what? All any college can do for us is to provide a time, a place, and a curriculum for study—we have to do the real work of education ourselves."[43]

But the problem of misplaced college anxiety cut deeper. True to his therapeutic sensibility, Carnegie was especially distressed by its psychological impact. "I have talked to thousands of men who had needless inferiority complexes because they never went to college. They had the impression that somehow, something vital and mysterious inevitably happens to you in college," he related. "Nonsense! The only thing that college can do is to help you educate yourself." While Carnegie certainly valued his own college experience—"I can hardly imagine what my life would have been without it," he once said—the lack of such training should not cause a psychological syndrome. Higher learning certainly could enrich one's mind, he granted, but opportunities for learning existed in numerous places outside of a college campus. "In the last analysis, all education is self-education," he declared. One need only take advantage and feelings of inferiority would be replaced by feelings of accomplishment and self-esteem.[44]

Also true to his therapeutic leanings, Carnegie encouraged a new focus for modern education: the shaping of personality. He argued that "the outstanding purpose of high school is to develop personality" in students. A friendly, solicitous, confident personal image—exactly the kind he had formulated in How to Win Friends—would help students find and keep jobs when they left the classroom for the workforce. The connection between education and personal development was vital, so "regardless of what our schooling has been, the first step in achieving the cultivated, well-rounded personalities we all desire is to realize this need for continuing to learn as long as we live." He offered the example of patients choosing a doctor. "You don't ask what college he attended, how many degrees he obtained, and the number of years he's been practicing, do you? No, the average person is guided largely by the impression a certain physician—and it applies to other professions as well—gives," he argued. "Does he have a pleasing personality? Is he the kind of chap who pats you on the shoulder, sympathizes with your troubles; who has a pleasing smile; who is an easy conversationalist?"[45]

Therein lay the problem with Carnegie's prescriptions for academic reform: a narrow perspective that tended to substitute job training for genuine learning, to replace hard-won skills and bona fide expertise with personal charm. While no one would disagree with the need for vocational guidance, must it come at the expense of doing away with many areas of study? Is exploring the mental discipline of mathematics, the imaginative delights of art, the broadened perspective that accompanies the study of the French language really of no use whatever to the young person who wants to find a satisfying career? Simultaneously, no one could question the importance of a pleasant, friendly manner in a physician. But is medical training and experience really of no concern whatever to the patient? Thoughtful people might wonder.

Thus, in the 1940s Carnegie excelled as an entrepreneur and inspiring teacher in the expansion of his famous course on self-improvement. But the role of sage—the venerated individual who provided wise insights into public issues of the day—proved much harder to fill. His commentary, both on global political tensions and on education reform at home, appeared glib, or occasionally foolish, as often as it did shrewd and penetrating. It also revealed the limitations of Carnegie's therapeutic worldview. Winning friends and influencing people might have a powerful impact on personal life and success, but it provided little guidance for understanding the titanic convulsions of World War II or the complex nature of human learning. Such matters required different, and deeper, kinds of thinking.

15

"He Has the Whole World with Him"

As Dale Carnegie stood at the pinnacle of public fame in the 1940s, his personal life entered a fascinating new stage. Now in late middle age, he had achieved a confident maturity. Behind the national expansion of the Carnegie Course, the nonstop lecture tours, the radio show and newspaper column, and the continued popularity of *How to Win Friends and Influence People* stood a man who finally had come to terms with the elements of his experience—the rural Midwestern Protestant heritage, the ambitious success impulse, the urbane sophistication, the positive-thought optimism—and melded them into a complete whole. He reached a point of secure adult identity, as described by Erik Erikson, where the individual banishes feelings of stagnation or disengagement and embraces his own "generativity," or sense of active, positive contribution to the world.[1]

As a result, Carnegie's personality achieved a conspicuous coherence and force during the 1940s and left a striking impact. The traits he demonstrated—self-effacing charm, enthusiasm for life, warmth, a common touch—truly influenced others and won their friendship. Carnegie, now in his fifties, seemed utterly happy with himself and what he was doing. He radiated the conviction that he was carrying a valuable message to society, one that would ease the way to happiness and fulfillment. In the mid-1940s, relaxing in a hotel suite with a group of Carnegie Course instructors in Chicago, he revealed his pride and satisfaction. "You know, the first 35 years of my life were spent in an effort to earn money, and I almost starved to death," he reflected. "It wasn't until I discovered the idea of rendering a genuine service to humanity that I began to enjoy life and have a real sense of accomplishment."[2]

Perhaps the culminating sign of personal contentment came when Carnegie finally settled into a marriage and orderly domestic life at age fifty-six. He formed a romantic and professional partnership with an intelligent, attractive, and forceful young woman twenty-four years his junior. He became, instantly, the loving father of a stepdaughter, while at the same time continuing to discreetly support and nurture the girl he believed to be his biological daughter. He made it all work. The 1940s would mark the apex of Carnegie's life and career when he achieved the compelling personality and mature influence that he had long pursued.

"Dale Carnegie was a big surprise to me," admitted a *Look* magazine reporter when he met the modern success guru for a feature story in 1947. "I expected a row of gleaming white teeth bared in a forced smile, a bone-crunching handshake, and a yes-man manner," he wrote. "I found instead a sober little man who smiled in moderation, offered a mild hand, and could get mad without any trouble." Many people had similar reactions. Rather than a high-powered, charismatic, polished, breezy character, they found an unassuming man of subtle qualities, an easygoing, average-seeming person whose comfortable presence reminded them of a favorite uncle.[3]

His physical appearance in his fifties conveyed an understated maturity. Of modest height, slender, with a ruddy complexion, alert eyes, and a head of steel-gray hair fading to white around the edges, Carnegie wore clear-plastic framed glasses that were more substantial and less severe than the wire-rims he had favored in earlier years. A traditional, if somewhat natty dresser, he was partial to black or gray double-breasted suits, or occasionally three-piece tweed suits, restrained but expensively tailored, and crisp white shirts. As one journalist observed, they were "not unlike the robes worn by distinguished bankers and successful embalmers. But now and then Dale's individuality, triumphantly putting sartorial conservatism to rout, will assert itself with a tie that flashes like a lighthouse." The same impulse produced his fondness for two-toned saddle shoes. Carnegie's voice, a quiet, slightly nasal Missouri drawl in normal conversation, reinforced the gentle, avuncular demeanor.[4]

Upon first making his acquaintance, many noted a certain discrepancy between the private man and the public man. With individuals or small groups he tended to be quiet, chatting easily in a friendly style but not pushing himself forward, and having a "horror of exhibitionists" who were always trying to draw attention to themselves, as one observer described. He tended to engage strangers with quirky conversational hooks. For example, Carnegie would ask a new acquaintance if he knew what kept him from being an idiot, and when the puzzled man said no, would reply that "a nickel's worth of iodine" in the body's chemistry did so. Or he would pepper conversation with oddities, observing that it was against the law to shake dustrags out of windows in New York, or that about one billion minutes had passed since the birth of Christ.[5]

With larger groups or crowds, however, he threw off any reserve and displayed a "perpetual effervescence and ever-ready handshake" that a journalist described as "the organized charm

of a Sunday School superintendent." When speaking to an audience, his unassuming qualities disappeared as he took command
of the room with a quiet authority. Eschewing grand gestures,
studied poses, and bombastic rhetoric, he spoke instead in a conversational, engaging yet forceful style that conveyed an "almost
hypnotizing assurance," in the words of one enthralled listener. "It
is not inconceivable that Carnegie could lead an army off a high
cliff with his enthusiasm," he wrote. As another reporter described,
when going onstage "he becomes the real Carnegie—the Carnegie
with the Alert Posture and the Self-Confident Air."[6]

But as those who knew him well discovered, Carnegie's unassuming daily appearance and his compelling stage presence encased a
magnetic personality. Subtle rather than powerful, it attracted and
inspired in equal measure as people found themselves drawn into
his orbit before they realized what had happened. For example,
Brick Brickell, a course instructor, first met Carnegie in 1946 when
he was invited to the founder's hotel suite after a lecture. Carnegie
inquired into his background and chatted amiably, and soon "I was
conversing freely with Dale Carnegie and doing so without fear,"
Brickell said. "He had a knack for making people feel at ease." Such
encounters became legion.[7]

Carnegie conveyed a cheerful zeal for life that most people
found contagious. After spending several days in his company, a
Collier's reporter concluded, "Enthusiasm, in fact, is his most en-
dearing quality." Friends and family frequently encountered this
same gusto for new experiences and passion for fresh ideas. Brickell marveled that Carnegie possessed "that spiritual wonder drug
called enthusiasm."[8]

At a course convention in Chicago in 1945, Carnegie was observed carrying around a quart-size paper container leaking an
orange liquid. When friends inquired, he waxed eagerly about a

wonderful new product, condensed frozen orange juice, being developed by an old friend of his. Most people rolled their eyes at such an impractical idea, but it turned out that the old friend was Clarence Birdseye, and his product soon took the national food market by storm. As a colleague summarized, Carnegie inspired others to follow him "from defeat to victory, from fear to confidence . . . He was a whole-hearted man."[9]

Carnegie's sincere interest in others, combined with a genial demeanor and puckish sense of humor, endeared him to many. John Spindler first met him in 1946 during a speaking engagement in Los Angeles, and Carnegie soon had him talking about his family as if they were old friends. It was the beginning of a lifelong friendship. Another colleague reported that during an animated conversation, Carnegie suddenly got a twinkle in his eye and said, "You amaze me. You remind me so much of Einstein." When the instructor replied that he must be kidding, Carnegie delivered the punch line: "No, I'm not. Einstein once said that he was wrong 99% of the time."[10]

Carnegie's enthusiasm for people and life even shaped his work schedule, which was anything but routine. Whether laboring at home or traveling the country, he did not submit to the restrictions of a nine-to-five schedule but lived his work. Marilyn Burke, who became his personal secretary in the mid-1940s, soon found that her duties were highly unconventional and unstructured. "There were no rigid hours, no set routines, no daily rituals. You never knew what new venture he would dream up for you," she explained. "And this was part of the charm of the man." From one day to the next, she might find herself fixing breakfast for Carnegie and a visitor or flying to Kansas with her boss to visit the ranch of an oilman seeking an investment in his operation. She concluded, "Dale expected much of the people who worked for him, much that was not related to their jobs. But he gave far more than he took."[11]

Yet throughout the 1940s, while expanding his network of friends and colleagues, Carnegie maintained his old friendships. His boyhood chum Homer Croy lived nearby and Carnegie regularly spent Sunday afternoons with him where, according to one observer, they would go for hours "walking in the woods, loafing in comfort, eating impossible food in impossible restaurants, or raiding the icebox—just having fun in an irresponsible, relaxed, boyish fashion." They also traveled to Missouri on occasion where they made for an interesting contrast—Croy, the wisecracking practical joker, who told a banquet in Maryville that while Carnegie had a new book coming out at the cost of $3.00, the thrifty reader should wait a few more weeks when he could buy *his* new book for only $2.75; and the low-key, self-deprecating Carnegie, who joked that Croy had urged him to talk about himself "since that was my favorite subject anyway."[12]

Carnegie also cherished his relationship with Lowell Thomas. He still visited Thomas at his upstate farm for softball games or weekends of relaxation, and they enjoyed getting together whenever Thomas came to New York. They exchanged signed copies of their new books, attended Broadway plays when they could arrange it, and were featured on each other's radio shows. With typical thoughtfulness, Carnegie purchased a special gift for Thomas's Pawling estate by buying hardwood trees and having them planted along the driveway leading to the house to create a spacious natural canopy.[13]

Throughout the 1940s, Carnegie persisted in many of his lifelong hobbies and interests. He remained devoted to the theater, attending numerous plays and shows, often with an attractive woman on his arm. He even participated on occasion. In 1949, he turned up as a "supernumerary," or an extra, in the ballet *Scheherazade* at the New York City Center, along with Croy. Dressed in faded blue robes, they played the parts of the sultan's soldiers. According to one of the lead dancers, when the pair came charging onstage waving wooden sabers, "they looked so solemn they made *me* laugh. I was supposed to be stabbing myself to death at the time, so you might say I died laughing. They got a dollar apiece for being supers."[14]

Carnegie remained an inveterate traveler. He regularly visited the Canadian Rockies, often at Lake Louise in Alberta, and sailed to Europe whenever he could find the time. In 1948, for instance, he spent several weeks touring France and England. But Carnegie's yen for travel involved more than recreation, as he eagerly sought to soak up varied experiences around the world and to foster personal self-improvement. In 1943, for example, he followed his own advice about lifelong education by enrolling for summer courses at the University of Wyoming. While vacationing in the area to engage in horseback riding and hiking, he decided to extend his stay by taking classes in astronomy, mental hygiene, marriage and the family, and vernacular English. "I like western people," he told the Laramie newspaper. "I have lived for 16 years so close to some people in New York that I could throw an apple into their yard, but I have never spoken to them. Out here, where people are sparsely settled, there is a friendly atmosphere that I like."[15]

Yet Carnegie, for all of his attractive qualities, also had certain shortcomings that rankled him, perhaps, more than others. He fretted about his inability to consistently follow his own dictates of human relations. Although friendly, considerate of others, fulsome in his praise, and an attentive listener, he frequently grew impatient, argumentative, even angry about others' foibles. He would stalk around the house after some frustrating encounter, glance balefully at his staff, and fall to brooding. In addition, a colleague

Carnegie engaged in one of his favorite hobbies, camping and hiking in the Rockies, in the 1940s.

was startled to overhear Carnegie, at a staff meeting, lean over to Abbie Connell and quietly inquire about the name of a teacher who had been with him for almost twenty years. When the colleague inquired, Connell replied with a laugh, "Sure, Mr. Carnegie can't remember names." Carnegie was trustful to the point of naïveté. He set up his organization with little oversight regarding money, and after his death, family and colleagues were shocked to discover a complete absence of financial controls. In the words of one of them, "had the staff not been scrupulously honest, the company could have been stolen blind!"[16]

But such personal flaws seemed petty as Carnegie won over nearly everyone he encountered, not least because of his unpretentious manner and common touch. A deep sympathy for ordinary people seeped out of him at every turn. In articles, he described a university professor in one of his courses as lifeless while praising a common sailor whose talks "had the sweep and salt and tang of the sea." On teacher-training trips, he avoided fancy restaurants and ate at common diners, such as one in Los Angeles that specialized in buttermilk pancakes. "I love buttermilk pancakes," he told his hosts. When he appeared before thousands of people at the Pasadena Civic Auditorium, his host said he had prepared introductions of ten minutes, five minutes, and two minutes. But Carnegie remonstrated, "Can you do it in ten seconds." So the man simply said, "Ladies and gentlemen, Dale Carnegie."[17]

A powerful inspiration for Carnegie's common touch came from his reverence for the rural values of his youth. When he was on the road lecturing and teaching, he would have his driver stop at fruit stands so he could sample the local produce. He would frequent farmers' markets and exchange stories about rural life with proprietors of the various stalls. While most Americans saw Carnegie as a symbol of modern urbanity, one journalist said he was left with the impression of passing the time with a genial farmer after spending several days in Carnegie's company. Much of the philosophy in *How to Win Friends*, the journalist concluded, was merely an outgrowth of "the deep-seated courtesy, the respect for human dignity, the appreciation for the rarely seen and therefore appreciated neighbor which is practiced by country people."[18]

Indeed, Carnegie did everything he could to keep in touch with his rural past. He returned frequently to his boyhood stomping grounds in Maryville and Warrensburg, Missouri, throughout the 1940s to give talks and visit old friends. After World War II, Carnegie strengthened his rural ties by purchasing a 1,250-acre farm in Belton, Missouri, where he raised Brangus cattle, a combination of the Brahman and Angus breeds. He hired a distant cousin to manage the place but snuck away from his professional duties every few months to stay for several days. Riding horses, pitching hay, repairing fences, and planting hedges to stop soil erosion, he reveled in the joys of rural life. He liked visiting with neighbors, sitting on a front porch and talking over a Coke. He still felt at home in the country. "Most of my relatives are farmers. My parents are buried on the farm," Carnegie told *Look* magazine in 1948. "And when I die, I expect to spend eternity there beside them." This rural sensibility carried over to his home in suburban New York, where he became an avid gardener and loved to get his hands dirty. One afternoon, after Marilyn Burke spied her boss coming in from planting flower bulbs on a rainy afternoon, happily covered in mud, she came to an important realization. Carnegie was "a very different person from the one I thought I worked for—not the sophisticated New Yorker, the erudite author, lecturer, and educator—but rather a very homey, down-to-earth human being."[19]

A love of the outdoors flavored Carnegie's daily life. He took long walks several times a week in Forest Park, a large tract of tree-filled public land not far from his home. A reporter for *Collier's* accompanied him on one of these jaunts and described his habit of "constantly exclaiming over the wonders of nature." An accompanying photograph showed Carnegie resting on a park bench, dressed warmly in a wool overcoat and holding a tweed fedora, contentedly gazing out at the huge trees, scattered leaves, and stark beauty of a winter landscape. In the 1940s, his love for nature encompassed a new interest: dinosaurs. He became fascinated with paleontology—contemplating vast expanses of time and extinct creatures seemed to have left him in a state of awe—and he pursued the topic with typical enthusiasm. When in Los Angeles, he asked to visit the famous La Brea Tar Pits, and his host listened as he talked knowledgeably about dinosaurs, woolly mammoths, and saber-toothed cats as they rode along Wilshire Boulevard. He even contacted Yale University and purchased a set of dinosaur tracks embedded in shale and stone and installed them in his backyard garden. Carnegie always showed them to visitors, proudly announcing, "I have a letter from the curator of the Peabody Museum, saying those tracks were made 180 million years ago."[20]

But Carnegie's home life would become even more settled in the mid-1940s. On one of his lecture-and-teaching tours, he had an engagement in Tulsa, Oklahoma, with a Carnegie Course sponsor. There he met an attractive, charming, articulate young woman. Both felt a spark of attraction, and within a few months a relationship had flourished. A little more than a year after their initial introduction, Carnegie, the confirmed bachelor, took a step that surprised many.

Dorothy Vanderpool did not want to go. She was tired after work and not especially eager to hear the great Dale Carnegie speak in her hometown of Tulsa in the fall of 1943, even though she had graduated from his course. But she and her mother had been invited by Everett Pope, an old family friend and the Carnegie sponsor in Tulsa, and her mother, a forceful woman, insisted on attending the event. So off they went and she found herself captivated. It was "amazing" to hear Carnegie speak as he radiated a quiet charisma and held the rapt attention of the audience, she said. Afterward, Dorothy was taken to meet Carnegie, and she, along with her mother and Pope, ended up joining the famous visitor for coffee. The young woman enjoyed his company and found him interesting and attractive, but thought little of the encounter except to tell friends about her brush with fame.

Carnegie, however, found much more in this casual get-together. He pressed Pope for details about Dorothy after her departure and secured her address. After returning home, he began sending her letters that were, in her words, "not romantic exactly, but they were a little warmer than business letters." After several weeks of correspondence, he invited her to New York to join his organization doing secretarial work as well as some ghostwriting for him. She accepted, moved, and took up her new duties in January 1944. Dorothy and Dale began to date and developed a serious relationship throughout the spring and summer before announcing their impending marriage in the fall. "I used a puppy's method to win her," Carnegie joked later. "You know, a puppy shows an interest in you and that makes you get interested in him."[21]

Dorothy Price Vanderpool came from a heartland background that appealed to Carnegie in a visceral way. In fact, he told a magazine writer that her mother had boarded briefly with his parents at their farm in Missouri when he was a very small boy. Dorothy was born on November 3, 1912, the only child of Henry and Victoria Price. He worked as a minor public official in Spavinaw, Oklahoma, a small town in the northeast corner of the state, and the family soon moved to Tulsa. Henry was a quiet, gentle man whom Carnegie later would memorialize in one of his books as someone who "tries to live by the Golden Rule; and he is incapable of doing anything mean, selfish, or dishonest." Victoria, on the other hand, was a tough, strong-willed, outspoken woman who ruled the Price household with a firm hand. Her daughter would inherit many of these qualities.[22]

By her teenage years, Dorothy, an intelligent and popular girl, had developed varied interests and joined many clubs at her high school. In particular, she had thrown herself into journalism with the hopes of someday becoming a writer. By the time she was a senior at Central High School in 1930, she had become involved in the Press Club, School Life Club, Quill and Scroll, Junior Honor Society, and Advertising Board. In the yearbook she was described as "An imaginative personage with inclinations toward vagabonding and pencraft." Slender, pretty, with auburn hair and a determined look frequently on her face, she was also very tall—she stood about five foot ten—and this often left her, with typical teenage angst, feeling awkward, "like a giant."[23]

After graduation, Dorothy began taking classes at a local college when she met Louis Vanderpool, a handsome, blond-haired young man who was a student at the University of Oklahoma in Norman. A whirlwind romance resulted. Dorothy got pregnant, dropped out of school, and the couple married. A daughter, Rosemary, was born on July 2, 1933, in Norman while the young parents worked as caretakers of a university fraternity house over the summer. The marriage lasted only a short time. Louis drank enthusiastically and wanted to socialize while Dorothy had career ambitions, and they separated and divorced. She would later describe it as "one of those unfortunate teenage marriages." Cut adrift, Dorothy and her infant daughter moved back home to live with her parents in Tulsa.[24]

Motherhood proved to be an awkward fit. Dorothy nurtured strong aspirations in the working world and showed scant interest in being a single parent. She found a job in the Tulsa office of the Gulf Oil Corporation and began to climb the corporate ladder. Her efforts eventually landed a position as senior secretary in the executive suite, a promotion no doubt aided by her completion of a Carnegie Course under Pope. The communication skills she learned there, along with her outgoing personality and forceful manner, won her the presidency of Tulsa's Young Republicans Club. She began to give "humorous-type talks to men's civic club luncheons," she recalled later. "They even got reported in the papers." At the same time, Dorothy largely turned over the raising of her daughter to Henry and Victoria, who became surrogate parents for the girl. Rosemary always called her Dorothy, never "mother" or "mom" or "mommy." Dorothy had a conflicted attitude. Later she commented that her daughter's habit had been encouraged by Victoria, and that it hurt her. At the same time, Dorothy would always say, "she had a name and Rosemary should use it." In either event, the maternal role proved difficult. Straining against the confines of her life, the young career woman desperately dreamed of leaving her hometown for a bigger arena.[25]

This was her situation when Carnegie arrived for his fateful visit. Smitten immediately, he convinced Dorothy to move to New York where the infatuation evolved into something more serious. Throughout 1944, they gradually fell in love, and the nature of their mutual attraction was obvious. For Carnegie, the young woman offered obvious physical enticements with her tall, lithe figure and good looks. But her intellectual qualities proved equally important—a sparkling intelligence, a gift for writing, an irreverent zest for life, and a tough-minded determination to succeed. She was a Midwesterner like him, someone with whom he instinctively felt comfortable. And unlike Frieda Offenbach, she was not entangled in a complicated marriage but was available for a deeper relationship. As for Dorothy, she embraced a suitor who was famous, charming, mature, and wealthy, someone with a kind and generous spirit who seemed ready to settle down to domestic life at the age of fifty-six. He also offered her an opportunity for escape to an exciting life in the cultural, social, and economic hub of the nation's largest city. So in addition to the personal spark between them, Dale and Dorothy very much met each other's broader emotional needs.

Their courtship, not surprisingly given the two strong personalities at play, was sometimes tempestuous. Most of the time, Dale was his amiable, considerate, and solicitous self while Dorothy used her wit and intelligence to great effect. But occasionally, as often happens with two willful individuals, tensions turned into conflicts and arguments erupted. According to one observer, a crisis threatened as "Dorothy once quit her job after a spat with Carnegie and started to pack and go home, only to have him turn on the how-to-win-friends charm and influence her into staying." By the fall of 1944, the couple decided they were right for each other and sent out an official wedding announcement in October, which was picked up by newspapers all over the country. It also appeared in *Time* magazine, along with Dale's quip that even after writing *How to Win Friends* "it took me eight years to influence a woman to marry me."[26]

Dale and Dorothy married on November 5, 1944, in Tulsa at the Boston Avenue Methodist Church with a small group of family and friends in attendance. Before the ceremony began, Harry O. Hamm, serving as an usher, was with Dale in the groom's room as they heard selections from the musical *Oklahoma* being played in the church sanctuary. According to Hamm, "Dale Carnegie turned to Everett Pope and me and said, 'If they play "People Will Say

We're in Love," I'll just cry.' Well, they did play that song but Dale managed to stay dry-eyed. How? He was so excited about marrying Dorothy that he never even heard the song."[27]

After the ceremony, Dorothy moved into Dale's house on Wendover Road in Forest Hills and the couple settled into domestic life. Dale continued to work at home, a fact that made for a difficult adjustment for his new wife. In an advice book for women she wrote a few years later called *How to Help Your Husband Get Ahead in His Social and Business Life,* Dorothy included a chapter entitled

The wedding of Dale Carnegie and Dorothy Vanderpool in Tulsa, Oklahoma, on November 5, 1944.

"How to Keep from Going Crazy if He Works at Home." "Any woman who must gear her entire home routine around a man who is constantly underfoot deserves a special award of merit," she wrote. "Imagine having to tiptoe around that closed room where your lord is at work, having him ask you to turn off the vacuum when you are only half through, or never being able to entertain your friends at luncheon because the cackle disturbs the master." Nonetheless, Dorothy urged the wife to accommodate her work-at-home husband's needs, make him comfortable, forget his presence and go about your own daily tasks, assume a good-humored demeanor, and avoid interrupting him. She added, "For eight years of our marriage, my husband did all of his work at home, so I know whereof I speak."[28]

As Dorothy grew accustomed to her new life, she quickly became an efficient manager of a household that included two secretaries and a housekeeper. As a magazine article noted, however, the housekeeper "gets little chance to demonstrate her Middle European cuisine because the Carnegies prefer Middle Western dishes." Settling into marriage, Dale and Dorothy knit together their interests to create a contented, harmonious life. He remained an avid backyard gardener and she shared this enthusiasm, eagerly working in the yard and becoming a specialist in growing tulips and irises. The couple shared a love of the theater, regularly attending performances in New York. They loved to travel and took numerous trips to the Canadian Rockies, the ranch country of Wyoming, and Europe, where they toured England, France, and Italy. In general, Dale and Dorothy manifested an enthusiasm for life that made their relationship congenial. Lee Maber, one of Carnegie's secretaries, who along with her husband joined them for dinner in New York's Chinatown, recalled a memorable ride home on an elevated train. "The car we were on was deserted and one of us started to sing a song about New York," Maber reported. "Suddenly Dale said, 'Let's go!' and waltzed Dorothy down the aisle. George and I joined them and we all continued to sing together. We had a wonderfully light-hearted time."[29]

Now established in an affluent suburb of New York, Dorothy pursued a wide array of interests that revealed the breadth of her intelligence, talent, and enthusiasm for life. She loved to read, with mysteries quenching her lighter tastes and Shakespeare becoming a passion. She pored over the Bard's many plays, and eventually became president of the Shakespeare Club of New York City, an organization with which she maintained close ties for the rest of her life. "My wife is entranced with the study of Shakespeare and his plays," Dale wrote proudly; "she says old age has no terrors for her because it will give her more time for study." Dorothy became an avid cook, although her culinary skills never quite matched her ardor, and played the piano with gusto, gathering friends and family around the keyboard to sing carols during the Christmas season. Influenced by her Oklahoma background, she was a skilled horsewoman and a crack shot at the rifle range. She became interested in fencing and for a time was a member of a fencing team in Forest Hills.[30]

Dorothy proved adept at handling her husband and establishing a position of equality in the relationship. She came to understand his occasional dark moods. When he appeared sour and uncooperative, an observer noted, she would jokingly recall that she "once spent $76 to take the [Carnegie] course, laughingly demands her money back, and this usually straightens him out." This tactic occasionally failed. A visitor once observed Dale stalking about the house quietly seething in anger, and described Dorothy's roguish reaction: "'There,' said Mrs. Carnegie, arching an eyebrow, 'goes the man who wrote The Book.'" But Dorothy, a confident and outspoken woman, did not shrink from standing up to her famous husband when she felt it necessary. "She never backed down from an argument, and that included Dale," observed a family member. "Abbie [Connell], who was Dale's secretary, and then later Dorothy's, told me there were times that their arguments would increase to yelling, but always by the end they would have some resolution. They were a very normal married couple." Carnegie, who came to accept and appreciate his wife's assertive nature, would joke about how the realities of marriage forced an alteration of his human relations principles. A colleague once adopted Carnegie's tactic of "avoiding the acute angle" during a dinner party when his wife strongly expressed a controversial opinion and he commented, "Dear, you could be right." Immediately, Carnegie chimed in with a laugh: "No, no, no! When it is your wife, you say, 'Darling, you are *absolutely* right!'"[31]

While determined to carve out a position of equity in their marriage, Dorothy also worked to accommodate her husband's enthusiasms and activities. For example, although a bit mystified at first, she quickly accepted his close friendship with Homer Croy. The two spent every Sunday afternoon together horsing around, going to low-rent eateries, telling jokes, and sharing old memories. Dorothy came to enjoy Croy's rambunctious personality, as well as the company of his wife, Mae, and to appreciate his salutary influence on her husband by helping him to unwind. In 1945, as a good-natured joke, Dorothy even composed a satirical poem about Dale's best friend after *The New York Times* pilloried Croy in a book review as a "professional rube." She sent the verses to be published in the *Maryville Forum* just as the two men were making a joint appearance in their hometown:

HOMER, SWEET HOMER

or

THE BAREFOOT BOY WITH CUSTOM-MADE SHOES ON

By Dorothy Carnegie

He's just an unspoiled village lad, with hayseed in his hair,
Bewildered by the Great White Way, and choked by city air.
His heart is back in Maryville, he sings the simple life.
He writes of small-town heroes, and eats peas with his knife.
But this homesick rube is baffled, by a problem grim and
    stark
He can't make hay in hayfields, like he can in old New York!
Missouri boasts no Player's Club, where jolly wights can
    meet,
And country roads aren't quite so smooth, as Forty-Second
    Street.
So Croy sticks to the city, with its sin and strife and glare.
And just writes about the country, and thanks God he isn't
    there.[32]

But Dorothy's influence on her husband went beyond their personal life. She became his partner on the business front as well. In 1945, only a few months after they married, Carnegie reorganized his enterprise by creating Dale Carnegie and Associates, Inc., a private-stock company, with himself as president and Dorothy as vice president. With her combination of intelligence, assertiveness, and business savvy, she immediately began to expand her role in the operation. While on one of their vacations early in their married life, an important new idea germinated. "We had been to the Canadian Rockies three or four times previously; he liked to hike over the trails and sit and admire the scenery," she explained. "I got tired of this outdoor life. At night, when I wanted to dance, he

Carnegie at a banquet with lifelong friend Homer Croy seated three chairs to his left.

wanted to go to bed early so he could get up at dawn and look at more scenery. I could ride those trails on horseback in my sleep. Finally he came up with a plan to keep me happy: 'Why don't you write a class for women?' he asked. I agreed, and started right to work." This produced the Dorothy Carnegie Course in Personal Development for Women, which would remain an important part of the Carnegie enterprise for the next fifteen years.[33]

In fact, Dorothy's business acumen clearly exceeded her husband's. While at heart he was a teacher and writer, she had financial and organizational skills, as well as a hardheaded instinct for assessing the bottom line of profit, which proved invaluable in a corporate setting. According to an inside observer, Dorothy was an ambitious businesswoman who had "the killer instinct. She was the one who really put the wheels under the Carnegie company . . . She knew where she wanted to go and damn the torpedoes, full speed ahead." With her background at Gulf Oil in Tulsa, as well as her shrewd judgment in business matters, Dorothy clearly influenced the 1945 incorporation, a move that rationalized Carnegie's somewhat haphazard teaching and publication endeavors.[34]

His 1944 marriage brought an additional new element into Carnegie's life: Dorothy's daughter, Rosemary. The new husband and the eleven-year-old took an immediate liking to each other and forged a strong bond over the next few years. Dale introduced the girl to travel, arranging for her to accompany them on vacations to the west and on a cruise ship to Europe in 1948. He referred to her as his daughter, never his stepdaughter, and enjoyed becoming a parent. At the same time, he deferred to her mother in matters of discipline. Carnegie was proud of the girl and liked to brag about her. "My daughter, Rosemary, at the age of twelve, had no interest in rocks and minerals, until a friend gave her some fossils when we were vacationing in the Canadian Rockies," he told a magazine. "She began to notice rocks and pay attention to them. Then she saved her own money and bought herself a textbook. Next, she got some specimens of her own. Now she has a fine mineral collection and dreams of becoming a geologist when she grows up."[35]

For her part, Rosemary "thought the world" of her new father. Many years after his death, she launched a project to gather reminiscences from many of his relatives, friends, and colleagues and published them as a tribute. She recalled his enthusiasm for new ideas and inventions, describing "how delighted he was with the first ball point pens when they came out." She remembered how he showed her "my first television, which he had purchased in the mid-thirties. It was a huge mahogany chest much like a monster. The top opened to reveal a mirror because the picture came in reverse and thus had to be viewed with the aid of a mirror." She described how he carefully displayed old family pictures from his boyhood days in rural Missouri and had a penchant for rewriting numerous drafts of his articles and books as he sought to find "what he wanted to express in the way he wanted it to be read."[36]

At the same time, Rosemary's unconventional relationship with her mother produced a certain tension in the family dynamic. Dorothy struggled with melding motherhood and strong career aspirations. When she moved to New York to take up her new duties with the Carnegie Institute, she left Rosemary behind with her grandparents in Tulsa. When the eleven-year-old girl came to Wendover Road nearly a year later, it was only for a short time. Dorothy sent Rosemary to an exclusive boarding school in upstate New York not long after her arrival, and the girl returned to Forest Hills for holidays and an occasional weekend. Growing rebellious, Rosemary at age sixteen flatly rejected any kind of debutante activities in New York, a decision that sorely disappointed Dorothy. So while mutual respect prevailed between mother and daughter, a certain distance kept the relationship somewhat strained.[37]

Nonetheless, as with all parents and children, accommodations were reached and compromises negotiated. And at the end of the decade, the Carnegie family presented themselves to America on behalf of *World Book Encyclopedia*. In a full-page, color magazine advertisement, a large photograph depicted a smiling Dale, Dorothy, and Rosemary seated on a divan against a book-lined wall in their home. A caption blared, "Dale Carnegie asks, 'Are you helping your child win success?'" The text claimed that even though schools may be crowded and good teachers in short supply, parents could help by purchasing an encyclopedia "to give their children the kind of mental stimulation that gets results." Carnegie observed that while teachers had students only 9 percent of the time, "it's often what you do during the 91% of the time that your child is at home that creates the thirst for knowledge, the desire to learn. It was because we realized this that we selected World Book Encyclopedia for our daughter, Rosemary. She finds constant pleasure and inspiration in it."[38]

Dale, Dorothy, and Rosemary featured in a national advertisement for *World Book* in 1950.

Thus Carnegie's personal and domestic life settled into a comfortable and fulfilling pattern in the 1940s. A fabulously successful writer and legendary teacher, and now in possession of a stable family life, he was very content. His endeavors had made him financially prosperous, but he had no great desire to become richer. "If I had all the money in the world, I couldn't wear more clothes, and I live exactly where I want to live," he would say. Yet one complicated issue remained, a holdover from an earlier period, which continued to attract Carnegie's attention and pull at his heart.[39]

"All in all, I think you are about the sweetest little girl that God ever sent to New Haven," said the letter to Linda Dale Offenbach, dated July 3, 1944. "I wish I could see you more often. You are most fortunate to have the wise, understanding father you have, [and] the sweet, charming, unselfish mother," the writer added in a typically ambiguous reference to her paternity. He praised the girl on the eve of her sixth birthday for her "remarkable personal charm," "energy and enthusiasm," "sincere smile," "good looks," and "extraordinary intelligence." "I am constantly surprised at your ability to use words and at your ability to read. And how you love to read to me," he added. Offhandedly, the writer mentioned that he had purchased for her several shares of "Humble Oil Stock," observing that while inflation might dilute the money he already had given her for a college education, the stock's value would rise accordingly and always hold its value. The letter closed, "With eternal love, Linda, I am your uncle, Dale Carnegie."[40]

Written in the middle of the successful author's courtship of Dorothy Vanderpool, this letter highlighted a continuing conundrum in his life. Carnegie believed that Linda Dale Offenbach was his daughter, the offspring of his half-hidden relationship with Frieda

Offenbach. Throughout the 1940s, much of this peculiar arrangement continued, with Linda regularly visiting Carnegie's home on Wendover Road in Forest Hills, Queens. The situation remained as murky and complex as ever.

Carnegie and Frieda maintained their romantic relationship through the early 1940s. Her letters contained outpourings of love to "my dearest," musings that "it must be heavenly where you are," and wishes "to be at your side, my darling." He responded in kind, filling letters with words of affection for Frieda and hopes of seeing her whenever it could be arranged. In the summer of 1943, while vacationing in Wyoming, he wrote to Linda, "How I wish you and your lovely mater could be here, too. I am lonely for both of you . . . I give you, Linda Dale, all my love and tenderness—give it to you and your lovely mother." Carnegie occasionally made sojourns to New Haven and stayed overnight in the Offenbach home. But arranging such liaisons could be difficult. "I quite understand why it isn't convenient for you to have me come today," he wrote at one point. "As soon as the visitors leave and you are feeling yourself again, please let me know, and I will be seeing you." In Canada, he wrote that he kept "looking every day for a letter from you," and added, in a sarcastic jab at Isador, "And how is your Lord and Master?"[41]

Carnegie even featured Frieda in one of his daily newspaper columns titled, somewhat ironically, "Self-Control." "The best thought I have picked up this week came from Mrs. Isador Offenbach, who lives at 58 Gordon St., Hamden, Connecticut," he wrote. "I have always admired her exquisite poise, her ability to get things done without hurry or nerve." When he asked how she was able to remain so unruffled and graceful under even the most pressing conditions, she had replied, "I never do anything important enough to get nervous about." Carnegie thought about the answer, and concluded, "Come to think about it, neither do I. And the chances are, you don't either. None of the trivial things we do day by day are important enough." This became the basis for a homily on the need to control our emotions, gain mastery over our thoughts, and thus steer ourselves toward happiness. Frieda's comment, however, carried a deeper layer of meaning for those who knew her: It suggested the underlying sadness in her life as she remained loyal to a disabled husband, unable to have a real relationship with Carnegie.[42]

But the romance between Dale and Frieda began to fade. She gave birth to a second child, Russell, on October 14, 1942, and there seems to have been no question of paternity—Carnegie mentioned little about the boy and did not shower him with gifts and money as he did the sister. In fact, the issue of sibling favoritism became so awkward that Isador finally asked Carnegie to give more presents to Russell to lessen his growing jealousy of Linda. It is hard to pinpoint the reasons for the cooling of Dale and Frieda's relationship. Her steadfast refusal to leave Isador must have contributed, and Carnegie also may have wearied of the psychodrama attending this complicated entanglement. Then, with Dale's wooing of and marriage to Dorothy in 1944, any physical relationship between Dale and Frieda definitely came to an end.[43]

Regarding Linda, however, Carnegie's feelings of paternal obligation remained strong throughout the 1940s, even after his marriage. As with any proud father, he reminisced about their times together and doted on her childish adventures and achievements. After his visits to New Haven, he would write and remind the girl how she had fallen out of her bed in the middle of the night, or how they had played together on the floor as she "got on my back and rode me as your horse." In 1943, he reminded her of a recent visit when they took a long walk in a New Haven park and "you spent most of your time picking red clover and wild flowers and running out into the wet grass to do it . . . [You] insist on sitting in the swing by yourself and being pushed high." Carnegie's visits to the Offenbach home continued until at least late 1948.[44]

Throughout the decade, Carnegie sent a steady flow of gifts and money into the Offenbach household. He established a college education fund for the girl and regularly sent checks to deposit in it. Perhaps most remarkably, however, a document typed on his personal stationery and dated July 24, 1942, indicated Carnegie's profound concern for Frieda and Linda's financial well-being:

> For $100.00 and other good and valuable consideration which I hereby acknowledge, I sell to Mrs. Frieda Offenbach all the stock I own both A and B Shares in the following corporations:
> Dale Carnegie Publishing and Service Corporation
> Dale Carnegie Courses Corporation
> Dale Carnegie Institute of Effective Speaking and Human Relations, Inc.

It was signed by Carnegie and witnessed by Abigail M. Connell, his trusted assistant. The legal status and import of this document is unclear—it was never put into effect nor probated after Carnegie's death—but it clearly suggested the depth of his commitment.[45]

As for Linda's visits to the Carnegie house at Wendover Road, they continued through the late 1940s. After coming to New York on the train, she would spend the weekend with Carnegie, and he would take her to museums, plays, the circus, or any other activity he thought she might enjoy. "You recently visited me here in Forest Hills. You and Pat, the little girl next door, played together in my garden," he wrote, adding proudly, "Pat is your age, yet she can't use one tenth as many words as you can. She is either dumb or you are bordering on—your mother's ability." As late as 1949, at age eleven, Linda was still coming to Forest Hills for weekend visits. In July, Carnegie sent a letter of regret upon hearing that she had been sick with a cold. "I had looked forward to seeing you on Sunday," he wrote. "After you get well, come down some other Sunday and we will have an exciting time."[46]

Beginning in 1944, with his marriage to Dorothy, Carnegie seems to have scheduled Linda's visits to coincide with Dorothy's absences. Having assumed an ever more prominent role in the Carnegie company, his wife traveled occasionally on teaching and business trips, as well as visiting Tulsa to see her family. Dale seems to have explicitly brought Linda to Wendover Road when Dorothy was away. Later, the girl recalled seeing Dorothy only once during her many stays with Dale, and the experience was unpleasant—Linda committed a minor faux pas at the dinner table, wherein Dorothy laughed loudly and caused the girl great embarrassment. There is no evidence of what Dale told his wife about the visiting "niece," but around 1950 Linda's visits to New York stopped abruptly. Frieda told her daughter, without providing details, that Mrs. Carnegie had "banned" the Offenbachs from the Carnegie home. One suspects that Dorothy may have discovered incriminating evidence of some kind regarding Dale and Frieda, or even that Dale may have confessed the truth about the situation. Regardless, Carnegie's overt relationship with Frieda and Linda ran up against a strong barrier.[47]

But it did not end. In September 1950, Carnegie wrote a long letter to Frieda noting that several years ago he had given Linda "a one-half interest in the building located at 250-02 Northern Boulevard, Little Neck." But now he had purchased an adjoining tract of land and contracted with the U.S. government to build a post office on it. Part of the building would intrude onto the property half owned by Linda. So Carnegie asked Frieda to return the deed to the property, and in return "I will give Linda outright a four-story apartment house in Little Neck. It would cost about $35,000 to build it today." Clearly he was still maneuvering to insure the girl's future economic security. At the end of the letter to Frieda, he added, "I'll be seeing you in October or November." Then at Christmas 1950, as a gift he sent Linda a copy of his book *Biographical Roundup: Highlights in the Lives of Forty Famous People*. He inscribed it, "To the sweetest young woman this side of paradise, Linda Dale Offenbach, from one of her most ardent admirers. 'Uncle' Dale Carnegie."[48]

Despite such complications, Carnegie's life and career flourished during the 1940s. In fact, his personal contentment, stability, and prosperity in many ways mirrored the larger condition of the United States. With the fading of the Depression and the successful conclusion of World War II, events had ushered in a new era of confidence and economic expansion. This convergence of personal status and public aspiration set the stage for Carnegie's last great contribution to American culture. In the late 1940s, he wrote another best-selling book that reflected the currents of material abundance, religiosity, domestic togetherness, and suburban conformity sweeping through American life in the postwar era. But it also captured much of its underlying anxiety.

16

"Businessmen Who Do Not Fight Worry Die Young"

I n the aftermath of World War II, America entered a new era of abundance. With the demise of the Great Depression and the successful prosecution of the global conflict against fascism, the United States emerged as the world's most powerful nation, both militarily and materially. A booming wartime economy shifted gears to consumer production after 1945 to meet the swelling demand for goods among a citizenry eager to be done with the privations of economic depression and the sacrifices of national crisis. With material aspirations growing, middle-class Americans began a popular love affair with suburban homes and lawn mowers, washing machines and vacuum cleaners, automobiles and barbecue grills. Prosperity was in the air.

America's glossy, photograph-laden, big-format magazines took the lead in promoting and examining this new ethos. Publications such as *Life* and *Look*, with their millions of subscribers, served as barometers of public opinion, and they began to examine the country's booming consumer economy. In May 1948, for example, *Look* proclaimed "The Miracle of America." The article was the brainchild of the Advertising Council, a nonpartisan group of business leaders, advertisers, union representatives, media managers, and public figures who sought to promote tighter cooperation among business, government, and organized labor. It included figures such as Evans Clark, the executive director of the Twentieth Century Fund; James B. Conant, the president of Harvard University; Alan Gregg, a director of the Rockefeller Foundation; Boris Shishkin, an economist with the American Federation of Labor; Eugene Meyer, the publisher and chairman of the board of *The Washington Post*; Clarence Francis, the chairman of the board of General Foods Corporation; and Reinhold Niebuhr, the noted theologian and political philosopher. This *Look* piece presented the central message of the group: postwar America had created a dynamic consumer economy that was bringing abundance to all and making class divisions archaic.[1]

In an opening statement, the article contended that "our economic system and democratic way of life have enabled us to produce more and better goods at lower cost and give the American people a standard of living far surpassing that of any totalitarian country in the world." It detailed the glories of an American way of life: personal freedom, political democracy, free and competitive business endeavors, machine technology, worker productivity, and "government action when necessary" to protect the "public welfare" through unemployment insurance, vocational training, public works, and family welfare programs. This system had created the modern "miracle of America," said the Advertising Council, which guaranteed "the good things for all which our economic system can give us."[2]

In the same year, *Life* addressed an unexpected, vexing issue that had accompanied this explosion of material abundance. America's expanding consumer utopia, for all of its material advantages, had not eased the achievement of happiness. While the end of the Great

Depression had guaranteed economic survival for most, postwar
prosperity had not automatically created personal fulfillment and
emotional satisfaction. In fact, for many that goal seemed more
elusive than ever. So in the early summer of 1948, *Life* convened a
special gathering of some of America's leading thinkers, businessmen, lawyers, government officials, and writers to take up this cultural issue. The results appeared in a July 12, 1948, cover story
entitled "A *Life* Roundtable on the Pursuit of Happiness."[3]

This group, which met for a three-day symposium, was an all-
star panel of eighteen prominent figures from many areas of public
life. It included Henry Luce, the editor of *Time*, *Life*, and *Fortune*;
Sidney Hook, the famous political philosopher from New York
University; Father Edmund Walsh of Georgetown University, the
author of books on totalitarianism; Charles Luckman, the president of Lever Brothers; William Milliken, the director of the Cleve-
land Museum of Art; Thomas D'Arcy Brophy, the president of the
American Heritage Foundation; Beatrice Gould, the co-editor of
Ladies' Home Journal; Joseph Scanlon, a leader of the United Steelworkers of America; Stuart Chase, an economist and social critic;
and the noted psychoanalytic theorist Erich Fromm. The roundtable discussed a central question: whether modern Americans were
"pursuing happiness in such a way as to promote the fulfillment
of our own lives and of our democracy." The group agreed that
according to numerous opinion polls, contemporary Americans *believed* they were happy. At the same time, much evidence suggested
otherwise—for example, the divorce rate was soaring, juvenile delinquency was rising, and roughly one American in ten was wrestling with serious mental illness. Thus the seminar saw a paradox:
While the United States had created a society where prosperity had
flourished with widespread material goods, "we don't know how

to use them, don't really know how to live . . . There is a failure in America to achieve genuine happiness."[4]

After a spirited intellectual exchange, the *Life* roundtable reached a consensus. Their final report contended that ultimately happiness could only be found in the "inner lives" of men and women rather than in external economic, political, and social circumstances. The group admitted that this position reflected a "change in the thinking of our time" following the Depression:

> Had this Table met 10 years ago it is safe to guess no such agreement would have been reached: the entire debate . . . would have centered around "outer" reforms and particularly the economic question. Today it is becoming apparent to millions that economics does not in itself hold the answers to the underlying problems of democratic society . . . People are searching themselves and their society for deeper answers than the outer world alone is able to reveal.

Americans must cherish their democratic freedom to define and pursue happiness in their own way, the roundtable concluded. But "mere pleasure or self-indulgence" should be avoided by cultivating a firm basis of morality, a respect for labor, an appreciation of the arts, a hostility to censorship, and a "practical idealism, highly characteristic of Americans, which relates the individual to humanity as a whole." In the summation of one participant, "Happiness is primarily an inner state, an inner achievement . . . I would like to close by saying that the Kingdom of God is within us."[5]

Dale Carnegie stepped into the middle of this important discussion. As postwar America struggled to come to terms with abundance and its implications, he once again demonstrated his acumen for gauging the popular mood. Like the intellectual heavyweights and opinion shapers gathered by *Life* and *Look*, he was struck by Americans' paradoxical struggle to find happiness amid material plenty. Thus Carnegie published another blockbuster book that addressed this crucial question head on. While in the 1930s he had presented *How to Win Friends and Influence People* as a guidebook for those seeking success in an age of deprivation, now he offered a text pointing a way forward through the thicket of emotional issues attending postwar economic prosperity. Once again, it resonated powerfully with the public, who made it the second-ranking best seller of 1948, just behind Dwight Eisenhower's memoir of the war, *Crusade in Europe*, and just ahead of Alfred Kinsey's controversial study, *Sexual Behavior in the Human Male*. It would go on to sell six million copies in subsequent years. Its great popularity reinforced the author's lofty position as a trusted social and cultural guide for millions of ordinary Americans.

In the spring of 1948, Simon and Schuster published Dale Carnegie's *How to Stop Worrying and Start Living*, a long-awaited follow-up to his enormously popular book of the late 1930s. The author noted that he had decided to write this volume when, after listening to thousands of students in his public-speaking classes, "I realized that one of the biggest problems of these adults was *worry*." Intrigued, he went to the New York City Public Library only to discover a handful of books listed under "worry" (in contrast, astonishingly, the nearby topic "worms" had one hundred and eighty-nine books) and none of them were appropriate for use in his classroom. So he decided to fill the void. Listening to his students as they talked about their problems, reading biographies, interviewing successful individuals, and even dipping into philosophy, he began to compose a volume on how to banish worry.

It was vintage Carnegie. Filled with snappy prose and abundant anecdotes, it drew lessons from real individuals who had succeeded at overcoming stressful problems that threatened their lives. Above all, it was down-to-earth and useful. "I have tried to write a fast-moving, concise, documented report on how worry has been conquered by thousands of adults," he wrote. "One thing is certain; this book is practical. You can set your teeth in it."[6]

In many ways, the new book mimicked the structure and approach of *How to Win Friends and Influence People*. In true Carnegie style, it offered an array of principles, always formulated in a practical vein, for anxious readers: "Nine Suggestions on How to Get the Most Out of This Book," "Live in 'Day-tight Compartments,'" "Co-operate with the Inevitable," "How to Eliminate Fifty Per Cent of Your Business Worries." Then he seasoned these directives with bursts of inspiration ("Eight Words That Can Transform Your Life," "A Magic Formula for Solving Worry Situations") and perky, offbeat humor ("Don't Try to Saw Sawdust," "Remember That No One Ever Kicks a Dead Dog"). Finally, he leavened the text with a host of biographical snippets showing how individuals, some ordinary and some celebrities, had overcome pressing concerns in their lives. The book concluded with a collection of thirty-one brief, inspirational essays by figures such as J. C. Penney, Gene Autry, Homer Croy, Jack Dempsey, and Connie Mack.

Time magazine, in a long review of *How to Stop Worrying and Start Living*—it was accompanied by an interview with the author—agreed that Carnegie had found a suitable target for his talents. "Stretched taut as a wet clothesline by nervous tension, studded with warts of worry, perforated by ulcers, 20th-century man lives his much-cartooned life sandwiched between the deep blues and high blood pressure," the review observed. "Starting this month, he may take a new lease on life; his problems have been taken in hand by the author of the century's best-selling success story." It noted that Carnegie aimed to prod readers into adopting commonsense strategies for dealing with a pervasive problem of modern life. The purpose of the book, he told *Time*, was to jolt the reader out of complacency and "kick you in the shins."[7]

But it became clear that Carnegie was doing more than simply giving a wake-up call to stressed-out modern individuals. He was confronting the same troubling issue faced by the expert panels of *Life* and *Look*: In the postwar age of abundance, many of Americans' problems were no longer economic but overwhelmingly mental and emotional. In Carnegie's view, an epidemic of "nervous troubles" had swept through America. "But medical science has been unable to cope with the mental and physical wrecks caused, not by germs, but by emotions of worry, fear, hate, frustration, and despair," he wrote. "Casualties caused by these emotional diseases are mounting and spreading with catastrophic rapidity." As *How to Stop Worrying* soon revealed, both the analysis and the solution to this looming cultural catastrophe were complex matters.[8]

Carnegie offered a vivid description of America's modern plague of anxiety. "More than half of our hospital beds are occupied by people with nervous and emotional troubles," he reported. Statistics indicated that "one person out of ten now living in these United States will have a nervous breakdown—induced in the vast majority of cases by worry and emotional conflict." Many individuals were scrambling to find appropriate slots in a complex modern economy, making it no "small wonder that insecurity, worry, and 'anxiety neuroses' are rampant at times among the white-collar fraternity!" In fact, the malady of worry was spreading throughout modern society with severe consequences. "Businessmen who do not know how to fight worry die young," the author wrote. "And so do housewives and horse doctors and bricklayers."[9]

Carnegie offered a bold diagnosis: The very material growth and social advancement of Americans in the 1940s had *caused* this crisis. The welcome advancement of abundance after the Depression had brought an unexpected by-product of stress, worry, and angst. As financial concerns had lessened, emotional ones had increased. And the higher the rise, the worse the pressures. Citing a Mayo Clinic study of a hundred and seventy-six business executives in their forties, Carnegie reported that one in three suffered from "ailments peculiar to high-tension living—heart disease, digestive-tract ulcers, and high blood pressure before they even reach forty-five." He noted the recent death of a wealthy industrialist. "The best-known cigarette manufacturer in the world recently dropped dead from heart failure while trying to take a little recreation in the Canadian woods. He amassed millions—and fell dead at sixty-one. He probably traded years of his life for what is called 'business success,'" wrote Carnegie. *How to Stop Worrying* made clear that Americans needed to turn their attention from seeking success in the old-fashioned material sense, and train it on the personal, emotional, often unanticipated costs it generated. Ironically, the twentieth century's greatest avatar of success now declared, "What price success!"[10]

Carnegie pinpointed several areas where economic abundance had generated worry. The bureaucratic nature of modern corporate life had created enormous tension by entangling individuals in complicated webs of procedure and decision-making. "I spent almost half of every business day holding conferences, discussing problems. Should we do this, or that—or nothing at all?" explained one weary businessman. "We would get tense; twist in our chairs, walk the floor; argue and go around in circles. When night came,

I would be utterly exhausted." Carnegie also noted the tensions caused by finances, referring to a recent survey in *Ladies' Home Journal* indicating that 70 percent of all modern worries were caused by money. This was not a matter of financial need, as in the 1930s, but a situation where modern people *"don't know how to spend the money they have!"* Budgets, income management, financial planning, and the temptation to abuse easily available credit were unfamiliar issues that created new headaches for prosperous Americans.[11]

Even leisure time, one of the great boons of modern consumer life, had brought unexpected pain. During the workday, activity occupied the mind and left no time for fretting. "But the hours after work—they are the dangerous ones. Just when we're free to enjoy our own leisure, and ought to be the happiest—that's when the blue devils of worry attack us," Carnegie observed. "That's when we begin to wonder whether we are getting anywhere in life; whether we're in a rut; whether the boss 'meant anything' by that remark he made today; or whether we're getting bald." He ruefully quoted an aphorism of George Bernard Shaw: "The secret of being miserable is to have the leisure to bother about whether you are happy or not."[12]

What was Carnegie's remedy for curing the debilitating emotional anxiety and worry sweeping through modern America? Boldly, once again, he proposed a new cultural ethic: live for today and seek emotional self-fulfillment. In the opening chapter of *How to Stop Worrying*, he passionately denounced the tendency to be emotionally imprisoned by bad decisions or unfortunate circumstances in the past, or, conversely, dreams of a perfect future. Sometimes the syndrome worked in reverse, with people spinning golden memories of an earlier period or outlandish fears of looming disasters to come. In either event, instead of clinging to "dead yesterdays" or "unborn tomorrows," Carnegie insisted that the proper approach was to enjoy the present. Too many modern Americans "have collapsed under the crushing burden of accumulated yesterdays and fearful tomorrows," he wrote.

> You and I are standing at this very second at the meeting place of two eternities: the vast past that has endured forever, and the future that is plunging on to the last syllable of recorded time. We can't possibly live in either of those eternities—no, not even for one split second. But, by trying to do so, we can wreck both our bodies and our minds. So let's be content to live the only time we can possibly live: from now until bedtime.

In other words, happiness involved living in the moment.[13]

Finding self-fulfillment, Carnegie insisted, involved finding work that was not only productive but emotionally satisfying. Only a few years before, of course, many Americans would have been delighted to find work of any kind, an outlook that stretched back to an earlier economy of scarcity in the nineteenth century. But now, with a booming consumer economy bringing material abundance within the reach of most, a new calculus was required. And Carnegie codified it in a section of *How to Stop Worrying* entitled "How to Find the Kind of Work in Which You May Be Happy and Successful." He maintained that finding a vocation was one of the two great decisions in modern life—the other was choosing a mate—and it was imperative to find satisfying, even joyful labor. As a prominent businessman put it, a successful career was based on "having a good time at your work. If you enjoy what you are doing, you may work long hours, but it won't seem like work at all. It will seem like play." So job seekers should proceed carefully, in Carnegie's view: think carefully about your own temperament in light of the tasks required, seek vocational guidance, consider the likelihood of being able to make a living, do extensive research on occupations in which you are interested. But the goal was worth reaching, he concluded, when you pause to think "how many of our worries, regrets, and frustrations are spawned by work we despise."[14]

Carnegie spent much time proposing various techniques to help people overcome worry and find happiness in their jobs, their homes, and their lives. As he stated frankly in the book's preface, if readers did not "acquire a new power and a new inspiration to stop worry and enjoy life" from the practical suggestions in its pages, "then toss this book into the ashcan. It is no good for you." In wrestling with the difficulties of obtaining personal self-fulfillment in an age of prosperity, however, he turned in a familiar direction. As in his earlier work, Carnegie sought safety and solace by sailing in the direction of psychology. Once again, he found a comfortable harbor in therapeutic culture.[15]

At the beginning of *How to Stop Worrying and Start Living*, as he gauged the toll taken by worry on human health and happiness, Carnegie quoted from an old inspiration, a man he described as "the father of applied psychology," William James: "The Lord may forgive us our sins, but the nervous system never does." It was a revealing reference as once again Carnegie turned to psychology for an explanation.[16]

Defining the vagaries of modern life almost exclusively in terms of mental adjustment, Carnegie opened the book on an autobiographical note by discussing his own attempts to escape the wave of "disappointment, worry, bitterness, and rebellion" that had nearly crushed him as a young man struggling to find his way in New York. But now such cases had multiplied dramatically, with some experts suggesting that "one American in every twenty now alive will spend a part of his life in an institution for the mentally ill." Carnegie rallied to his side a host of psychiatrists, therapists, and physicians, many of them giants in the field, who stressed the mental aspects of modern discontent. He cited figures such as "the famous British psychiatrist, J. A. Hadfield"; "the Mayo brothers of psychiatry," Karl Menninger and his equally prestigious sibling, William; "the great psychologist, Alfred Adler"; "one of the most distinguished of psychiatrists," Carl Jung; the director of the Psychological Service Center in New York, Henry C. Link; the noted psychoanalyst, A. A. Brill; and of course, numerous times, William James. Under their influence, Carnegie concluded that the anxiety eroding postwar American happiness had created an epic psychological crisis.[17]

Carnegie's diagnosis identified several psychological flash points. He related the story of a GI who came out of the war exhausted, unhappy, and unfocused. Worrying constantly about his future, this soldier began to suffer crying spells and weight loss that culminated in a breakdown. Finally he ended up in the hospital where a doctor concluded that his "problems were mental" and offered counseling that set him on the path to recovery. Carnegie pointed to the business arena, where people were so intent on crowding forward in search of advancement and material possessions that it was no "small wonder that insecurity, worry, and 'anxiety neurosis'" were running rampant. He found another danger zone in America's postwar prosperity, where he quoted a *Ladies' Home Journal* survey indicating that "seventy percent of all our worries are about money." This variety of pressures attending modern life—particularly their tendency to encourage worry about future problems, dreams of future bliss, or regret about things done in the past—led Carnegie to a stark denunciation. The "emotional sickness of worry" had become ubiquitous, in his view, causing "ten thousand times more damage than smallpox." American society presented a startling picture of "how we destroy our bodies and minds by anxiety, frustration, hatred, resentment, rebellion, and fear."[18]

This pressing array of emotional maladies prompted Carnegie to search for a cure from the world of psychology. He endorsed psychoanalysis (in a diluted version) because of its "healing power of words. Ever since the days of Freud, analysts have known that a patient could find relief from his inner anxieties if he could talk, just talk . . . All of us know that 'spitting it out' or 'getting it off our chest' brings almost instant relief. So the next time we have an emotional problem, why don't we look around for someone to talk to?" More often, however, Carnegie turned to commonsense strategies that involved a clear-minded assessment of mental problems and a realistic forging of solutions. He advocated a tactic of accepting the worst possible outcome that might flow from a problem, and then working on improving things from there. He quoted William James: "Be willing to have it so . . . [because] acceptance of what has happened is the first step in overcoming the consequences of any misfortune." Carnegie added, "Psychologically, it means a new release of energy! When we have accepted the worst, we have nothing more to lose. And that automatically means—we have *everything* to gain!" He advocated the time-tested technique of losing yourself in work and activity as an antidote to anxiety. " 'Occupational therapy' is the term now used by psychiatry when work is prescribed as though it were a medicine," he wrote. "Any psychiatrist will tell you that work—keeping busy—is one of the best anesthetics ever known for sick nerves."[19]

But Carnegie's favorite psychological solution to worry came from a longtime influence on his thinking: the positive-thought tradition, which stressed that focusing mental resources could shape social reality. In part four of *How to Stop Worrying*, he turned once again to the therapeutic powers of positive thinking. Entitled "Seven Ways to Cultivate a Mental Attitude That Will Bring You Peace and Happiness," this section explained the "mental attitudes that lead to inner security and happiness." Carnegie grew passionate. "The longer I live, the more deeply I am convinced of the tremendous power of thought," he exclaimed. "I know men and women can banish worry, fear, and various kinds of illnesses, and can transform their lives by changing their thoughts. I know! I know!! I know!!!"[20]

For Carnegie, the basis for this deep conviction lay in the unity of mind and body, the mental and the physical. For support he cited great thinkers ranging from Plato ("the mind and the body are one and should not be treated separately") to Marcus Aurelius ("Our life is what our thoughts make it") to William James ("Action seems to follow feeling, but really action and feeling go together; and by regulating the action, which is under the more direct control of the will, we can indirectly regulate the feeling, which is not"). Thus thinking positive thoughts and banishing negative attitudes, Carnegie believed, created an atmosphere in which self-fulfillment would flourish. "Yes, if we think happy thoughts, we will be happy. If we think miserable thoughts, we will be miserable. If we think fear thoughts, we will be fearful. If we think sickly thoughts, we will probably be ill. If we think failure, we will certainly fail," he wrote. "If we wallow in self-pity, everyone will want to shun us and avoid us. 'You are not,' said Norman Vincent Peale, 'you are not what you think you are; but what you *think*, you are.'"[21]

Carnegie shifted into high inspirational gear to insist that worry could be eradicated by utilizing "the magic power of thought." He urged readers to embrace the idea that peace of mind and a joyful sense of living stemmed "solely from our mental attitude. Outward conditions have very little to do with it." Happiness was a state of mind. "Put a big, broad, honest-to-God smile on your face; throw back your shoulders; take a good, deep breath; and sing a snatch of song. If you can't sing, whistle. If you can't whistle, hum," Carnegie exhorted. "You will quickly discover what William James was talking about—that it is physically impossible to remain blue or depressed while you are acting out the symptoms of being radiantly happy!"[22]

With an ironic twist, Carnegie buttressed this positive-thought formula with a relic from his past. As a young man, he had rejected his mother's stern Protestant doctrines from his childhood and then in adulthood he spoke rarely of religion, either in his private life or writings. But now, in *How to Stop Worrying*, he returned to spiritual belief. It was less a case of going *back* to religion, however, and more a realization of its emotional utility. "I have gone *forward* to a new concept of religion. I no longer have the faintest interest in the difference in creeds that divide the churches," he explained.

> But I am tremendously interested in what religion does for me, just as I am interested in what electricity and good food and water do for me. They help me to lead a richer, fuller, happier life. But religion does far more than that. It brings me spiritual values. It gives me, as William James put it, "a new zest for life . . . more life, a larger, richer, more satisfying life." It gives me faith, hope, and courage. It banishes tensions, anxieties, fears, and worries.[23]

In other words, Carnegie now embraced religion for its therapeutic function. Matters of salvation, the trinity, and the Gospel never came up. Instead, he argued that spirituality and psychology, religion and science, had converged in a modern approach to achieving happiness and fulfillment. Many psychiatrists, for example, endorsed the notion that prayer and religious faith helped eradicate many of the anxieties and strains of life. "The newest of all sciences—psychiatry—is teaching what Jesus taught," he wrote. "Today, psychiatrists are becoming modern evangelists . . . they are urging us to lead religious lives to avoid the hell-fires of this world—the hell-fires of stomach ulcers, angina pectoris, nervous breakdowns, and insanity." Carnegie called several prestigious psychologists as witnesses. Carl Jung had written that among his patients "there has not been one whose problem in the last resort was not that of finding a religious outlook on life. It is safe to say that every one of them felt ill, because he had lost that which the living religions of every age have given to their followers, and none of them has really healed who did not regain his religious outlook." William James agreed: "Faith is one of the forces by which men live, and the total absence of it means collapse."[24]

Carnegie took these admonitions to heart. In his own life, he confessed, he often felt rushed, stressed, and anxious as he dashed about the country for teaching and speaking appearances. So he adopted the habit of dropping by a church—whichever one was at hand—on a weekday afternoon for a period of quiet contemplation. "I say to myself: 'Wait a minute, Dale Carnegie, wait a minute. Why all the feverish hurry and rush, little man? You need to pause and acquire a little perspective,'" he confided. "I find that doing this calms my nerves, rests my body, clarifies my perspective, and helps me revalue my values."[25]

Eventually, this therapeutic sensibility led Carnegie toward another major issue in postwar America. A decade earlier, in *How to Win Friends and Influence People*, he had promoted a new

paradigm of personality keenly attuned to demands of bureaucratic interaction, consumer expectation, and leisure aspiration in
modern America. Now, in the postwar period, he confronted the
consequences produced by the new-model individual he had done
so much to invent. This encounter placed Carnegie in the middle of
a debate that, because it cut so deeply into the grain of American
behavior and beliefs, attracted a great deal of attention.

In 1950, David Riesman published *The Lonely Crowd: A Study
of the Changing American Character*, one of the most influential
books of social analysis ever written in modern America. A sociologist at the University of Chicago with additional training in the
law and literature, Riesman had become fascinated with a new
social type he believed had been called forth in the modern age.
In an older nineteenth-century society devoted to production and
entrepreneurialism, he contended, an "inner-directed personality"
of strong moral values, sturdy personal character, and a dogged
work ethic had guided individuals through life. By the early twentieth century, however, an increasingly complex economy propelled
by consumerism, bureaucratic forms of labor, and leisure opportunities had called forth the emergence of a new "other-directed
personality." This modern ideal type, operating in an atmosphere
of constant human interaction, relied on a charismatic personality
and skilled human relations to meet goals and advance through
life.[26]

Riesman carefully described the traits of this modern ideal type.
Unlike his inner-directed forebear, who tended to go it alone according to internalized principles implanted by family, church, and
economic creed, the more cosmopolitan and urban individual who
had emerged by about 1920 came into contact with and responded

to a much wider array of influences. "[O]ther-direction is becoming the typical character of the 'new' middle class—the bureaucrat, the salaried employee in business," Riesman asserted.

> What is common to all other-directed people is that their contemporaries are the source of direction for the individual—either those known to him or those with whom he is indirectly acquainted, through friends and through the mass media . . . While all people want and need to be liked by some of the people some of the time, it is only modern other-directed types who make this their chief source of direction and chief area of sensitivity . . . Social mobility depends less on what one is and what one does than what others think of one— and how competent one is in manipulating others and being oneself manipulated . . . [D]rives for mobility are still embedded in [the other-directed's] character. But the product now in demand is neither a staple nor a machine; it is a personality.[27]

These traits—processing signals from diverse sources, cultivating bureaucratic skills, needing to be liked, engaging in self-manipulation, shaping personality—created a new formula for success. The modern individual's "interactional qualities," in Riesman's words, were key. "He wants to be loved rather than esteemed; he wants not to gull or impress, let alone oppress, others but, in the current phrase, to relate to them . . . [to gain] assurance of being emotionally in tune with them."[28]

Riesman illustrated the historical shift from inner-directed to other-directed individualism with a brilliant metaphor. The nineteenth-century individual, seeking goals according to his own principles, was directed psychologically by a "gyroscope," a compass-like mechanism set in place by parents and other authorities that always kept its holder on course regardless of external circumstances. But the other-directed individual operated in a broader world defined by interactions with others. So he "must be able to receive signals from far and near; the sources are many, the changes rapid." Rather than being guided by an internalized gyroscope, the other-directed person moved according to a more elaborate psychological mechanism that "instead of being like a gyroscope, is like a radar." Now one's personal radar plotted a course through life by constantly bouncing signals off of others.[29]

Riesman stressed that the broader culture, in all of its historical forms, always sought to control the character types it had called forth. The tradition-directed type—an archaic variant that appeared in agricultural societies of small, tight-knit communities and was nearly extinct—suffered the sanction of *shame* when violating approved standards of conduct. The entrepreneurial inner-directed type, operating by internal piloting, suffered *guilt* when veering off course. But the modern other-directed type, in scrambling to interpret the numerous, rapid, and often varied signals constantly coming in from others, suffered *anxiety* as he sought to move toward success. Constantly adjusting his own emotional tuning to others, "his anxieties, as child consumer-trainee, as parent, as worker and player, are very great," wrote Riesman. "He is often torn between the illusion that life should be easy, if he could only find the ways of proper adjustment to the group, and the half-buried feeling that it is not easy for him."[30]

The Lonely Crowd touched a powerful cultural nerve in postwar America. It captured the anxieties of an age done with economic depression and war, but confused by suburban affluence and the emotional demands of status chasing. The book sold 1.5 million copies, an unheard-of figure for an academic tome, and landed its author on the cover of *Time* magazine, an even more unprecedented achievement for a university professor. The magazine cover displayed a photograph of the earnest, probing "Social Scientist David Riesman" surrounded by sketches of a bewhiskered Victorian entrepreneur confidently striding forward with a gyroscope strapped to his back and a modern businessman beseeching others as he moved onward carrying a radar dish. *Time* described Riesman's ideas as a response to an age of rapid postwar change where "the American self-picture has gone out of focus." Many people were desperately looking for ways to understand modern life that went beyond older conceptions of class struggle or the frontier thesis, *Time* asserted, and "Riesman seems to be leading thousands of Americans on this quest." His interpretation had achieved "already a kind of classic status."[31]

Indeed, by the late 1940s American culture seemed awash in anxiety suffered by the other-directed personality. The 1948 *Life* roundtable, with its panel of experts, dissected the frustrated pursuit of happiness in postwar America. Leonard Bernstein presented Symphony No. 2: *The Age of Anxiety*, in 1949 while the same year saw *Death of a Salesman*, Arthur Miller's Pulitzer Prize–winning play, premiering on Broadway with its heartbreaking tale of Willy Loman, a failed disciple of human relations who, desperate to be liked but incapable of selling himself, grew so anxious that he committed suicide. Rabbi Joshua Liebman's best-selling book, *Peace of Mind* (1946), offered a self-help formula of spiritual values and psychological self-esteem to overcome unhappiness, while the existential psychologist Rollo May explored these issues in *The Meaning of Anxiety* (1950). In the practical world of politics, Arthur Schlesinger Jr.'s tremendously influential book *The Vital Center* (1949) opened with a chapter entitled "Politics in an Age of Anxiety."[32]

Unquestionably the greatest exemplar of Riesman's other-directed modernity, however, was Dale Carnegie. His 1930s bestseller, *How to Win Friends and Influence People*, had heralded this modern personality type with its clear delineation of radar-like skills—making others feel important, projecting a pleasant personal appeal, winning others to your way of thinking, being sensitive to group dynamics—needed to navigate through the bureaucratic, consumer maze of modern American life. Now with his 1948 best seller, Carnegie addressed the upshot of this new cultural milieu—what Riesman had described as the gnawing anxiety besetting the other-directed individual as he struggled to process a vast array of external signals picked up on his radar. Riesman, in fact, noted in *The Lonely Crowd* a connection with the popular writer, pointing out that Carnegie's first book had recommended "self-manipulation exercises for the sake not only of business success but of such vaguer, non-work goals as popularity." Now Carnegie's second best seller, Riesman observed, addressed not only "the change from depression to full employment" after World War II but the pressures to use self-manipulation "in a solipsistic way to adjust one to one's fate and social state."[33]

Riesman's sense of intellectual camaraderie was accurate. Indeed, *How to Stop Worrying and Start Living* broadcast the clearest, most far-reaching cultural signal of concern about the anxiety-ridden, other-directed individual in postwar America. Having earlier created the urtext of this personality type, Carnegie now turned instinctively to eradicating the emotional problems that had come in its wake. He suggested two remedies. First, other-directed types needed to adjust their radar to differentiate between the true signals that would lead to happiness and the dangerous static that would throw them off course. Second, they needed to adjust more smoothly to social demands, a maneuver that would create emotional reconciliation rather than alienation.

A concern for finely calibrating one's personal radar permeated Carnegie's text. Elaborating on his earlier principles of human relations, he contended that happiness often lay in coming to terms with the ups and downs of personal interactions. For example, the successful individual needed to cope creatively with, rather than bridle at, negative behavior among co-workers, friends, and family. Human ingratitude, jealousy, and envy was natural, Carnegie counseled, and individuals should expect it. Even Jesus, after healing the lepers, had received scant thanks, so should we "expect more thanks for our small favors than was given Jesus Christ?" The lesson was clear: "Human nature has always been human nature—and it probably won't change in your lifetime. So why not accept it? . . . Let's not expect gratitude. Then, if we get some occasionally, it will come as a delightful surprise. If we don't get it, we won't be disturbed." Such an attitude was essential to avoiding stress and heartache. Instead of hating your enemies and obsessing over criticism, try to forgive and forget. Cultivate a sense of serenity and poise, and a lively sense of humor. When Jesus said "love your enemies," he was "not only preaching sound ethics. He was also preaching twentieth-century medicine," wrote Carnegie. "Jesus was telling you and me how to keep from having high blood pressure, heart trouble, stomach ulcers, and many other ailments."[34]

In fact, Carnegie maintained that the wise person should actively seek out criticism. He noted his personal "Damned Fool Things I Have Done" file and urged readers to embrace Elbert Hubbard's dictum: "Every man is a damn fool for at least five minutes every day. Wisdom consists in not exceeding that limit." Listen to opposition or denunciation and discern if it has any validity. "We all tend to resent criticism and lap up praise, regardless of whether either the criticism or the praise is justified," he pointed out. But the serene, healthy individual would say, "Maybe I deserve this criticism. If I do, I ought to be thankful for it, and try to profit from it." Carnegie offered one of his trusty principles for avoiding anxiety: "Let's keep a record of the fool things we have done and criticize ourselves ... let's ask for unbiased, helpful, and constructive criticism."[35]

But the emotionally healthy individual also needed to reach beyond himself and promote the happiness of others as a way to promote his own. By tuning one's radar to an awareness of other's search for fulfillment, contentment, and validation, and then trying to provide it, one could shed personal unhappiness as if by magic. The happy individual did not wallow in self-pity and demand to be the center of attention. He did not go about, in the words of George Bernard Shaw, as "a self-centered, little clod of ailments and grievances complaining that the world would not devote itself to making him happy." Instead, he cultivated sensitivity to others. "What about the grocery boy, the newspaper vendor, the chap at the corner who polishes your shoes? These people are humans bursting with troubles, and dreams, and private ambitions. They are also bursting for the chance to share them with someone," Carnegie instructed. "But do you ever let them? Do you ever show an eager, honest interest in them or their lives? You don't have to become a Florence Nightingale or a social reformer to help improve the world—your own private world; you can start tomorrow morning with the people you meet! What's in it for you? Much greater happiness! Greater satisfaction and pride in yourself!" Everyone longs to be loved, he concluded, but the only way to get love was "to stop asking for it and to start pouring out love without hope of return."[36]

Typically, Carnegie enlisted an army of prominent psychologists to provide support on this point. After years of psychiatric practice, Henry C. Link concluded, "No discovery of modern psychology is, in my opinion, so important as its scientific proof of the necessity of self-sacrifice or discipline to self-realization and happiness." Carl Jung had written that approximately one-third of his patients were suffering not from a clinically definable neurosis but from "the senselessness and emptiness of their lives," a condition often ameliorated by striving to "get interested in helping others." The "great psychiatrist" Alfred Adler had proposed a solution to melancholia in his book *What Life Should Mean to You*: "Try to think every day of how you can please someone . . . It is the individual who is not interested in his fellow man who has the greatest difficulties in life." Such sage advice led Carnegie to his own proposition: "Thinking of others will not only keep you from worrying about yourself; it will also help you to make a lot of friends and have a lot of fun . . . Let's forget our own unhappiness—by trying to create a little happiness for others. When you are good to others, you are best to yourself."[37]

If creating a more sensitive personal radar was Carnegie's first remedy for the anxiety of the other-directed individual, his second lay in becoming well-adjusted. Pressing social demands and unaccustomed emotional strains, Carnegie insisted, were best met by understanding and calm acceptance rather than bitterness or resentment. A key chapter in *How to Stop Worrying* was entitled "Co-operate with the Inevitable," and in it he made the case for coming to terms with life's pressures. "As you and I march across the decades of time, we are going to meet a lot of unpleasant situations that are so. They cannot be otherwise," he wrote. "We have our choice. We can either accept them as inevitable and adjust ourselves to them, or we can ruin our lives with rebellion and maybe end up with a nervous breakdown."[38]

It was an individual decision. The onus of adjusting to the world lay on each of us, Carnegie believed, and how we responded to adversity determined our emotional fate. "Obviously, circumstances alone do not make us happy or unhappy. It is the way we react to circumstances that determines our feelings. Jesus said that the kingdom of heaven is within you. That is where the kingdom of hell is, too," he warned. One could rant or stew about life's tribulations or unfairness, or one could try to make the best of what you have, or as he put it in another chapter title, "If You Have a Lemon, Make a Lemonade." In fact, he contended, adversity often spurred improvement or achievement if one only came to grips with it. Alfred Adler had posited that one of the most valuable gifts given to human beings was "their power to turn a minus into a plus." William James had agreed: "Our very infirmities help us unexpectedly."[39]

But Carnegie understood that sometimes things could not be changed for the better; sometimes circumstances were not malleable. In those cases, the individual came face-to-face with a lesson "all of us will have to learn sooner or later: namely, that we must accept and cooperate with the inevitable." Here, he said, the words of Schopenhauer were instructive: "A good supply of resignation is of the first importance in providing for the journey of life." But Carnegie made an important distinction. "Am I advocating that we simply bow down to *all* adversities that come our way? Not by a long shot! That is mere fatalism," he insisted. "As long as we can save a situation, let's fight. But when common sense tells us that we are up against something that is so—and cannot be otherwise— then, in the name of our sanity, let's not 'look before and after and pine for what is not.'"[40]

The trick, of course, was to delineate between improvable situations and intractable ones. Here Carnegie passed on to readers the "best single piece of advice about worry that I have ever discovered." It was a prayer—"twenty-seven words that you and I ought to paste on our bathroom mirror so that each time we wash our faces we could also wash away all worry from our minds." The famous theologian Reinhold Niebuhr had composed it: "God grant me the serenity to accept the things I cannot change; the courage to change the things I can; and the wisdom to know the difference."[41]

Ultimately, Carnegie's advice for anxious, other-directed individuals culminated in an overarching therapeutic dictum: nurture self-esteem. Developing a more sensitive personal radar and smoothly adjusting to pressing social demands were important, of course, but the final conqueror of anxiety was a sense of self-worth. This theme saw Carnegie at his most inspirational. "No matter what happens, always be yourself . . . You and I have such abilities, so let's not waste a second worrying because we are not like other people. You are something new in this world," he enjoined. He urged anxious individuals to respect their own talents and gifts: "You can sing only what you are. You can paint only what you are. You must be what your experiences, your environment, and your heredity have made you. For better or worse, you must cultivate your own little garden . . . Let's not imitate others. Let's find ourselves and be ourselves."[42]

About halfway through *How to Stop Worrying*, Carnegie summarized his self-esteem advice in a therapeutic program. Entitled "Just for Today" and aimed at relieving the anxieties of the other-directed individual, it consisted of a step-by-step procedure for securing personal peace and happiness:

1. Just for today I will be happy . . . Happiness is from within; it is not a matter of externals.
2. Just for today I will try to adjust myself to what is, and not try to adjust everything to my own desires. I will take my

family, my business, and my luck as they come and fit myself
to them.

3. Just for today, I will take care of my body. I will exercise it,
   care for it, nourish it . . .

4. Just for today, I will try to strengthen my mind. I will learn
   something useful . . .

5. Just for today, I will exercise my soul in three ways: I will do
   somebody a good turn . . . [and] I will do at least two things I
   don't want to do, as William James suggests, just for exercise.

6. Just for today, I will be agreeable. I will . . . criticize not at
   all, nor find fault with anything, and not try to regulate nor
   improve anyone.

7. Just for today, I will try to live through this day only, not to
   tackle my whole life problem at once . . .

8. Just for today, I will have a program . . . I may not follow it
   exactly, but I will have it. It will eliminate two pests, hurry
   and indecision.

9. Just for today, I will have a quiet half-hour all by myself and
   relax. In this half-hour sometimes I will think of God, so as to
   get a little more perspective into my life.

10. Just for today, I will be unafraid, especially I will not be afraid
    to be happy, to enjoy what is beautiful, to love, and to believe
    that those I love, love me.

Here was a prototype for countless twelve-step programs that
would inundate American culture in the years to come, all of them
aimed at achieving self-esteem.[43]

So in the same way that Carnegie's *How to Win Friends and
Influence People* captured a cultural moment in 1930s America
when desperate citizens were seeking a path upward through the
bureaucratic maze of modern life, his *How to Stop Worrying and*

Start Living addressed the anxieties besetting materially affluent but emotionally confused citizens in the postwar era. With the first book, he provided a trusted guidebook for an age troubled by economic privation and outdated principles of success. With the second, he offered a soothing therapeutic manual for an age troubled by the unexpected perils of prosperity.

17

"Enthusiasm Is His Most Endearing Quality"

As Dale Carnegie entered the 1950s, he had abundant reasons for happiness. Now in his sixties, this beloved teacher and popular author enjoyed the fruits of fame as they poured in from an affectionate public. Traveling about the country giving inspirational talks and stepping in to teach sessions in the famous Carnegie Course, he unfailingly drew large and enthusiastic crowds for the former and adoring students for the latter. His celebrity status attracted attention in the daily rounds of life. "People would recognize him on the street, having seen his picture on the book or in the newspaper," said his wife, Dorothy. Carnegie clearly reveled in the attention and respect showered on him. In typical self-effacing style, however, he made light of his popularity. "Now that Clark Gable has come along, my big ears are just the fashion," he often joked.[1]

Moreover, Carnegie's private life had become a picture of contentment. Married to an intelligent, attractive, forceful younger woman since the mid-1940s and settled into a lovely home in Forest Hills, he enjoyed the stability of a comfortable domestic life. As he began to cut back on his demanding schedule of teaching, writing, and public speaking with advancing age, Dorothy assumed an increasingly greater role at Carnegie and Associates, especially in business matters. Spending less time with professional pursuits, Carnegie enjoyed a kind of semiretirement that provided the best of both worlds, work and home. Then, in the midst of this halcyon scene, his personal life changed dramatically. At the age of sixty-three, he unexpectedly became the father of a little girl, an experience that filled his life with newfound delights.

Sadly, however, while standing at the pinnacle of public esteem and domestic happiness in the early 1950s, Carnegie began to lose his footing. After some peculiar behavior, it gradually became apparent to family and friends that something was seriously wrong with this beloved public figure. Carnegie clearly was suffering from some kind of malady. This mysterious illness brought mental and physical deterioration and sent him into a downward spiral by mid-decade. But not before his legacy had been cemented in American culture.

As Carnegie eased into the 1950s, his professional life became one long parade of acclamation and praise. Befitting his status as one of the most famous Americans of the era, invitations for inspirational talks poured in and he became, in the words of a long newspaper profile, "in constant demand everywhere as a lecturer." He traveled the country for such appearances, speaking without a script, or even notes, relying instead on his trademark six-by-eight-inch cards. When Carnegie spoke in Minneapolis, a member of the audience came up afterward for a handshake and noticed that half a dozen of these cards were laid out on the podium, upon each of which was printed a single word. Carnegie "said he had quite a number of these cards and he simply picked out the ones that he wanted to use as an outline for his comments," the audience member reported. "Because he used anecdotal material so effectively, he felt that he needed no elaborate outlines to bring out the points he wanted to make."[2]

The message of Carnegie's talks usually came from his best-selling books, and it highlighted one of his famous principles about winning friends and finding success, or thwarting worry and finding peace of mind. But it was the style, rather than the substance, that held the key to his charm and appeal. Honed over many years at the lectern, his low-key, conversational manner attracted and held the listeners' attention. "People sensed that here was a real person talking to them, someone who was being himself. He was full of humor, down to earth, genial, not stuffy at all," an observer explained. "Here was someone you could trust." Carnegie's speaking style was animated by a certain cheerfulness, a gusto for living, a joie de vivre. While onstage he came alive with enthusiasm and, time and again, won over crowds with his Midwestern twang, self-effacing humor, storytelling, and appreciation for life's possibilities.[3]

Carnegie gave many memorable speaking performances. Several months after the publication of *How to Stop Worrying and Start Living*, a group of Boston businessmen invited him to present a talk in the city's hallowed Symphony Hall. J. Gordon MacKinnon, the sponsor of the Carnegie Course in eastern New England and chair of the group, had organized the appearance. Carnegie spoke for an hour to a receptive audience and received a standing ovation, which so impressed him that he agreed to come back after a fifteen-minute break and take questions. Not one person left, and the speaker was still responding to queries an hour later. "I have shared the platform with many famous people," MacKinnon observed. "All that he shared with us that evening—his warmth, his interest in the audience, and his vast knowledge of people—has never been equaled by another speaker in my forty years of attending meetings."[4]

A few years later, at a Carnegie Course annual convention, the concluding banquet began with a talk by Paul Harvey, the popular radio personality. He was so dynamic that many feared Carnegie had an impossible act to follow. But Carnegie tread his usual subtle path. He faced the crowd with a big smile and exclaimed, "Wasn't that a wonderful example of a man on fire, a speaker really in love with his message!" He praised Harvey's speech to the heavens, and then delivered his own remarks. As one listener noted, "because of the sincerity with which Dale praised Paul, I knew that here was a man who had so much self-confidence that he did not have to worry about following such a dynamic speaker." By the time Carnegie had finished, the listener had forgotten about Harvey. In his words, "All I could do was to marvel at what Dale Carnegie had done. He not only enhanced Harvey's presentation but also he made me truly appreciate what a great man he, himself, was. A highly successful, famous man, yet a man who was humble."[5]

But Carnegie's first love remained teaching and he continued to play a large role in the Carnegie Course—appearing at sessions around the country, instructing and inspiring students, mentoring instructors, and imbuing everyone with his principles for self-confidence and success. "What he really liked to do best was teach. He would turn down a well-paying engagement if it would keep him away from his teaching," said Dorothy. "He was brilliant. The miraculous way he had with people, I've never seen anything quite like it. People would blossom, right there where they were speaking. He was helping them to grow to the limit of their capacities. He was inspiring . . . He had a gift for teaching. He was magnificent."[6]

Students marveled at his teaching skills. Richard Stomstead, later a Carnegie Course instructor, saw Carnegie speak on human relations to a group of course graduates in the early 1950s in Kansas City at the Bellerive Hotel. The founder's ability to "be himself" and his spontaneous humor impressed Stomstead deeply. Fred White, who took the course in 1952, found Carnegie to be "superb, kind but firm. He commented, coached, and commented again, constantly teaching and inspiring. To say that Mr. Carnegie 'breathed' sincerity and enthusiasm could be considered an understatement." Carnegie's kindness also appeared frequently, as in July 1950 when a teacher-training course convened in New York for several weeks. Some of the trainees from the area were able to go home on weekends, but Carnegie made a point of looking after the out-of-towners by taking them all to lunch and a Broadway play every weekend.[7]

In his supervisory role, Carnegie continued to closely monitor his course to assure that it was up to his demanding standard. In 1952, when he learned that some of his instructor trainers were using gimmicks in certain educational sessions, he wrote a stern memo to the course managers. "Our main job is to help our instructors help our students build courage and confidence in themselves and to use better human relations," he insisted. "The less time we spend on supplying 'gimmicks' and the more time we spend on inspiring our instructors, the more help we will be to the men and women who come to us for courage and self-confidence and leadership ability. I am intensely eager that we stress this point over and over and over again at our instructors' schools, our refreshers, our conventions, and to ourselves daily."[8]

Carnegie maintained close ties with many of his course sponsors around the country. Bill Stover, the holder of the Carnegie Course franchise in Washington, D.C., became a close friend and recalled visiting him on his Missouri farm in 1953. He observed that Carnegie went there "to escape pressures and relive childhood memories." Stover was deeply touched when Carnegie, who was planning a trip abroad, and "knowing I was suffering from throat cancer, repeatedly urged me to join him on the trip for a needed rest." Stover was even more touched when Carnegie offered to pick up the bill.[9]

In fact, the Carnegie operation was so successful that it required an expansion of facilities. With classes filled to overflowing in nearly every major city in the United States, and with the regional franchises flourishing, the booming enterprise could no longer be run out of the Carnegie home in Forest Hills. Thus on February 27, 1953, the Dale Carnegie Institute of Effective Speaking and Human Relations opened new headquarters in a five-story, converted brownstone at 22 West Fifty-Fifth Street in New York. Carnegie, along with Dorothy and other course managers, appeared at the evening dedication ceremony. The festivities were presided over by Theodore R. McKeldin, the governor of Maryland, who had achieved national prominence with a rousing speech nominating Dwight Eisenhower for president at the Republican convention in 1952. A graduate of the Carnegie course, McKeldin frequently declared that the principles he learned there had propelled him to political success.[10]

Despite such successes, advancing age caused Carnegie to ease up on his public activities in the early 1950s. He began to accept fewer invitations, and when speaking he contented himself with giving a few stock talks. Carnegie made a notable appearance, however, in the pulpit of the church where his old friend Norman Vincent Peale served as pastor. New York ministers had agreed to schedule an occasional Sunday service when a layman would speak, so Peale invited Carnegie to address the congregation at his Marble Collegiate Church. Sitting next to him in the pulpit, Peale heard his friend deliver a powerfully emotional talk. Carnegie spoke about the poverty of his youth and the spiritual strength of his mother. "When there was nothing to eat in the house, she was calm and unworried. 'The Lord will provide,' she said quietly. Under these circumstances she just went about the house singing the old hymns of faith, such as 'What a Friend We Have in Jesus,'" Carnegie said. "Then he stopped speaking," Peale recounted. "The great congregation sat hushed while Dale struggled to regain his composure as tears ran down his face. Finally, still choked up, he said, 'My parents gave me no money nor financial inheritance, but they gave me something of much greater value, the blessing of faith and sturdy character.'" Peale declared, "It was one of the most moving and affecting speeches I have ever heard."[11]

In the twilight of his career, Carnegie thus enjoyed many benefits—public respect, goodwill, and gratitude—that he had earned over four decades as a teacher of self-confidence and an author on getting ahead in the world. With his course attracting tens of thousands of students every year, and his celebrity as an author attracting considerable attention, he continued to inspire ordinary Americans around the country with visions of personal success. These glowing pictures of self-fulfillment and material abundance painted for others, however, were not mere fantasies. They described Carnegie's own life, which had become a portrait of contentment.

In the aftermath of his second blockbuster book in 1948, *How to Stop Worrying and Start Living*, Carnegie settled into a rich, full domestic life. Ensconced at 27 Wendover Road in Forest Hills with Dorothy, he enjoyed a wide variety of hobbies and activities. The couple continued to travel widely—to the American West, to the Canadian Rockies, to Europe, and occasional jaunts to his western Missouri farm. Dale went alone to Italy in 1951 and Japan in 1953.

They shared a love of the theater, eating at good restaurants, hosting small dinner parties for friends, and reading as they filled the house with books. At gatherings, Dorothy often played the piano as others sang—Dale did so with gusto, especially on old hymns like "Bringing in the Sheaves." Their marriage was a strong one, characterized by mutual love and respect. Yet their personalities diverged in certain ways. Dale was a pack rat while Dorothy tended to be tidy and efficient. She loved to remodel the house at every opportunity while he preferred a stable arrangement of things. His taste in furnishings ran to traditional, heavy, wooden items while she liked a sleek, modern style. But Dale and Dorothy shared a strong will. Once Dale brought home a large ocean fish given to him by an acquaintance that he hoped to have for a weekend meal. It was so odiferous that Dorothy made him leave it in the wood box outside. After they went to bed, however, he waited until she seemed to be asleep before sneaking down to put it in the refrigerator. But she heard him, waited until *he* was asleep, and then tiptoed down to put it back outside. This continued throughout the night. In the morning, Dorothy finally threw in the towel but they both laughed in recognition of their mutual stubbornness.[12]

As he cut back on professional activities, Carnegie occasionally found time to dip an oar into public affairs. In 1953, he had a feisty exchange of letters with Herbert H. Lehman, a U.S. senator from New York. Carnegie had read John T. Flynn's book *The Road Ahead: America's Creeping Revolution* (1949), which maintained that the United States was falling prey imperceptibly to socialism, much as England had a few decades earlier. Carnegie described the volume as "one of the most important books ever written in the western world" and included an excerpt that had appeared in *Reader's Digest*. A week later, he received a form letter from Lehman thanking him for his input. Deeply annoyed, Carnegie

replied that he appreciated Lehman's lack of time to reply personally to every letter he received, but this issue deserved his personal
attention because the nation was in peril of bankruptcy due to excessive deficit spending. "It seems to me that we are now engaged
in a program of spending that sounds like something out of Gilbert
and Sullivan," he wrote. "Take the farmers, for instance. I certainly
am in sympathy with them. My mother and father spent their entire lives on a Missouri farm. I, myself, own a Missouri farm which
is just four miles from where Harry Truman used to farm. But, the
idea of this government paying the farmers $1.86 a bushel to raise
potatoes and then burning them, is financial insanity." The senator
wrote back a week later, assuring Carnegie that he opposed waste-
ful government spending and only supported "appropriations
which I consider to be necessary for the national health, welfare,
and security."[13]

Meanwhile, Dorothy's daughter, Rosemary, who had gone off to
college at the University of Wyoming, enlarged the Carnegie family
circle when she became engaged to Oliver Crom, a bright and engaging fellow student, in 1952. She brought the young man home
at Christmas that year, where Carnegie greeted him with typical
graciousness. Crom was studying to become certified as a seller of
mutual funds, and his future father-in-law immediately expressed
an interest. Crom told him about his company, its good track record, and his optimism about a career. He then let the matter drop,
figuring Carnegie was just being polite. The next day, however,
Carnegie said, "Aren't there some papers we have to fill out?" Crom
expressed a bit of confusion, and the older man said, "If I'm going
to invest some money, don't we have to file some forms?" Still clue-
less, Crom replied that he wouldn't be licensed to sell until January. Carnegie smiled and said, "Well, can't we date it in January?"
When a nervous Crom observed that he wasn't sure how to fill out

the forms, the older man, smiling patiently, said, "Well, maybe the two of us working together can do it!" So after a bit of prompting, Carnegie became Crom's first buyer of mutual funds and helped start a career that culminated with the younger man becoming the president of Dale Carnegie and Associates many years later.[14]

Enjoying the comforts of domestic life, Carnegie turned much of his energy to gardening. He had pursued this activity for many years, but now, in his sixties and with a more relaxed schedule, he threw himself into it with a passion. He was especially proud of the flagstones bearing the imprint of dinosaurs' feet and the fossilized stumps from Wyoming that now accented his many plants and bushes. Carnegie hired Patrick McKenna, a well-known horticulturalist from Hunter College, to design a spectacular tulip border at the rear of his property. Nine feet wide and fifty feet long, it featured clusters of different-colored tulips interspersed with perennials such as Scotch bluebells, columbine, and bearded irises, all set against a cedar fence garlanded with Rambler roses. Then in 1952 he purchased an empty lot a few doors down the street and, again with McKenna's assistance, built an even larger garden enclosed by a fence. It included a dense screen of shrubs around the perimeter; climbing roses and vines on trellises; a broad, curving section filled with roses, annuals, and perennials for all-season blooms; and a central pool for water lilies and goldfish. At the far end of the garden, on a raised, paved terrace, sat a table and benches where, according to one observer, "Mr. Carnegie can sit, meditate, and look out upon the colorful garden picture he loves."[15]

So impressive were Carnegie's gardens that *American Home* magazine visited Wendover Road in 1955 for a feature story. It described the lush designs, examined the planning that lay behind them, offered several photographs of the grounds, and talked at length with the host about his devotion to gardening. Carnegie explained that he had come to love flowers as a farm boy in Missouri. "My mother was the gardener. I must have picked up her enjoyment of them . . . I got to know the flowers my mother grew from seeds and bulbs and bushes—tulips and daffodils, gladiolus, dahlias, zinnias, marigolds, roses, lilacs, and hollyhocks," he recalled. "I have always been especially fond of hollyhocks, perhaps because there's something farm-like about them that reminds me of my boyhood. I came to know weeds, too." He confessed that he still stopped to pull weeds out of his flower beds when he spotted any.[16]

But gardening, it became clear, did more than prompt memories of childhood and present an aesthetic appeal. It performed a therapeutic function in Carnegie's personal life. Marilyn Burke, his secretary, confided that when her boss was feeling tired or strained, "he would disappear from the office and slip out to the garden, to sit there, pull some weeds, look at the flowers, get his fingers into the soil, for a couple of hours. Always it seemed to rest and invigorate him." Carnegie was "a living testimonial of the philosophy he teaches—a philosophy of serenity combined with energy and determination; of ignoring or shedding things that do not matter and that he cannot do anything about; of putting himself in the other person's place and seeing the good in him; of having faith and confidence in what he is doing, and enthusiasm for it," concluded the article's author. "And I like to think that, even though he may not realize it, the plants and flowers in his garden are subtly strengthening him in the philosophy."[17]

Carnegie's cultivation of plants, however, receded before a more serious kind of husbandry that threw his life, as well as his psyche, into temporary disarray. For a number of years after their marriage in 1944, he and Dorothy had tried to conceive a child but were unsuccessful. So later in the decade they tried to adopt an infant but were rejected because they were too old. So the couple reluctantly reconciled themselves to the situation. In a letter to Lowell Thomas in 1947, Carnegie congratulated his old friend on the success of his son but added mournfully, "I often wonder if I haven't missed the most important thing in life: children."[18]

To the couple's mutual astonishment, however, Dorothy became pregnant in 1951. Dale was thrilled, at times ecstatic, at this unexpected development. Because his wife feared a miscarriage due to her age, they agreed to keep the news secret for as long as possible. But only a few days after confirming her pregnancy, Dorothy was shocked to see the minister of their church show up on the doorstep at 27 Wendover Road, carrying flowers and offering congratulations on this happy news. She knew immediately that Dale had been unable to keep quiet. In fact, the father-to-be told just about all of his friends (and even casual acquaintances) about the pregnancy. Dorothy forgave his enthusiasm, but then grew consternated when he announced the news to the world without informing her. While on a long-planned trip to Italy in September 1951, he publicly proclaimed the impending birth of a child while being interviewed in Rome: "Author-lecturer Dale Carnegie today disclosed that he is going to become a father at the age of 63. Carnegie, who wrote *How to Win Friends and Influence People*, said his wife expects a child in December." The press release quickly circled the globe and appeared in hundreds of newspapers before he returned home in October.[19]

Later in the fall, an anxious Carnegie struggled to meet scheduled speaking engagements but his mind was elsewhere. He dashed off to Kansas City to deliver a talk on human relations on his birthday, November 28. "I recall his excitement," said the local sponsor of the Carnegie Course. "It was his birthday and he was anxious to go home because his first child was expected to be born the next day." This expectation was off by only a bit. Donna Dale Carnegie was born on December 11, 1951. Her father was delighted if a bit nonplussed. He immediately phoned Rosemary about the birth but was so nervous that he could not recall any details about the baby's size or weight.[20]

Dale was the proudest of fathers. After receiving a note of congratulations from Lowell Thomas, he happily described "the little angel who has come into our family," and then joked, "You are right, Tommie. I expect to have them at the rate of one a year for the next fifteen years." At the same time, the experience of fatherhood left him somewhat bewildered. At sixty-three years of age and having no experience whatsoever with a crying infant, diapers, feeding, and burping, his efforts often proved fumbling. For months after Donna Dale's birth, he would stop suddenly in the middle of daily activities and proclaim, "Can you believe there is a baby in this house?" His behavior, a mixture of joy, wonder, and overwrought concern, prompted this amused description from his wife: "you would have thought no one else had ever had a baby in the history of mankind."[21]

As Donna Dale grew from an infant into a toddler, Carnegie became an even more doting father. He adored her and, since he was in semiretirement and Dorothy had moved into a leadership role in the company, he became something of a househusband. He served as Donna's primary caregiver, spending much of the day playing with her around the house, in the backyard, or pushing her in a baby carriage (or, a bit later, walking her) to his elaborate garden down the street. Rosemary would see them together when she visited from college and noticed their daily rituals. "He loved to push her carriage into the garden where he liked to work each afternoon, just to be near her. He found Donna to be an enchanting wonder," she observed. "Every morning, he would carry her downstairs and point out pictures of a cow and Abraham Lincoln.

When she would respond with 'Gow,' he knew she was saying real words." Then he would chuckle and announce that his precocious daughter knew the difference between Mr. Lincoln and the cow.[22]

Sometimes Carnegie was overly protective. One Sunday afternoon two older gentlemen, members of one of Dorothy's clubs, stopped by with their small dog for a visit. Dale welcomed them graciously, of course, but then made them tie the dog up in the backyard to avoid presenting any danger to Donna. Dorothy was mortified, but her husband would not be swayed. Dale made up for such overprotectiveness, however, with a steady flow of love toward his daughter: putting her on a pony for the first time, teaching her to tend the flower garden, getting her a cocker spaniel named Birdie. He also delighted in taking her to his Missouri farm in the summertime where he hoped, in his words, she would "learn to love

Dale and Dorothy Carnegie with their daughter, Donna, in 1953.

Carnegie, his health and mental acuity fading, spent increasing time at home with his adored daughter, Donna.

the little calves and pigs and chickens; and the song of the thrush and the whistle of the bobwhite." Years later, Donna recalled fond images of being a toddler with her father: "sitting in his lap, eating ham off his plate, pulling weeds in the garden . . . walks with him, to the office, on his farm in Missouri bringing back painted turtles to free in the yard."[23]

Another sign of his deep feelings came several weeks after Donna's birth. In January 1952, Carnegie began composing an autobiographical memoir entitled "Letters to My Daughter," which he worked on sporadically over the next several years. The opening revealed much about his state of mind as a new father. "To my darling daughter, Donna Dale Carnegie. As I write this sentence, you have been on this earth only fifty days. I have been here for sixty-three years. Yet I am surprised at how little more I know at sixty-three than I knew at twenty-three," he wrote. "But this I do know: I love you, so I am writing to tell you about the experiences I had when I was a child. Maybe in the year two thousand, when you are forty-nine years old, you may be interested in some of the things your old daddy did as a child."[24]

Carnegie clearly adored Donna Dale, and her arrival provided an unanticipated charge of emotional fulfillment late in his life. He saw her presence as almost a miracle and sought to give her the happiest life possible. At the same time, this blissful situation was complicated by the existence of Linda Dale Offenbach and her mother, Frieda, who, while now at the margins of his serene family life, remained in his emotional field of vision. Secretly, they continued to draw his concern, support, and love.

As he enjoyed domestic life at Wendover Road in Forest Hills, Carnegie carefully maintained contact with the Offenbachs in New Haven. While Dorothy had banned Linda's visits to the Carnegie home around 1950, her husband skirted this directive in subsequent years. He wrote the girl regularly, arranged to meet her in New York when she was able to visit, and kept in touch with Frieda by phone, letter, and occasional trips to her home. Facing a precarious situation, he maneuvered dexterously to preserve his family happiness with Dorothy, and then Donna, on the one hand, while keeping alive the loving relationship with Linda and Frieda, on the other hand. He managed this delicate balancing act throughout the early 1950s.

Carnegie was enormously proud of Linda's great success in school. A highly intelligent girl, she excelled in academic studies and he praised her efforts at every opportunity. "My darling Linda, I was delighted to hear that your grades averaged 94. I do not remember ever having achieved that average. I am mighty proud of you," he wrote in November 1950. In 1954, upon learning that she had been voted the outstanding junior in her class of seven hundred, he exclaimed, "I wanted to run down the street and button hole every stranger I met and say, 'Have you heard the thrilling news?'" Carnegie also delighted in Linda's musical talent. "So are you playing Rachmaninoff Prelude in C# Minor?" he wrote. "How I envy you. How I wish I had taken music in college. But it didn't seem important to me at the time . . . I had no time for music. I miss it now."[25]

As in earlier years, Carnegie continued to shower his "niece" with gifts. Now that Linda was a teenager, however, it became more difficult to find appropriate gifts for her. He confessed, "I find it hard to believe you are already sixteen . . . I would have loved to keep you a little girl for much longer." At one point, he inquired plaintively, "Please be sure to give me the titles of a dozen teenage romances that you would like." He finally enlisted the services of Marilyn Burke, who wrote to Linda suggesting that Carnegie could "bring you some of the Louisa May Alcott books such as *Little Women, Little Men, Fight Cousins, Rose in Bloom, Joe's Boys* . . . These were my favorites when I was twelve and thirteen years old. I read them over and over again and still have them on my bookshelves now."[26]

Carnegie also issued a constant stream of invitations for Linda to meet him in New York for various activities. She accepted some of them, occasionally accompanied by her brother. In 1950, he wrote, "It was a real pleasure to have you and Russell go to the rodeo with me. We will go to the circus when it comes in the spring." Once, learning that she would be on vacation from Christmas to New Year's, he said, "I imagine that you would like to come down to New York to see a show and perhaps to do some shopping. I would love to be your beau that day." Linda's trips often focused on a special commemoration date for Carnegie: her birthday. In 1954, when he was forced to cancel her visit because of a company convention, he implored, "Please let me know when you can come. Why don't you come down to New York to celebrate your birthday on July 8?" Trying to arrange for them to attend a matinee performance of *Kismet*, he inquired, "could you come to New York on either Saturday the 10th or Wednesday the 14th? I am distressed that we cannot celebrate your birthday closer to the real date, but Fate took a hand this year."[27]

Linda, now a teenager, had become more reluctant to visit Carnegie. Increasingly aware of the strange, complex, mysterious nature of the relationship among this famous man, her mother, her father, and herself, she wondered about the lavish attention Carnegie paid to her. It was around this time that Linda pointedly asked her mother about the reason for his intense interest, and Frieda evaded direct answers. In addition, the girl increasingly saw her visits to New York as tiresome and annoying. An adolescent becoming sensitive to the nuances of social life, she felt that while Carnegie tried to please her, he never really tried to understand her as a real person. Linda was fond of this larger-than-life older man, but had come to see him, in her words, "as something of a phony, a master of the grand gesture but really not in touch with me in a genuine, authentic way."[28]

Unaware of Linda's feelings—or perhaps attributing them to the onset of teenage angst—Carnegie remained solicitous of the girl. A letter from Marilyn Burke to Linda assured her, "You'll see your Uncle Dale over the weekend." A missive from Carnegie noted that he had received a handwritten note from President Truman that he would show her "when I come up. I hope that won't be too long . . . My regards to your charming mother and your brilliant

daddy." Offhand references in letters to Linda also revealed that
Carnegie stayed in touch with Frieda on a steady basis. In 1954,
for instance, he praised the girl for her academic performance
and mentioned that he had learned of her latest accomplishments
"when I received a letter from your mother." Describing her as a
lovely and adorable girl, he asked, "How do I know? Because your
mother tells me so." As he worked to arrange her visits to New
York, he would comment on possible free times and add, "Your
mother tells me that you will be on vacation."[29]

On several occasions, Carnegie's letters made clear that contact
with Linda and Frieda was occurring without Dorothy's knowledge. In a 1954 letter, he carefully instructed the girl to use a special
telephone number: "If you phone me, please call me at Boulevard
8-4000." The same held true for Frieda, as Carnegie told Linda,
"Please tell your mother to phone me at Boulevard 8-4000 the next
time she is coming to New York to shop." He also gave special instructions regarding letters, telling Linda, "Please write me at once
to 155 Ascan Ave., New York City." This was an address in Queens
about a mile from the Carnegie home, where he had established an
office on the upper floor of a friend's house.[30]

While his family remained unaware, some of Carnegie's friends
knew about his ongoing relationship with Linda and Frieda Offenbach. "Your Uncle Dale has talked so much about you that I feel
as though I already know you. I hope someday to be lucky enough
to meet such a nice little girl," Marilyn Burke wrote Linda in 1950.
"I'm sure you've chalked up a remarkable record for good behavior, at least according to the reports that I get from your Uncle
Dale." In 1955, Homer Croy received a letter from Isador Offenbach, and responded in a familiar, joking style. Offenbach had related that Linda had graduated from high school and was entering
college. "I don't believe that she [Linda] is in Vassar," replied Croy.

"How is Frieda Birk? I can't remember her married name. She was known as the Belle of Gaucher."[31]

A poignant moment came with Linda's graduation from high school in June 1955. Bursting with pride, Carnegie reacted emotionally. He noted that he had read about her outstanding record in a newspaper clipping from the *New Haven Register*, doubtless forwarded by Frieda. The article listed her achievements as "Outstanding Senior, Hillhouse High; Honor Student four years; Graduation Speaker; Treasurer, Student Council; News Editor, *The Sentinel*" and various other activities in Latin Club, Debating Club, and French Club. The article observed that Linda "will enter Vassar." Carnegie wrote the girl, warmly assuring her that she had "already entered my heart. Frankly, I had to catch my breath when I read all the things you had accomplished. You ought to be proud, very proud of such a record." Then on June 15, the day of the graduation ceremony, he sent a telegram to her home: "I am very proud of the brilliant work you have done in school. I wish I could be present tonight for your graduation. I am sure you will be the outstanding speaker of the evening. Best wishes and love always, Uncle Dale."[32]

Carnegie's carefully camouflaged relationship with Linda and Frieda Offenbach remained an important part of his life, even as his life with Dorothy and Donna Dale flourished. But in the early 1950s, a difficulty slowly emerged that steadily overshadowed everything—his connections with family and friends, his work, even his personality and abilities. Eroding his faculties and undermining his judgment, this silent malady sent the famous author and teacher into an inexorable decline.

The problem began with small things. Not long after Donna's birth, her father started exhibiting lapses in memory and confusion about ordinary incidents and day-to-day issues. One of the first times was when the fastidious Carnegie arrived home from New York having left an expensive brand-new overcoat on the subway. Rather than being perturbed about the situation when Dorothy probed, he first seemed uncomprehending about the loss, and then said it was unimportant. His wife found this behavior very odd "because Dale would have hunted that coat down only a few months prior." Then she noted that her husband began having trouble with the telephone, mixing up the numbers even a moment after looking them up, and then becoming frustrated and upset. Colleagues noticed that Carnegie occasionally grew confused over teaching and administrative matters, and had increasing trouble recalling names and appointments. The routine of caring for his beloved daughter even became troublesome as he would walk the toddler down the street to his auxiliary garden, forget that she was with him, and come home alone. Dorothy would gently scold him—"Dale, you can't leave Donna by herself, she may drown in that fish pond!"— and they would dash up the street to get her. Eventually, they were forced to fill in the pond and plant rosebushes to prevent a mishap.[33]

Forgetfulness also began to affect Carnegie's public-speaking appearances. An associate described a scene in Wichita, Kansas, when he addressed the graduates of the local Carnegie Course, with some people driving two hundred miles to hear the famous speaker. "He was 30 minutes late and after he got there he couldn't find his notes," the local sponsor reported. After much time, he finally found them in his overcoat pocket but the host described it as "a memorable disaster." Another time, Carnegie began a speech in Los Angeles in his usual confident fashion: "I started this course of mine . . ." But then he paused for an uncomfortable stretch of time, and continued, "I think it was in 1912." He had recited this founding date hundreds of times over the years and it seemed odd that now he would stumble over it. As such instances multiplied, Dorothy helped her husband cope. She assisted him in trimming down his presentations to four stock speeches—"Enthusiasm," "Public Speaking," "Avoiding Worry," and "Human Relations"— and he became so well versed in them that he avoided most slips and remained "the Dale Carnegie that everyone knew."[34]

Journalists also began to notice a change. Long a master of public relations and handling the press, Carnegie still displayed flashes of down-home wit and self-effacing charm in interviews. But now there were lapses. A reporter from the *Kansas City Star* observed that he appeared somewhat listless at times during their discussion and "told us his story in a voice that was low and diffident." During the long interview with *American Home* magazine on his gardening activities, he energetically led the reporter on a tour of his various flower beds and plant arrangements, before making a curious

Carnegie in the last year of his life.

observation. Stooping over to show him a chunk of pale gray rock, laced with intricate and convoluted markings, called "brain coral," Carnegie commented that the unusual name was "what I sometimes think *my* brain is turning into."[35]

Carnegie had fallen victim to Alzheimer's disease. His symptoms of dementia, not well understood at the time, were attributed to hardening of the arteries, according to Dorothy, but later they would be diagnosed more clearly with the advancement of medical science. As his forgetfulness and confusion steadily accelerated by 1954, doctors finally told his wife that at some point he would require custodial care. The family, however, for both personal and business reasons, carefully kept Carnegie's problem from the public.[36]

With her husband's condition steadily worsening, Dorothy stepped forward and took charge of his business enterprise as well as his personal care. With their marriage in 1944, of course, she had become a partner in his endeavors, developing the Dorothy Carnegie Course for Women and playing a major role in the incorporation and expansion of Carnegie and Associates. In 1945, Dale had appointed her vice president of the company. Now, with her husband's growing infirmity, she took the helm and steered its course in all business matters. The fact that she was a woman provided no barrier. "Dorothy believed that any woman with talents, with gumption, with any ability should not be embarrassed to be a woman. She saw no deterrent to achieving whatever she wanted to achieve," said her son-in-law, Oliver Crom. "She felt she was equal to, maybe better than, any man. She could walk into a room and make tough men quake in their boots. She was strong!" Her granddaughter described Dorothy's temperament piquantly: "Dorothy was liberated before anyone knew what that meant."[37]

Dale and Dorothy Carnegie in the early 1950s as she assumed a larger role in the business and he slowly withdrew.

Dorothy's business ascendency contained considerable irony. In 1953, she published a book entitled *How to Help Your Husband Get Ahead in His Social and Business Life*, a text for women (by "Mrs. Dale Carnegie") that extolled the virtues of motherhood and domestic tasks. Reflecting the conformist sensibility of the 1950s suburban family, and written in the mold of her husband's famous advice books, this volume offered formulas on "Four Ways to Give Him an Extra Boost," "Help Him Decide Where He Is Going," "How to Give Him a Home, Sweet Home," and "How to Make People Like Him." Dorothy's central argument was that a woman must bend to the task of helping her husband succeed, because upon him depended her well-being and that of their family. Wives, both actual and aspiring, must adhere to this rule: "Be willing to give up a career of your own if it conflicts with your husband's

happiness and best interests." In her words, "Let's face it girls. That
wonderful guy in your house—and mine—is building your house
and your happiness and the opportunities that will come to your
children. So maybe it's time you started thinking more seriously
about how you can improve his act."[38]

But the steel beneath this sentimental, self-sacrificing façade occasionally showed through and revealed the real Dorothy Carnegie. As she wrote in *Better Homes and Gardens*, in a brief extract
from her book, a wife "can't be a silent partner in this business
called marriage. She must use her brains—and her brawn, if necessary." In another passage, she insisted that shaping one's husband
was not that hard. "Ever hear about the power of a woman? Of
course you have," she exclaimed. "Women have been shown to be
powerful enough to build new schools, change a town's political
administration, wipe out crime and corruption." Some years later,
she revealed her self-confidence and ambition with a quip. The demands of running the Carnegie operation were not overwhelming,
this no-nonsense Oklahoman told a reporter, but they were considerable enough that "I have no time to sit and whittle and spit."[39]

So even though its founder was struggling with a serious af-
fliction, Dale Carnegie and Associates, because of the steady, firm
leadership of his wife, did not flounder. By 1955, however, Carnegie's situation had worsened noticeably. As his mental faculties
slipped away, he became increasingly susceptible to an array of
physical ailments. For a man who had seldom experienced sickness
of any kind, life became a growing travail.

In June 1955, among the many invitations for speaking appearances
that poured into Carnegie's office, one thrilled him to the core.
His alma mater, Central Missouri State College in Warrensburg,

Missouri, had decided to award him an honorary Doctor of Letters degree, the first ever awarded in its history. The institution asked Carnegie to attend the summer 1955 graduation ceremony and, moreover, to give the commencement address. Eager to return to the town where he had spent his adolescence, he replied, "I appreciate the honor you have paid me in asking me to make this address at my Alma Mater. I hope the students who listen to it enjoy it half as much as I am going to enjoy being there." As one of his colleagues noted, he would not have been more pleased if the honor had come from Harvard or Oxford.[40]

Carnegie arrived on the Central Missouri State campus to deliver his talk on July 29 and spent the day. He was driven to and from Warrensburg by Harold Abbott, a Carnegie Course associate in Kansas City. Agreeing to attend a graduation luncheon at the college, Carnegie happily greeted dignitaries, faculty, and former classmates in attendance. *Newsweek*, covering the event, observed that the honorary degree validated a distinguished and influential career. "Today, Dale Carnegie is an institution of worldwide influence," it wrote. "*How to Win Friends and Influence People*, the most popular book of nonfiction since the Bible, appears in 31 languages. Five million copies are in English alone. In addition, 450,000 disciples have graduated from his Institute for Effective Speaking and Human Relations since he started it in 1912."[41]

It became evident, however, that Carnegie was laboring under some duress. His physical appearance had changed noticeably from even a few years before. Now with a head of snow-white hair that was much receded and thinning, he had lost weight and his features appeared almost gaunt behind dark-framed glasses. While still a natty dresser—he appeared in Warrensburg wearing a beautifully tailored, light-colored summer suit with a bow tie—the clothes hung more loosely upon his slight frame. Overall, he appeared frail while his normally alert eyes sometimes seemed vacant. An acquaintance remarked, "Oh, how tragic it is to see the disintegration of what has been a well-tuned and effective personality." He also noted that one of Carnegie's friends had confided that, given his declining health, "only Dale's extreme affection for his school could have induced him to appear again in public."[42]

Even more shockingly, Carnegie read his commencement address from printed pages. For decades, he had counseled his students to talk naturally, enthusiastically, and from the heart in a fashion that would project their personalities. "Don't read, and don't attempt to memorize your talk word for word," he had advised as far back as 1926 in *Public Speaking: A Practical Course for Business Men.* "The whole exhibition will be stiff and cold and colorless and inhuman." But now, even after laboring on his talk for several weeks, Carnegie was unable to remember even the outline and direction of his remarks. So he was forced to read it.[43]

But first, Carnegie sat on the dais at the ceremony in Hendricks Hall as the head of the college's Board of Regents read a glowing citation:

An individual who came to this campus from his nearby farm home; who here, by his own efforts and determination, developed from a timid, reserved farm boy into a skilled public speaker who won contest after contest; who through difficulties and adversity became renowned as a teacher of public speaking and applied psychology and gained world recognition as an author in those fields; who has been welcomed in many parts of the world as a benefactor of mankind who has helped thousands to conquer their fears and develop their innate abilities and self-confidence; a man who is now known and will be remembered, almost as a legend, by the entire world

as contributor to human happiness and development; I present
to you for the degree, Doctor of Letters, Dale Carnegie.

Then Dr. George W. Diemer, the president of the college, conferred
the degree on Carnegie, and Mrs. J. Howard Hart, a regent and
former classmate of the honoree, added a few words. "It occurs to
me that no other alumnus has more completely fulfilled the meaning of the motto of this college, 'Education for Service,' than has
Mr. Carnegie," she said. "He has given to men and women alike,
throughout the world, faith in themselves, hope in their future, and
joy and confidence in their relationships with their fellow man."[44]

Carnegie a few months before his death, proudly accepting an honorary degree in July
1955 from his alma mater, Central Missouri State College.

Carnegie then arose to read his speech on "The Value of Enthusiasm," a favorite topic. Mustering some of the mental energy that had sustained him for years, he contended that enthusiasm was a little-recognized key to success and quoted the late Frederick E. Williamson, then president of the New York Central Railroad Company: "The longer I live, the more certain I am that enthusiasm is the little recognized secret of success . . . [A] man of second-rate ability with enthusiasm will often outstrip a man of first-rate ability without enthusiasm." Carnegie told one of his favorite stories about a student, many years ago, who made a speech about how he threw wood ashes into his yard and got bluegrass the next spring, and spoke so passionately on the point that the students actually believed him. "If enthusiasm can make a group of apparently intelligent businessmen believe that you can produce bluegrass with nothing but hickory wood ashes, what can't enthusiasm produce if you have a tiny molecule of common sense behind what you are saying?" he said.[45]

But Carnegie also suggested, unintentionally in a lighthearted passage, that the power of enthusiasm had a downside. It could be used to scam people. He recalled his days as a young salesman, when he came across a crowd at a street corner in a small, South Dakota town where a street barker was pushing a product with great enthusiasm. The barker proclaimed that men who wore thick-soled shoes became bald because they did not establish good electrical connections with the earth. His product, a small steel plate to be tacked to the heels of men's shoes, would remedy this and stave off baldness. Carnegie described how some people were buying it, then joked, "I had spent four years in college and I knew that this claim was absolutely ridiculous. But the man was so enthusiastic that . . . Well, I did just what you think. And look, it worked!" He pointed to his own head of hair.[46]

After extolling the virtue of being eagerly committed to your work—"Yes, to an enthusiastic man, his work is always part play, no matter how hard or demanding it is"—Carnegie ended on a note of therapeutic uplift. He observed that Douglas MacArthur, a man who had made himself into a great American general, had led troops through many dark days of fierce fighting before triumphing in the Pacific theater during World War II. The plaque hanging on the wall of his office told the secret of his success: "You are as young as your faith; as old as your doubt; as young as your self-confidence; as old as your fear; as young as your hope; as old as your despair. Years may wrinkle the skin, but to give up enthusiasm wrinkles the soul."[47]

Carnegie sat down as the crowd responded with a loud ovation. The reporter for *Newsweek* concluded, "He spoke with his usual firmness and enthusiasm, in an accent still of the Midwest. His natural body gestures were well timed, and his persuasive content was high. No doubt only the dignity of the occasion restrained his listeners from encouraging shouts of 'Atta boy?'" Appropriately, given his treasured Midwestern roots, Carnegie's address in Warrensburg would be his last public appearance.[48]

Over the next few months, Carnegie deteriorated rapidly. He developed a bad case of shingles and this painful condition seemed to sap his strength. He slowly recovered, however, and Dorothy decided to take him to Bermuda for rest and recuperation, hoping that sunshine and sea air would restore some of his energy. Later, Donna Dale would recall "evenings in Bermuda, the sand and drinking milk on the front porch with him and picnics on the beach." But instead he grew weaker, and after a few days had to be flown back to a New York hospital on a chartered airplane, where uremia, an acute illness triggered by kidney failure, swept through his system.[49]

After an operation proved unsuccessful, Carnegie suffered an infection that brought on an intense, unrelenting fever. When it became obvious that he was dying, Dorothy brought him home to Wendover Road. Homer Croy, his best friend, visited his bedside. "Dale's later days were sad, indeed," he wrote a short time later. "The last nine days I went out to see him, he did not know me, so greatly did the fever have him. If infection from the operation had not come upon him, he would have fought off everything else and survived. But day after day of fever, fever that no powerful drug could allay. Very sad." Carnegie died at 6:10 in the morning on November 1, 1955, three weeks before his sixty-seventh birthday.[50]

A funeral service was held at the Church-in-the-Gardens in Forest Hills. Condolences and flowers arrived from all over the world, and Croy noted that prominently displayed was "a great wreath—from one of his classes in South Africa. The radio had carried the word, and the class had cabled money to a New York florist." During his remarks, the pastor observed that while Carnegie had idolized Abraham Lincoln, he also had displayed many of "the Lincolnesque qualities of wisdom, patience, tolerance, humor, humility, and faith." Obituaries appeared in *Newsweek*, *Time*, the *Kansas City Star*, and *The New York Times*, all of which noted that his influence had spread from the United States around the world. Perhaps the most insightful summing up came in an obituary in a Washington newspaper. "In his books and in his classes, he sought to teach the average man how to overcome his feelings of inadequacy, how to speak," it said. "Dale Carnegie solved none of the profound mysteries of the universe. But, perhaps more than anyone of his generation, he helped human beings learn how to get along together—which seems to sometimes to be the greatest need of all."[51]

Befitting his heritage and unassuming manner, Carnegie's body was transported to Belton, Missouri, after the funeral where he was buried next to his parents in a small graveyard. The plain marble slab marking the site was inscribed simply "Dale Carnegie, 1888–1955." This modest interment belied the great significance of the man. In fact, his teaching and writing over several decades had profoundly influenced the development of modern American culture. He had taken the lead in fomenting a revolution in values and attitudes, manners and morals that had arisen in the early decades of the twentieth century. In the years after his death, it would sweep through modern life with irresistible force.

Epilogue

The Self-Help Legacy
of Dale Carnegie

On September 23, 2001, almost two weeks after the devastating terrorist attacks that brought down the twin towers of the World Trade Center, a commemoration service was held at Yankee Stadium. Tens of thousands of grieving citizens, along with dozens of national dignitaries such as former president Bill Clinton and Senator Hillary Clinton, Senator Edward Kennedy, Governor George Pataki, and Mayor Rudolph Giuliani, filed somberly into the stadium. The crowd, waving American flags and clutching photos of the victims, listened tearfully to a program of speeches, songs, and prayers that honored the victims of the most deadly attack on the United States in six decades.

One aspect of the gathering stood out. Organizers had appointed as master of ceremonies Oprah Winfrey, an African American talk-show host and self-help guru whose empathetic, inspiring, and charismatic style had galvanized millions and made her the most popular woman in the country. After introducing a parade of speakers and performers, she read aloud from her own "A Prayer for America." The country had been attacked, but "we, Americans, refuse to be shattered," she declared. "What was meant to divide us has drawn us together and we shall not be moved." But the lessons of the assault also ascended to a higher plane. "When you lose a loved one, you gain an angel whose name you know," she explained. "May we leave this place determined to now use every moment that we yet live to turn up the volume in our own lives, to create deeper meaning, to know what really matters." Winfrey closed her remarks with a trademark combination of pathos and uplift: "We all know for sure now how fragile, how uncertain, yet extraordinary life can be. May we always remember."[1]

It was a telling moment. In this time of national tragedy, instead of a political or religious leader striding forward to seize the moment, it was America's leading representative of the modern self-help culture who salved the nation's wounds and affirmed its highest aspirations. Such a thing would have seemed preposterous in the aftermath of Pearl Harbor in 1941, or even after the assassinations of John F. Kennedy or Martin Luther King Jr. in the 1960s. But it seemed perfectly appropriate at the dawn of the twenty-first century. For many Americans, a self-help ideology of self-esteem, personal growth, mental health, and positive thinking had become deeply embedded in their worldview. It provided a natural framework for coming to grips with the devastation that had descended on the United States on that September day. Winfrey expressed this pervasive worldview brilliantly.

This incident also revealed the legacy of Dale Carnegie. He had established the template for the modern self-help culture in the 1930s and 1940s with *How to Win Friends and Influence People, How to Stop Worrying and Start Living*, and his popular adult-education courses. He had linked success and happiness to the individual's capacity to develop several characteristics—a compelling personality, positive thinking, tightly focused mental resources, vague spirituality, and skill in human relations. Carnegie popularized the notion that pleasure and satisfaction flowed from fulfilling, rather than repressing, one's internal needs and desires. In his hands, character and moral certitude gave way to personality and the search for an abundant life, both materially and emotionally. The scope and significance of this sea change in American culture became increasingly evident in the years after his death.

In mid-twentieth-century America, signs of Carnegie's spreading influence appeared everywhere on the cultural landscape. His famous course produced businessmen such as Warren Buffett and Lee Iacocca, both of whom attributed their success and influence to their Carnegie training in the 1950s. In a very different venue, both President Lyndon Johnson and radical Jerry Rubin, bitter enemies during the great political upheavals of the 1960s, drew upon the Carnegie model. Johnson's assertive, powerful personality had gained a boost from his efforts as a Carnegie instructor in Houston in 1930 and '31. Rubin, radical leader of the Youth International Party (Yippies) and one of the Chicago Seven, imbibed Carnegie's *How to Win Friends* to help overcome his dread of making political speeches. In popular culture, Carnegie's ideas triggered several parodies—always a signal of influence—that appeared to great acclaim. Shepherd Mead's *How to Succeed in Business Without Really Trying* (1952), first a best-selling book and then a fashionable Broadway musical, poked fun at Carnegie's success methods, while controversial comedian Lenny Bruce's *How to Talk Dirty and Influence People* (1965) played off the success writer's bestselling book title to present a scathing critique of middle-class social conventions.[2]

Carnegie also anticipated several developments in modern cognitive psychology and neuropsychology that reached out to a broader audience. His emphasis on discerning and appreciating the submerged emotional needs and processes of human beings surfaced in several popular, influential works appearing around the end of the twentieth and the beginning of the twenty-first century: Daniel Kahneman's *Thinking, Fast and Slow*; Daniel Goleman's *Emotional Intelligence: Why It Can Matter More Than IQ*; Daniel Gilbert's *Stumbling on Happiness*; Richard H. Thaler and Cass R. Sunstein's *Nudge: Improving Decisions About Health, Wealth, and Happiness*; and Malcolm Gladwell's *Blink: The Power of Thinking Without Thinking*. In various but complementary ways, these works have suggested that the cognitive processes of human beings, rather than their rationality, help them navigate through society according to wants and needs they understand only dimly, if at all. In parallel fashion, adherents of modern "positive psychology"—such as Martin Seligman in *Authentic Happiness: Using the New Positive Psychology to Realize Your Potential for Lasting Fulfillment*, and Ed Diener and Robert Biswas-Diener in *Happiness: Unlocking the Mysteries of Psychological Wealth*—have followed a Carnegian path in arguing that an embrace of close-knit social ties, spirituality, and the interpersonal virtues of kindness, sincerity, gratitude, and the capacity for love paves the psychological path to human happiness.[3]

In a broader and deeper vein, however, the therapeutic culture of self-help pioneered by Carnegie became his greatest legacy. Throughout the second half of the twentieth century, a host of disciples carried versions of it into every nook and cranny of modern life and wove it into the fabric of American values. This crusade demolished the last vestiges of an older Victorian standard of self-control and hardy, self-reliant morality and nurtured a fresh set of values based on the search for personal growth, abundant health, and radiant personality. By adopting a model of psychological sickness and recovery, advocates of therapeutic self-help posed the individual's struggle to overcome victimization and establish self-esteem as the central drama of life. They presented emotional empowerment as the key to happiness. Of course, Carnegie was not the only inspiration for this cultural revolution—other important contributors included the "positive thinking" preacher and author Norman Vincent Peale; the psychologist and sociologist of modern work Elton Mayo; the advertising executive and biographer Bruce Barton; and the child-rearing expert Dr. Benjamin Spock. But Carnegie, the wildly popular success writer and teacher, served as its leader, its formulator, and its greatest popularizer.

In the realm of success literature, several popular figures carried forward the torch lit by Carnegie. In an avalanche of how-to-succeed publications, they advocated myriad psychological strategies aimed at creating self-confidence, enhancing personality, thinking positively, and marshaling emotional resources in order to achieve social and material advancement. In 1967, for example, Thomas Harris's *I'm Okay, You're Okay*, which swept to the top of the best-seller list, advocated a technique of "transactional analysis" to help individuals adjust their relationships with others and overcome psychological debilitation. Some years later, Tony Robbins, in books such as *Unlimited Power* (1986) and *Awaken the Giant Within* (1992), as well as in hundreds of infomercials and seminars on "Personal Power" and "Power Talk," promoted a strategy of neurolinguistic programming, or light-trance hypnosis, to rewire the subconscious in order to eliminate fear, enhance self-confidence, and acquire profits, a fuller life, and better relationships. Susan Jeffers, a PhD in psychology who has been dubbed the "Queen of Self-Help," used *Feel the Fear and Do It Anyway* (1987) as a springboard to launch her message of positive thinking and overcoming timidity. Dr. Joyce Brothers in *How to Get Whatever You Want Out of Life* (1978), Dr. Wayne W. Dyer in *Your Erroneous Zones: Step-by-Step Advice for Escaping the Trap of Negative*

Thinking and Taking Control of Your Life (1976), and Rhonda Byrne in *The Secret* (2006) are only a few among the host of self-help gurus garnering popular acclaim for their psychology-tinged formulas to achieve success.[4]

Another genre of popular books descended from the Carnegie cultural bloodline made self-esteem the central component of modern happiness and achievement. Melody Beattie's *Codependent No More: How to Stop Controlling Others and Start Caring for Yourself* (1986)—this runaway bestseller began, "This book is dedicated to me"—urged readers to overcome "co-dependency" with others and concentrate on cultivating their own emotional lives. John Bradshaw, in *Homecoming: Reclaiming and Championing Your Inner Child* (1990), argued that individuals needed to work their way through the pain, neglect, shame, or grief of childhood in order to achieve "recovery" and find self-esteem. Jack Canfield's *Chicken Soup for the Soul* book series, first launched in 1993 and now numbering more than two hundred titles with total sales of five hundred million volumes, compiled inspirational stories for readers. Canfield, the head of the Foundation for Self-Esteem and convener of numerous Self-Esteem Seminars, employed the *Chicken Soup* volumes to nurture that quality. Indeed, the self-esteem paradigm became so pervasive that in the 1990s *Saturday Night Live* featured a comedy sketch starring comedian Al Franken (now a U.S. senator from Minnesota) as Stuart Smalley, a hapless young man addicted to recovery programs. With his life in shambles but inspired by numerous support groups, he faced every difficulty by looking in the mirror and intoning his mantra: "I'm good enough, I'm smart enough, and doggone it, people like me!"[5]

Modern religion increasingly displayed Carnegie's imprint of spirituality as therapy. In 1993, a perplexed *Christianity Today* noted that a powerful "therapeutic revolution" had transformed modern Protestantism: "Almost without anyone paying attention, Christian psychology has moved to the center of evangelicalism." Norman Vincent Peale had pioneered this trend, of course, first establishing the influential Religio-Psychiatric Clinic at Marble Collegiate Church, then writing the 1952 best seller *The Power of Positive Thinking*, which became the foundation of a vast organization. Other ministers followed in his wake. They included Robert Schuller, with his "Theology of Self-Esteem" and *Hour of Power* television broadcasts from his Crystal Cathedral in Southern California, and televangelist Joel Osteen, the pastor of the mammoth Lakewood Church in Houston and author of *Your Best Life Now: 7 Steps to Living at Your Full Potential* (2004). Another important stone in the edifice of therapeutic religion came from M. Scott Peck, whose massively popular book *The Road Less Traveled: A New Psychology of Love, Traditional Values and Spiritual Growth* (1988) promoted a nondenominational, nonjudgmental fusion of psychology and spirituality. By the early twenty-first century, observers such as Kenda Creasy Dean, in *Almost Christian: What the Faith of Our Teenagers Is Telling the American Church* (2010), concluded that "moralistic therapeutic deism" had become the centerpiece of modern Christianity. This vague, psychologized, non-theological spirituality, cut from Carnegie cloth, comprised a "gospel of niceness" wherein God appeared as a benevolent power for boosting the self-esteem of believers. It also featured, in many cases, a variant of the "prosperity gospel," which claimed that faith in God would bring financial blessings. In this modern model of Christianity, the standard of judgment shifted from sin to sickness as spiritual longing transformed into a recovery movement combining self-help, material abundance, and mental health.[6]

By the mid-twentieth century, modern education was adopting much of Carnegie's therapeutic self-help model. In the 1960s, experts began building self-esteem into the curriculum nationwide as they linked students' self-image to their educational attainment. Punishment, authority, and strict standards were increasingly branded as harmful in the classroom while identity reinforcement and interpersonal relations were deemed essential to achievement. Educational leaders insisted that "lowered self-esteem" among students made them "more submissive and withdrawn, though occasionally veering to the opposite extreme of aggression and domination." With the psychological development of students moving to the fore in curriculum and pedagogy, new paradigms emerged. Schools increasingly stressed extra-academic activities where children could demonstrate competence or mastery, or new kinds of testing, such as portfolio programs, which encouraged self-expression and were sensitive to different "learning styles." Meanwhile, teachers were urged to reinforce good behavior rather than to castigate bad behavior, and to provide positive commentary on student work to encourage self-confidence. In this new landscape of progressive, child-centered education, building the self-worth of students emerged as the central goal. Thus in 1990, a special California task force on education issued an influential report entitled "The Social Importance of Self-Esteem," which argued that "lack of self-esteem" lay at the heart of most modern social and personal problems and that educational reforms placing student self-affirmation at the heart of the curriculum provided the remedy. In that same year, the New York State Board of Regents endorsed "A Curriculum of Inclusion," a report claiming that traditional school curricula had damaged the psyches of young people, particularly females and minorities, and that a new multicultural model was needed to instill "higher self-esteem and self-respect" among students.[7]

Carnegian principles influenced modern child-rearing models. Dr. Benjamin Spock's popular *Baby and Child Care* (1946), which he described as a combination of "sound pediatrics with sound psychology," provided a benchmark in this development with its guidelines for parents on fostering interpersonal relations, social skills, and spontaneous personality in their offspring. In subsequent years, child-rearing literature continued to shift emphasis away from an older, moral stress on learning right from wrong, building character, and recognizing community responsibility and toward a new therapeutic calculus of emotional fulfillment, personality development, and mental health. By 1970, experts such as Dorothy C. Briggs, in *Your Child's Self-Esteem: The Key to His Life*, were offering parents a step-by-step process for building "a solid sense of self-worth in your child," insisting that if he "has high self-esteem, he has it made." Adele Faber and Elaine Mazlish's popular *How to Talk So Kids Will Listen and Listen So Kids Will Talk* (1980) stressed "the importance of acknowledging youngsters' feelings," while Louise Hart, in the popular *The Winning Family: Increasing Self-Esteem in Your Children and Yourself* (1987), told parents that "self-esteem is the greatest gift you can give your child . . . [I]t is the cornerstone of mental health, learning, and happiness."[8]

Great swaths of corporate America steadily adopted Carnegie's ethos of emotional sensitivity and mental health. As early as the 1920s, Elton Mayo, in his famous study of a General Electric plant in Chicago, had advanced a "human relations" model of management that underlined the importance of group relationships and a sense of belonging. By the 1950s, Peter Drucker had formulated an influential management model based on decentralization and the empowerment of laborers, wherein managers helped liberate modern "knowledge workers" and guided them in a common direction. Then TQM (total quality management) reformers such as W. Edwards Deming advocated a therapeutic environment defined by "worker empowerment," cooperative work groups, and "win-win" thinking. Tom Chappell, in *Managing Upside Down: The Seven Intentions of Values-Centered Leadership* (1999), offered a later version of the sensitized corporation where self-actualized individuals found meaning in their work, sought human connection, and pledged to be aware of others' feelings. But Stephen Covey eventually swept the field to become the king of modern business gurus. In *The 7 Habits of Highly Effective People* (1990), he promoted a psychologized management approach based on self-awareness, emotional empathy, and personal transformation. He stressed the need for reexamining how we interact with the world (a "paradigm shift") and working creatively and collaboratively with others ("synergize"). Covey's seventh and final "habit," which he termed "sharpen the saw," expressed a salient value of Carnegie's broader self-help agenda: use the lessons of experience to foster constant self-renewal.[9]

In fact, Carnegie's vision of therapeutic self-help flourished just about everywhere on America's modern cultural landscape in the last half of the twentieth century. It pushed New Age thinkers such as Deepak Chopra to the top of the best-seller list and television therapists such as Dr. Phil McGraw to a pinnacle of media popularity. It informed conservative crusades such as the Promise Keepers, which aimed to nurture "Godly men" through a combination of Biblical teaching, emotional empowerment, and support-group bonding. It influenced feminist thinking, where theorists such as Carol Gilligan, in *In a Different Voice: Psychological Theory and Women's Development* (1982), and Gloria Steinem, *Revolution From Within: A Book of Self-Esteem* (1993), stressed therapeutic issues of identity and emotional recovery as key to women's advancement. It shaped racial formulations, where figures such as Cornel West argued that African Americans needed not only an activist agenda of democratic socialism and revolutionary Christianity but a program of self-love to counteract the "profound sense of psychological depression, personal worthlessness, and social despair" that has devastated their community. Similarly, it inspired the Million Man March in October 1995, where African American males embraced a remedy of identity politics, male bonding, and recovery-group atonement. Even political discourse increasingly adopted a sensibility of therapeutic remedy and personal uplift. Bill Clinton, for example, swept into the White House announcing "I Feel Your Pain" and then, during subsequent crises during his presidency, summoned self-help gurus and New Age advisers such as Tony Robbins, Marianne Williamson, and Stephen Covey to meet him at Camp David for personal revitalization sessions.[10]

A telling set of statistics reveals the extent to which Carnegie's vision of therapeutic self-improvement has come to dominate modern values and sensibility. In the late 1940s, the United States had roughly 2,500 clinical psychologists, 30,000 social workers, and less than 500 marriage and family therapists. Sixty years later in 2010, however, the country had 77,000 clinical psychologists, 192,000 clinical social workers, 105,000 mental health counselors, 50,000 marriage and family therapists, 17,000 nurse psychotherapists, and 30,000 life coaches. Recently the omnivorous appetite for therapeutic self-help has prompted therapeutic entrepreneurs to develop "psychotherapy apps" for the treatment of various anxieties and emotional problems. Patients, by working through smartphone programs twice a week for four to six weeks, have been promised marked progress in overcoming their mental health issues.[11]

But the victory of therapeutic, self-help values in American culture has become most evident, perhaps, in that female figure who presided over the New York City memorial service in the aftermath of 9/11. It is now, incontrovertibly, the Age of Oprah. Beginning in the 1980s, Oprah Winfrey emerged as an unparalleled cultural force in modern America. With a top-rated, nationally syndicated television talk show bringing enormous influence and profits (she would be, perhaps, the wealthiest woman in the world by 2002), Winfrey branched out to found her own production company that churned out a long list of movies, television miniseries, inspirational seminars, radio shows, books, and magazines. She also gained plaudits as a high-profile philanthropist. Appearing on the cover of magazines such as *Newsweek*, *Vogue*, *The Saturday Evening Post*, *The New Republic*, *Ladies' Home Journal*, and *People*, she was crowned the "Queen of All Media" in a 1998 *Time* cover story.

But the secret of Winfrey's remarkable career and tremendous influence lay in the unique way she has synthesized a compelling creed of therapeutic self-fulfillment and New Age spirituality. Shaping her television show into a vast group-therapy session, she dealt with a tremendous variety of personal problems afflicting her guests while confessing her own struggles to overcome child abuse, crack cocaine, and compulsive weight gain. She invoked a litany of inspirational concepts for her vast audience—"Live Your Best Life," "Be More Splendid, More Extraordinary," "Evolve into the Complete Person You Were Intended to Be"—and emerged as *the* spokesperson for the modern self-help tradition. With her message of personal empowerment, Winfrey became America's therapist. Historically, she has completed what Dale Carnegie began in the first half of the twentieth century.[12]

So what does the final balance sheet indicate about Carnegie's far-reaching cultural legacy? By the dawn of the twenty-first century, the worldview of therapeutic self-help developed by this modest Missourian stood triumphant in modern America. Due to his writing and teaching efforts—as well as those of his disciples and other like-minded figures—mental health replaced morality, personality replaced character, human relations replaced authority, sensitivity replaced virtue, and self-esteem replaced community expectations as guides to behavior. Psychologized values permeated dominant institutions and liberation movements alike. This cultural transformation brought weighty consequences.

On the one hand, Carnegie's ethos of therapeutic self-help has produced notable benefits. First, by helping to alleviate individual pathologies and private misery, which too often were left to fester in earlier eras, it has encouraged a greater sensitivity to human emotional needs. In new ways, Carnegie and his followers sought to aid ordinary people in remedying the torments of personal life. Second, this ethos has erected a standard of "psychological man" in modern life, a more capacious model for understanding human behavior and impulses than earlier notions of "religious man" or "economic man" or "ideological man," where loyalties and endeavors were seen as narrowly spiritual, materialistic, or political. Third, in a practical vein, Carnegie's broad principles have encouraged a social standard of kindness, sensitivity, good humor, and patience with the foibles of others. This is no small achievement. In a modern environment too often shaped by careerism, arrogance, greed, and disregard for others, or hamstrung by social ineptness and ignorance, the prospect of well-adjusted personalities, solicitous conduct, and mentally healthy individuals has its attractions. Finally, the Carnegie vision of the good life as one of abundance, both emotionally and materially, draws upon deep wellsprings in American life. Since the founding of the colonies in the seventeenth century, and reinforced by the founding of the republic in the late eighteenth century, the notion of America as a land of opportunity for striving individuals to find prosperity and contentment has drawn tens of millions of immigrants from all over the globe. It is, perhaps, the central component of America's self-definition and Carnegie became one its most influential advocates.

On the other hand, however, the triumph of Carnegie's therapeutic model of self-help has come at a heavy cost. It has created an omnivorous, perpetual appetite for "feeling good about yourself." Like drug addicts who must ingest larger and larger doses to get high, too many modern Americans harbor outlandish emotional expectations that require ever more self-fulfillment to achieve satisfaction. This unrealistic mind-set encourages wild swings between a grandiose pole of "empowerment," where individuals believe they can generate the personal capacity to do anything, and a pathetic pole of "victimization," where outside forces consistently conspire to frustrate one's entitlement to bliss. Moreover, the Carnegie code has undermined people's capacity to think about the world in terms that transcend personal feelings. Its stress on human relations, sensitivity, and nonjudgmentalism has pushed aside frameworks of morality, social justice, and even economic well-being while the needs of emotionally injured individuals become paramount.

In a Carnegie world, where advancement and achievement are often the result of psychological maneuver, a fear of insincerity and emotional gamesmanship has been woven into our modern cultural fabric. The shift from character to personality has drawn a very fine line—indeed, it often seems to disappear entirely—between appreciation and flattery, sensitivity and artful control, human relations and human manipulation. Most broadly, perhaps, the culture of therapeutic self-help has isolated the individual from a larger sense of community. With concern focused so intensely on the private emotional needs of the self, many modern Americans have found it difficult, if not impossible, to conceptualize their relationship to common concerns. In the modern culture of self-fulfillment, notions of legitimate authority or civic obligation or community standards have become nearly oxymoronic.

Thus Carnegie's capture of modern American culture has encouraged a democratization of feelings where everyone has an equal right to happiness. At the same time, it has encouraged a pathologizing of democracy where private baggage is transported wholesale into the public realm. Personal desires, fears, and problems tend to overwhelm all considerations of the public good as much human interaction and governance is forced into the mold of the psychotherapy session or the support group or the therapeutic state.

In the face of this overwrought modern scene dominated by therapeutic self-help, a certain redress beckons. A more balanced, nuanced view of human endeavor appreciates reason as well as emotion, healthy instincts as well as dysfunctional states, dangerous impulses that require correction as well as self-esteem that deserves enhancement. It emphasizes morality and justice as grounds for acting upon the world and brings them into parity with claims of emotional need. It sees the complex, multifaceted connection between public and private realms and understands private life as an arena where values and traits are shaped in preparation for our shared social life, and not merely as a seedbed for personal pathologies and identity issues to be foisted on others. It recognizes duty as well as dysfunction, achievement as well as angst, the value of a useful life as well as recovery from emotional distress, the need for limitation as well as endless self-fulfillment.[13]

But regardless of any critical assessment of Carnegie's influence, there can be no question of his enormous impact on modern American life. Born into a late-Victorian culture of self-control, he played a leading role in constructing a modern culture of self-fulfillment. The messiah of the modern self-help movement, he created the framework for our contemporary commitment to therapeutic uplift and abundant living. His books and teachings revealed both the evident strengths (a sensitivity to people's emotional needs) and abiding weaknesses (a narcissistic preoccupation with the self) of this creed. Whatever one makes of the therapeutic culture of self-esteem, one must acknowledge the crucial efforts of a modest farm boy from Missouri in shaping its powerful role. Long ago, Thomas Jefferson coined that most American of phrases: "the pursuit of happiness." Dale Carnegie defined its modern meaning.

Acknowledgments

I am delighted to acknowledge the many debts incurred in the completion of this biography. Several members of Dale Carnegie's family and organization kindly assisted me during the process of research and writing. Brenda Leigh Johnson, his granddaughter, helped me get started, hosted several research trips to Long Island, shared her extensive knowledge of Carnegie's life and career, and funneled many useful materials my way. Donna Carnegie, his daughter, staunchly supported the project, provided a very informative interview and extensive written comments, and offered much warm encouragement and help in the book's final stage of completion. Oliver Crom, Carnegie's son-in-law, sat for an interview and shared many insights into Dale and Dorothy Carnegie and their enterprise. Muriel Goldstein stepped in near the end to provide invaluable help in gathering photographs for the book.

Special appreciation is extended to Linda Polsby, who graciously opened to a stranger a cache of previously unknown letters between Carnegie and her, and Carnegie and her mother, Freida Offenbach. She also was generous enough to discuss—at length, in detail, and with great honesty—the long and extremely complex relationship between Carnegie and her family. At the end, she granted the use of several family photographs. Her assistance proved invaluable as it helped open a new window on the life and career of this important cultural figure. Thanks also to Vivian Richardson, who assisted with gathering materials on Carnegie's college career at the Arthur F. McClure II Archives at the University of Central Missouri, and to John Ansley and Nancy Decker at the Marist College Archives and Special Collections for forwarding material on Carnegie from its Lowell Thomas Collection.

At the Other Press, Judith Gurewich performed the role of editor with great enthusiasm and intellectual zest. In many fascinating and provocative conversations, she prodded me to think about Carnegie, modern intellectual history, and American culture in big ways. Then in more detailed work on the manuscript itself, she offered much shrewd advice on organizing a mountain of material and clearly expressing the ideas within. A bit later in the process, Marjorie DeWitt deployed her considerable editorial skills to help trim and tighten the prose and clarify the argument. My appreciation extends to Yvonne E. Cárdenas and Tynan Kogane, who handled a host of production tasks. And, as usual, my friend and agent, Ronald Goldfarb, did yeoman's work in making this book happen. From its inception through its completion, he tendered much good advice on matters contractual, authorial, and personal.

A number of friends and colleagues kindly read the manuscript and provided insightful comments and suggestions: Armando Favazza, Mary Jane Gibbon, Cindy Sheltmire, Jonathan Sperber, Don Tennant, and John Wigger. Coming at the book from a variety of perspectives, their insightful advice improved it in countless ways. Melinda Lockwood deployed her extensive computer skills to assist with many matters great and small. But greatest thanks, of course, go to my family. Olivia Watts took time away from her own busy schedule of reading, drawing, Barbies, horseback riding, piano practice, and pet care to ask many interesting questions about Dale Carnegie and to put her special stamp of approval on the colorful book jacket design. Patti Sokolich Watts carefully read drafts of the manuscript, talked with me countless times about many of its most complicated and interesting issues, and offered a host of very useful suggestions. She is a star.

Notes

The following abbreviations have been used in the notes:

DC Dale Carnegie

DCA Dale Carnegie Archives, located at Dale Carnegie and Associates, Hauppauge, New York on Long Island

LPA Linda Polsby Archive (letters between Dale Carnegie and Frieda Offenbach, Isador Offenbach, and Linda Offenbach now in her possession)

Unless noted otherwise, all unpublished primary source materials involving Dale Carnegie—letters, talks, autobiographical notes and fragments, essay manuscripts, novel manuscripts, company pamphlets, diaries, scrapbooks— are located in the DCA.

Introduction: Helping Yourself in Modern America

1 See Lowell Thomas's description of this event in his introduction to DC, *How to Win Friends and Influence People* (New York, 1936), 1–2.

2 DC to Mrs. Roy Lippman, March 12, 1937, which included verbatim a "just received" letter from Leon Shimkin, DCA.

3 DC, *How to Win Friends*, page entitled "Twelve Things This Book Will Help You Achieve," before dedication and title pages at the front of the book.

4   "Books That Changed People's Lives," *The New York Times*, November 20, 1991; "Most Influential Americans of the Twentieth Century," *Life* (September 1, 1990); and Jonathan Yardley, "Ten Books That Shaped the American Character," *American Heritage* (April–May 1985): 24–31.

1. Poverty and Piety

1   DC, *How to Win Friends and Influence People* (New York, 1936), 34, 67.

2   DC, *How to Stop Worrying and Start Living* (New York, 1948), 154, 157–58.

3   DC, "When I Lived in Harmony" and "Dale's Heart Is in Nodaway," two installments from his 1930s newspaper series, Dale Carnegie's Daily Column, undated, DCA; Carnegie, *How to Stop Worrying*, 150–51; and DC, "Letters to My Daughter" (January 1952–1955), 11, 12, 32, DCA.

4   DC, "Letters to My Daughter," 7.

5   Ibid., 5–6, 8, 38; and "Ancestry of Dale Carnegie," compiled by William Addams Reitwiesner, available at http://wargs.com/other/carnegie.html. Reitwiesner relied on U.S. Census data.

6   See Theron L. Smith, "Harbison Ancestors of Dale Carnegie," available at http://archiver.rootsweb.ancestry.com; and Reitwiesner, "Ancestry of Dale Carnegie." Like Reitwiesner, Smith relied on U.S. Census data. On Abraham Harbison being drafted, see *Past and Present of Nodaway County*, vol. 2 (Indianapolis, 1910), 1,024.

7   DC, "Letters to My Daughter," 8–10.

8   Ibid., 4.

9   Ibid., 23, 26–27, 28, 30; and May Evans, a childhood friend, in Rosemary Crom, ed., *Dale Carnegie—As Others Saw Him* (Garden City, NY, 1987), 18.

10   DC to James and Amanda Carnagey, February 24, 1913, DCA; and DC, "Letters to My Daughter," 12, 21, 19, 63, 22.

11   DC, "Letters to My Daughter," 21; and Harold B. Clemenko, "He Sells Success," *Look* (May 25, 1948): 68.

12   DC, "Boyhood Days in Nodaway County," *Morning Star* (Concepcion, Missouri), February 21, 1938; and DC, "Letters to My Daughter," 23, 2–3, 48–55.

13   DC, "Letters to My Daughter," 29, 27, 30; and DC, *How to Stop Worrying*, 226.

14   DC, "Letters to My Daughter," 31–32.

15   DC, *How to Stop Worrying*, 149; and DC, "Mass Meeting Talk," September 29, 1937, in *A Public Presentation of the Dale Carnegie Course*, 2–3, DCA.

16 DC, "Letters to My Daughter," 57–58, 39–40. A shorter account of this traumatic episode also appeared in DC, *How to Stop Worrying*, 67.

17 DC, "Letters to My Daughter," 42–43.

18 Ibid., 37; DC, *How to Stop Worrying*, 149; and Homer Croy, "The Success Factory," *Esquire* (June 1937): 240.

19 DC, *How to Stop Worrying*, 226, 149; and DC, "Letters to My Daughter," 35, 37, 41, 47.

20 DC, "Letters to My Daughter," 43–44; and DC, "Boyhood Days in Nodaway County."

21 DC, "Letters to My Daughter," 44; and "Life in Bedison Is More Thrilling Than in Paris," newspaper clipping, handwritten date October 18, 1924, no citation, DCA. For treatments of the Populist revolt, see Lawrence Goodwyn, *The Populist Moment: A Short History of the Agrarian Revolt in America* (New York, 1978); Robert C. McGrath, *American Populism: A Social History, 1877–1898* (New York, 1993); and Charles Postel, *The Populist Vision* (New York, 2007).

22 DC, *How to Stop Worrying*, 150; and DC, "Letters to My Daughter," 43–44.

23 DC, *How to Stop Worrying*, 151; and DC, "Letters to My Daughter," 18, 19, 12, 63.

24 DC, "Letters to My Daughter," 64, 21, 6; and Croy, "The Success Factory," 240.

25 DC, *How to Stop Worrying*, 112; and Norman Vincent Peale quoted in Crom, *Dale Carnegie*, 24.

26 William A. H. Bernie, "Popularity, Incorporated," *New York World-Telegram Weekend Magazine* (February 27, 1937); DC, *How to Stop Worrying*, 151; and DC, *How to Win Friends*, 15.

27 DC, "Letters to My Daughter," 11, 64.

28 Ibid., 12, 26.

29 Ibid., 24, 13–14; and DC, *How to Stop Worrying*, 61.

30 DC, "Letters to My Daughter," 34, 18.

31 Crom, *Dale Carnegie*, 11; DC, "Daniel Eversole Is More Impressive Than Cuno, Says a Former Resident," *Nodaway Democrat-Forum*, September 25, 1933; "Two Well-Known Writers Recall Their Boyhood Days in Missouri," *Kansas City Star*, January 1, 1936; and DC, "Letters to My Daughter," 26.

32 DC, "Letters to My Daughter," 64; and DC quoted in Margaret Case Harriman, "He Sells Hope," *The Saturday Evening Post* (August 14, 1937): 13.

33 DC, "When I Lived in Harmony," Dale Carnegie's Daily Column, undated, DCA; and DC, "Letters to My Daughter," 45–47.

34 DC, *How to Win Friends*, 30.

35 DC, "Letters to My Daughter," 14–15.

2. Rebellion and Recovery

1 DC, *How to Win Friends and Influence People* (New York, 1936), 52–54, 110–12.

2 Ibid., 93, 103, 81, 36.

3 *The History of Johnson County, Missouri* (Kansas City, MO, 1881), 388–448; and Erving Cockrell, *History of Johnson County, Missouri* (Topeka, KS, 1918), 102–5.

4 *Sandstones of Time: A Campus History of Central Missouri State University* (Warrensburg, MO, 1995), 5–8; *The History of Johnson County, Missouri* (1881), 290–314; Cockrell, *History of Johnson County*, 143–50; and *Annual Catalogue of the State Normal School and Announcements for 1907–1908*, sketch of campus across from title page, 21–22, McClure Archives, Kirkpatrick Library, University of Central Missouri.

5 Monia C. Morris to Richard M. Huber, December 7, 1955, McClure Archives, Kirkpatrick Library, University of Central Missouri; and *Annual Catalogue of the State Normal School for 1907-1908*, 22–23, 43–50.

6 DC, "Letters to My Daughter" (January 1952–1955), 15, DCA.

7 DC, "Mass Meeting Talk," September 29, 1937, in *A Public Presentation of the Dale Carnegie Course*, 2–3, DCA; Joseph Kaye, "A Youth's Timidity Led Him to World Influence," *Kansas City Star*, July 24, 1955; and DC, "Letters to My Daughter," 16.

8 DC, "Letters to My Daughter," 16–17; and DC, "Mass Meeting Talk," 3.

9 DC, "Mass Meeting Talk," 3; and DC, *How to Stop Worrying and Start Living* (New York, 1944), 61.

10 DC, *How to Stop Worrying*, 151–52.

11 DC to Amanda Carnagey, October 17, 1910; DC to James and Amanda Carnagey, May 16, 1913; and DC to James and Amanda Carnagey, no month or day, 1913: all DCA.

12 DC, "Letters to My Daughter," 65; and DC, "Mass Meeting Talk," 4.

13 DC, "Letters to My Daughter," 65–66; and Margaret Case Harriman, "He Sells Hope," *The Saturday Evening Post* (August 14, 1937): 13, 30.

14 DC, "Letters to My Daughter," 65; and DC, "Mass Meeting Talk," 4.

15 Morris to Huber, December 7, 1955; and *Annual Catalogue of the State Normal School and Announcements for 1907-1908*.

16 *The Rhetor, 1908*, 8, McClure Archives, Kirkpatrick Library, University of Central Missouri; DC, "Letters to My Daughter," 65; and DC, "Mass Meeting Talk," 5.

17 Homer Croy, "The Success Factory," *Esquire* (June 1937): 240; "The History Place, Great Speeches Collection: George Graham Vest," available at www. historyplace.com/speeches/vest.htm; and DC, "Carnegie Recalls Important Years Here in Reprinting Eulogy to a Dog," undated newspaper column from the 1930s, DCA.

18 DC, "Letters to My Daughter," 66–67; Harriman, "He Sells Hope," 30; and Lowell Thomas, "Introduction," in DC, *Public Speaking and Influencing Men in Business* (New York, 1953 [1926]), vi, 358–60.

19 Croy, "The Success Factory," 240; DC, "Mass Meeting Talk," 5; and DC, "Letters to My Daughter," 66–67.

20 *The Rhetor, 1907*, 58, 157, McClure Archives, Kirkpatrick Library, University of Central Missouri.

21 *The Rhetor, 1908*, 161, 163, 164, 165, 170; and Collie Small, "Dale Carnegie: Man with a Message, *Collier's* (January 15, 1949).

22 Daniel J. Boorstin, *The Americans: The Democratic Experience* (New York: Vintage Books, 1973), 463–66.

23 Ibid., 466–67.

24 See two essays in Karl R. Wallace, *History of Speech Education in America: Background Studies* (New York, 1954): Claude L. Shaver, "Steele MacKaye and the Delsartian Tradition," 202–18, and Edyth Renshaw, "Five Private Schools of Speech," 301–25.

25 For broad analyses of this cultural shift in Progressive Era America, see Morton White, *Social Thought in America: The Revolt Against Formalism* (New York, 1976 [1947]), and Louis Menand, *The Metaphysical Club: A Story of Ideas in America* (New York, 2001). Renshaw, in "Five Private Schools of Speech" (322–23), suggests some of the modern impulses in the Delsarte System, while Joseph Fahey, in "Quiet Victory: The Professional Identity American Women Forged Through Delsartism," *Mime Journal* (2004–2005), explores the role of Delsartism in liberating women from Victorian restraint in the theater.

26 See the faculty biography of Abbott in *The Rhetor, 1908*, 21; and Leslie Anders, *Education for Service: Centennial History of Central Missouri State College* (Warrensburg, MO, 1971), 36, 44.

27 See Abbott's testimonial for Southwick's book in *Werner's Readings and Recitations No. 8* (New York, 1892), 212; and F. Townsend Southwick, *Elocution and Action* (New York, 1897), 6, 15, 130–31.

28 DC, *Public Speaking and Influencing Men in Business*, 197–98, 204, 212, 241; and DC quoted in Joseph Kaye, "A Youth's Timidity."

29 DC to James and Amanda Carnagey, February 1913; and DC to James and Amanda Carnagey, February 24, 1913: both DCA.

30 DC, "Letters to My Daughter," 15; DC, *How to Stop Worrying*, xii; and DC, "How Businessmen Are Acquiring Self-Confidence and Convincing Speech," Supplement to Syllabus B-15—Public Speaking, YMCA, October 15, 1919, DCA.

3. Selling Products, Selling Yourself

1 DC, *How to Win Friends and Influence People* (New York, 1936), 47, 16, 40, where DC quoted from Harry O. Overstreet.

2 Ibid., 57–103, 135–36, 201–3.

3 DC, "Letters to My Daughter" (January 1952–1955), 67, DCA.

4 Ibid., 68, 22.

5 Ibid., 67–68.

6 See James D. Watkinson, " 'Education for Success': The International Correspondence Schools of Scranton, Pennsylvania," *Pennsylvania Magazine of History and Biography* (October 1996): 343–69.

7 Ibid.

8 DC, "Letters to My Daughter," 68–69; and Joseph Kaye, "A Youth's Timidity Led Him to World Influence," *Kansas City Star*, July 24, 1955.

9 DC, "Letters to My Daughter," 68–69; and Kaye, "A Youth's Timidity."

10 DC to Amanda Carnagey, January 11, 1909; DC to Amanda Carnagey, July 2, 1910; DC to Amanda Carnagey, February 2, 1910; Benjamin L. Seawell to J. W. Carnagey, February 5, 1911; and DC, "Letters to My Daughter," 80: all DCA. Seawell taught biology at the State Normal School in Warrensburg from 1897 to 1909, according to the *Central Missouri State Teacher's College Semi-Centennial Number, 1871–1921*, McClure Archives, Kirkpatrick Library, University of Central Missouri.

11 DC, "Letters to My Daughter," 69–70.

12 Watkinson, " 'Education for Success,' " 350, 358.

13 Kaye, "A Youth's Timidity"; and DC, "Letters to My Daughter," 70–71.

14 See Rudolf A. Clemen, *The American Livestock and Meat Industry* (New York, 1923), 149–56, 387–90, 456–57.

15 DC, "Letters to My Daughter," 71.

16 Among a large number of books and articles examining the turn-of-the-century growth of consumer capitalism, see T. J. Jackson Lears, "From Salvation

to Self-Realization: Advertising and the Therapeutic Roots of the Consumer Culture, 1880–1930," in Richard Wrightman Fox and T. J. Jackson Lears, eds., *The Culture of Consumption: Critical Essays in American History, 1880–1980* (New York, 1983), 3–38; William Leach, *Land of Desire: Merchants, Power, and the Rise of a New American Culture* (New York, 1993); Daniel Horowitz, *The Morality of Spending: Attitudes Toward the Consumer Culture in America, 1875–1950* (Baltimore, 1985); Simon J. Bonner, ed., *Consuming Visions: Accumulation and Display of Goods in America, 1880–1920* (New York, 1989); Olivier Zunz, *Making America Corporate, 1870–1920* (Chicago, 1995); and Steven Watts, *The People's Tycoon: Henry Ford and the American Century* (New York, 2005).

17   Suggestive works on the emergence of modern advertising include T. J. Jackson Lears, "From Salvation to Self-Realization," and his *Fables of Abundance: A Cultural History of Advertising in America* (New York, 1994); Roland Marchand, *Advertising the American Dream: Making Way for Modernity, 1920–1940* (New York, 1985); and Pamela W. Laird, *Advertising Progress: American Business and the Rise of Consumer Marketing* (Baltimore, 1998).

18   Walter A. Friedman, *Birth of Salesman: The Transformation of Selling in America* (Cambridge, MA, 2004), 4–6, 12–13, 7.

19   DC to Mrs. J. W. Carnagey, February 21, 1910; DC to Amanda Carnagey, February 2, 1910; DC to Mrs. J. W. Carnagey, January 4, 1909; and DC, "Letters to My Daughter," 84, 71: all DCA.

20   DC to Amanda Carnagey, August 24, 1909, DCA; and DC, "Letters to My Daughter," 73.

21   DC, "Letters to My Daughter," 71–72; and Kaye, "A Youth's Timidity."

22   DC, "Letters to My Daughter," 73, 81; and DC to Amanda Carnagey, July 2, 1910, DCA.

23   DC to Amanda Carnagey, February 2, 1910; DC to James and Amanda Carnagey, February 21, 1910; and DC to Amanda Carnagey, April 11, 1910: all DCA.

24   DC to Amanda Carnagey, August 24, 1909; DC to Amanda Carnagey, February 2, 1910; DC to James and Amanda Carnagey, February 21, 1910; and DC to Amanda Carnagey, July 2, 1910: all DCA.

25   See "Birth of the American Salesman: Q & A with Walter Friedman," *Harvard Business School Working Knowledge* (April 19, 2004), available at http.//hbswk.hbs.edu/cgi-bin/print/4068.html.

26   DC to Amanda Carnagey, August 24, 1909, DCA.

27   DC to Mrs. J. W. Carnagey, January 4, 1909; and DC to James and Amanda Carnagey, February 21, 1910: both DCA.

28 DC to Amanda Carnagey, January 11, 1909; DC to Amanda Carnagey, July 2, 1910; DC to James and Amanda Carnagey, February 21, 1910; and DC to Amanda Carnagey, October 17, 1910: all DCA.

29 DC, "Letters to My Daughter," 86–88.

30 Kaye, "A Youth's Timidity"; and DC, "Letters to My Daughter," 71, 89, 73.

31 DC, "Letters to My Daughter," 73–74.

32 DC to Amanda Carnagey, October 17, 1910, DCA; and DC, "Letters to My Daughter," 90.

33 DC, "Letters to My Daughter," 89–90.

34 See Benjamin Franklin, *The Autobiography and Other Writings* (New York, 1961), 38–39; Horatio Alger, *Ragged Dick and Mark the Match Boy* (New York, 1973 [1867]), 102–4; and Horatio Alger, *Ragged Dick and Struggling Upward* (New York, 1985 [1890]). For an insightful exploration of this cultural motif, see Karen Halttunen, *Confidence Men and Painted Women: A Study of Middle-Class Culture in America, 1830–1870* (New Haven, CT, 1982), particularly 11–13.

35 DC, "Letters to My Daughter," 90–91.

4. Go East, Young Man

1 DC, *How to Win Friends and Influence People* (New York, 1936), 70, 166.

2 Ibid., 59–60, 165–66, 171, 86. For a brilliant analysis of how the market and the theater emerged side by side in the early modern period and were deeply entangled with each other, see Jean-Christophe Agnew, *Worlds Apart: The Market and the Theater in Anglo-American Thought, 1550–1750* (Cambridge, 1988).

3 For insightful examinations of cultural change in early twentieth-century America, see John F. Kasson, *Amusing the Million: Coney Island at the Turn of the Century* (New York, 1978); Lary May, *Screening Out the Past: The Birth of Mass Culture and the Motion Picture Industry* (Chicago, 1980); and Lewis A. Erenberg, *Steppin' Out: New York Nightlife and the Transformation of American Culture, 1890–1930* (Chicago, 1981).

4 DC, "Letters to My Daughter" (January 1952–1955), 91–92, DCA.

5 Ibid.

6 Ibid., 92, 90; and Margaret Case Harriman, "He Sells Hope," *The Saturday Evening Post* (August 14, 1937): 30.

7 On the history of the academy, see Gerard Raymond, "125 Years and Counting: The American Academy of Dramatic Arts Celebrates a Special

Anniversary," *Backstage* (November 26–December 2, 2009): 6–7, and James H. McTeague, *Before Stanislavsky: American Professional Acting Schools and Acting Theory, 1875–1925* (Metuchen, NJ: Scarecrow Press, 1993), 45–93.

8 Franklin H. Sargent, "The Preparation of the Stage Neophyte," *New York Dramatic Mirror* (July 10, 1911): 5; and McTeague, *Before Stanislavsky*, 73.

9 McTeague, *Before Stanislavsky*, 80–84, 67.

10 Ibid., 67, 58; and Sargent, "Preparation of the Stage Neophyte," 5.

11 Garff B. Wilson, *A History of American Acting* (Bloomington, IN, 1966), 100–1.

12 Ibid., 103; McTeague, *Before Stanislavsky*, 48, 55, 65; Sargent, "Preparation of the Stage Neophyte," 5; and Algernon Tassin, "The American Dramatic Schools," *The Bookman* (April 1907): 161.

13 Harriman, "He Sells Hope," 30; and DC to Amanda and James Carnagey, April 1, 1911, DCA.

14 DC to Amanda and James Carnagey, April 1, 1911, DCA.

15 DC, *How to Stop Worrying and Start Living* (New York, 1944), 124.

16 Sargent is quoted in McTeague, *Before Stanislavsky*, 72, 91, 93.

17 DC to Amanda Carnagey, August 17, 1911, DCA; Margaret Mayo, *Polly of the Circus: A Comedy-Drama in Three Acts* (New York, 1933); and "Polly of the Circus (1907)," in *Oxford Companion to American Theatre* (New York, 2004), 504.

18 DC, "Letters to My Daughter," 74; and DC to Amanda Carnagey, August 17, 1911, DCA.

19 DC, "Letters to My Daughter," 74–75; and Howard Lindsay, letter to author quoted in Richard M. Huber, *The American Idea of Success* (New York, 1971), 233.

20 DC to Amanda Carnagey, January 5, 1912, DCA.

21 DC to Amanda Carnagey, August 17, 1911, DCA; Howard Lindsay letter to author, quoted in Huber, *American Idea of Success*, 233; and DC to Amanda Carnagey, March 8, 1912, DCA.

22 DC, "Letters to My Daughter," 75–76; William A. H. Bernie, DC quoted in "Popularity, Incorporated," *New York World-Telegram Weekend Magazine* (February 27, 1937), 9; and Harriman, "He Sells Hope," 30.

23 DC to Amanda Carnagey, March 8, 1912, DCA.

24 For two good overviews of the main trends of the Progressive Era, see Steven Diner, *A Very Different Age: Americans of the Progressive Era* (New York, 1998), and Robert H. Wiebe, *The Search for Order, 1877–1920* (New York, 1967).

25 For two broad analyses of the automobile's impact on American life, see James J. Flink, *The Car Culture* (Cambridge, MA, 1975), and Steven Watts, *The People's Tycoon: Henry Ford and the American Century* (New York, 2005).

26 DC, "Letters to My Daughter," 88–89.

27 DC to Amanda Carnagey, May 5, 1912, DCA.

28 DC, "Letters to My Daughter," 76, 89; DC to Amanda Carnagey, December 12, 1912; and DC to Carnagey family, February 1913: all DCA.

29 DC to Amanda Carnagey, February 1, 1913, DCA.

30 Ibid.; DC to Carnagey family, February 17, 1913; DC to Carnagey family, February 24, 1913; DC to Carnagey family, March 4, 1913; and DC to Amanda Carnagey, March 18, 1913: all DCA.

31 DC to Amanda Carnagey, March 18, 1913, DCA.

32 DC to Baptist Young People's Group, Pierre Baptist Church, April 1, 1911; DC to Amanda Carnagey, January 5, 1912; DC to Amanda Carnagey, December 12, 1912; DC to Carnagey family, January 14, 1913; DC to Carnagey family, February 1913; and DC to Carnagey family, June 16, 1913: all DCA.

33 DC to Carnagey family, undated 1913, DCA.

34 DC to Carnagey family, March 25, 1913; DC to Carnagey family, February 17, 1913; and DC to Carnagey family, May 16, 1913: all DCA.

35 DC to Amanda Carnagey, March 8, 1912; DC to Carnagey family, January 14, 1913; DC to Amanda Carnagey, March 18, 1913; DC to Carnagey family, March 25, 1913; and DC to Carnagey family, February 17, 1913: all DCA.

36 DC to Amanda Carnagey, August 17, 1911; and DC to Amanda Carnagey, March 8, 1912: both DCA.

37 DC to Amanda Carnagey, December 12, 1912; and DC to Amanda Carnagey, February 1, 1913: both DCA.

38 DC, "Letters to My Daughter," 76; and DC, *How to Stop Worrying*, xi.

39 DC to Carnagey family, undated, 1913, DCA; DC to Carnagey family, May 16, 1913, DCA; DC quoted in James Kaye, "A Youth's Timidity Led Him to World Influence," *Kansas City Star*, July 24, 1955; and DC, "Letters to My Daughter," 76.

40 DC to Carnagey family, October 19, 1913, DCA; and DC, *How to Stop Worrying*, xi.

41 DC to Amanda Carnagey, February 1, 1913; and DC to Carnagey family, June 16, 1913: both DCA.

42 DC to Carnagey family, February 24, 1913; DC to Carnagey family, March 25, 1913; DC to Carnagey family, March 4, 1913; and DC to Carnagey family, October 19, 1913: all DCA.

43 DC to Carnagey family, June 16, 1913, DCA; and DC, *How to Stop Worrying*, xii.

44 DC to Carnagey family, June 16, 1913; DC to Carnagey family, June 3, 1913; DC to Carnagey family, July 8, 1913; DC to Amanda Carnagey, March 18, 1913; and DC to Carnagey family, October 19, 1913: all DCA.

45 DC to Carnagey family, March 4, 1913; DC to Carnagey family, undated, 1913; DC to Carnagey family, June 16, 1913; DC to Carnagey family, undated, 1913; and DC to Carnagey family, July 8, 1913: all DCA.

46 DC to Carnagey family, February 17, 1913, DCA.

47 DC to Carnagey family, October 19, 1913; and DC to Carnagey family, undated 1913: both DCA.

5. Teaching and Writing

1 DC, *How to Win Friends and Influence People* (New Yor, 1936), 12–15, 56.

2 Ibid., 12–17.

3 DC, *How to Stop Worrying and Start Living* (New York, 1944), xi–xii; and DC, "Mass Meeting Talk," September 29, 1937, in *A Public Presentation of the Dale Carnegie Course*, 6, DCA.

4 DC, "Letters to My Daughter" (January 1952–1955), 93–94, DCA; Margaret Case Harriman, "He Sells Hope," *The Saturday Evening Post* (August 14, 1937): 30; James Kaye, "A Youth's Timidity Led Him to World Influence," *Kansas City Star*, July 24, 1955; and Richard M. Huber, *The American Idea of Success* (New York, 1971), 233–34.

5 DC, "Letters to My Daughter," 76–77.

6 Kaye, "A Youth's Timidity"; DC, *How to Stop Worrying*, xii; and DC, "Mass Meeting Talk," 7.

7 For the best examination of this institution, see Nina Mjagkij and Margaret Spratt, eds., *Men and Women Adrift: The YMCA and the YWCA in the City* (New York, 1997); quotes are from page 3.

8 DC, "Letters to My Daughter," 77; John Janney, "Can You Think Fast on Your Feet?," *American Magazine* (January 1932): 94; and Kaye, "A Youth's Timidity."

9 DC identified October 22, 1912, as his first class in several places over the years, including DC, "Mass Meeting Talk," 7; DC quoted in Arthur R. Pell, *Enrich Your Life the Dale Carnegie Way* (Garden City, N, 1979), 37; and DC, "Letters to My Daughter," 96, 77.

10 Harriman, "He Sells Hope," 30; and DC, "Letters to My Daughter," 94–98.

11 Janney, "Can You Think Fast on Your Feet?," 94; and DC, "Letters to My Daughter," 77, 98.

12 DC to Amanda Carnagey, February 1, 1913; DC to Carnagey family, February 1913; and DC to Carnagey family, May 16, 1913: all DCA.

13 DC to Carnagey family, October 19, 1913, DCA; DC to Carnagey family, March 4, 1913, DCA; DC to Amanda Carnagey, December 12, 1912, DCA; Dale Carnagey and J. Berg Esenwein, *The Art of Public Speaking* (Springfield, MA, 1915), title page; Harriman, "He Sells Hope," 30; DC to Carnagey family, February 24, 1913, DCA; and DC to Carnagey family, June 3, 1913, DCA.

14 DC to Carnagey family, October 19, 1913, DCA; and DC, "War," *Leslie's Illustrated Weekly* (October 16, 1913): 365. DC also identified the *Leslie's* editorial as his work and reprinted it in Carnagey and Esenwein, *The Art of Public Speaking*, 84–86.

15 DC to Carnagey family, October 19, 1913, DCA.

16 For trenchant discussions of the new magazines, see Richard Ohmann, *Selling Culture: Magazines, Markets, and Class at the Turn of the Century* (New York, 1996); Matthew Schneirov, *The Dream of a New Social Order: Popular Magazines in America, 1893–1914* (New York, 1994); and Christopher P. Wilson, "The Rhetoric of Consumption: Mass-Market Magazines and the Demise of the Gentle Reader, 1880–1920," in Richard Wrightman Fox and T. J. Jackson Lears, eds., *The Culture of Consumption: Critical Essays in American History, 1880–1980* (New York, 1983), 39–64.

17 DC, "Fighting for Life in Antarctic Ice," *Illustrated World* (September 1915): 22–26; DC, "The World's Best Known Hobo," *American Magazine* (October 1914), unpaginated; DC, "Mrs. Atwood—The Laborer's Big Sister," *Illustrated World* (February 1916): 808–9; and DC, "America's Champion Money Raiser," *World Outlook* (February 1917): 3–4, 26.

18 DC, "Sharpshooting the Future," *Illustrated World* (December 1915): 507–9.

19 DC, "Money Made in Writing for the Movies," *American Magazine* (June 1916): 32; DC, "Rich Prizes for Playwrights," *American Magazine* (April 1916): 65–66; and DC, "How I Laid the Foundation for a Big Salary," *American Magazine* (August 1916): 16.

20 DC, "Rich Prizes for Playwrights," 34; DC, "Money Made in Writing for the Movies," 32; and DC, "How I Laid the Foundation for a Big Salary," 16.

21 DC, "America's Champion Money Raiser," 26; DC, "Mrs. Atwood," 808; DC, "Rich Prizes for Playwrights," 68; and DC, "How I Laid the Foundation for Big Salary," 16–17.

22 DC, "America's Champion Money Raiser," 3–4; and DC, "Show Windows That Sell Goods," *American Magazine* (October 1917): 126–30.

23 DC, "Rich Prizes for Playwrights," 70; DC, "Mrs. Atwood," 808; DC, "Delivered One Lecture 5,000 Times," *American Magazine* (September 1915): 55; DC, "Fighting for Life," 26; and DC, "How I Laid the Foundation for a Big Salary," 17.

24 DC, "My Triumph Over Fears That Cost Me $10,000 a Year," *American Magazine 5,000* (November 1918):–51, 137–39.

25 Ibid.

26 DC's reprinting of this article is noted and analyzed in J. M. O'Neill, "The True Story of $10,000 Fears," *Quarterly Journal of Speech Education* (March 1919): 128–37.

27 DC to Carnagey family, May 16, 1913, DCA.

28 Carnagey and Esenwein, *The Art of Public Speaking*.

29 "Home Study Under College Professors," *Primary Education* (November 1910): 535; "Miscellaneous Classes of Schools," *College and Private School Directory of the United States*, vol. 6 (New York, 1913), 177; and Frank H. Palmer, "Correspondence Schools," *Education* (September 1910): 49–51.

30 "Esenwein, Joseph Berg," in Thomas William Herringshaw, *Herringshaw's National Library of American Biography*, vol. 2 (New York, 1909), 395; "Esenwein, Joseph Berg," in *Who's Who in America, 1906–1907* (Chicago, 1906), 561; "Esenwein, Joseph Berg," Wikipedia, quoting *New International Encyclopedia* (New York, 1914–1916); and J. Berg Esenwein, "Can You Too Have the Rewards of Authorship?," *Atlantic Monthly* (June 1922): 47.

31 Carnagey and Esenwein, *The Art of Public Speaking*, 5, 8, 80, 272, 358.

32 Ibid., 356, 357–58, 359.

33 Ibid., 109, 3, 94, 106–7, 95.

34 Ibid., 88, 83, 91.

35 Ibid., 4, 107, 301–2, 374–76.

36 Ibid., 102–3, 101, 262, 263–67, 270, 275–76, 273.

37 Ibid., 355, 357, 358.

38 Ibid., 356, 358, 361, 360.

6. Mind Power and Positive Thinking

1 DC, *How to Win Friends and Influence People* (New York, 1936), "Twelve Things This Book Will Help You Achieve" on first printed page in the text (no pagination), 10, 14, 17.

NOTES

2 Ibid., 29, 58, 70, 135, 48, 71.
3 DC, "Letters to My Daughter" (January 1952–1955), 48, DCA.
4 DC, *Public Speaking: The Standard Course of the United Y.M.C.A. Schools*, Book II (New York: Association Press, 1920), 17–20.
5 Ibid., Book III, 127–28.
6 Ibid., 127–28, 129–30, 131; and Homer Croy, "The Success Factory," *Esquire* (June 1937): 241. A brief discussion of the Chautauqua Course of Reading can be found in *The Encyclopedia of Social Reform* (New York, 1909), 162, while a more extended analysis appears in John C. Scott, "The Chautauqua Movement: Revolution in Popular Higher Education," *Journal of Higher Education* (July–August 1999): 389–412.
7 On New Thought, see Donald Meyer, *The Positive Thinkers: A Study of the American Quest for Health, Wealth, and Personal Power from Mary Baker Eddy to Norman Vincent Peale* (Garden City, NY, 1966 [1965]); Richard M. Huber, *The American Idea of Success* (New York, 1971), 124–76; Richard Weiss, *The American Myth of Success: From Horatio Alger to Norman Vincent Peale* (Urbana, IL, 1988), 195–240; and Beryl Satter, *Each Mind a Kingdom: American Women, Sexual Purity, and the New Thought Movement, 1875–1920* (Berkeley, 1999).
8 See Meyer, *Positive Thinkers*, 51; Huber, *American Idea of Success*, 235; Weiss, *American Myth of Success*, 131–210; Warren I. Susman, "Personality and the Making of Twentieth-Century Culture," in his *Culture as History* (New York, 1984), especially 277–79; and Steven Watts, *The People's Tycoon: Henry Ford and the American Century* (New York, 2005), 323–24.
9 Dale Carnagey and J. Berg Esenwein, *The Art of Public Speaking* (Springfield, MA: The Home Correspondence School, 1915), 189, 80, 197–98, 359.
10 Margaret Case Harriman, "He Sells Hope," *The Saturday Evening Post* (August 31, 1937): 30, 33; and Giles Kemp and Edward Claflin, *Dale Carnegie: The Man Who Influenced Millions* (New York, 1989), 121. In a letter from DC to Edward Frank Allen, April 8, 1916, the letterhead stationery shows his address as "Studio 824, Carnegie Hall," DCA.
11 Frank Bettger, *How I Raised Myself from Failure to Success in Selling* (New York, 1992 [1947]), 5–6, 15–16.
12 A 1917 advertising pamphlet for the Carnagey Course in Public Speaking, DCA; and DC, *Public Speaking: The Standard Course*, Books I–IV.
13 DC, *Public Speaking: The Standard Course*, Book III, 119, 122, 133, and Book I, 1–2, 21.

14   Russell H. Conwell, "Acres of Diamonds," reprinted in DC, *Public Speaking: The Standard Course*, Book III, 3–28. For excellent biographical sketches of Conwell, see Huber, *American Idea of Success*, 55–61, and Judy Hilkey, *Character Is Capital: Success Manuals and Manhood in Gilded Age America* (Chapel Hill, NC, 1997), 58, 92, 102–3.

15   Russell H. Conwell, "What You Can Do with Your Will Power," *American Magazine* (April 1916): 16, 96–100; Russell H. Conwell, *What You Can Do with Your Willpower* (New York, 1917), 42–43; Carnagey and Esenwein, *The Art of Public Speaking*, 82–83; and DC, *Public Speaking: The Standard Course*, Book III, 26, 84, 87–88, and 2–28.

16   Elbert Hubbard, "A Message to Garcia," as reprinted in DC, *Public Speaking: A Practical Course for Business Men* (New York: Association Press, 1926), 553–57. On Hubbard's life, see Huber, *American Idea of Success*, 79–85.

17   Elbert Hubbard, *The Book of Business* (East Aurora, NY, 1913), 89, 158; Carnagey and Esenwein, *The Art of Public Speaking*, 3–4; Elbert Hubbard, *Love, Life and Work* (East Aurora, NY, 1906), 43–44, a quotation that DC reprinted at even greater length in his *How to Win Friends*, 71–72. Weiss, in *American Myth of Success*, 189, 191, stresses Hubbard's emergence as a New Thought advocate in the early 1900s.

18   See "James Allen: Unrewarded Genius, 1864–1912," at James Allen Home-page, available at jamesallen.wwwhubs.com; and Mitch Horowitz, "James Allen: A Life in Brief," in James Allen, *As a Man Thinketh* (New York, 1909).

19   Allen, "As a Man Thinketh," reprinted in DC, *Public Speaking: The Standard Course*, Book IV, Part II, 2–23.

20   Arthur J. Forbes, editor of the journal *The Business Philosopher*, to DC, November 8, 1921, DCA; and DC, quoted in *Public Speaking: The Standard Course*, Book III, 122.

21   On Marden's life and career, see Huber, *American Idea of Success*, 145–64, and "Orison Swett Marden (1850–1924): Founder of *Success Magazine*," available at orisonswettmarden.wwwhubs.com. Susman, in *Culture as History*, 279, discusses Marden's shift in emphasis from "character" to "personality" in his writings on success.

22   See the following books by Marden: *Little Visits with Great Americans* (New York, 1903), 11; *Peace, Power, and Plenty* (New York, 1909), viii, x; and *The Miracle of Right Thought* (New York, 1910), ix–x.

23   DC, *Public Speaking: The Standard Course*, Book I, 7, Book III, 129–30, Book III, 1, and Book III, 32. Surviving editions of this volume, presented in several

different formats, indicate Marden's "special lecture" in the table of contents but do not include the actual text. But most likely this lecture was a chapter from *Pushing to the Front* (New York, 1911 edition) entitled "Public Speaking," 411–23; the quotations are from 411.

24   On psychotherapy in early twentieth-century America, see Weiss, *American Myth of Success*, 195–214; Nathan G. Hale, *Freud and the Americans: The Beginnings of Psychoanalysis in the United States, 1876–1917* (New York, 1995), especially chapters IV–VII; and Meyer, *Positive Thinkers*, 65–75. Satter also analyzes the intersection of New Thought and psychology in the early 1900s in chapter 7, "New Thought and Popular Psychology," in his *Each Mind a Kingdom*, 217–47.

25   Carnagey and Esenwein, *The Art of Public Speaking*, 8, 80, 308, 360.

26   DC, *Public Speaking: The Standard Course*, Book III, 37, and Book IV, 6, 67–68, 78, 24–35.

27   Ibid., Book II, 16, Book III, 44, and Book IV, 24.

28   William James, *The Varieties of Religious Experience: A Study in Human Nature* (New York, 1905), 94–95, 115, 108; and William James, "The Powers of Men," *American Magazine* (November 1907): 57–65; reprinted (and delivered as a talk) in several other venues under the title "The Energies of Men."

29   DC, *Public Speaking: The Standard Course*, Book III, 136, and Book IV, 18–19.

30   H. Addington Bruce, "Masters of the Mind," *American Magazine* (November 1910): 71–81. See also H. Addington Bruce, "The New Mind Cure Based on Science," *American Magazine* (October 1910): 773–78, and several books by Bruce: *The Riddle of Personality* (New York, 1908), *Scientific Mental Healing* (Boston, 1911), *Nerve Control and How to Gain It* (New York, 1919), and *Self-Development: A Handbook for the Ambitious* (New York, 1921). For biographical information on Bruce, see Satter, *Each Mind a Kingdom*, 244.

31   DC, *Public Speaking: The Standard Course*, Book I, 26.

32   Ibid., Book III, 28–29, and Book IV, 19, 2, 69.

33   Ibid., Book III, 125–26, where DC described and quoted from *Invictus*, by William Ernest Henley.

34   Dale Carnagey, Draft Registration Card No. 59, 10th District, Draft Board 44 and Registrar's Report 31-9-44-A, June 5, 1917, in *World War I Selective Service Draft Registration Cards, 1917–1918* (Washington, D.C.: National Archives); "Yaphank Greets New Army Recruits," *The New York Times*, September 20, 1917; and "Camp Upton," *Brookhaven History*, available at http:www.bnl.gov/bnlweb/history/camp_upton1.asp.

35 DC, "Letters to My Daughter," 19–20.
36 DC, *Public Speaking: A Practical Course*, 353, 355–56.
37 Charles Whann, Captain, 23rd Precinct, Metropolitan Canvass Committee to Adj. General M. McCaim, July 12, 1918; DC to Amanda Carnagey, December 3, 1918; and DC to Mrs. J. W. Carnagey, January 29, 1919: all DCA.
38 DC to Mrs. J. W. Carnagey, January 29, 1919; and DC to Mrs. J. W. Carnagey, May 11, 1919: both DCA.
39 DC, "How Businessmen Are Acquiring Self-Confidence and Convincing Speech," Supplement to Syllabus B-15—Public Speaking, YMCA, October 15, 1919, DCA.
40 DC, "My Triumph Over Fears That Cost Me $10,000 a Year," *American Magazine* (November 1918): 50–51, 137–39; and J. M. O'Neill, "The True Story of $10,000 Fears," *Quarterly Journal of Speech Education* (March 1919): 128–37.
41 O'Neill, "The True Story of $10,000 Fears," 132, 135–36.
42 Ibid., 136, 137.
43 DC, *Public Speaking: The Standard Course*, Book III, 117–34.

7. Rebellion and the Lost Generation

1 DC, *How to Win Friends and Influence People* (New York, 1937), 12, 111, 17.
2 Ibid., 16, 15, 26.
3 DC, *How to Stop Worrying and Start Living* (New York, 1948), 134, 121–22, 123–24.
4 Margaret Case Harriman, "He Sells Hope," *The Saturday Evening Post* (August 31, 1937): 33; and Lowell Thomas, *Good Evening Everybody* (New York, 1976), 109.
5 Lowell Thomas to Mr. H. W. Turner, March 8, 1917, reprinted in 1917 advertisement for Carnagey's course in Baltimore, DCA.
6 Joel C. Hodgson, *Lawrence of Arabia and American Culture: The Making of a Transatlantic Legend* (Westport, CT, 1995), 11–26.
7 Ibid., 11, 28–30.
8 Harriman, "He Sells Hope," 33; Thomas, *Good Evening Everybody*, 200; and DC, autobiographical note, untitled and undated, DCA.
9 DC to Amanda Carnagey, August 1919, DCA; Thomas, *Good Evening Everybody*, 200; and DC to Amanda Carnagey, July 31, 1919, DCA.
10 Thomas, *Good Evening Everybody*, 200–1; and DC, *Public Speaking and Influencing Men in Business* (New York, 1953 [1926]), 194.

11   Thomas, *Good Evening Everybody*, 201–2; DC to Amanda Carnagey, August 18, 1919, DCA; DC, autobiographical fragment, DCA; Hodgson, *Lawrence of Arabia and American Culture*, 30–31; and *Lloyd's Weekly News* and *The Times* quoted in *With Allenby in Palestine* publicity pamphlet, DCA. A complete description of the show can be found in Hodgson, *Lawrence of Arabia and American Culture*, 33–35.

12   *With Allenby in Palestine* publicity pamphlet; and DC to Amanda Carnagey, August 1919: both DCA. DC outlined the scope of his job several years later in a letter to Professor A. B. Williamson, February 2, 1925, DCA.

13   DC to Amanda Carnagey, August 1919; DC to Carnagey family, undated, fall 1919; DC to Amanda Carnagey, January 27, 1920; and DC to Amanda and James Carnagey, March 12, 1920: all DCA.

14   DC to Amanda and James Carnagey, December 1920; DC to Amanda Carnagey, August 1919; and DC to Amanda and James Carnagey, March 12, 1920: all DCA.

15   Hodgson, *Lawrence of Arabia and American Culture*, 41; DC, autobiographical fragment, DCA; and DC to Amanda and James Carnagey, May 14, 1920, DCA.

16   DC to Amanda and James Carnagey, May 26, 1920, DCA; and Harriman, "He Sells Hope," 33.

17   Thomas, *Good Evening Everybody*, 219.

18   DC to Amanda and James Carnagey, December 1920, DCA.

19   Ibid.; DC to Professor A. B. Williamson, February 2, 1925; and *The Ross Smith Flight: From England to Australia* publicity pamphlet: all DCA.

20   "Dale Carnagey Married," *Belton Herald*, August 4, 1921; and Marriages Registered in July, August, and September 1921, *England and Wales, Marriage Index: 1916–2005*, available at Ancestry.com.

21   Lolita B. Carnagey, passport application in Rome, May 10, 1922, *U.S. Passport Applications, 1795–1925*, available at Ancestry.com; National Archives and Records Administration; Charles C. Harris, *1900 United States Federal Census*, available at Ancestry.com; and *1910 United States Federal Census*, available at Ancestry.com.

22   "Dale Carnagey Married"; Charles C. Harris, *1920 United States Federal Census*, available at (database, Ancestry.com); Lolita Carnagey, passport application; and Dorothy Carnegie, videotaped interview, 1996, DCA, who related facts about her husband's first marriage based on conversations with him.

23   Various postcards, photographs, and letters from DC to his parents during the 1920s, DCA.

24 "Interesting News Received from Mr. Dale Carnagey," *Belton Herald*, February 10, 1922; Lolita Carnagey, passport application; and DC, "Dale Carnagey, Spending Summer in Europe, Writes of Life There," *Maryville Tribune*, October 22, 1922.

25 DC, "Daniel Eversole Is More Impressive Than Cuno," *Maryville Democrat-Forum*, September 25, 1923; DC, *Public Speaking: A Practical Course for Business Men* (New York: Association Press, 1926), 174–75; and undated postcard, DCA.

26 Series of undated postcards, DCA; DC, "Dale Carnagey Says Nodaway County Girls Would Charm Heart of Iron Man," *Maryville Democrat-Forum*, November 13, 1924; and DC, "Letters to My Daughter" (January 1952–1955), 20–21, DCA.

27 DC, "Dale Carnagey Says Nodaway County Girls Would Charm."

28 "Life in Bedison Is More Thrilling Than in Paris," newspaper clipping dated by hand "Oct. 18, 1924," no citation, DCA; DC, "Dale Carnagey Says Nodaway County Girls Would Charm"; and DC letter to himself, undated but probably written in late 1920s, DCA.

29 DC, "Dale Carnagey, Spending Summer in Europe"; DC to Amanda and James Carnagey, December 1920, DCA; Thomas H. Nelson to Mr. Percy Peixotto in Paris, undated, DCA; "Would You Like to Speak in Public? Learn to Think When on Your Feet," *New York Herald* (European edition: Paris), November 25, 1924; and DC to Prof. A. B. Williamson, February 2, 1925, DCA.

30 *Carnagey Shepherd Breeding and Training Farm* undated pamphlet, DCA; and James Carnagey, "Closing Out Sale" announcement, undated but refers to his "nearing" seventy-fourth birthday in January 1926, obviously written by DC, DCA. The DCA also has about one dozen photos of German shepherds with Lolita's handwriting on the back.

31 Charles Kemp and Edward Claflin, *Dale Carnegie: The Man Who Influenced Millions* (New York, 1989), 128; DC, "Damned Fool Things I Have Done" file, December 31, 1927, and undated entry, DCA.

32 DC, "Damned Fool Things I Have Done" file, December 9, 1927; DC, "Dale Carnagey, Spending Summer in Europe"; and undated postcard, DCA.

33 Harriman, "He Sells Hope," 33–34; and DC, *Lincoln the Unknown* (New York, 1959 [1932]), 51, 55–56, 71–72.

34 DC, *Lincoln the Unknown*, 55–56, 77, 84, 86.

35 Lolita Carnegie to DC, March 16, 1932, DCA. DC applied for a passport on January 5, 1928, and spent some time later that year traveling in Germany,

Switzerland, Norway, and France with Lolita. Records indicate that on October 5, he left Cherbourg, France, for New York City alone.

36   "Dale Carnagey Entering Rank of Writing Celebrities," *Maryville Democrat-Forum*, December 6, 1914.

37   DC, *How to Win Friends*, 62; and DC, *How to Stop Worrying*, 77.

38   "Dale Carnagey Entering Rank of Writing Celebrities"; DC, "Daniel Eversole Is More Impressive Than Cuno"; and DC, "Dale Carnagey Says Nodaway County Girls Would Charm."

39   Malcolm Cowley, *Exiles Return: A Literary Odyssey* (New York, 1975 [1934]), 9. For insightful analyses of the Lost Generation of writers, see also Craig Monk, *Writing the Lost Generation: Expatriate Autobiography and American Modernism* (Iowa City, 2008), and an older treatment by Alfred Kazin, "Into the Thirties: All the Lost Generations," in his *On Native Grounds: An Interpretation of Modern American Prose Literature* (New York, 1942).

40   See Carl Van Doren, *Contemporary American Novelists, 1900–1920* (New York, 1922), 146; and Kazin, "The New Realism: Sherwood Anderson and Sinclair Lewis," in *On Native Grounds*.

41   "All That I Have" unpublished manuscript, DCA.

42   Ibid., 3, 4, 31–32.

43   Ibid., 101–2.

44   Ibid., 183–84.

45   Ibid., 20–21, 100.

46   Ibid., 10–12.

47   Ibid., 38, 88.

48   DC, "Former Nodaway Countian, Now Writer, Declares He Still Knows His ABC's," *Maryville Democrat-Forum*, October 1925; "Armistice Novel" sketch, DCA; DC's clippings on writing, DCA.

49   DC, *How to Stop Worrying*, 77–78.

50   Ibid.; and DC, "Letters to My Daughter," 21.

51   DC to Amanda and James Carnagey, May 14, 1920, DCA; DC to Amanda and James Carnagey, May 26, 1920, DCA; and DC, "Dale Carnagey Says Nodaway Girls Would Charm."

8. Business and Self-Regulation

1   DC, *How to Win Friends and Influence People* (New York, 1937), 2–3, 12.

2   Ibid., 54, 68–69, 42–43, 34, 126, 160, 179, 98, 160, 190.

3 DC, "Dale Carnagey Says Nodaway County Girls Would Charm Heart of Iron Man," *Maryville Democrat-Forum*, November 13, 1924; DC, "Former Nodaway Countian, Now Writer, Declares He Still Knows His ABC's," *Maryville Democrat-Forum*, October 1925; and DC, *Public Speaking: A Practical Course for Business Men* (New York: Association Press, 1926).

4 Margaret Case Harriman, "He Sells Hope," *The Saturday Evening Post* (August 31, 1937): 36; and Adolph E. Meyer, "How Dale Carnegie Made Friends, Etc.," *The American Mercury* (July 1943): 44.

5 Harriman, "He Sells Hope," 36.

6 DC to Prof. A. B. Williamson, February 2, 1925; William F. Hirsch, the executive secretary of United YMCA Schools, to DC, December 2, 1920; and DC to Hirsch, January 8, 1921: all DCA.

7 DC, "Dale Carnagey, Spending Summer in Europe, Writes of Life There," *Maryville Tribune*, October 10, 1922.

8 DC, *Public Speaking: A Practical Course*, 201, 37, 38–40, 153–54, 175.

10 Coolidge quoted in William Allen White, *A Puritan in Babylon* (New York, 1938), 253, and in James Prothro, *The Dollar Decade* (New York, 1954), 224.

11 Ford quoted in Steven Watts, *The People's Tycoon: Henry Ford and the American Century* (New York, 2005), 120–22. For a trenchant summary of 1920s prosperity, see Paul Boyer et al., *The Enduring Vision: A History of the American People* (Lexington, MA, 1996), 772–73.

12 William Leach, *Land of Desire: Merchants, Power, and the Rise of a New American Culture* (New York, 1988), xiii–xiv. Among a voluminous literature on the new consumerism, see also Warren I. Susman, *Culture as History: The Transformation of American Society in the Twentieth Century* (New York, 1984), and Daniel Horowitz, *The Morality of Spending: Attitudes Toward the Consumer Society in America, 1875–1950* (Baltimore, 1985). On domestic science, see Bettina Berch, "Scientific Management in the Home: The Empress's New Clothes," *Journal of American Culture* (Fall 1980): 440–45, and Glenna Matthews, "The Housewife and the Home Economist," in her *Just a Housewife: The Rise and Fall of Domesticity in America* (New York, 1987), 145–71.

13 Ellis Hawley, *The Great War and the Search for a Modern Order* (New York, 1979), v, 80, 99; Kim McQuaid, "Corporate Liberalism in the American Business Community, 1920–1940," *Business History Review* (Autumn 1978): 342–68; and Leach, *Land of Desire*.

14   DC, *Public Speaking: The Standard Course of the United Y.M.C.A. Schools* (New York, 1920), Book III, 16, 19, and Book IV, 69–71, 72; and *Public Speaking and Self-Confidence,* 1917 advertising pamphlet, DCA.

15   DC to Prof. A. B. Williamson, February 2, 1925, DCA.

16   DC, *Public Speaking: A Practical Course,* 3–5, 12.

17   Ibid., 31, 228.

18   Ibid., 31, 172–73.

19   Ibid., 47, 82, 332, 395–96.

20   Ibid., 134, 166, 192.

21   Ibid., 401–2.

22   Ibid., 48–49.

23   Ibid., 247, 37.

24   Susman, *Culture as History,* 274, 280.

25   Olivier Zunz, *Making America Corporate, 1870–1920* (Chicago, 1990), 201–2. See also, in a vast literature on the "organizational synthesis," Alfred D. Chandler, *The Visible Hand: The Managerial Revolution in American Business* (Cambridge, 1977); Richard R. John, "Elaborations, Revisions, Dissents: Alfred D. Chandler, Jr.'s *The Visible Hand* After Twenty Years," *Business History Review* (Summer 1997): 151–200; and Louis Galambos, "Technology, Political Economy, and Professionalization: Central Themes of the Organizational Synthesis," *Business History Review* (Winter 1983): 471–93.

26   DC, "How Businessmen Are Acquiring Self-Confidence and Convincing Speech," Supplement to Syllabus B-15—Public Speaking, YMCA, October 15, 1919, DCA; and DC, *Public Speaking: The Standard Course,* Book IV, 66–67, 85–87.

27   DC, *Public Speaking: A Practical Course,* 143–44.

28   Ibid., 203.

29   Ibid., 225, 226.

30   Ibid., 228, 229, 230, 238, 239, 242.

31   Ibid., 423–24.

32   Ibid., 298–99, 425, 391.

33   Richard Weiss, *The American Myth of Success: From Horatio Alger to Norman Vincent Peale* (Urbana, IL, 1988), 196; and DC, *Public Speaking: A Practical Course,* 389.

34   DC, *Public Speaking: A Practical Course,* 240, 175, 389.

35   Ibid., 386, 474–75.

36   Ibid., 387–88.

37 Coolidge quoted in Frank Presbrey, *The History and Development of Advertising* (New York, 1929), 620, 622, 625.

38 DC, *Public Speaking: A Practical Course*, 470, 387.

39 Bruce Barton, *The Man Nobody Knows* (New York, 2000 [1925]), 5, 18, 50, 66, 33–35, 13–18, 19–25, 42. For an exceptionally insightful analysis of Barton and the new culture of personality, see T. J. Jackson Lears, "From Salvation to Self-Realization: Advertising and the Therapeutic Roots of the Consumer Culture, 1880–1930," in Richard Wrightman Fox and T. J. Jackson Lears, eds., *The Culture of Consumption: Critical Essays in American History, 1880–1980* (New York, 1983), 3–38, especially 29–38.

40 DC, *Public Speaking: A Practical Course*, 429–30.

41 See, among many others, two books that suggest this interpretive paradigm: John G. Cawelti, *Apostles of the Self-Made Man* (Chicago, 1965), and Judy Hilkey, *Character Is Capital: Success Manuals and Manhood in Gilded Age America* (Chapel Hill, NC, 1997).

42 Entries quoted here and in the following paragraphs are all from "Damned Fool Things I Have Done" file, DCA.

43 DC, *Public Speaking: A Practical Course*, 33, 65, 140, 68, 135, 231.

44 *What Can a Course in Public Speaking Do for Me?*, 1930 publicity pamphlet, DCA.

45 "The Engineers Club of Philadelphia: Here Is How New York and Philadelphia Engineers Have Profited by Dale Carnegie's Course," 1930 advertisement, DCA.

46 DC, "Why a Banker Should Study Public Speaking," *Bulletin of the American Institute of Banking* (January 1927): 23–30.

47 See the following "How They Got That Way" installments in *American Magazine*: (September 1929): 88, 174; (October 1929): 78, 192; (December 1929): 73; (January 1930): 144; (April 1930): 208; (May 1930): 204; (July 1930): 82, 94, 124; and (January 1931): 80. For a brief sketch of Albert T. Reid, see the Kansas Historical Society website, available at Kansapedia: kshs.org/kansapedia/albert-t-reid/12182.

48 "How They Got That Way," *American Magazine* (November 1929): 80.

9. "Do the Thing You Fear to Do"

1 For statistics on the impact of the Great Depression, see Robert L. Heilbroner, *The Economic Transformation of America* (New York, 1977), 179, 185.

2 Rosemary Crom, ed., *Dale Carnegie—As Others Saw Him* (Garden City, NY: D. Carnegie, 1987), 10, 12; DC to Homer Croy, September 15, 1931, Homer

Croy Papers, State Historical Society of Missouri; and Homer Croy's sad story in DC, *How to Stop Worrying and Start Living* (New York, 1948), 266–68.

3 See Abbie Connell's reminiscences in Crom, *Dale Carnegie*, 25; and DC to Amanda and James Carnagey, December 31, 1930, DCA.

4 See Warren I. Susman's essays in his *Culture as History: The Transformation of American Society in the Twentieth Century* (New York, 1984), in particular "Culture and Commitment," 196–98, and "The Culture of the Thirties," 154, 164.

5 For a concise treatment of FDR's first inaugural address, see David M. Kennedy, *Freedom from Fear: The American People in Depression and War, 1929–1945* (New York, 1999), 133–34.

6 DC, "Grab Your Bootstraps," *Collier's* (March 5, 1938): 14–15.

7 Ibid., 14, 15, 37.

8 See DC's reminiscences on China in Crom, *Dale Carnegie as Others Saw Him*, 25; and DC, "Grab Your Bootstraps," 14, where he reiterated his views on that country and America's Great Depression.

9 DC, *The Dale Carnegie Course in Effective Speaking and Influencing Men in Business*, 1934, 12.

10 DC to Lowell Thomas, May 21, 1934, Lowell Thomas Papers, Marist College Archives and Special Collections; "How to Increase Your Income and Develop Leadership," full-page newspaper advertisement for the Carnegie course, 1932–1935, DCA; and DC, *Topics for Talks and Schedule of Sessions: Dale Carnegie Course*, 1934, 27.

11 DC, *Topics for Talks*, 12.

12 Ibid., 41–47.

13 John Janney, "Can You Think Fast on Your Feet?," *American Magazine* (January 1932): 94, 41.

14 "How to Increase Your Income and Develop Leadership"; "Are You Strangled by Fear?," full-page ad for the Dale Carnegie Course in Effective Speaking and Influencing Men in Business, *Newsweek* (August 17, 1935); and Margaret Case Harriman, "He Sells Hope," *The Saturday Evening Post* (August 14, 1937): 34.

15 *What Can I Get Out of This Course in Effective Speaking? 11 of Your Questions Answered by Dale Carnegie*, early 1930s promotional pamphlet, DCA; "How to Increase Your Income and Develop Leadership"; *What Can a Course in Public Speaking Do for Me?*, 1930 promotional pamphlet, DCA; DC, "We Have with Us Tonight," *Reader's Digest* (November 1936): 56; and Janney, "Can You Think Fast on Your Feet?," 92.

16 "How to Increase Your Income and Develop Leadership"; *What Can I Get Out of This Course in Effective Speaking?*; *What Can a Course in Public Speaking Do for Me?*; DC, *The Dale Carnegie Course in Effective Speaking*, 15, 16; and endorsement letter from H. B. Le Quatte, vice president of the Advertising Club of New York, to businessmen of New York City, 1933, DCA.

17 Harriman, "He Sells Hope," 12; Janney, "Can You Think Fast on Your Feet?," 94; and Lowell Thomas introduction in DC, *Public Speaking and Influencing Men in Business* (New York, 1953 [1926]), 6.

18 DC, *Lincoln the Unknown* (New York, 1959 [1932]), vii.

19 Homer Croy to DC, April 7, 1931, Homer Cory Papers, State Historical Society of Missouri; and DC, *Lincoln the Unknown*, viii.

20 DC, *Lincoln the Unknown*, 43, 48–49, 78, 99.

21 Ibid., 133, 186–88.

22 Ibid., 44, 145, 90.

23 Ibid., 32, 27–28, 42.

24 Ibid., 29, 35, 96, 192.

25 Ibid., 155–56, 170.

26 Susman, "Culture and Commitment," 192, 199.

27 On "sentimental Populism," see Steven Watts, *The Magic Kingdom: Walt Disney and the American Way of Life* (Boston, 1997), 63–100, and Watts, *The People's Tycoon: Henry Ford and the American Century* (New York, 2005), 401–26. Other treatments of 1930s populism include Alan Brinkley, *Voices of Protest: Huey Long, Father Coughlin, and the Great Depression* (New York, 1982), and Erika Doss, *Benton, Pollock, and the Politics of Modernism: From Regionalism to Abstract Expressionism* (Chicago, 1991). The quote is from Susman, "Culture and Commitment," 205.

28 Gertrude Emerick, "Dale Carnegie: The Man Who Made an Adventure of Knowing Lincoln," *Brooklyn Eagle*, January 9, 1936; and DC, *Lincoln the Unknown*, ix. On the reconstruction of New Salem, see Benjamin Thomas, *Lincoln's New Salem* (Springfield, IL, 1934), particularly chapter 3.

29 DC, *Lincoln the Unknown*, 21, 31, 22, 36, 55.

30 Ibid., 104, 189.

31 "Dale Carnegie to Be Heard in Air Talks," news clipping, August 1933, DCA; and Luther F. Sies, *Encyclopedia of American Radio, 1920–1960* (Jefferson, NC, 2000), 335.

32 DC to Lowell Thomas, August 26, 1934, Lowell Thomas Papers, Marist College Archives and Special Collections; Samuel C. Croot Advertising Company to Lowell Thomas, July 7, 1933, Lowell Thomas Papers, Marist College

Archives and Special Collections; and DC, *Little Known Facts About Well Known People* (New York, 1934), 115.

33 DC to Lowell Thomas, August 28, 1933, Lowell Thomas Papers, Marist College Archives and Special Collections; and J. R. Bolton, manager of the Advertising Club of New York, to DC, August 23, 1933, DCA.

34 DC, "Letters to My Daughter" (January 1952–1955), 82; and "NBC Personalities—Dale Carnegie," September 16, 1934, DCA.

35 "Carnegie Says Radio Hardest," *Lawrence Telegram*, March 10, 1937; and Jo Ransom, "Wherein Dale Carnegie of Forest Hills Discusses Merits of Certain News Commentators," *Brooklyn Daily Eagle*, March 28, 1937.

36 The broadcast transcripts for this show have not survived, so examples have been cited from the book, which collected and published them in only slightly revised form. See DC, *Little Known Facts About Well Known People*, 213, 189, 57, 77, 81.

37 DC, *Public Speaking: A Practical Course for Business Men* (New York, 1926), 428; and Ransom, "Wherein Dale Carnegie of Forest Hills Discusses Merits of Certain News Commentators."

38 DC, *Little Known Facts About Well Known People*, 199, 228, 65, 105–7; and Daniel Boorstin, *The Image, or What Happened to the American Dream* (New York, 1962), 57.

39 DC to Homer Croy on December 19 and December 14, 1933, and on May 31, 1934, Homer Croy Papers, State Historical Society of Missouri.

40 Maury Klein, "Laughing Through Tears: Hollywood Answers to the Depression," in Steven Mintz and Randy Roberts, eds., *Hollywood's America: Unites States History Through Its Films* (New York, 2008), 87; and Andrew Bergman, *We're in the Money: Depression America and Its Films* (New York, 1972), xvi, 167–68. See also Karen Sternheimer, *Celebrity Culture and the American Dream: Stardom and Social Mobility* (New York, 2011), especially "Pull Yourself Up by Your Bootstraps: Personal Failure and the Great Depression," 72–94; and C. David Heymann, *Poor Little Rich Girl* (New York, 1983).

41 Sies, *Encyclopedia of American Radio, 1920–1960*, 335; "Little Known Fact About Well Known People," *New York Journal*, undated, DCA; "Little Known Fact About Well Known People," Redding, California, *Courier Free Press*, undated, DCA; and "Biography by Radio," *New York Herald Tribune*, November 24, 1934.

42 NBC Artists Services promotion, included in DC, *The Dale Carnegie Course in Effective Speaking*, 36; and "NBC Personalities—Dale Carnegie."

10. "Men and Women, Hungry for Self-Improvement"

1 Lolita Baucaire to DC, March 16, 1932; Lolita Baucaire to DC at time of Amanda Carnagey's death in 1939; and Dorothy Carnegie, videotaped interview, 1996: all DCA.

2 Amanda Carnagey to DC, August 10, 1931; and DC, "Letters to My Daughter" (January 1952–1955), 9–10: both DCA.

3 "Leon Shimkin, Guiding Force at Simon & Schuster, Dies at 81," *The New York Times*, May 26, 1988; and interview with Leon Shimkin, May 26, 1967, in Rosemary F. Carroll, "The Impact of the Great Depression on American Attitudes Toward Success: A Study of the Programs of Norman Vincent Peale, Dale Carnegie, and Johnson O'Connor" (PhD Dissertation, Rutgers University, 1968), 102–3.

4 Leon Shimkin's reminiscence in Rosemary Crom, ed., *Dale Carnegie—As Others Saw Him* (Garden City, NY: D. Carnegie, 1987), 25; and Shimkin interview in Carroll, "The Impact of the Great Depression," 103.

5 Harold B. Clemenko, "He Sells Success," *Look* (May 25, 1948): 62; Homer Croy, "The Success Factory," *Esquire* (June 1937): 239; and DC, *Topics for Talks and Schedule of Sessions: Dale Carnegie Course*, 1934, 17.

6 DC, "Notes for an Autobiography," early 1950s, DCA.

7 The advertisement and coupon are included in a special Simon and Schuster inset promotion for the book in *Publishers Weekly* (January 23, 1937). See also the discussion of Schwab's ad in Julian L. Watkins, *The One Hundred Greatest Advertisements: Who Wrote Them and What They Did* (New York, 1959), 92–93; and "*How to Win Friends and Influence People* Campaign," available at www.dalecarnegie.com.

8 Simon and Schuster insert, *Publishers Weekly*, 2; Margaret Case Harriman, "He Sells Hope," *The Saturday Evening Post* (August 14, 1937): 33; figure of 4,520,000 copies sold on dust jacket of 1949 edition of DC, *How to Win Friends and Influence People* (New York, 1949); and "Dale Carnegie: The Man Who Succeeded by Preaching Success," *Look* (December 21, 1937): 41. Schwab explained the book's successful advertising campaign in "An Ad That Sold a Million Books," *Printers' Week Monthly* (November 1939): 50–52.

9 DC, "Notes for an Autobiography"; Shimkin's reminiscence in Crom, *Dale Carnegie*, 25; and DC quoted inClemenko, "He Sells Success," 62.

10 DC, *How to Win Friends*, 56; and Harriman, "He Sells Hope," 12, 33.

11 DC, *How to Win Friends*, 3, 12, 13, 15.

12 Ibid., 201–2.

13　Ibid., 19, 123, 88, 74, 170.

14　Ibid., 154, 94, 110–11.

15　Ibid., 77–78.

16　Ibid., 55, 12–13, 28, 79.

17　Ibid., 29, 31, 93, 154.

18　Ibid., 93, 39, 40–41, 51.

19　Terkel's interviews quoted in Warren I. Susman, *Culture as History: The Transformation of American Society in the Twentieth Century* (New York, 1984), 194–95.

20　Steven Watts, *The Magic Kingdom: Walt Disney and the American Way of Life* (New York, 1997), 69–82.

21　Susman, *Culture as History*, 154–60; and FDR quoted in Andrew Bergman, *We're in the Money: Depression America and Its Films* (New York, 1971), 167.

22　DC, *How to Win Friends*, 16, 52, 54, 17, 102.

23　William A. H. Bernie, "Popularity, Incorporated," *New York World-Telegram Weekend Magazine* (February 27, 1937); and Harriman, "He Sells Hope," 12.

24　On other success writers in the 1930s, see Carroll, "The Impact of the Great Depression."

25　DC, "How They Got That Way: Charles Schwab, Foremost Living Steel Magnate," *American Magazine* (November 1929): 80. See also Kenneth Warren, *Industrial Genius: The Working Life of Charles Michael Schwab* (Pittsburgh, 2007).

26　DC, *How to Win Friends*, 67, 168–69, 177.

27　Ibid., 34–35. See also 50, 67, 81, 129.

28　T. J. Jackson Lears, "From Salvation to Self-Realization: Advertising and the Therapeutic Roots of the Consumer Culture, 1880–1930," in Richard Wrightman Fox and T. J. Jackson Lears, eds., *The Culture of Consumption: Critical Essays in American History, 1880–1980* (New York, 1983), 8; and DC, *Public Speaking: A Practical Course for Business Men* (New York: Association Press, 1926), 225.

29　DC, *How to Win Friends*, 68.

30　Ibid., 57–103.

31　DC, *Public Speaking: A Practical Course*, 228–29.

32　DC, *How to Win Friends*, 12–13; and advertisement for *How to Win Friends* in *Publishers Weekly* (January 23, 1937).

33　DC, *How to Win Friends*, 30, 51.

34   Ibid., 196–99.

35   Ibid., 25–26, 71, 42–43, 60–61, 216, 157–58, 101.

11. "We Are Dealing with Creatures of Emotion"

1   DC, *How to Win Friends and Influence People* (New York, 1936), 10, 14; "How to Get Along with People," *The Literary Digest* (November 21, 1936): 28; and Homer Croy, "The Success Factory," *Esquire* (June 1937): 112.

2   DC, *How to Win Friends*, opening page, 27.

3   Philip Rieff, *Freud: The Mind of the Moralist* (Chicago, 1979 [1959]), 356–57.

4   *What Can I Get Out of This Course in Effective Speaking? 11 of Your Questions Answered by Dale Carnegie*, early 1930s promotional pamphlet, 5, 12; "Admit Two: First Session of the Dale Carnegie Course," promotional flyer, 1933; and "How to Increase Your Income and Develop Leadership," full-page newspaper advertisement for the Carnegie course, 1932–1935: all DCA.

5   See the listing of DC's psychological associates in William A. H. Bernie, "Popularity, Incorporated," *New York World-Telegram Weekend Magazine* (February 27, 1937), and in Croy, "The Success Factory," 239.

6   Harry A. Overstreet, *Influencing Human Behavior* (New York, 1925), vii, 43; and Eduard C. Lindeman's review, "Psychology Put to Work," *The New Republic* (May 26, 1926): 40–41.

7   Overstreet, *Influencing Human Behavior*, 2, 3, 4, 17–18, 45–46.

8   Ibid., 44, 49, 69.

9   DC, "Damned Fool Things I Have Done" file, 1928, DCA, which also cites the Overstreet article "Remodeling Wives and Husbands," *McCall's* (August 1928). Overstreet's role as a Carnegie course lecturer is related in Croy, "The Success Factory," 239, while his impact on Carnegie was confirmed by Richard M. Huber, who writes, "Perhaps the most important influence was H. A. Overstreet's *Influencing Human Behavior* (1925), which contains most of the principles of applied psychology advanced by Carnegie in his book": see Richard M. Huber, *The American Idea of Success* (New York, 1971), 235.

10   On Link's life and career, see Richard S. Tedlow, "Essay on Industrial Psychologist Henry C. Link," in *Dictionary of American Biography* (New York, 1977), 433–34; Donald Meyer, *The Positive Thinkers: A Study of the American Quest for Health, Wealth, and Personal Power from Mary Baker Eddy to Norman Vincent Peale* (Garden City, NY, 1966), 224–30; and Frank Goble,

The Third Force: The Psychology of Abraham Maslow (New York, 1970), 149–51. Link's role is also noted in Paul S. Achilles, "The Role of the Psychological Corporation in Applied Psychology," *American Journal of Psychology* (November 1937): 229–47.

11 Henry C. Link, *The Return to Religion* (New York, 1936), 89, 11, 13, 69, 70. See also Meyer, *Positive Thinkers*, 226.

12 Link, *Return to Religion*, 39–40, 49, 33–34.

13 Link's position as a special lecturer in the Carnegie course is noted in Croy, "The Success Factory," 239; and DC, *How to Win Friends*, 66.

14 Vash Young, *A Fortune to Share* (Indianapolis, 1931), 20–21, 35, 49, 77, 85, 46–47.

15 Vash Young, *The Go-Giver: A Better Way of Getting Along in Life* (New York, 1934), 15–16, 39–40, 18.

16 Ibid., 18, 244.

17 DC, *How to Win Friends*, 47–48; and Young, *The Go-Giver*, 241.

18 See Arthur Frank Payne, *Methods of Teaching Industrial Subjects: A Companion Volume to Administration of Vocational Education and Organization of Vocational Guidance* (New York, 1926); and Arthur Frank Payne, "The Scientific Selection of Men," *Scientific Monthly* (July–December 1920): 544–47.

19 See Arthur Frank Payne, *My Parents: Friends or Enemies* (New York, 1932). On Payne's radio efforts, see Peter J. Behrens, "Psychology Takes to the Airways: American Radio Psychology Between the Wars, 1926–1939," *American Sociologist* (2009): 214–27; Payne's participation in the Carnegie course is noted in Bernie, "Popularity, Incorporated."

20 For information on Bisch's early career, see dossiers.net/louis-e-bisch/; Louis E. Bisch, "Science and the Criminal," *Popular Science Monthly* (April 1916): 555–58; and Burns Mantle, *The Best Plays of 1924–1925* (New York, 1926).

21 See the following by Louis E. Bisch: "Defense Barrier Is a Sign of Weakness," *Mansfield News*, September 17, 1928; "Successful Men's Sons Often Failures," *Kokomo Tribune*, April 23, 1928; and "The Relationship of the Inferiority Complex to Orthodontia," *Dental Cosmos* (July 1928): 697–98. For other Bisch articles, see "Psycho-Analyzing the Hollywood Divorce Epidemic," *Screen Book* (October 1933); "Psychiatry and Advertising: Why Copy Should Appeal to Human Emotions," *Printers' Ink* (January 6, 1938); "Turn Your Sickness into an Asset," *Reader's Digest* (November 1937); "Have All Actors an Inferiority Complex?," *Photoplay* (August 1927); and "Why Hollywood Scandals Fascinate Us," *Photoplay* (January 1930).

22 Louis E. Bisch, *Be Glad You're Neurotic* (New York, 1936), 5–13.

23 Ibid., 55, 60, 223, 230. Bisch's participation in the Carnegie course is noted in Croy, "The Success Factory," 239.

24 DC, *How to Win Friends*, 151, 159.

25 Ibid., 216, 229, 230.

26 Ibid., 29, 30, 230, 58–59.

27 Ibid., 48, 112, 27.

28 Ibid., 63, 75, 172, 204–5.

29 Ibid., 17, 189, 71, 70, 190.

30 On Peale, see Carol V. R. George, *God's Salesman: Norman Vincent Peale and the Power of Positive Thinking* (New York, 1993), 88–93; Huber, *The American Idea of Success*, 315–25; and Meyer, *Positive Thinkers*, 239–75.

31 Napoleon Hill, *Think and Grow Rich* (New York, 1963 [1937]), 27, 85, 36, 68, 248. For treatments of Hill's life and career, see John G. Cawelti, *Apostles of the Self-Made Man* (Chicago, 1988 [1965]), 209–18, and J. M. Emmert, "The Story of Napoleon Hill," *Success Magazine* (January 6, 2009).

32 For two good treatments of Adler that examine both his life and ideas, see Josef Rattner, *Alfred Adler* (New York, 1983), and Manes Sperber, *Masks of Loneliness: Alfred Adler in Perspective* (New York, 1974). For a more critical assessment of Adler, see Russell Jacoby, *Social Amnesia: A Critique of Conformist Psychology from Adler to Laing* (Boston, 1975), 21–40.

33 See Susan Quinn, *A Mind of Her Own: The Life of Karen Horney* (New York, 1987).

34 Nathan G. Hale Jr., *The Rise and Crisis of Psychoanalysis in the United States: Freud and the Americans, 1917–1985* (New York, 1995), 139; Warren I. Susman, *Culture as History: The Transformation of American Society in the Twentieth Century* (New York, 1984), 166, 203; and Richard H. Pells, *Radical Visions and American Dreams: Culture and Social Thought in the Great Depression* (New York, 1973), 114. Eli Zaretsky, in *Secrets of the Soul: A Social and Cultural History of Psychoanalysis* (New York, 2004), 208–11, argues for a more radical reading of Horney as a feminist and advocate of Popular Front leftism.

35 Hale, *Rise and Crisis of Psychoanalysis*, 173, 139. For a fine biography of Sullivan, see Helen Swick Perry, *Psychiatrist of America: The Life of Harry Stack Sullivan* (Cambridge, MA, 1982).

36 See Christopher Lasch, *Haven in Heartless World: The Family Besieged* (New York, 1977), 75; and Hale, *Rise and Crisis of Psychoanalysis*, 175–76. For criticism of Sullivan's "psychology of interpersonal relations" as a key

benchmark in America's "transformation of psychoanalysis into a cult of personal health and fulfillment," see Christopher Lasch, *The Minimal Self: Psychic Survival in Troubled Times* (New York, 1984), 209–10. Ralph M. Crowley treats Sullivan's use of self-esteem in "Harry Stack Sullivan as Social Critic," *Journal of the American Academy of Psychoanalysis* (1981), 211–26.

37   Pells, *Radical Visions and American Dreams*, 113–14; Zaretsky, *Secrets of the Soul*, 278–79; and Richard Gillespie, *Manufactured Knowledge: A History of the Hawthorne Experiments* (Cambridge, MA, 1991).

38   Susman, *Culture as History*, 166.

39   DC, *How to Win Friends*, 58, 66.

40   Ibid., 40, 159, 36.

41   Ibid., 92, 145, 221, 127, 145, 150, 58.

42   Ibid., 135–36.

43   Susman, *Culture as History*, 200.

44   DC, *Topics for Talks and Schedule of Sessions: Dale Carnegie Course*, 1934, 39; and DC, *The Dale Carnegie Course in Effective Speaking and Influencing Men in Business*, 1934, 9.

45   Bernie, "Popularity, Incorporated"; and Lowell Thomas' Introduction, DC, *How to Win Friends*, 4.

46   Jack Alexander, "A Reporter at Large: The Green Pencil," *The New Yorker* (December 11, 1937): 56, 57; "The Engineers Club of Philadelphia: Here Is How New York and Philadelphia Engineers Have Profited by Dale Carnegie's Course," 1930 advertisement, DCA; Frank Bettger, *How I Raised Myself from Failure to Success in Selling* (New York, 1986 [1947]), 6; Ormond Drake, reminiscence manuscript entitled "Meeting Mr. Carnegie," 2, DCA; and testimonials published in *How to Win Friends* promotional insert, *Publishers Weekly* (January 23, 1937), 6.

47   T. J. Jackson Lears, "From Salvation to Self-Realization: Advertising and the Therapeutic Roots of the Consumer Culture, 1880–1930," in Richard Wrightman Fox and T. J. Jackson Lears, eds., *The Culture of Consumption: Critical Essays in American History, 1880–1980* (New York, 1983), 4.

48   Christopher Lasch, *The Culture of Narcissism: American Life in an Age of Diminishing Expectations* (New York, 1978), 250, 13; Lears, "From Salvation to Self-Realization," 29; and Richard Weiss, *The American Myth of Success: From Horatio Alger to Norman Vincent Peale* (Urbana, IL, 1988), 201–2.

49   DC, *How to Win Friends*, 28, 29, 52.

50   Ibid., 15, 69, 16, 37.

51 Philip Rieff, *The Triumph of the Therapeutic: The Uses of Faith After Freud* (New York, 1968), 3, 5, 13, 252; and Rieff, *Freud: The Mind of the Moralist*, 356–57.

12. "Every Act You Ever Performed Is Because You Wanted Something"

1 Doris Blake, "Praise Gets Results," *New York Daily News*, March 14, 1937; Margaret Marshall, "Columnists on Parade: Dale Carnegie," *The Nation* (March 19, 1938): 328; and "Soft Answers," *The New York Times*, February 27, 1937.

2 DC, questions and answers with Carnegie course trainees entitled "How to Teach Effective Speaking and Human Relations," May 21, 1938, 5, 3, DCA.

3 DC, *How to Win Friends and Influence People* (New York, 1936), 154, 102, 40.

4 "*Funnymen,*" *Time (September 20, 1937)*.

5 Irving Tressler, *How to Lose Friends and Alienate People* (New York, 1937), 14, 19, 23–24.

6 "Tressler, Irving Dart," *Who's Who in America* (Chicago, 1943), 2, 199; and T. J. Davis, interview with Anne Kendall Tressler (widow), at teedysay. blogspot.com, accessed August 15, 2011.

7 Tressler, *How to Lose Friends*, 36–37, 42, 45.

8 Ibid., 38, 96, 41, 47.

9 Ibid., 80, 101, 108, 111, 160.

10 Ibid., 93, 155–56.

11 "Pastor Raps Best Seller," *Brooklyn Reading Eagle*, March 18, 1938.

12 "Soft Answers"; Blake, "Praise Gets Results"; and James Aswell, "My New York," *Paterson Morning Call*, March 12, 1937.

13 James Thurber, "The Voice with the Smile," *Saturday Review of Literature* (January 30, 1937): 6; and DC, *How to Win Friends*, 92.

14 W. W. Woodruff to Dale Carnegie, February 26, 1942, LPA.

15 Heywood Broun, "It Seems to Me," *Atlanta Journal* (March 2, 1937); and William A. H. Bernie, "Popularity, Incorporated," *New York World-Telegram Weekend Magazine* (February 27, 1937).

16 DC, *How to Win Friends*, 221.

17 Ibid., 228.

18 Ibid., 13, 70.

19 Ibid., 54–55.

20 Ibid., 36–37, 208.

21 Ibid., 37, 92–93.

22 DC, "How to Teach Effective Speaking and Human Relations," 3, 4.

23 For an insightful analysis of the rise of the confidence man in American life, see Karen Halttunen, *Confidence Men and Painted Women: A Study of Middle-Class Culture in America, 1830–1870* (New Haven, 1982). I have been influenced by her discussion of Carnegie on pages 208–10.

24 Sinclair Lewis, "Car-Yes-Man," *Newsweek* (November 15, 1937): 31.

25 Dale Carnegie and J. Berg Esenwein, *The Art of Public Speaking* (Springfield, MA, 1915), 103–4, 263; and Bernie, "Popularity, Incorporated."

26 Tressler, *How to Lose Friends*, 43, 246–47.

27 Ibid., 189, 180, 186. Mencken had coined "booboisie" in 1922 to denigrate the American middle class and its religious, consumerist, and moralizing proclivities. A monthly collection of quotations from the booboisie became one of the most popular features of Mencken's column in *The American Mercury*. See Terry Teachout, *The Skeptic: A Life of H. L. Mencken* (New York, 2003).

28 Lewis, "Car-Yes-Man," 31.

29 Sinclair Lewis, "One Man Revolution," *Newsweek* (November 22, 1937): 33. Mark Schorer, in his biography *Sinclair Lewis: An American Life* (New York, 1961), 634, explains that Lewis included his denunciation of Carnegie as the "Bard of Babbittry" in many of his lectures throughout the late 1930s.

30 DC, *How to Win Friends*, 13, 16, 52, 69; and "Dale's Heart Is in Nodaway," an installment from his 1930s newspaper series, Dale Carnegie's Daily Column, undated, DCA.

31 "Pastor Raps Best Seller."

32 Fillmore Hyde, "Your Cue," *Cue* (June 3, 1939): 11.

33 DC, *How to Win Friends*, 127–28.

34 For a discussion of this labor clash, see Ron Chernow, *Titan: The Life of John D. Rockefeller* (New York, 1998), chapter 29, and Thomas G. Franklin, *Killing for Coal: America's Deadliest Labor War* (Cambridge, MA, 2008).

35 DC, *How to Win Friends*, 13, 75.

36 Ibid., 184, 198.

37 Ibid., 60, 73–74, 197.

38 "Pastor Raps Best Seller"; and Marshall, "Columnists on Parade."

39 Lewis, "Car-Yes-Man," 31; and Marshall, "Columnists on Parade," 328.

13: "Give a Man a Fine Reputation to Live Up To"

1 For Whiting's reminiscences about this event, see William Longgood, *Talking Your Way to Success: The Story of the Dale Carnegie Course* (New York, 1962), 227–28.

2   "Author Dale Carnegie ... Knew Days of Poverty," *Akron Times-Press*, April 13, 1937; and DC, "Notes for an Autobiography," early 1950s, DCA.

3   "A Business Messiah," *Wichita Beacon*, October 12, 1940; "Author Dale Carnegie ... Knew Days of Poverty"; and "Friend Maker Arrives" and "Dale Carnegie Demonstrates His Art of Influencing People," both *Commercial Appeal*, January 13, 1941.

4   *Asheville Citizen*, March 23, 1939.

5   Margaret Case Harriman, "He Sells Hope," *The Saturday Evening Post* (August 4, 1937); Homer Croy, "The Success Factory," *Esquire* (June 1937); "How to Win Friends ... and Influence People," *Look* (April 1937): 34–35; "One Minute Biographies," *Look* (June 8, 1937): 12; and "Dale Carnegie: The Man Who Succeeded by Preaching Success," *Look* (December 21, 1937): 31–32.

6   Harold B. Clemenko, "He Sells Success," *Look* (May 25, 1948): 68.

7   Harriman, "He Sells Hope," 34; and Carl Anderson, *Henry: America's Funniest Youngster*, *New York Daily Mirror*, November 13, 1939.

8   Ad campaign for Turret Cigarettes, DCA.

9   DC, "Notes for an Autobiography"; and Abbie Connell's reminiscences in Rosemary Crom, ed., *Dale Carnegie—As Others Saw Him* (Garden City, NY: D. Carnegie, 1987), 12.

10 Luther F. Sies, *Encyclopedia of American Radio, 1920–1960* (Jefferson, NC, 2000), 148; and Giles Kemp and Edward Claflin, *Dale Carnegie: The Man Who Influenced Millions* (New York, 1989), 142–43.

11 Lowell Thomas and Ted Shane, *Softball! So What?* (New York, 1940), 98–106.

12 Ibid., 106–11, 125.

13 Ibid., 101, 116–17, 225–26.

14 Ibid., 71, 104, 6, 118.

15 Homer Croy to DC, March 30, 1940, DCA; and Thomas and Shane, *Softball! So What?*, 12, 13, 137.

16 Thomas and Shane, *Softball! So What?*, 10–11.

17 DC, *Public Speaking: A Practical Course for Business Men* (New York: Association Press, 1926), 428; and DC, *How to Win Friends and Influence People* (New York, 1936), 14.

18 DC diary entry, April 24, 1939, DCA.

19 DC, "Notes for an Autobiography."

20 Ibid.

21 DC quoted in Kemp and Claflin, *Dale Carnegie*, 160.

22 DC to Homer Croy, October 31, 1938, Homer Croy Papers, State Historical Society of Missouri; Crom, *Dale Carnegie*, which also features a number of

photographs of Carnegie's home; and author's interviews with Linda Offenbach Polsby, June 6–8, 2011, who recounted her memories of Carnegie's home
from numerous childhood visits.

23 Author's interview with Brenda Leigh Johnson, March 23, 2011; and DC to
Lowell Thomas, February 20, 1936, Lowell Thomas Papers, Marist College
Archives and Special Collections.

24 DC to Amanda Carnagey, February 18, 1938, DCA.

25 See Clifton Carnagey to DC, December 20, 1939; and DC to Clifton Carnagey, December 23, 1939: both DCA.

26 See newspaper clippings and obituaries from the Maryville newspaper in Dale
Carnegie Scrapbook, Nodaway County Historical Society; and DC to Isador
and Frieda Offenbach, December 8, 1939, LPA.

27 1938 newspaper clippings and scrapbook on DC's 1939 Japanese trip, DCA

28 DC diary entries, May 11 and 12, 1939, DCA.

29 Author's interviews with Polsby.

30 Ibid. Polsby reported the Cuban cruise connection from the recollection of an
older relative. The inscribed copy of *Little Known Facts* is in her possession.

31 File on the Berkowitz/Burke family available at at ancestry.com; and author's
interviews with Polsby.

32 Author's interviews with Polsby.

33 Ibid.; and Frieda Burke file available at ancestry.com.

34 Author's interviews with Polsby; Isador Edmond Offenbach file available at
ancestry.com; and "Shalom (Soloman) Offenbach" available at familytree-
maker.genealogy.com, which contains an extensive reminiscence by Isador
Offenbach, recorded in the 1980s, about his father's life and his own childhood in the early 1900s.

35 Author's interviews with Polsby.

36 Ibid.; and author's interview with Carol Kur, December 15, 2011.

37 Frieda Offenbach to DC, summer of 1942, DCA.

38 DC diary entry, spring of 1939, DCA; Frieda Offenbach, "Virulence in Relation to Early Phases of the Culture Cycle," *Proceedings of the Society for
Experimental Biology and Medicine* 35 (November 1936): 385–86; and DC
to [Linda] Dale Offenbach, July 12, 1938, LPA.

39 Frieda Offenbach to DC, summer 1942, DCA; author's interviews with
Polsby; DC to Frieda Offenbach, telegram dated August 26, 1940, LPA; and
DC to Frieda Offenbach, August 22, 1940, LPA.

40 Frieda Offenbach to DC, summer 1942; Frieda Offenbach to DC, fall 1942;
and Frieda Offenbach to DC, early summer 1941: all DCA.

41 Frieda Offenbach to DC, early summer 1941, DCA; DC to Frieda Offenbach, December 22, 1939, LPA; and DC to Frieda Offenbach, November 24, 1940, LPA.

42 Photograph of DC and Frieda Offenbach, LPA.

43 Author's interviews with Polsby.

44 DC to Isador Offenbach, December 20, 1939, LPA.

45 DC to Miss Offenbach/Care Mrs. Isador Offenbach, Western Union Telegram, June 8, 1938; and DC to Linda Dale Offenbach, July 12, 1938: both LPA.

46 DC to Linda Dale Offenbach, July 8, 1939; DC to Linda Dale Offenbach, December 3, 1939; DC to Linda Dale Offenbach, April 1, 1940; DC to Linda Dale Offenbach, July 6, 1940; and DC to Linda Dale Offenbach, September 9, 1940: all LPA.

47 DC to Linda Dale Offenbach, July 8, 1939; and DC to Linda Dale Offenbach, June 1955: both LPA.

48 Author's interviews with Polsby.

49 DC to Isador and Frieda Offenbach, December 8, 1939; DC to Frieda Offenbach, September 8, 1940; DC to Linda Dale Offenbach, April 1, 1940; and DC to Linda Dale Offenbach, July 6, 1940: all LPA.

14. "Find Work That You Enjoy"

1 Adolph E. Meyer, "How Dale Carnegie Made Friends, Etc.," *The American Mercury* (July 1943): 40, 44–45; Collie Small, "Dale Carnegie: Man with a Message," *Collier's* (January 15, 1949): 36; and Harold B. Clemenko, "He Sells Success," *Look* (May 25, 1948): 67–68.

2 "4-Month Backbiting Moratorium Urged by Carnegie," *Chattanooga Daily Times*, March 11, 1940; "Dale Carnegie School Opens," *Wichita Beacon*, October 14, 1940; and "The Junior Chamber of Commerce Brings Dale Carnegie to Kansas City," advertisement, *Kansas City Journal*, April 3, 1940.

3 DC to President Franklin D. Roosevelt, May 20, 1940, DCA; and Rosemary Crom, ed., *Dale Carnegie—As Others Saw Him* (Garden City, NY, 1987), 19.

4 See movies.amctv.com on *Jiggs and Maggie in Society*.

5 See tcm.com on *The Magnificent Dope*.

6 David L. Cohn, *The Good Old Days: A History of American Morals and Manners as Seen Through the Sears, Roebuck Catalogs 1905 to the Present* (New York, 1940), 469.

7 Jack Alexander, "A Reporter at Large: The Green Pencil," *The New Yorker* (December 11, 1937): 42.

8   Ibid., 42, 43.

9   Ibid., 58, 60.

10 Ibid., 50, 55, 58, 50–52, 62.

11 Ibid., 42; and Homer Croy, "The Success Factory," *Esquire* (June 1937): 241.

12 *A History of Dale Carnegie Training: 1912–1997* (New York: Dale Carnegie and Associates, 1997), 8, DCA; and Croy, "The Success Factory," 112.

13 Croy, "The Success Factory," 112, 236; and William A. H. Bernie, "Popularity, Incorporated," *New York World-Telegram Weekend Magazine* (February 27, 1937).

14 *A History of Dale Carnegie Training*, 8; and DC, "Notes for an Autobiography," early 1950s, DCA.

15 DC, "Notes for an Autobiography."

16 Arthur Secord to Rosemary Crom, October 11, 1985, DCA; DC, *How to Stop Worrying and Start Living* (New York, 1948), 83; and author's interview with Oliver Crom, March 2, 2012, who confirmed Carnegie's mistake with the building.

17 DC, "Notes for an Autobiography."

18 William Longgood, *Talking Your Way to Success: The Story of the Dale Carnegie Course* (New York, 1962), 51–52, 9.

19 Alexander, "The Green Pencil," 43, 60, 62; J. P. McEvoy, "He Makes a Fortune Out of Fear," *Your Life* (November 1948): 25; *A History of Dale Carnegie Training*, 910; DC, "Notes for an Autobiography"; and Ormand Drake, "Meeting Dale Carnegie," 4, DCA.

20 Clemenko, "He Sells Success," 62, 65.

21 McEvoy, "He Makes a Fortune Out of Fear," 23–24.

22 Crom, *Dale Carnegie*: Redd Story, 27; Pat Jones, 21; and John Burger, 8.

23 Ken Bowton to Rosemary Crom, November 29, 1986, DCA.

24 Brick Brickell, "Reminiscence," 1980s, DCA.

25 Ken Bowton to Rosemary Crom, November 29, 1986, DCA; and Brickell, "Reminiscence."

26 Ken Bowton to Rosemary Crom, November 29, 1986, DCA; and R. G. Sanderson to Rosemary Crom, February 5, 1985, DCA.

27 Crom, *Dale Carnegie*: Roger Jackson, 20–21; and Arthur Secord, 25.

28 Ibid., Harry O. Hamm, 19; and Redd Story, 27.

29 John Burger to Rosemary Crom, March 28, 1985, DCA.

30 William A. D. Millison, "An Appraisal of the Teaching Methods of Dale Carnegie," *Quarterly Journal of Speech* 27, 1 (1947): 67–73. See also Alan Nichols, "Ray Keeslar Immel," *Quarterly Journal of Speech* 32, 1 (1946): 31–33.

31   "The Salesman's Viewpoint," *Asheville Citizen*, March 26, 1939; and "Winning the Nazis," *Geneva Times* (Geneva, NY), April 12, 1939.

32   "Dale Carnegie Says His Book Has Big German Sale but Probably Doesn't Help," *Knoxville News-Sentinel*, November 20, 1941.

33   "Dale Carnegie Expects More U.S. War Aid," *Vancouver Sun*, November 18, 1940; and "Dale Carnegie Says His Book Has Big German Sale."

34   "Dale Carnegie Fears He Couldn't Do Much with Hitler's Personality—'It Isn't Normal,'" *Chattanooga News-Free Press*, March 10, 1941; and "Guns Only Cure for Hitler's Ilk, Carnegie Admits," *Daily Oklahoman*, January 26, 1941.

35   "Philosophy of Successful Life," *Los Angeles Evening Herald-Express*, September 21, 1939.

36   "Japan Removed Nazi Flags, Says Dale Carnegie" and accompanying cartoon, *New York Daily Mirror*, October 6, 1939.

37   "Philosophy of Successful Life"; and "World Woes Cause Told," *Portland Oregonian*, September 1940.

38   "'How to Win Friends' Author Isn't Worrying About Any Big Bad Wolf—Even if It's Hitler," *Palm Beach Post*, February 18, 1941.

39   War Bond advertisement, *The Washington Post*, May 3, 1943.

40   "Dale Carnegie Says His Book Has Big German Sale"; Andy Logan and Russell Maloney, "The Talk of the Town: Friends and Influence," *The New Yorker* (March 20, 1943): 14; Meyer, "How Dale Carnegie Made Friends, Etc.," 48; and 1947 advertising campaign flyers, clippings scrapbook, DCA.

41   "Dale Carnegie Tells College Girls How to Get and Hold a Husband," *The Student* (Central Missouri State Teachers College), April 9, 1940; and "Carnegie Scores Nation's Schools as Ineffectual," *Orlando Sentinel-Star*, March 2, 1941.

42   "Guidance of Youth Urged by Carnegie," *Beaumont Journal*, March 15, 1939.

43   "Are You Suffering from an Inferiority Complex Because You Never Went to College?," article manuscript, 1940s, 1–2; and DC, "I Never Had a Chance to Go to College," article manuscript, 1940s, 3: both DCA.

44   "Are You Suffering from an Inferiority Complex," 12–13, 15–16.

45   "Praise Still Comes from Carnegie," *New Orleans Item*, April 2, 1939; "I Never Had a Chance to Go to College," 10; and "Carnegie Scores Nation's Schools as Ineffectual."

15. "He Has the Whole World with Him"

1   See Erik Erikson, *Identity and the Life Cycle* (New York, 1980 [1959]), 103–4.

2   Brick Brickell, "Reminiscence," 1980s, DCA.

3   Harold B. Clemenko, "He Sells Success," *Look* (May 25, 1948): 60.

4   Ibid., 68; and Adolph E. Meyer, "How Dale Carnegie Made Friends, Etc.,"
    The American Mercury (July 1943): 46–47.

5   Clemenko, "He Sells Success," 65; and Collie Small, "Dale Carnegie: Man
    with a Message," *Collier's* (January 15, 1949): 70.

6   Meyer, "How Dale Carnegie Made Friends, Etc.," 46–47; and Small, "Dale
    Carnegie: Man with a Message," 70.

7   Brickell, "Reminiscence."

8   Small, "Dale Carnegie: Man with a Message," 70; and Brickell, "Reminiscence."

9   Rosemary Crom, ed., *Dale Carnegie—As Others Saw Him* (Garden City, NY:
    D. Carnegie, 1987), 12–13; and Brickell, "Reminiscence."

10 Crom, *Dale Carnegie*, 26; and Brickell, "Reminiscence."

11 Marilyn Burke to Rosemary Crom, May 13, 1985, DCA.

12 Dorothy Carnegie, *How to Help Your Husband Get Ahead in His Social
    and Business Life* (New York, 1953), 171–72; Ormand Drake, "Meeting Mr.
    Carnegie," 5, DCA; and "Rotary Observes 20th Birthday," *Maryville Daily
    Forum*, June 4, 1948.

13 See the following letters in the Lowell Thomas Papers, Marist College Ar-
    chives and Special Collections: DC to Lowell Thomas, June 1, 1940; DC to
    Lowell Thomas, January 1, 1942; DC to Lowell Thomas, April 11, 1944; and
    DC to Lowell Thomas, December 17, 1947. Author's interview with Oliver
    Crom, March 2, 2012.

14 Lindsay Howard, "The Talk of the Town: Dale the Super," *The New Yorker*
    (March 26, 1949): 18–19.

15 "Recreation Facilities and West's Hospitality Brought Carnegie Here," *Lara-
    mie Boomerang*, June 18, 1943.

16 Small, "Dale Carnegie: Man with a Message," 70; and Arthur Secord to Rose-
    mary Crom, October 11, 1985, DCA.

17 DC, "Are You Suffering from an Inferiority Complex," article manuscript,
    1940s, 7–8, DCA; Crom, *Dale Carnegie*, 26; and Harry Hamm to Rosemary
    Crom, February 27, 1985, DCA.

18 Harry Hamm to Rosemary Crom, February 27, 1985, DCA; Crom, *Dale
    Carnegie*, 26; and Clemenko, "He Sells Success," 65–66.

19 *Maryville Daily Forum*, March 25, 1940, and "Inspiration of Mother Guides
    Dale Carnegie in His New Book," *Maryville Daily Forum*, June 4, 1948. On
    DC's trips to Missouri, see also "Dale Carnegie Is Here for a Few Days of
    Rest," *Maryville Daily Forum*, May 29, 1941; "Dale Carnegie Tells College
    Girls How to Get a Husband," *The Student* (Central Missouri State Teacher's

College), April 9, 1940; "Dale Carnegie Here on a Visit," *Maryville Daily Forum*, October 15, 1945; and "Rotary Celebrates 20th Anniversary." Giles Kemp and Edward Claflin, *Dale Carnegie: The Man Who Influenced Millions* (New York, 1989), 166; Clemenko, "He Sells Success," 66; and Marilyn Burke to Rosemary Crom, May 13, 1985, DCA.

20 Small, "Dale Carnegie: Man with a Message," 36, 70; Crom, *Dale Carnegie*, 26; and DC, *How to Stop Worrying and Start Living* (New York, 1948), 83.

21 Brenda Leigh Johnson to the author, February 7, 2012; author's interview with Oliver Crom; William Longgood, *Talking Your Way to Success: The Story of the Dale Carnegie Course* (New York, 1962), 52–53; and Clemenko, "He Sells Success," 68.

22 Small, "Dale Carnegie: Man with a Message," 70; Brenda Leigh Johnson to the author, February 7, 2012; DC, *How to Stop Worrying*, 154; and author's interview with Oliver Crom.

23 Brenda Leigh Johnson to the author, February 7, 2012; and *Central High School Yearbook* (Tulsa), 1930.

24 Brenda Leigh Johnson to the author, February 7, 2012; 1931 *University of Oklahoma Yearbook*, 139; "Dorothy Carnegie's Road to Success Is Right on Course," *Palm Beach Post* (reprinted from *The New York Times*), May 29, 1973; and author's interview with Oliver Crom.

25 Brenda Leigh Johnson to the author, February 7, 2012; "Dorothy Carnegie's Road to Success"; "Dorothy Carnegie Rivkin, 85, Ex–Dale Carnegie Chief, Dies," *The New York Times*, August 8, 1998; author's interview with Oliver Crom; and author's interview with Donna Carnegie, August 1, 2012.

26 Longgood, *Talking Your Way to Success*, 53; *Maryville Daily Forum*, October 23, 1944; Kemp and Claflin, *Dale Carnegie: The Man Who Influenced Millions*, 162; and marriage announcements, *Time* (November 13, 1944): 42.

27 Crom, *Dale Carnegie*, 19.

28 Dorothy Carnegie, *How to Help Your Husband Get Ahead*, 107–10.

29 Clemenko, "He Sells Success," 68; Brenda Leigh Johnson to the author, February 8, 2012; and Crom, *Dale Carnegie*, 22.

30 Brenda Leigh Johnson to the author, February 6, 2012; and DC, "I Never Had a Chance to Go to College," article manuscript, 1940s, 11, DCA.

31 Small, "Dale Carnegie: Man with a Message," 70; Brenda Leigh Johnson to the author, February 16, 2012; and author's interview with Oliver Crom.

32 "Dale Carnegie Here on a Visit."

33 Longgood, *Talking Your Way to Success*, 51–54; and *A History of Dale Carnegie Training: 1912–1997* (New York: Dale Carnegie and Associates, 1997), 9, DCA.

34 Author's interview with Oliver Crom.

35 Brenda Leigh Johnson to the author, February 8, 2012; author's interview with Oliver Crom; and DC, "I Never Had a Chance to Go to College," 11.

36 Crom, *Dale Carnegie*, 13–14.

37 Brenda Leigh Johnson to the author, February 8 and March 6, 2012; author's interview with Oliver Crom.

38 *Life* (May 1, 1950): 9.

39 Crom, *Dale Carnegie*, 14.

40 DC to Linda Dale Offenbach, July 3, 1944, LPA.

41 Frieda Offenbach to DC, early summer 1941 and summer 1942, DCA; DC to Linda Dale Offenbach, July 3, 1944, LPA; DC to Linda Dale Offenbach, July 7, 1942, LPA; DC to Linda Dale Offenbach, July 7, 1943, LPA; DC to Linda Dale Offenbach, July 7, 1941, LPA; DC to Frieda Offenbach, July 8, 1942, LPA; and DC to Frieda Offenbach, August 18, 1942, LPA.

42 "Dale Carnegie: Self-Control," *Spokane Daily Chronicle*, July 5, 1939.

43 Author's interviews with Linda Offenbach Polsby, June 6–8, 2011.

44 DC to Linda Dale Offenbach, July 7, 1941; DC to Linda Dale Offenbach, July 7, 1942; DC to Linda Dale Offenbach, July 7, 1943; and DC to Linda Dale Offenbach, December 6, 1948: all LPA.

45 DC to Linda Dale Offenbach, July 7, 1941; DC to Linda Dale Offenbach, July 7, 1942; and untitled, signed document dated July 24, 1942: all LPA.

46 DC to Linda Dale Offenbach, February 17, 1949; and DC to Linda Dale Offenbach, July 7, 1942: both LPA.

47 Author's interviews with Polsby.

48 DC to Frieda Offenbach, September 1, 1950, LPA; and Linda Offenbach Polsby's inscribed copy of DC, *Biographical Roundup: Highlights in the Lives of Forty Famous People* (Forest Hills, NY, 1944), inscribed by DC at Christmas 1950.

16. "Businessmen Who Do Not Fight Worry Die Young"

1 "The Miracle of America," *Look* (May 25, 1948): 56–57. See also Robert Griffith, "The Selling of America: The Advertising Council and American Politics, 1942–1960," *Business History Review* (Autumn 1983): 388–412.

2 "The Miracle of America," 56, 57.

3 "A *Life* Roundtable on the Pursuit of Happiness," *Life* (July 12, 1948): 95–113.

4 Ibid., 95, 97.

5 Ibid., 112–13.

6 DC, *How to Stop Worrying and Start Living* (New York, 1948), xiii–xiv.

7 "A Kick in the Shins," *Time* (June 14, 1948): 101.

8 DC, *How to Stop Worrying*, 20–21.

9 Ibid., xiii, 219, 18.

10 Ibid., 19–20.

11 Ibid., 38, 225–30.

12 Ibid., 49, 53.

13 Ibid., 2–3, 6.

14 Ibid., 214–21, especially 214–15, 217.

15 Ibid., xv.

16 Ibid., 13, 25.

17 Ibid., xi–xiii, 21. On Hadfield, 91; the Menningers, 21, 217; Adler, 128, 138, 139; Jung, 142, 156; Link, 143–44, 153; Brill, 153; James, 13, 67–68, 97, 99, 152, 154, 157.

18 Ibid., 4–6, 219, 225, 18, 21.

19 Ibid., 190–91, 13, 48–49.

20 Ibid., 89–148, especially 93.

21 Ibid., 20, 89, 97, 90.

22 Ibid., 91, 89, 95, 97.

23 Ibid., 152–53.

24 Ibid., 153, 157.

25 Ibid.,157–58.

26 David Riesman, *The Lonely Crowd: A Study of the Changing American Character* (New Haven, CT, 1973 [1950]).

27 Ibid., 20, 21, 22, 25, 45–46.

28 Ibid., xxxii.

29 Ibid., 16, 15. See also 45, 47.

30 Ibid., 24–25, 160. See also 47–48, 51, 261.

31 *Time* (September 27, 1954): cover title "Social Scientist David Riesman: What Is the American Character?" and inside story "Freedom—New Style," 22–25 (quotes are from 22). For an insightful analysis of the historical and cultural impact of *The Lonely Crowd*, see Todd Gitlin, "How Our Crowd Got Lonely," *The New York Times*, January 9, 2000.

32 This material is skillfully outlined in William S. Graebner, *The Age of Doubt: American Thought and Culture in the 1940s* (Boston, 1991), 101–3.

33 Riesman, *The Lonely Crowd*, 149–50.

34 DC, *How to Stop Worrying*, 110–11, 172–73, 101–2.

35　Ibid., 175–78.
36　Ibid., 137, 143, 111.
37　Ibid., 143–44, 142, 138, 148.
38　Ibid., 66–75, especially 67.
39　Ibid., 69, 128, 133, and 128–34.
40　Ibid., 69, 71.
41　Ibid., 75.
42　Ibid., 122–24, 126–27.
43　Ibid., 100.

17. "Enthusiasm Is His Most Endearing Quality"

1　Dorothy Carnegie, videotaped interview, 1996, DCA.
2　James Kaye, "A Youth's Timidity Led Him to World Influence," *Kansas City Star*, July 24, 1955; and John Burger to Rosemary Crom, March 28, 1985, DCA.
3　Dorothy Carnegie, videotaped interview; and author's interview with Oliver Crom, March 2, 2012.
4　Rosemary Crom, ed., *Dale Carnegie—As Others Saw Him* (Garden City, NY: D. Carnegie, 1987), 22.
5　Ibid., 8.
6　Dorothy Carnegie, videotaped interview.
7　Crom, *Dale Carnegie*, 22, 29, 6.
8　DC memo, April 30, 1952, "How to Speak Inspirationally" file, DCA.
9　Bill Stover, "Dale Carnegie: The Man Behind the Legend," *Success Unlimited* (April 1976): 38–39.
10　Invitation sent to Lowell Thomas, Thomas Papers, Marist College Archives and Special Collections.
11　Kaye, "A Youth's Timidity"; and Crom, *Dale Carnegie*, 24.
12　Dorothy Carnegie, videotaped interview; author's interview with Oliver Crom; and author's interview with Donna Carnegie, August 1, 2012.
13　See exchange of letters between DC and Lehman on May 17, May 25, and June 1, 1950, in "The Special File of Herbert H. Lehman," Lehman Papers, Columbia University, Digital Edition. On Flynn's odyssey from left-wing supporter of the New Deal to critic of "creeping socialism," see John Moser, *Right Turn: John T. Flynn and the Transformation of American Liberalism* (New York, 2005).
14　Author's interview with Oliver Crom.

15 R. I. D. Symour, "How to Win Friends and Influence Tulips," *American Home* (October 1955): 156, 64, 69. See also Kaye, "A Youth's Timidity."

16 Symour, "How to Win Friends and Influence Tulips," 64, 156.

17 Ibid., 156.

18 DC to Lowell Thomas, November 11, 1947, Thomas Papers, Marist College Archives and Special Collections; and Dorothy Carnegie, videotaped interview.

19 Dorothy Carnegie, videotaped interview; and Brenda Leigh Johnson to the author, February 16, 2012. The press release from Rome appeared in September 26, 1951, editions of newspapers throughout the United States, such as the *Cumberland Evening Times* and the *Fairbanks Daily News Miner*. DC returned to New York on October 15, 1951, on the *Constitution* from Naples, Italy, as recorded in "New York Passenger Lists, 1820–1957" at ancestry.com.

20 Crom, *Dale Carnegie*, 27, 13.

21 DC to Lowell Thomas, January 7, 1952, Thomas Papers, Marist College Archives and Special Collections; Crom, *Dale Carnegie*, 13; and Dorothy Carnegie, videotaped interview.

22 Brenda Leigh Johnson to the author, February 16, 2012; author interview with Oliver Crom; and Crom, *Dale Carnegie*, 13.

23 Dorothy Carnegie, videotaped interview; Symour, "How to Win Friends and Influence Tulips," 64; DC, "Letters to My Daughter" (January 1952–1955), 33, DCA; and Crom, *Dale Carnegie*, 4.

24 DC, "Letters to My Daughter," 1.

25 DC to Linda Dale Offenbach, November 18, 1950; DC to Linda Dale Offenbach, June 8, 1954; and DC to Linda Dale Offenbach, November 18, 1950: all LPA.

26 DC to Linda Dale Offenbach, June 12, 1954; DC to Linda Dale Offenbach, November 18, 1950; and Marilyn Burke to Linda Dale Offenbach, December 13, 1950: all LPA.

27 DC to Linda Dale Offenbach, November 9, 1950; DC to Linda Dale Offenbach, December 7, 1954; DC to Linda Dale Offenbach, June 16, 1954; and DC to Linda Dale Offenbach, June 25, 1954: all LPA.

28 Author's interviews with Linda Offenbach Polsby, June 6–8, 2011.

29 Marilyn Burke to Linda Dale Offenbach, December 13, 1950; DC to Linda Dale Offenbach, November 9, 1950; DC to Linda Dale Offenbach, June 8, 1954; and DC to Linda Dale Offenbach, December 7, 1954: all LPA.

30 DC to Linda Dale Offenbach, June 8, 1954, LPA; DC to Linda Dale Offenbach, June 25, 1954, LPA; DC to Linda Dale Offenbach, June 16, 1954, LPA; and author's interview with Donna Carnegie, August 1, 2012.

31   Marilyn Burke to Linda Dale Offenbach, December 13, 1950, LPA; and Homer Croy to Isador Offenbach, late fall of 1955, Homer Croy Papers, State Historical Society of Missouri.

32   DC to Linda Dale Offenbach, early June 1955; and DC telegram to Linda Dale Offenbach, June 15, 1955: both LPA.

33   Dorothy Carnegie, videotaped interview; Brenda Leigh Johnson to the author, February 16, 2012; and author's interview with Oliver Crom.

34   R. G. Sanderson to Rosemary Crom, February 5, 1985, DCA; author's interview with Oliver Crom; and Brenda Leigh Johnson to the author, February 16, 2012.

35   Kaye, "A Youth's Timidity"; and Symour, "How to Win Friends and Influence Tulips," 156.

36   Dorothy Carnegie, videotaped interview; and author's interview with Oliver Crom.

37   Brenda Leigh Johnson to the author, February 6, 2012; author's interview with Oliver Crom; and Brenda Leigh Johnson to the author, February 7, 2012.

38   Dorothy Carnegie, *How to Help Your Husband Get Ahead in His Social and Business Life* (New York, 1953), 114; and extract from the book in Mrs. Dale Carnegie, "How to Help Your Husband Succeed," *Better Homes and Gardens* (April 1955): 24. Another extract appeared in Mrs. Dale Carnegie, "How to Help Your Husband Get Ahead," *Coronet* (January 1954): 65–74.

39   Mrs. Dale Carnegie, "How to Help Your Husband Succeed," 24; and "Dorothy Carnegie's Road to Success Is Right on Course," *Palm Beach Post*, May 29, 1973.

40   DC to Dr. G. W. Diemer, the president of Central Missouri State College, June 21, 1955, Arthur F. McClure II Archives, University of Central Missouri; and William Longgood, *Talking Your Way to Success: The Story of the Dale Carnegie Course* (New York, 1962), 55. The letter of invitation, dated June 17, 1955, and others related to arrangements for the visit, dated June 29, June 30, and July 21, 1955, are also in the archives at the University of Central Missouri.

41   DC to Dr. G. W. Diemer, the president of Central Missouri State College, July 25, 1955, Arthur F. McClure II Archives, University of Central Missouri; "College Awards Famous Alumnus Honorary Degree," *Central Missouri State College Bulletin* (October 1955): 2; and "Friend with Influence," *Newsweek* (August 8, 1955): 71.

42   Reese Wade to Dr. George W. Diemer, August 2, 1955, Arthur F. McClure II Archives, University of Central Missouri.

43 Longgood, *Talking Your Way to Success*, 55; and DC, *Public Speaking: A Practical Course for Business Men* (New York: Association Press, 1926), 82.

44 "College Awards Famous Alumnus Honorary Degree," *Warrensburg Daily Star Journal*, July 29, 1955; and "Central Missouri State College, July 29, 1955, Citation of Dale Carnegie," Arthur F. McClure II Archives, University of Central Missouri.

45 "The Value of Enthusiasm," DC address at Central Missouri State College, Warrensburg, Missouri, July 29, 1955, DCA.

46 Ibid.

47 Ibid.

48 "World of Carnegie," *Newsweek* (August 8, 1955): 70.

49 Dorothy Carnegie, videotaped interview; author's interview with Oliver Crom; and Crom, *Dale Carnegie*, 4.

50 Dorothy Carnegie, videotaped interview; author's interview with Oliver Crom; and Homer Croy to Isador Offenbach, late fall 1955, State Historical Society of Missouri.

51 Homer Croy to Isador Offenbach, late fall 1955, State Historical Society of Missouri. See the following obituaries: *Time* (November 14, 1955): 114; "The Friendly Man," *Newsweek* (November 14, 1955): 41–42; "Dale Carnegie Is Dead," *Kansas City Star*, November 1, 1955; and "Dale Carnegie, Author, Is Dead," *The New York Times*, November 2, 1955. The Washington newspaper obituary was quoted in Stover, "Dale Carnegie: The Man Behind the Legend," 40.

Epilogue: The Self-Help Legacy of Dale Carnegie

1 For accounts of the ceremony, see "A Nation Challenged: The Service," *The New York Times*, September 24, 2001, and "Thousands Fill Yankee Stadium with Prayer," *Chicago Tribune*, September 24, 2001. A transcript of the entire Yankee Stadium service, including Winfrey's "A Prayer for America" is available at transcripts.cnn.com/TRANSCRIPTS.

2 "BBC Presents Warren Buffett on Dale Carnegie," posted on YouTube, December 4, 2009; "Lee Iacocca on Dale Carnegie Leadership," available at dalecarnegie.com; Robert Caro, *The Years of Lyndon Johnson: The Path to Power* (New York, 1990), 212; Jerry Rubin, *Growing (Up) at 37* (New York, 1976), 89; Shepherd Mead, *How to Succeed in Business Without Really Trying* (New York, 1952); and Lenny Bruce, *How to Talk Dirty and Influence People* (New York, 1965).

3   See Daniel Kahneman, *Thinking, Fast and Slow* (New York: Farrar, Straus and Giroux, 2011); Daniel Goleman, *Emotional Intelligence: Why It Can Matter More Than IQ* (New York, 1995); Daniel Gilbert, *Stumbling on Happiness* (New York, 2005); Richard H. Thaler and Cass R. Sunstein, *Nudge: Improving Decisions About Health, Wealth, and Happiness* (New York, 2008); Malcolm Gladwell, *Blink: The Power of Thinking Without Thinking* (New York, 2005); Martin Seligman, *Authentic Happiness: Using the New Positive Psychology to Realize Your Potential for Lasting Fulfillment* (New York, 2002); and Ed Diener and Robert Biswas-Diener, *Happiness: Unlocking the Mysteries of Psychological Wealth* (New York, 2008).

4   Thomas Harris, *I'm Okay, You're Okay: A Practical Guide to Transactional Analysis* (New York, 1967); Tony Robbins, *Unlimited Power: The New Science of Personal Achievement* (New York, 1986), and *Awaken the Giant Within: How to Take Immediate Control of Your Mental, Emotional, Physical, and Financial Destiny* (New York, 1992); Susan Jeffers, *Feel the Fear and Do It Anyway: Dynamic Techniques for Turning Fear, Indecision, and Anger into Power, Action, and Love* (New York, 1987); Dr. Joyce Brothers, *How to Get Whatever You Want Out of Life* (New York, 1978); Dr. Wayne W. Dyer, *Your Erroneous Zones: Step-by-Step Advice for Escaping the Trap of Negative Thinking and Taking Control of Your Life* (New York, 1976); and Rhonda Byrne, *The Secret* (New York, 2006).

5   Melody Beattie, *Codependent No More: How to Stop Controlling Others and Start Caring for Yourself* (Center City, MN, 1986); John Bradshaw, *Homecoming: Reclaiming and Championing Your Inner Child* (New York, 1990); Jack Canfield and Mark Victor Hansen, *Chicken Soup for the Soul: 101 Stories to Open the Heart and Rekindle the Spirit* (Deerfield Beach, FL, 1993); and Steven Denning, "How Chicken Soup for the Soul Dramatically Expanded Its Brand," available at Forbes.com/sites/stevedenning/2011/04/28/how-chicken-soup-for-the-soul-dramatically-expanded-its-brand/. Stuart Smalley clips from *Saturday Night Live* are available on YouTube, while a written taste of his therapeutic endeavors can be found in Al Franken, *I'm Good Enough, I'm Smart Enough, and Doggone It, People Like Me: Daily Affirmations by Stuart Smalley* (New York, 1992).

6   Tim Stafford, "The Therapeutic Revolution: How Christian Counseling Is Changing the Church," *Christianity Today* (May 17, 1993): 24–32; Carol V. R. George, *God's Salesman: Norman Vincent Peale and the Power of Positive Thinking* (New York, 1993); Dennis Voscull, *Mountains into Goldmines: Robert Schuller and the Gospel of Success* (New York, 1983); Joel

Osteen, *Your Best Life Now: 7 Steps to Living Your Full Potential* (New York, 2004); M. Scott Peck, *The Road Less Traveled: A New Psychology of Love, Traditional Values and Spiritual Growth* (New York, 1988); and Kenda Creasy Dean, *Almost Christian: What the Faith of Our Teenagers Is Telling the American Church* (New York, 2010).

7   Stanley Coopersmith, *The Antecedents of Self-Esteem* (San Francisco, 1967), 45; California State Department of Education, "A Curriculum of Inclusion" (1990); and New York State Department of Education, "A Curriculum of Inclusion" (1990). For criticism of this trend, see Charles J. Sykes, *Dumbing Down Our Kids: Why American Children Feel Good About Themselves but Can't Read, Write, or Add* (New York, 1995), and Maureen Stout, *The Feel-Good Curriculum: The Dumbing Down of America's Kids in the Name of Self-Esteem* (New York, 2001).

8   Dr. Benjamin Spock, *Baby and Child Care* (New York, 1946); Dorothy C. Briggs, *Your Child's Self-Esteem: The Key to His Life* (New York, 1970), 2–3; Adele Faber and Elaine Mazlish, *How to Talk So Kids Will Listen and Listen So Kids Will Talk* (New York, 1980); Louise Hart, *The Winning Family: Increasing Self-Esteem in Your Children and Yourself* (New York, 1987), 5. For a broad survey of modern child-rearing literature, see Peter N. Stearns's historical survey *Anxious Parents: A History of Modern Childrearing in America* (New York, 2004).

9   Richard Gillespie, *Manufacturing Knowledge: A History of the Hawthorne Experiments* (Cambridge, MA, 1991); Peter Drucker, *The Practice of Management* (New York, 1954); Mary Walton, *The Deming Management Method* (New York, 1988); Tom Chappell, *Managing Upside Down: The Seven Intentions of Values-Centered Leadership* (New York, 1999); and Stephen Covey, *The 7 Habits of Highly Effective People* (New York, 1990). For a broad critical survey, see John Micklewait and Adrian Woolridge, *The Witch Doctors: Making Sense of the Management Gurus* (New York, 1998).

10   Deepak Chopra, *Seven Spiritual Laws of Success: A Practical Guide to the Fulfillment of Your Dreams* (New York, 1994); Dr. Phil McGraw, *Self Matters: Creating Your Life from the Inside Out* (New York, 2001); Dane S. Claussen, *The Promise Keepers: Essays on Masculinity and Christianity* (Jefferson, NC, 2000); Hanna Rosin, "Promise Weepers," *The New Republic* (October 27, 1997): 11–12; Carol Gilligan, *In a Different Voice: Psychological Theory and Women's Development* (Cambridge, MA, 1982); Gloria Steinem, *Revolution from Within: A Book of Self-Esteem* (New York, 1993); Cornel West, *Race Matters* (Boston, 1993), 12–13, 17; Clarence Page, "Promise Keepers and

Million Man March," *Chicago Tribune*, September 7, 1991; "We're Bringing Back Self-Respect," *The Boston Globe*, October 20, 1995; and on Bill Clinton, see "Chronicles," *Time* (January 23, 1995): 9, and Bob Woodward, "At a Difficult Time, First Lady Reaches Out, Looks Within," *The Washington Post*, June 23, 1996.

11   See Ronald W. Dworkin, "The Rise of the Caring Industry," *Policy Review* (June 1, 2010); and Benedict Carey, "The Therapist May See You Anytime, Anywhere," *The New York Times*, February 14, 2012.

12   See Kitty Kelley, *Oprah: A Biography* (New York, 2010) for the most complete factual account of her life, and Janice Peck, *The Age of Oprah: Cultural Icon for the Neoliberal Era* (New York, 2008), for an interesting political analysis of her broader role in American life. Much of my view of this important cultural figure comes from my own long-term book project tentatively entitled "What Lies Within: Oprah Winfrey and America's Pursuit of Happiness."

13   My critical assessment of the therapeutic culture has been influenced by a number of perceptive critics, including Christopher Lasch, *The Culture of Narcissism: American Life in an Age of Diminishing Expectations* (New York, 1979); Wendy Kaminer, *I'm Dysfunctional, You're Dysfunctional: The Recovery Movement and Other Self-Help Fashions* (Reading, MA, 1992); and Eva S. Moskowitz, *In Therapy We Trust: America's Obsession with Self-Fulfillment* (Baltimore, 2001).

Index